ALSO BY MICHELLE MALKIN

Who Built That:
Awe-Inspiring Stories of America's Tinkerpreneurs

Culture of Corruption:
Obama and His Team of Tax Cheats, Crooks, and Cronies

Unhinged:
Exposing Liberals Gone Wild

In Defense of Internment:
The Case for Racial Profiling in World War II and the War on Terror

Invasion:
How America Still Welcomes Terrorists, Criminals,
and Other Foreign Menaces to Our Shores

Sold Out

How High-Tech Billionaires & Bipartisan Beltway Crapweasels Are Screwing America's Best & Brightest Workers

MICHELLE MALKIN

AND JOHN MIANO

31652002924612

THRESHOLD EDITIONS/MERCURY INK

New York   London   Toronto   Sydney   New Delhi

Threshold Editions/Mercury Ink
An Imprint of Simon & Schuster, Inc.
1230 Avenue of the Americas
New York, NY 10020

First Threshold Editions/Mercury Ink hardcover edition November 2015

THRESHOLD EDITIONS and colophon are trademarks of
Simon & Schuster, Inc.

GLENN BECK is a trademark of Mercury Radio Arts, Inc.

For information about special discounts for bulk purchases,
please contact Simon & Schuster Special Sales at 1-866-506-1949
or business@simonandschuster.com.

The Simon & Schuster Speakers Bureau can bring authors to your
live event. For more information or to book an event contact the
Simon & Schuster Speakers Bureau at 1-866-248-3049 or visit our
website at www.simonspeakers.com.

Interior design by Renato Stanisic

Manufactured in the United States of America

10 9 8 7 6 5 4 3 2 1

Library of Congress Cataloging-in-Publication Data

Names: Malkin, Michelle, author.
Title: Sold out : how high-tech billionaires & bipartisan beltway crapweasels
    are screwing America's best & brightest workers / Michelle Malkin and
    John Miano.
Description: New York : Threshold Editons/Mercury Ink, [2015] | Includes
    bibliographical references and index.
Identifiers: LCCN 2015035723| ISBN 9781501115943 (alk. paper) |
    ISBN 9781501115967 (ebook : alk. paper) | ISBN 9781501115950 (pbk. : alk.
    paper)
Subjects: LCSH: Labor policy—United States. | Labor market—United
    States. | Foreign workers—Government policy—United States. | Professional
    employees—United States. | Business and politics—United States. | United
    States—Economic policy—2009–
Classification: LCC HD8072.5 .M345 2015 | DDC 331.6/20973—dc23 LC
    record available at http://lccn.loc.gov/2015035723

Contents

PART III: THE BIG GOVERNMENT–BIG BUSINESS BETRAYERS OF AMERICA'S BEST AND BRIGHTEST WORKERS

Introduction

"Walt Disney World information technology workers laid off"[1]

"Qualcomm lays off 4,500 workers while demanding more H-1Bs"[2]

"Intel to cut over 5,000 jobs"[3]

"Cisco execs try to put best face on 6,000 layoffs"[4]

"Cargill to outsource IT services; 900 jobs affected"[5]

"Microsoft won't lay off H-1B before U.S. workers"[6]

"Bank of America planning to cut 16,000 jobs by year end"[7]

"Southern California Edison IT workers 'beyond furious' over H-1B replacements"[8]

"Harley-Davidson cuts IT staff; shifts some to Infosys"[9]

"[Northeast Utilities] cuts IT workforce; hires Indian outsourcers"[10]

"Did Pfizer force its staff to train their H-1B replacements?"[11]

"Best Buy hit with lawsuit over layoffs of IT workers"[12]

"Foreign workers fill hundreds of Sacramento-area IT jobs"[13]

"Outsourced at home: U.S. workers 'pissed' at H-1B visa program"[14]

From the "Happiest Place on Earth" at Walt Disney World in Florida to Silicon Valley and across the heartland, America's skilled workers are getting screwed. Brutally, insidiously, and comprehensively screwed.

We're going to show you who the worst perpetrators are, how and why they're doing it, and what we must do to stop them.

The plight of Disney employees—and of tens of thousands like them nationwide—is a real-world nightmare that even Hollywood's finest screenwriters couldn't concoct. Disney managers summoned hundreds of their American information technology workers (called "cast members") to mysterious meetings in October 2014. The data systems programmers and engineers had just completed an IT project; several proudly bore blue ID badges identifying them as Disney "Partners in Excellence." One of these Disney professionals told us he had received a big pay raise before the meeting, along with the highest possible performance review.

But he and his colleagues didn't walk into a fairy-tale celebration of their accomplishments. They walked into a professional death sentence—and their bosses handed them the shovels to dig their own graves. One by one, the Disney cast members heard their bosses read from the same grim script informing them that they would be laid off by January 30, 2015. The evil twist? Before getting the boot, they would be forced to participate in "Knowledge Transfer" sessions with their younger, cheaper, less-skilled replacements imported from India.

We reviewed two internal Disney documents informing workers about the elimination and outsourcing of their jobs to a "managed service provider." Each American IT team member was offered a "stay bonus" of 10 percent of their base salary—but only "contingent upon your continued satisfactory performance of your job duties and responsibilities." One memo warned that workers would lose their bonuses and be terminated before their "separation dates" if they violated "Company policy" or engaged in "misconduct" (e.g., failure to comply with nondisparagement and confidentiality clauses).

Another laid-off Disney IT worker at the Magic Kingdom reported: "Some of these folks were literally flown in the day before to take over the exact same job I was doing." He had little choice but to train his successor from India "on site, in our country."[15]

"If you do not cooperate," supervisors warned, "you will not get a severance or retention bonus."

Orlando's WESH-TV first reported on the brutal layoffs and replacement training scheme in late January 2015.[16] It took months for the mainstream media to follow up. The *Orlando Sentinel* produced a bland report that completely omitted the outsourcing angle,[17] but thanks to veteran tech journalist Patrick Thibodeau at *Computerworld*,[18] the Disney workers exposed to a national audience how they had been thrown under the bus at their worksite. As the layoff date neared, one worker told Thibodeau, "I really felt like a foreigner in that building."[19]

While those employees struggled to complete their last, humiliating assignment and find new work, Disney CEO Bob Iger and his fellow cochairs of a corporate front group called the Partnership for a New American Economy lobbied in Washington, D.C., for increases in temporary worker visas—and baldly denied to Congress that they were sacking American workers in favor of cheap foreign labor.

Not until June 2015 did the *New York Times* finally deem the Disney nightmare newsworthy with a front-page article headlined "Pink Slips at Disney. But First, Training Foreign Replacements."[20] By then, the Disney workers had been cut loose by their bosses, who prevented any contractor that worked with the entertainment empire from hiring the fired workers for twelve months.[21] In a face-saving move, Disney canceled plans for even more American tech worker layoffs in its New York City and Burbank offices.[22] But it came too late for the cast-off cast members in Orlando. To put this all in perspective, the combined salaries of all the 320 "cast members" Disney replaced is much lower than the $46.5 million the company paid to CEO Iger in 2014.[23]

"There is no future in IT for Americans. So why continue?" one of the victims told us.

FOLLOW THE MONEY

Who in Washington will stand up for our nation's best and brightest?

We know who stands with American tech companies and their off-shore outsourcing partners in championing low-cost foreign workers:

President Barack Obama and the Senate's so-called Gang of Eight—Sen. Michael Bennet (D-Colo.), Sen. Richard Durbin (D-Ill.), Sen. Jeff Flake (R-Ariz.), Sen. Lindsey Graham (R-S.C.), Sen. John McCain (R-Ariz.), Sen. Bob Menendez (D-N.J.), Sen. Marco Rubio (R-Fla.), and Sen. Chuck Schumer, (D-N.Y.)—side with the CEOs of Disney, Intel, Cisco, Facebook, Google, and Microsoft.

News Corp. founder Rupert Murdoch, GOP megadonor Sheldon Adelson, former New York mayor Michael Bloomberg, and liberal billionaire hedge fund mogul George Soros all support the Big Tech, open-borders agenda.

Revolving-door operatives on both the Left and Right, such as Virginia governor Terry McAuliffe (D), Hillary Clinton brother Tony Rodham, former Michigan senator Spencer Abraham (R), Grover Norquist of Americans for Tax Reform, and former Mississippi governor Haley Barbour (R), have made millions consulting for foreign governments, investors, and visa seekers.

The Republicrats and Demopublicans in D.C. pay lip service to improving the twenty-first-century American workforce. They've got fancy blueprints and buzzword-filled plans for helping the American middle class and encouraging American students to pursue college and advanced degrees in science, technology, engineering, and math (described by lobbyists and educrats using the buzzword "STEM").[24] They say they oppose tax breaks for offshoring and want to "Bring Jobs Home."[25] Yet untold thousands of skilled U.S. workers have been laid off, replaced, and forced to train their imported replacements—and most politicians embrace "solutions" that will only make things much, much worse.

As we'll show you, many brave whistleblowers have risked their livelihoods and lives exposing corporate betrayals and lobbyist-driven subversions of law. Yet defenders of the temporary guest worker racket—who rush to lionize every successful immigrant entrepreneur to bolster their case for bottomless tech visa handouts—scoff at Americans forced to dig their own graves.

At the center of the storm is H-1B, the foreign tech worker visa program that turns twenty-five years old in November 2015. It was supposed to be a program for high-skilled guest workers to alleviate shortages in specialty fields. While H-1B boosters in the U.S. hype the program as the "genius visa"[26] for "braniacs,"[27] the former commerce secretary of India, Kamal Nath, revealed the truth. H-1B, he said, "has become the outsourcing visa."[28] As we show you in *Sold Out*:

- With very few exceptions, the purported shortages of American workers don't exist.
- There is nothing special about the hundreds of thousands of H-1B visa holders flooding our workforce.
- Most H-1B workers are sponsored by companies that specialize in offshore outsourcing of U.S. jobs.
- Abuse of guest workers by both offshoring companies and their U.S. tech giant partners is rampant.
- Enforcement is a joke.
- The promises of U.S. worker protections were big fat whoppers.

"I was part of teams that trained our H-1B replacements at two different Fortune 500 firms," one U.S. worker informed the pro–open-borders *Wall Street Journal* in April 2015.[29] "Both times we were promised by management that we are training the H-1B workers so we could move on to the next big, high-priority, new technology project. What happened each time was the new project went to some other company and they laid us off. The third time this occurred, I realized the pattern and quit before the offshore team arrived."[30]

"They told us they could replace one of us with three, four, or five Indian personnel and still save money," a laid-off worker at Southern California Edison told the *Los Angeles Times*, recounting a group meeting with supervisors in 2014. "They said, 'We can get four Indian guys for cheaper than the price of you.' You could hear a pin drop in the room."[31]

In March 2015, in the wake of the American tech worker layoffs at Disney and elsewhere, the Senate Judiciary Committee held a hearing on H-1B abuse. The Republicans invited H-1B opponents as witnesses and the Democrats invited two H-1B supporters and one opponent. In the face of the Disney and Southern California Edison fiascos, the Democratic senators (including those sponsoring bills for more H-1B visas) were smart enough to remain largely silent, but a handful of Republicans danced for industry lobbyists. Sen. Hatch gave a lecture in support of H-1B visas, while Republican Sens. Jeff Flake of Arizona and John Cornyn of Texas threw softball questions to the *Democrats'* witnesses who supported H-1B.

They don't call it "the stupid party" for nothing, folks.

In April 2015, ten U.S. senators signed a letter asking the U.S. Department of Justice, the Department of Homeland Security, and the Labor Department to investigate the use of the H-1B program "to replace large numbers of American workers" at Southern California Edison (SCE) and other employers.[32] Two weeks later, the Labor Department refused to investigate because no "credible source" had complained and there was "no reasonable cause to believe the company violated the rules governing the visas."[33] Indeed, Congress itself bears the blame for facilitating the systematic replacement of American workers with temporary foreign guest workers. Immigration lawyers explicitly made it legal for employers to replace Americans with lower-paid H-1B workers in nearly all cases. The SCE workers are just the latest example of H-1B roadkill sanctioned by many of the lawmakers now complaining about it.[34] In fact, two of the senators who signed the complaint—Sens. Richard Blumenthal (D-Conn.) and Claire McCaskill (D-Mo.)—are cosponsors of legislation to *expand* H-1B without any meaningful American worker protection reforms.[35]

A SHORTAGE OF JOBS, NOT WORKERS

If you believe the constant Chicken Little rhetoric of the immigration expansionists, America suffers from a catastrophic dearth of talented, educated graduates and workers in science and technology. But in July 2014, the U.S. Census Bureau reported that an astonishing "74 percent of those who have a bachelor's degree in science, technology, engineering and math—commonly referred to as STEM—are not employed in STEM occupations."[36] That translates to roughly 11.4 million of 15 million Americans with STEM degrees who aren't working in STEM fields.[37]

Predictably, the pro–open-borders editorial board of the *Wall Street Journal*, owned by unrepentant immigration expansionist Rupert Murdoch, attacked Sen. Sessions for citing this devastating figure. To refute the census data, the paper's editors cited a contrary "study" by the "National Foundation for American Policy"—which, as we'll show you, is the one-man advocacy research shop of D.C. swamp creature and libertarian ideologue Stuart Anderson. He does not have a statistics or economics background, but boasts a well-connected Capitol Hill pedigree—and in typical circular fashion, proudly flaunts his credentials of having "published articles in," you guessed it, the *Wall Street Journal*.[38]

By contrast, three bona fide academics, Hal Salzman of Rutgers University, Daniel Kuehn of American University, and B. Lindsay Lowell of Georgetown University, determined that only one of every two U.S. college STEM graduates is hired into a STEM job each year. Most of the STEM graduates who don't enter the STEM workforce cite lack of STEM-related jobs or better job opportunities in non-STEM fields.

At the end of 2014, a leading employment-consulting firm reported that "despite the overall strength of the tech sector, employers in the computer industry saw the heaviest downsizing of the year, announcing a total of 59,528 planned layoffs. That is 69 percent more than a year ago."[39] Many of the companies calling for legislation to let in more foreign workers—Hewlett-Packard, Cisco Systems, United Technologies, American Express, Procter & Gamble, T-Mobile, Archer Daniels Midland, Verizon, and General Mills—have laid off thousands of Americans in recent years.[40] (See Appendix A for the demand letter to Congress signed by these and other U.S. companies seeking increases in foreign guest worker visas.)

Meanwhile, foreign guest workers account for one-third to one-half of all new IT hires.[41] By January 2015, guest workers made up 21 percent of software developers in the U.S.[42]

Employment site Bright.com examined H-1B labor condition application forms filed by companies during one quarter of 2013, crunched the numbers from its database of roughly one million active résumés, and matched its available candidate pool with available jobs geographically. "We had expected to find many areas where there was an insufficient supply" of domestic workers, David Hardtke, Bright's chief scientist, told *Entrepreneur* magazine.[43] Instead, the analysis found 1.34 qualified domestic workers for every one position where a company had indicated an intent to hire a foreign worker through the H-1B program. The study found 4.08 American job candidates for every one electronics-engineering job listed as an H-1B position. Not only did the data "overall show a plentiful supply of job candidates," but the analysis "also suggested the supply of American workers for these jobs will rise over time."[44]

If firms were so desperate to find IT workers, as immigration expansionists insist, wages in the sector would rise. Yet, wages for new computer science graduates are expected to plunge 9 percent during the coming year.[45] Professor Salzman observed that "average wages in the IT industry are the same as those that prevailed when Bill Clinton was president despite industry cries of a 'shortage.'"[46]

CONSPIRING AGAINST AMERICAN WORKERS

As stalwart Senate Immigration Subcommittee chairman Sen. Jeff Sessions (R-Ala.) notes, "The principal economic dilemma of our time is the very large number of people who either are not working at all, or not earning a wage great enough to be financially independent."[47] President Obama likes to blame automation, noting that some workers lost their jobs because of the advent of ATM machines and self-service kiosks at airports.[48] But there's a much more glaring and treacherous source of pain: government-engineered, corporate lobbyist–driven favoritism for cheap, immobile foreign workers over U.S. workers. The same politicians who preach about prosperity for all are stabbing talented, productive Americans in the back.

The U.S. Constitution does not say that the paramount duty of government is to "celebrate diversity" or to "embrace multiculturalism" or to give "every willing worker" in the world a job. It says our republic was established "to provide for the common defense, promote the general welfare, and secure the blessings of liberty."

Providing for the common defense does not mean obliterating guest worker visa caps whenever corporate lobbyists hit the panic button. Promoting the general welfare does not mean providing unlimited employment opportunities for all 7 billion people on our planet. Securing the blessings of liberty does not mean guaranteeing the blessings of low-wage workers for Microsoft, Facebook, and Google.

The "system" is not "broken," but America's will to enforce its laws, control its borders, and punish immigration violators is dying on the vine.

While multinational corporations clamor for ever-expanding immigration policies, it's worth pointing out that America remains generous—to a fault. We already grant one million legal permanent residencies ("green cards") to people from around the world every year. The number of new legal permanent residents is expected to increase by 10 million by 2025. That's more than the current combined population of Dallas, St. Louis, Denver, Boston, Chicago, Los Angeles, and Atlanta.[49]

The inflow of new green card holders is in addition to the upward of 30 million illegal aliens[50] poised to gain full work authorization and citizenship rights under various congressional and White House amnesty plans, along with an estimated annual influx of 70,000 asylees, 500,000 foreign students, and nearly 700,000 total foreign guest workers (both skilled and unskilled, not to mention their spouses, many of whom are allowed to work here as well).[51] More than 350,000 foreign high school and university students, researchers, physicians, and summer work travelers enter the country every year on J-1 exchange visitor visas.[52] Up to 66,000 visas are available for nonagricultural temporary foreign workers. In 2014, the Department of Labor approved nearly 117,000 positions for seasonal agricultural workers.[53] In addition, leaders in both parties and the White House support a fast-track trade agreement known as the Trans-Pacific Partnership (TPP), which reportedly includes expansions of temporary guest worker visas.[54]

The Departments of Homeland Security, State, and Labor have proved themselves serially incapable of handling the overload. By their own admission, their ability to monitor, collect, and analyze basic data about who gets in is completely overwhelmed. Decades' worth of U.S. Government Accountability Office and inspector general reports document repeated failures to enforce visa requirements, wage and non-displacement protections, and national security measures.

We take on the plight of high-skilled American workers and the visa programs that Big Business and Big Government cronies are abusing to line their pockets, undercut America's best and brightest, and curry favor with wealthy foreign investors and special interests. After a quarter century, the H-1B program's nominal worker protections have been completely eroded. Corporate lobbyists have infiltrated congressional backrooms to create circuitous paths around the laws and out of public view. Both U.S. companies and offshore outsourcing IT firms are exploiting alternative pipelines for cheap foreign workers.

In Part I of *Sold Out*, we completely dismantle the H-1B betrayal. It's the Grandfather of All American Worker Sellouts. Citizens need to know the sordid history of political tricks, Beltway influence peddlers, and legislative corruption behind the program. We introduce you to Jennifer Wedel, a spunky Fort Worth, Texas, mom who spoke truth to the H-1B powers in Washington. We debunk the myths about H-1B workers—the so-called "best and brightest"—manufactured by advocacy researchers and spread by lazy or complicit journalists.

We'll show you the rampant illegal schemes of "bodyshopping" and "benching," which allow companies to create a cheap, as-needed foreign workforce on American soil while tens of thousands of high-skilled American workers are being laid off. We'll shine light on how the disgraceful offshore outsourcing racket forces American workers to train their own foreign worker replacements.

We expose the fraud perpetrated by shady H-1B con artists and the abuse suffered not just by displaced American workers but also by exploited H-1B workers themselves. You'll learn about systemic discrimination against older American tech workers. You'll see how companies brazenly exclude Americans from applying for jobs specifically crafted for foreign H-1B visa holders.

In Part II, we'll expose the rest of the Foreign Worker Visa Racket from A to Z. There are a dizzying number of ways for companies to game the immigration and entrance system. Trust us, you have no idea how bad it really is. We'll detail how Indian software giant Infosys— the largest H-1B user—gamed the system to use B-1 temporary business traveler visas as entrance tickets for foreign workers as an end-run around H-1B caps. You'll learn about the death threats and discrimination faced by American tech workers who told the truth and forced Infosys into a $34 million work-visa settlement—the largest of its kind.

We'll take you on a tour of some of the most notorious F-1 student visa abusers—shady diploma mill operators who somehow won government approval from snoozing bureaucrats for their phony schools and bilked foreigners held hostage by the threat of deportation. We'll expose the shocking details of how bipartisan political cronies benefit from the corrupt EB-5 citizenship-for-sale scheme, which is a bonanza for immigration lawyers and foreign malefactors, enabled by an overwhelmed homeland security bureaucracy. And we'll walk you through the myriad ways that both U.S. and Indian companies are exploiting loopholes in the loosely regulated and little-scrutinized L-1 visa program to import foreign "business" transferees who are displacing Americans.

Executive branch abuse of the immigration system is not new. But radical transformer-in-chief President Obama has taken it to a new level. Under the Constitution, Congress defines the classes of aliens eligible to work in the United States, and the executive branch has the broad authority to determine the individual aliens within those classes who are authorized to work. Obama's Department of Homeland Security flipped this around and usurped the authority to allow any alien— legally or illegally in the country—to work unless Congress explicitly prohibits it.[55] The Obama administration first encroached upon congressional authority over immigration with the so-called Deferred Action for Childhood Arrivals (DACA) program, which allowed illegal alien children to remain in the United States. Next, he created the Deferred Action for Parents of Americans and Lawful Permanent Residents (DAPA) program, which granted illegal alien parents with children born in the United States the right to remain in the United States and work. Using the same twisted legal logic, in 2015 Obama started allowing certain spouses of H-1B workers (H-4 visa holders) to work in the United States.

If you thought these brazen illegal alien amnesties through executive order were bad, you ain't seen nothing yet.

We'll demonstrate how the administrations of both George W. Bush and Barack Obama sneakily expanded the foreign worker supply by administrative fiat, including expansion of the Optional Practical Training (OPT) program, through which 560,000 foreign "students" have been authorized to work in the U.S. It may well be America's largest guest-worker program, yet it has never been authorized by Congress. This backdoor H-1B visa increase allows foreign students to work with little monitoring, no wage protections, no payment of Social Security payroll taxes, and no requirement for employers to demonstrate labor market shortages. We'll show you how Microsoft lobbied the Bush White House for the program on the cocktail party circuit.

In Part III, we'll expose the legislative trickery and legal complexities that have enabled special interests to hijack the deliberative process and hoodwink the American public about the corporate sponsors' true intentions. We take you deep into the Beltway sewer and lead you through the bipartisan money trail that paved the way for sweeping immigration legislation and visa program expansions, which boosted Big Business and Silicon Valley's bottom lines—not to mention the campaign coffers of Capitol Hill water-carriers. We'll show you which cunning corporations are really benefiting and how shoddy (or completely nonexistent) the ostensible legislative protections for American workers really are. Like junkies desperate for their next heroin fix, high-tech billionaires and CEOs can't stop pestering D.C. dealers for new injections of cheap foreign workers supplied by H-1B visas.

We'll dive into the Trojan Horse of "comprehensive immigration reform," a vast legislative and propaganda vehicle that *worsens* and *compounds* the foreign guest worker programs' flaws and frauds, instead of *fixing* them. You'll learn how the Senate's so-called Gang of Eight served the needs and demands of immigration lawyers and corporations by gutting already-feeble protections against displacement of U.S. workers and depression of wages. And we'll show you all the Christmas-tree goodies stuffed into the bill to pay off the Senate's sellouts.

OUR SPECIAL INTEREST: YOU

Thirteen years ago, I wrote my first book, *Invasion: How America Still Welcomes Terrorists, Criminals, and Other Foreign Menaces to Our Shores.* It exposed all the ways in which Big Government and Big Business profited from open borders, while paving the way for the 9/11 Islamic jihadists. Their deadly recipe for threatening national security: lax enforcement of immigration laws, a deportation abyss designed to fail, repeated federal amnesties for illegal border-crossers, and institutional neglect of illegal visa overstayers.

Now the same political and corporate forces that support massive illegal immigration are pouring even more fuel on the fire. They're threatening our economic security. They're sabotaging the job prospects of our children and grandchildren. High-tech companies, university lobbyists, and powerful leaders in both parties have ramped up their plans to import unlimited numbers of legal foreign workers into our country through an alphabet soup of cheap labor visa programs.

My coauthor, John Miano, is a leading expert on the devastating effects of foreign labor on American technology workers. He has testified before Congress multiple times and his work on this issue has been printed and quoted widely in publications ranging from *USA Today* to *Computerworld* and *Information Week*. After receiving a BA in mathematics from the College of Wooster, John worked as a computer programmer for eighteen years. He founded the Programmers Guild, a professional organization for U.S. computer programmers, in 1998. But after suffering firsthand the adverse and absurd effects of the H-1B foreign guest worker program, he left his programming career to fight for American workers and graduated from Seton Hall Law School in 2005.

Now John represents a diverse clientele of employees on the front lines who have been adversely affected by foreign guest worker programs. His ground-breaking federal lawsuit on behalf of WashTech (a labor union of professional tech workers) against President Bush's regulatory expansion of the OPT program is, as *National Review*'s John Sullivan called it, "the first step of a long battle. The Obama administration, the U.S. Chamber of Commerce, and the corporate wing of the GOP are likely to fight it all the way to the Supreme Court if need be."[56] In April 2015, John and the Immigration Reform Law Institute filed another federal lawsuit in D.C., challenging President Obama's arbitrary and capricious regulatory expansion of work authorizations for H-1B workers' spouses (classified as H-4 visa holders). The plaintiff, Save Jobs USA, is a group of former Southern California Edison employees who were forced to train their foreign guest worker replacements before being laid off. As their complaint warns: "Corporate America is already seizing upon the opportunity created by DHS for more cheap labor. . . . Even before going into effect, the H-4 Rule has already created a market demand for aliens who possess an H-4 visa [and] these H-4 aliens are already directly competing with Save Jobs USA members."[57]

Though we come from very different backgrounds, John and I share a passion for seeking and sharing the truth about the Big Government/ Big Business alliances harming our country. Our shared special interest is the American worker, whose voice has been drowned out by the cheap labor lobby. This book is an indictment not only of bipartisan political corruption in Washington, but also of the advocacy research misconduct and journalistic malpractice that has provided cover for the sellouts.

It's time to trade the whitewash for solvent. American workers deserve better and the American public deserves the unvarnished truth.

Michelle Malkin
September 2015

PART I: THE H-1B BETRAYAL

⊣ 1 ⊢

When Barry Met Jennifer

A Texas Mom's Epic Reality Check for the White House

Jennifer Wedel describes herself as a "YouTuber" with "a sassy mouth."

The thirty-two-year-old Fort Worth resident has a Texas-sized personality to match. She's wild about her family, Schlotzky's sandwiches, and fart jokes. Jennifer is also a self-described "big, dorky nerd" about technology and social media. Her YouTube channel, "Momma Wedel," documents her family's "crazy Texas life" with home videos titled "TICKLED TO DEATH," "LITTLE GIRL PICKING HER BOOGERS," "NINJA MOM SNOOPS," "SILLY STRING PRANK," and "WEIGHT LOSS FAIL."[1]

On January 24, 2012, Jennifer departed from her usual wisecracking family fare. The vivacious online denizen had spotted a "little red telephone" symbol on her YouTube account dashboard.

"What the heck is that?" she thought.[2]

When she clicked on the icon, she was directed to a solicitation for citizen videos as part of a special event tied to President Obama's State of the Union Address. YouTube's parent company, Google, launched the public contest in cooperation with the White House—a high-visibility opportunity for the social media giant to promote its online video chat service, Google+ Hangout.

Jennifer read the invitation:

> If you could hang out with President Obama, what would you ask him? Would your question be about jobs or unemployment? The threat of nuclear weapons? Immigration reform? Whatever your question is, submit it on YouTube for the opportunity to ask the President directly in a special interview over a Google+ Hangout from the White House.[3]

Momma Wedel marched to her dimly lit bedroom and recorded a twenty-second video. With minimal makeup and noticeable bags under her eyes, the busy wife and mom of two young daughters pointed a wobbly camera toward herself, licked her lips, and began:

"Mr. President, my husband was laid off three years ago. He has an electrical engineering degree and has yet to find a job," she divulged, shaking her head.

"My question to you," Jennifer addressed the commander-in-chief bluntly with a slight southern drawl, "is how are you preventing foreigners with H-1B visas from getting American citizens' jobs?"

Foreign nationals who enter the U.S. legally are admitted as immigrants (aliens seeking permanent residence), nonimmigrants (such as students, diplomats, tourists, and workers), or refugees/asylees. The H-1B is a nonimmigrant guest worker visa created in 1990.[4] The employer—not the foreigner or a family sponsor—makes the visa application to the U.S. Citizenship and Immigration Services of the Department of Homeland Security. An initial H-1B visa is issued for three years. It can be renewed for another three years. If the H-1B worker's employer sponsors him or her for legal permanent residency, the H-1B visa can be extended in one-year increments until a green card is granted.

H-1B visas are restricted to "specialty" occupations that normally require a college degree or equivalent professional experience—plus, believe it or not, fashion models.[5] About three-fifths of H-1B visas go to workers in computer-related occupations. Most of the rest go to engineers, scientists, mathematicians, architects, surveyors, elementary and secondary school teachers, nurses, physical therapists, accountants, physicians, and those Beautiful People.

There are three steps required to get an H-1B visa. First, the employer files a Labor Condition Application (LCA) with the Department of Labor. The LCA certifies that an employer will comply with all the labor protection requirements of the H-1B program. Filing an LCA is a simple process that can be done online and costs nothing. Congress requires the Department of Labor to approval all LCAs within seven days as long as the form is filled out correctly. The Department of Labor is also prohibited from subsequently reviewing approved LCAs. As we'll explain in more detail later, the LCA process is nothing more than a meaningless paper-shuffling exercise. Next, the employer files an I-129 "Petition for Non-Immigrant Worker Form." This complex and costly process usually requires hiring a lawyer. If the petition is approved, the last step is for the worker to obtain the visa from the State Department. Consular offices may require an in-person visit, interview, fingerprinting, and document review. The successful applicant receives a visa stamp in his passport and can now enter the U.S.

The media often use inflated terms such as "best and brightest" and "highly-skilled" to describe H-1B workers. In reality the standards are low. A bachelor's degree, even a mail-order one from an Indian diploma mill, is all it takes to qualify.[6] As tech journalist Robert X. Cringely points out, "when Bill Gates complained about not being able to import enough top technical people for Microsoft, he wasn't talking about geniuses, just normal coders."[7]

There *is* a visa for the world's truly talented high achievers called the O visa, which is uncapped and available only to "individuals with extraordinary ability or achievement" in the fields of "sciences, arts, education, business, or athletics, or who has a demonstrated record of extraordinary achievement in the motion picture or television industry and has been recognized nationally or internationally for those achievements" who seek "to enter the United States to continue work in the area of extraordinary ability."[8] Google, Apple, and other top tech companies "will take as many of the O visa candidates as they can get, but there just aren't that many who qualify, which is why quotas aren't required," Cringely explained. "So when Microsoft—or Boeing, for that matter—says a limitation on H-1B visas is keeping them from getting top talent, they don't mean it in the way that they imply. If a prospective employee is *really* top talent—the kind of engineer who can truly do things others simply can't—there isn't much keeping the company from hiring that person under the O visa program. H-1B visas are about journeyman techies and nothing else."[9]

Darin Wedel's LinkedIn page is impressive.[10] Damned impressive. He's an American tech company's ideal job candidate. Or rather, he *should* be.

The science whiz graduated from Texas A&M in 1995 with a BS in electrical engineering. He worked as a process engineer for Hitachi Semiconductor and Dominion Conductor. In 2000, he joined Texas Instruments, the renowned chipmaker whose products range from your high school kid's graphing calculator to microcontrollers, data converters, processors, and integrated circuits used in touch screens, medical devices, surveillance cameras, tablets, and cars. He is "skilled in complex Electro-Mechanical, vacuum, gas delivery, materials, and quality control systems," "adept at learning complex hardware and software," and "skilled in leading edge manufacturing techniques: Six Sigma, SPC, DOE, ISO, FMEA, Predictive Maintenance, defect controls, material inspection, process optimization, capital equipment installation, and equipment development."

Wedel co-led a cutting-edge development project evaluating a "liquid chemical process precursor" for "next generation silicone nitride film."[11] Silicone nitride film, which resists moisture and oxygen, protects the surface of semiconductors. Wedel's work resulted in a valuable patented process for his company. Scaling the corporate ladder, he spearheaded development of more than forty complex electromechanical systems and manufacturing improvements.

The Texas Instruments electrical engineer prospered. He bought a nice home and lived the middle-class American dream, which talking heads in both political parties bloviate about every election cycle.

But after nine years of working hard and playing by the rules, Darin got laid off.

To the newspapers, he was just another bloodless statistic. "Layoffs spread to more sectors of the economy," the *New York Times* blandly reported in January 2009.[12] "Tech layoff parade continues: TI cuts 12 percent of workforce," ZDNet.com wrote.[13] The company slashed some thirty-four hundred positions through direct pink slips or "voluntary retirement" offers to "older" workers.

To his own company, he was a faceless liability. After nine successful years in the heart of the Dallas–Fort Worth tech corridor, the Lone Star State's own Silicon Valley, TI tossed forty-three-year-old Darin into the swirling currents of the highly skilled unemployed—and threw his family into financial and emotional chaos.

•   •   •

To fully appreciate the political fraud and continuing bureaucratic molestation of America's nonimmigrant visa programs, we must first travel back to the passage of the Immigration and Nationality Act of 1952 (known as the McCarran-Walter Act). Congress enacted the Democratic-sponsored bill over President Truman's veto to manage the flow of foreigners into America. With the Cold War and communist threat foremost on the nation's mind, an overwhelming majority of lawmakers approved McCarran-Walter's continuation of a national origins quota system (in place since 1924), combined with an orderly process to handle immigrants based on humanitarian reasons and a new set of visa preferences based on family reunification or skills.[14]

The law created two main guest worker visas: H-1 for guest workers with distinguished ability and H-2 for ordinary guest workers. (A third category was created for trainees.) The H-1 and H-2 visas had one feature in common and one major difference. Both visas were strictly guest worker programs. The alien had to maintain a foreign residence to qualify. The H-1 visa differed from the H-2 visa in that it did *not* require showing that Americans were not available for the job. It is clear from the legislative history[15] that Congress originally intended that the H-1 visa would be restricted to truly extraordinary people, such as distinguished professors and other "outstanding scholars, scientists, and teachers" of "exceptional ability whose services are needed in the country."[16] Lawmakers mistakenly assumed that for a small cadre of high-level intellectual elites and professional heavyweights, domestic protections would not be necessary.

If you read the plain text of the Immigration and Nationality Act of 1952, you would expect that a Nobel Prize winner coming to lecture at a university would fall into the H-1 category and an ordinary engineer would fall into the H-2 category. This turned out not to be the case. A series of backdoor agency decisions wiped out labor protections in the H-2 program for many U.S. workers. The then–Immigration and Naturalization Service (now the U.S. Citizenship and Immigration Services) unilaterally started classifying *anyone* in a profession as falling under the H-1 category. The INS decided that any alien engineer deserved to be classified as a worker with "distinguished merit and ability"—thus qualifying him for an H-1 visa, even though Congress clearly intended the H-2 visa for such workers. Through that process, the INS gutted the labor protections of the H-2 visa. Expansive and overbroad agency interpretations have persistently plagued our immigration system, empowering unelected bureaucrats at INS, its successor, USCIS, and the State Department to undermine and sabotage congressional intent.[17]

In 1990, Congress finally addressed the H-1 visa abuse epidemic. A House Judiciary Committee report noted at the time that administrative decision-making run amok "meant that little known entertainers and their accompanying crews [qualify] within this category, and aliens with nothing more than a baccalaureate degree have been deemed "distinguished.""[18] Politicians responded to the administrative sabotage of the previous H-1 program by placing specific limits on guest worker admissions.[19] The Immigration Act of 1990 amended the 1952 Immigration and Nationality Act to create the current H-1B visa program.[20]

Congress originally capped the number of H-1B visas at 65,000 per year, but the cap has changed several times thanks to the influence of the nonstop Cheap Foreign Labor Lobby. The absurdly named American Competitiveness and Workforce Improvement Act of 1998 increased the cap to 115,000 for fiscal year 1999 and fiscal year 2000. The American Competitiveness in the Twenty-First Century Act of 2000 (AC21) further increased the limit to 195,000 for fiscal year 2001 through fiscal year 2003. In addition, AC21 permanently exempted all foreign guest workers hired by institutions of higher education, as well as nonprofit and government-research organizations, from the cap. (See Figure 1.1.)

Beltway crapweasels in the House unanimously passed the 2000 bill on a voice vote that took place at night with only about forty members present. The vote took place after the leadership announced there would be no more votes for the day and most members had gone home.[21] It is not known who was present voting for the bill. The dark-of-night adoption of these anti–American worker statutes is a habit of feckless politicians in both parties. Congressional leaders take great pains to avoid having direct votes on H-1B.

In fiscal year 2004, the cap reverted to its original level of 65,000. But the H-1B Visa Reform Act of 2004 allowed for an additional 20,000 visas each year for foreign workers holding a master's degree or higher from an American institution of higher education to be exempted from the numerical cap limitation. In addition, in 2004, as a result of free trade agreements, more statutory changes allowed for up to 6,800 of the 65,000 H-1B visas to be set aside for workers from Chile and Singapore.[22] To prevent members from being held accountable, this H-1B expansion was buried in a massive budget bill.

FIGURE 1.1 CHANGES IN THE H-1B CAP OVER TIME

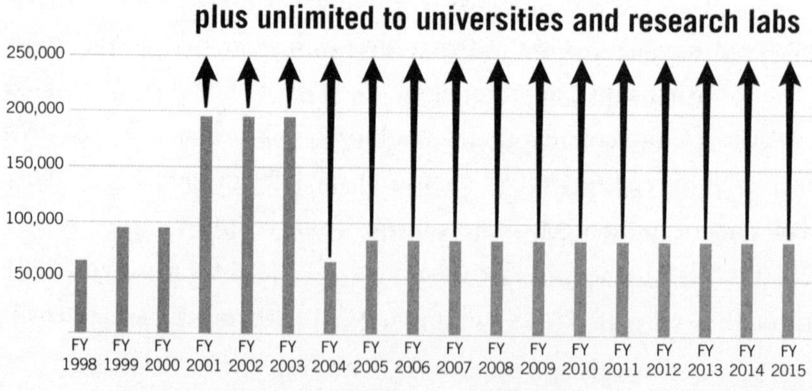

plus unlimited to universities and research labs

Old habits die hard. In 2015, Washington insiders again called on Congress to slip a new H-1B increase into a budget bill.[23] Sen. Charles Grassley rightly cautions against the Big Tech quota busters. "We'll hear arguments all day as to why the cap on H-1B visas should be raised, but nobody should be fooled," he said. "There are highly skilled American workers being left behind, searching for jobs that are being filled by H-1B visa holders."[24]

Across the country, American tech workers like Darin in their thirties and forties face rampant discrimination based on their age and citizenship status. (Yes, dear readers in your thirties and forties, welcome to geezerhood.)

U.S. computer workers forty and older are more likely to be laid off than those under forty; take longer to find a job after being laid off; and, when rehired, receive a substantial loss in wages.[25] The TechCrunch blog calls it "Silicon Valley's Dark Secret."[26] Recruiters and investors lust after the "cachet of the young entrepreneur."[27] At a tech conference in 2007 in which he advised companies not to hire workers over thirty, baby-faced Facebook CEO Mark Zuckerberg infamously bragged: "Young people are just smarter."[28] (Zuckerberg, by the way, turns thirty-one this year.)

Once they're out of their twenties, tech workers turn to makeover consultants and wardrobe stylists to maintain freshness. Piercings, biker boots, eyelid lifts. Whatever it takes.[29] And that's why the Botox-dispensing business is booming for San Francisco cosmetic surgeon Dr. Seth Matarasso, whose clientele now mainly consists of anxious American tech workers trying to rejuvenate their looks.[30]

"It's really morphed into, 'Hey, I'm forty years old and I have to get in front of a board of fresh-faced kids. I can't look like I have a wife and two-point-five kids and a mortgage,' " he divulged.[31]

Human resources departments have blatantly flouted anti–age discrimination laws by routinely excluding the applications of older workers on the grounds that the applicants have "experience beyond the range stated in the job ad." A "senior programmer" in job advertisements requires only three to five years of experience (e.g., a twenty-five- to twenty-seven-year-old).[32] *Fortune* magazine blew the whistle on job ads from Apple, Facebook, Yahoo, Dropbox, and video game maker Electronic Arts[33] explicitly favoring "recent grads" over older workers.

Caught with its pants down, Electronic Arts defended the ads to *Fortune* by claiming it hires people of all ages into its new grad program. "To prove the point," the magazine reported, "the company said those accepted into the program range in age from 21 to 35. But the company soon had second thoughts about releasing such information, which shows a total absence of middle-aged hires in the grad program, and asked *Fortune* to withhold that detail from publication."

Fortunately, the *Fortune* journalist did his job and disclosed the truth instead of burying it. But that's an exception, not the rule, in most mainstream media coverage of the Great American Tech Worker Sellout.

So, where are jobs like Darin's going? To younger, cheaper, foreign workers. About 75 percent of H-1B workers are under thirty-five years old.[34] Norman Matloff, a computer science professor at U.C. Davis, has extensively documented how "employers use H-1B to avoid hiring older (i.e., over age 35) U.S. citizens and permanent residents."

While Texas Instruments lays off thousands of American tech employees like Darin, its top officials have busied themselves pushing for "immigration reform"—Washington's overworn euphemism for opening up the pipeline to low-cost foreign workers.

•   •   •

Before 1990, there had been a clear distinction between nonimmigrant guest workers and immigrants. The Immigration and Nationality Act of 1952 required H visa holders to have "a residence in a foreign country which he has no intention of abandoning." The general rule was that a guest worker could not switch and become an immigrant without returning home.

The Immigration Act of 1990, by contrast, specifically authorized aliens with immigration intent to be admitted on H-1B guest worker visas.[35] The "dual intent" doctrine gave these guest workers the option to change their minds and change their status after they entered the country, but banned them from coming if their "sole intent" was to use their visa as a vehicle to immigrate permanently. What then is an H-1B worker—a nonimmigrant guest worker or an immigrant? Aliens should come to the U.S. either to visit or to immigrate. They should know where they stand when they arrive at our shores. Visitors should be required to return to their home before applying to be an immigrant. The current system of dual intent that permits "temporary" workers to apply for permanent immigration is inherently irrational. Allowing those admitted under the lower standard of nonimmigrant (tourists, students, etc.) then allowing them to apply for the higher standard of immigration creates backlogs by its very nature. It's like the New Jersey Turnpike merging from ten lanes to six lanes.

Appallingly but unsurprisingly, the federal government does not maintain an active count of unique H-1B visa holders. USCIS uses two separate computer systems that are incapable of exchanging data to track H-1B workers.[36] A rough estimate, based upon the number of visa approvals over three years, is that there are about 650,000 H-1B workers legally in the U.S.[37] Figure 1.2 shows the number of new H-1Bs approved over the last fifteen years.

FIGURE 1.2 H-1B PETITIONS APPROVED FOR INITIAL EMPLOYMENT

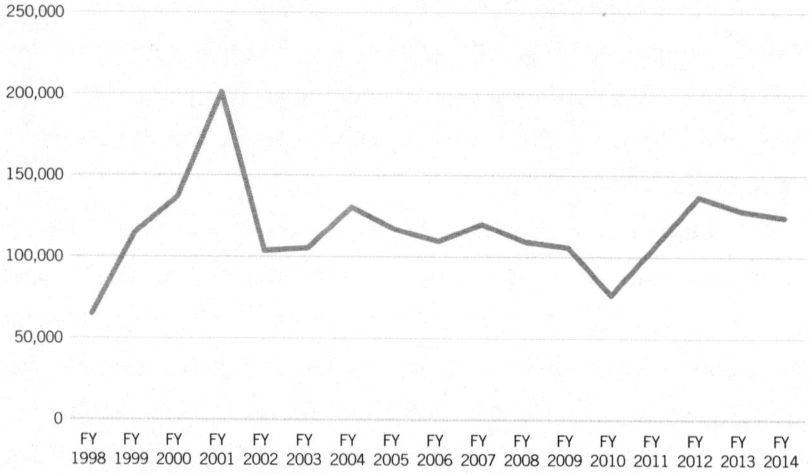

It is impossible to know how many people admitted on H-1B visas have overstayed their visas to become illegal aliens. As Michelle has documented in her book *Invasion* and in her syndicated columns for the past fifteen years, Congress has repeatedly mandated a nationwide visa entry-exit system to track legal short-term visa holders during the past two decades. But outrageously, one has yet to be built—even in the wake of the 9/11 terrorist attacks, which were perpetrated in part by several illegal alien visa overstayers—thanks to a toxic alliance of civil liberties absolutists, immigration lawyers, and ethnic lobbies.[38]

The current "US-VISIT" database, which processes biometric data upon foreign visitors' entry, suffers from widespread lack of data integrity and failed interoperability.[39] The Government Accountability Office reported a backlog of 1.6 million "unmatched" arrival records, which means they had yet to verify that those visa holders had actually departed.[40] To this day, there is *still* no *exit* control system in place, and DHS continues to drag its feet on planning and implementation. Universities, the travel industry, civil liberties absolutists, ethnic lobbies, and politicians in both parties have deliberately sabotaged efforts to get it up and running.[41]

An estimated 40–45 percent of the current illegal immigrant population in the U.S. consists of foreign visa overstayers who entered on valid visas and then never left.[42]

In 2008, the year before Darin lost his job, Texas Instruments spent $4 million on D.C. lobbyists,[43] many of them crusading "to increase visas for highly skilled foreign workers that the tech industry says is needed to fill vacant positions." It hired three lobbyists to push for eight different bills and one regulation designed to increase the amount of foreign labor. TI president Richard Templeton joined the "Compete America" coalition to push for more temporary H-1B work permits for foreigners and to sound the alarm about the so-called STEM worker "shortage." Paula Collins, then–vice president of government relations for Texas Instruments, became cochair of the industry group, which includes Accenture, Cisco, Google, Intel, and Microsoft.

Rather than focus on keeping their own high-skilled American workers, these business executives made retention of *foreign* visa holders their top priority. TI's Collins crusaded for legislation that would allow foreign-born college graduates with advanced technical degrees to be exempted from congressional H-1B visa caps. "To remain competitive," she claimed, "high-tech firms need to be able to hire and retain the best science and engineering talent in the world, especially graduates of U.S. universities."

But what about native-born, highly skilled, and experienced homegrown talents like Darin Wedel?

"Our own best and brightest are squeezed out of the market once they become 'expensive,' " Ron Hira, Economic Policy Institute research associate and associate professor at Howard University, has concluded. "The industry's claim that American kids don't study enough math and science is a red herring and is rank hypocrisy, with the layoffs of thousands of U.S. citizens and permanent residents who were math and science whizzes as kids."[44]

Texas Instruments' vice president of human resources, Darla Whitaker, admitted that her company did not have any problem finding Americans with bachelor's degrees in engineering.[45] At a congressional hearing on the alleged STEM worker shortage, she claimed the real problem was in finding Americans with advanced degrees (master's or doctorates) in engineering. When Congressman Ted Poe (R-Texas) asked her why Americans don't pursue graduate degrees, Whitaker replied, "I don't really know the exact reason why they don't."

According to *Science* magazine, the reason many engineers don't pursue graduate degrees is simple: The degrees aren't worth the money. "[I]n purely financial terms," the magazine reported, "the case for graduate training is not compelling, and the short- to medium-term sacrifices a career in science can demand cause even some passionate scientists and trainees to reconsider their plans before they reach the financial break-even point."[46]

In other words, salaries for engineers with advanced degrees aren't high enough to justify the investment. And why is that? Because the importation of foreign guest workers with advanced degrees is suppressing wages.

This is exactly what an internal report of the National Science Foundation predicted in 1989, when it forecast that a deluge of foreign doctoral students would hold salaries down—and drive American STEM bachelor's degree holders into better-paying jobs outside their fields of study after graduation.[47] This, NSF noted, would lead to a vicious cycle of American STEM PhDs seeking "alternative career paths" or educational pursuits outside their original areas of study, leading tech companies to clamor for more foreign PhD students to fill the gap they helped create.

And therein lies the answer to Rep. Poe's question to Ms. Whitaker. The diversion of talented American engineers away from graduate study is precisely the result of Big Tech's insatiable appetite for low-wage foreign workers.

As Roger Coker, Texas Instruments' director of staffing for the United States, told *U.S. News & World Report* back in 1999, the company was "using every trick in the book to fight labor cost creep" by lobbying Congress to "allow more foreign engineers and designers to take jobs in the United States on temporary H-1B visas."[48]

A decade later, Darin Wedel's number was up. The very same year he was laid off, Texas Instruments was lobbying President Obama to ease restrictions on foreign workers. And three years after getting the pink slip, the electrical engineer was *still* searching for permanent work.

Message from American tech companies to American tech workers: We're just not that into you.

Companies in the business of offshore outsourcing are the largest users of H-1B workers, accounting for more than 50 percent of the annual base visa cap of sixty-five thousand.[49] They use H-1B workers to help transition IT operations from the U.S. to overseas locations such as India, where wages are lower.

Table 1.1 lists the thirteen largest recipients of H-1B visas in 2013.[50] Of the thirteen, six are based in India: Infosys, Tata, Wipro, HCL America, Tech Mahindra, and Larsen & Toubro. One—Cognizant—was founded in India but moved its headquarters to the U.S. Five—Syntel, IBM, iGate, Deloitte, and Accenture (formerly Anderson Consulting)—offer offshoring services and have large presences in India. Even Microsoft entered the business of selling offshore development from India.[51] It has also moved internal development overseas. At an internal presentation titled "Thinking About India," Microsoft vice president Brian Valentine urged employees to "pick something to move offshore today."[52] coincidentally, a majority of H-1B workers—65 percent in fiscal year 2013—are from India.[53] In computer-related occupations, the proportion of Indian workers is even higher—nearly 86 percent in 2014, according to an August 2015 report published in *Computerworld*.[54] The magazine's analysis showed Tata, Cognizant, Infosys, Wipro, Accenture, Tech Mahindra, IBM, Syntel, Larsen & Toubro, and HCL as the top ten companies winning H-1B visa approvals for computer workers in 2014.[55]

TABLE 1.1   LARGEST RECIPIENTS OF H-1B VISAS IN FY 2013

Company	Visas	Offers Offshoring Services?
Infosys	6,298	Yes
Tata	6,258	Yes
Cognizant	5,186	Yes
Accenture	3,346	Yes
Wipro	2,644	Yes
HCL America	1,766	Yes
IBM	1,624	Yes
Mahindra Group	1,589	Yes
Larsen & Toubro	1,580	Yes
Deloitte	1,491	Yes
IGate	1,157	Yes
Microsoft	1,048	Yes
Syntel	1,041	Yes

A few days after she posted her "Dear Mr. President" YouTube clip, Jennifer received a phone call after work. The stay-at-home mom had taken a job at a nearby State Farm office—first as a secretary, then rising to full-time insurance agent—to help pay the bills while Darin searched for a new job. The caller? A Google employee who informed the young mom that she had been chosen to pose her challenge to President Obama. Face to virtual face.

Naturally, Jennifer took to YouTube.

"YAAAAAAY! WOO-HOO! I got chosen!"

Bubbling with excitement, Jennifer informed friends, family, and strangers on YouTube of the news in a January 28, 2012, video titled "I AM INTERVIEWING OBAMA." She talked into a dashboard camera while driving—and without missing a beat.

"If you don't know what an H-1B visa is," she breezily explained as trees and telephone poles flashed by, "it's basically a work visa. And not just any work visa. It's a work visa for foreigners who have college educations to get jobs [over here] that require at least a bachelor's degree or more."

With a small sigh, she distilled the core issue for American workers more astutely and succinctly than most elected officials in Washington.

"Well, the problem with *that* is," Jennifer grimaced, "when the economy [got] hit hard, a lot of big corporations laid off a lot of people, including my husband. And what they have started doing, because it's cheaper labor, is hiring people with H-1B visas. And it is completely and utterly wrong!

"I am not in any way bashing H-1B visa holders," Jennifer made clear. "And I very much believe in the American dream. Having foreigners come here and find freedom and find work, you know, that's what this country was founded on. So I'm not at all bashing anyone who is on the H-1B program. But what I am bashing is the government for not steppin' in and sayin' okay, well, we have a cap of sixty-five thousand a year, we need to lower this and let more Americans—especially ones who got laid off!—get a chance at getting these jobs and really kinda, you know, slap the hands of the corporations that are lobbying for this."

No doubt about it: Jennifer was ready for prime time and prepped to take on the president.

Given Google's own advocacy of increasing H-1B visas, you might wonder how in the world Jennifer's question got picked. Google Hangout host Steve Grove says the company took into account a combination of votes and other factors. In Jennifer's case, her bubbly personality and articulate delivery shone through.

The busy mom hurried home to set up for a rehearsal with Google employees sent to her house.

Jennifer told her YouTube viewers the day before her historic hangout that she was excited beyond belief. Though she identified herself as a Republican, she still relished the "once in a lifetime" opportunity to speak with the president, and she hadn't been happy with how either political party had dealt with H-1Bs. "I don't care if you voted for him or not. Talking to the president is cool. I mean, you know, how many people get to ask him a question? Not a lot of people get to do that."

Back in Washington, D.C., White House speechwriters huddled over President Obama's edits to his last State of the Union Address of his first term. Gene Sperling, a top economic adviser, explained in a "behind the scenes" video that his boss wanted to focus on "getting more Americans back to the top of high-paying, durable jobs that last."[56] Championing the "middle class" would be another big theme. (When is it not?)

Another Obama aide emphasized the need to give a sense of "humanity" and "reality" to the speech by highlighting real people to "make a concrete connection."[57] As an extra boost to sell the president's policies, the White House handpicked twenty-one special guests to sit in First Lady Michelle Obama's box during the address. The invitees were supposedly "representative of America." One of the lucky chosen: Instagram cofounder Mike Krieger.

"You don't say no to the White House," the tech startup guru excitedly told CNN when he received the call three days before President Obama's speech.[58] He flew into D.C. and immediately embarked on a whirlwind with the administration's top tech bureaucrats before joining the First Lady for the festivities—which, of course, he Instagrammed.

Why did the Obamas tap Mike Krieger and not, say, his cofounder Kevin Systrom, the American-born, Stanford University–trained engineer who originally conceived Instagram and recruited Krieger?[59] In its announcement of the First Lady's 2012 State of the Union guest list, the East Wing spotlighted Krieger's immigrant history. He was born in São Paulo, Brazil, and moved to California in 2004 to attend Stanford University, where he studied computer science and cognitive science on an F-1 student visa. After graduation, he worked for a year through the Optional Practical Training program, later applying for and receiving an H-1B visa at instant messaging firm Meebo. In 2010, Systrom enlisted him to cofound Instagram,[60] which they sold to Facebook for $1 billion in 2012. Three years later, Krieger secured a green card.[61]

The Instagram cofounder has lobbied Washington aggressively to raise the caps on H-1B visas, expand work training opportunities for foreign STEM students in the U.S., and increase green cards for foreign graduate students.[62] His personal history bolsters the popular Big Tech narrative that foreign H-1B workers are brilliant entrepreneurial resources, brimming with billion-dollar, job-creating startup ideas.

CNN dutifully explained that the Brazilian wunderkind's attendance at the 2012 State of the Union Address "represented the need for legislation that would assist non–U.S. citizen startup founders looking to build a company in America."[63] Perched in the First Lady's gallery, Krieger applauded as Obama lamented that foreign students who "staff our labs" and "start new businesses" come to the U.S. "to study business and science and engineering, but as soon as they get their degree, we send them home to invent new products and create new jobs somewhere else."

Obama shook his head and raised his hands in exasperation: "That doesn't make sense."[64]

The President's Council on Jobs and Competitiveness echoed White House and tech industry talking points with its sweeping assertion that "highly skilled immigrants create jobs, they don't take jobs."[65] Press reports trumpeted the factoid that "More Than a Third of the Top US Tech Companies Were Founded by People Born Outside the Country."[66] Chicken Little pundits wailed that "startups are starved for engineers and other workers."[67] Stanford University president John Hennessy complained that "forcing" foreign graduate students "to leave, rather than allowing them to stay and add their skills and knowledge to our economy, is one of the most short-sighted policies we have."[68]

As for those statistics on immigrants and tech companies, it all depends on how you slice it. The frequently cited figure from venture capitalist and H-1B crusader Mary Meeker, which purports to show that 36 percent of America's top twenty-five tech companies were founded by immigrants, misleads the casual reader into assuming that only 64 percent of companies were founded by native-born Americans. However, Ms. Meeker used a trick with numbers; she counted as "founded by immigrants" any company that has at least one of its often multiple founders who was born abroad. But that trick works both ways. All you have to do is flip her numbers around; instead of ignoring the native-born Americans, ignore the immigrants. From that, one can determine that native-born Americans founded 92 percent of the companies studied.[69]

Darin Wedel's former employer Texas Instruments, for example, had four founders: John Erik Jonsson (born in Brooklyn, N.Y.), Eugene McDermott (born in Brooklyn, N.Y.), Patrick Haggarty (born in Harvey, N.D.), and Cecil Green (born in Whitefield, England). Meeker ignored Jonsson, McDermott, and Haggarty in favor of Green and dubbed Texas Instruments a company founded by immigrants. Do the opposite and ignore Green. Voilà! Texas Instruments becomes a company founded by native-born Americans.

That statistical deception is only the first misstep in the argument. Next comes the non sequitur. The fact that Sergey Brin came to the United States as a child and years later became a cofounder of Google in no way supports the argument that America needs more H-1B guest workers.

Instagram's Krieger is an anomaly. Stringent employment rules bind H-1B visa holders to the companies that sponsor them. H-1B workers who want to start new businesses can only do so under limited circumstances in which the startup can "provide evidence that there is a separate Board of Directors which has the ability to hire, fire, pay, supervise or otherwise control the beneficiary's employment." This is because an H-1B worker must be an employee of the startup.[70]

Unfortunately for homegrown tech startup founders and displaced American tech workers, President Obama and his State of the Union speechwriting team had no interest in showcasing their stories. There is no Laid-Off American Worker Lobby to funnel cash into D.C. coffers. Obama's deep-pocketed tech industry donors, meanwhile, had been clamoring relentlessly for more H-1B visas and specialty green cards to feed their foreign worker pipeline. It bought them seats at the table, backstage access, and choice words on Obama's teleprompter.

As politicians in both parties applauded, Obama punctuated his 2012 State of the Union Address with a call for "comprehensive immigration reform"—that is, legislative action on behalf of foreign students, illegal aliens, and legal temporary foreign workers.

In the First Lady's box, Mike Krieger beamed proudly as the hand-picked representative of "immigrant-founded startups" that, in truth, are (1) as much American-founded as they are immigrant-founded; (2) not representative of the modest skills and achievements of most H-1B visa holders; and (3) expedient distractions from the dire impact that the foreign tech flood is having on American workers.

Outside the Beltway, families like the Wedels had no place or space in President Obama's manufactured reality. But six days after the 2012 State of the Union Address, Momma Wedel would burst that bubble—big time.

With pictures of her two young daughters hanging on a cheery, yellow-painted wall behind her, Jennifer faced a webcam in her living room and spoke directly to President Obama.

"Hi, Mr. President. My husband has an engineering degree with over ten years of experience, and he was laid off three years and has yet to find a permanent job in his field. My question to you is why does the government continue to issue and extend H-1B visas when there are tons of Americans just like my husband with no job?"

Obama, clearly flummoxed, immediately started to filibuster.

"Well, Jennifer," the president began, "I don't know your husband's specialty, but I can tell you that there's a huge demand around the country for engineers."

Well, yes: There's a huge demand. But only for cheaper, younger, foreign engineers.

"Now, obviously, there are different kinds of engineers," he babbled, before plugging his government infrastructure spending to put civil engineers to work. Then he pivoted like a Bolshoi Ballet dancer.

"Now, what industry tells me is that they don't have enough highly skilled engineers. If your husband's in that field, then we should get his résumé and I'll forward it to some of these companies that tell me they can't find enough engineers in this field."

The cameras cut to Google Hangout host Steve Grove chuckling. Jennifer, however, didn't think her hubby's job loss was a laughing matter. She astutely observed after the event: "I just think I stumped him a little and he wanted me to hush about it."[71]

Ignoring the facts just laid out to him by the wife of an engineer who couldn't find work for the last three years, President Obama yammered again that "as a basic matter, there's a huge demand for engineers around the country right now."

"Um, I understand that," Wedel tried to interject politely.

"And so . . ." Obama prattled on.

"But," Wedel jumped in, seizing the moment, "given the list [of job openings] that you're getting, *we're* not getting that. I mean, you said in the State of the Union for business leaders to ask themselves what can they do to bring jobs back to America."

"Right," Obama mumbled.

Wedel challenged the president: "But *why* do you think the H-1B is so popular with big corporations?"

Bull's-eye!

Instead of confronting the reality of the Big Tech preference for lower-wage foreign workers over Americans, Obama dodged.

"Jennifer, can I ask you what kind of engineer your husband is?"

"He's a semiconductor engineer."

Obama, unable to cope with the cognitive dissonance of what industry was telling him and what Darin had suffered, evaded Jennifer's question again.

"See, it's interesting to me," he started, then backtracked, "and I meant what I said, if you send me your husband's résumé, I'd be interested in finding out exactly what's happening right there, because the word that we're getting is that somebody in that kind of high-tech field, that kind of engineer, should be able to find something, uh, right away."

The president persisted in showing just how out of touch and clueless he was about how H-1B actually works.

"[T]he H-1B should be reserved only for those companies who say they cannot find somebody in that particular field," he said. "So, that wouldn't necessarily apply if, in fact, there are a lot of highly skilled American engineers in that position." While H-1B visas *should* be reserved for jobs that Americans are not filling, that is not how the program works. And when it comes to actual legislative change, Obama has only pushed for even *more* foreign workers with no changes to the broken system.

Jennifer again tried to inject reality, but the Google host wanted to move on. The next questioner, a young man from Detroit, started his question by thanking Obama for "saving the auto industry."

Twenty minutes later, Jennifer couldn't hold her tongue. President Obama was urging a group of high school students to get college degrees in order to secure good-paying jobs. When one young man expressed anxiety about not being able to find a job even after graduating from college, Obama bizarrely lectured the students not to "goof off" and to seek "growth areas" in higher education in order to "make a good investment."

Jennifer's husband did all the right things when he earned his electrical engineering degree at Texas A&M. A lot of good it was doing him now. She jumped in to point out that a lot of responsible kids "have seen their parents get laid off. . . . And because of the downturn . . . they see their father not even able to have a job . . . and it's affecting them!"

Following President Obama's gimmicky offer to help, the Wedels were inundated with press inquiries. Jennifer's gutsy willingness to take on the White House caught the attention of *Politico, The Atlantic,*

CNN, CNBC, Fox News, MSNBC, and every major Texas newspaper and TV station. The Republican National Committee exploited the opportunity to needle Obama the headhunter with a website soliciting résumés from other laid-off workers. But as the Wedels knew, the GOP was just as culpable as the Obama White House for enabling the H-1B racket.

After White House staffers passed his résumé around, Darin Wedel received a few job offers. But they came from out of state, in places like New York City, where the cost of living was prohibitive for a middle-class family of four. Another complication: A custody arrangement with one of Darin's daughters from a previous marriage prevented him from leaving North Texas. Some open-borders pundits used the Wedels' immobility as an excuse to dismiss Jennifer's confrontation with the president entirely. "Immigrants did not take your job," sneered a Cato Institute analyst, who blamed the family for sticking "to the Dallas–Fort Worth area where Jennifer held a job." Never mind that it was a job she was *forced* to seek because H-1B-hungry Texas Instruments laid off Darin in the first place.[72]

U.C. Davis professor Matloff points out that even with the Wedels' inability to move, "If the hype regarding a seller's market for engineers were true, Wedel should have been able to find something in that region"[73]—which, remember, is not just any swath of flyover country, but the fourth-largest metropolitan area in the U.S. and a dynamic technology region. By Texas Instruments president Richard Templeton's own estimate, "In Texas alone, the economy is poised to add nearly 760,000 STEM-related jobs within the next four years."[74] According to the *Dallas Business Journal*, twenty-one of the world's two thousand largest companies are based in the Dallas–Fort Worth metro area.[75]

Semiconductor firms with facilities in the area include not only Texas Instruments, but also Maxim Integrated Products, STMicroelectronics,

Quorvo/TriQuint Semiconductor, and Diodes Inc. All employ H-1B guest workers. None hired Darin Wedel.

Through the sheer force of her candid and bold questioning of President Obama, Jennifer Wedel succeeded in disrupting the administration's carefully crafted economic narratives. At a White House press briefing the day after the Google Hangout, press secretary Jay Carney opened by touting his boss's "Startup America initiative" and peddling "important visa reforms that remove undue obstacles for high-skill immigrants and recent graduates that contribute to our economic competitiveness."[76] Some of the reporters peppered Carney with questions about Darin's résumé:

> "Is this something that he plans to do now when he campaigns and hears people's individual stories, to get down to that level of collecting résumés? Is that something that he thinks is part of the job of President?"[77]
>
> "What exactly is going to happen to the résumé that—from this guy? And what are you going to do about the inevitable tens of thousands of résumés that are going to be sent here because of that?"[78]

Unlike Jennifer, alas, the professional journalists appeared to know nothing about the crux of the H-1B debate and squandered their opportunity to follow up with their own reality checks. Carney asserted that Obama's exchange with the Texas mom demonstrated his "sincere interest and concern in the experiences of folks out in the country and how they're dealing with what remains a very tough economy."[79] Yet, a day after his exchange with Jennifer, who asked President Obama to put American workers first, the White House announced multiple executive actions *loosening* foreign tech worker visa regulations. These included expanding eligibility for a seventeen-month extension of foreign student visas for students with a prior degree in a Science, Technology, Engineering and Mathematics (STEM) field and providing work authorization for spouses of certain H-1B holders. The White House also altered visa rules for "specialty occupation" foreign workers from Australia, Singapore, and China and unveiled plans for a new initiative to discuss how to maximize current immigration laws' potential to attract foreign entrepreneurial talent.[80]

The White House press corps could have challenged Carney to explain exactly how the president reconciled his "sincere" compassion for the Wedels with the actions he was taking to make it even harder for experienced American engineers like Darin to find full-time employment in their fields. Instead, an identity-politics zealot masquerading as a journalist asked this stunningly idiotic (and ungrammatical) question:

Is the President concerned that there might be a feeling of xenophobia or something going on out there when the economy is tight and there are some concerns that reflect in that question from the woman?[81]

How about the blatant reverse "xenophobia" of American companies publishing job ads excluding American workers? Under the Immigration and Nationality Act, U.S. workers, those legally entitled to work in the United States, are *supposed* to be a protected class. A decade ago, the Programmers Guild (John's group representing U.S. information technology workers) blew the whistle on employment listings at Dice .com and Monster.com that explicitly stated: "We require candidates for H1B from India," "We sponsor GC [green card] and we do prefer H1B holders," "We offer H1B services for L1 Visa Holders and new H1B for the right candidates in India" and "H1B -From India-Multiple positions."[82]

Here's another example: In 2006, iGate Mastech, a company with large Indian offshore centers, placed thirty online job ads asking for only H-1B visa holders, including this one for a Java programmer in the Midwest: "Only H-1s Apply, and should be willing to transfer H-1B."[83] In response to a complaint by the Programmers Guild, the Justice Department spanked iGate with a forty-five-thousand-dollar fine. But it's the tip of the iceberg. John filed about one hundred discrimination complaints against H-1B employers based on his groups' findings. About one-third of the complaints resulted in settlements. The rest of the companies were not covered by antidiscrimination provisions because they had fewer than four employees.

The Justice Department's fines have done little to deter violators since then. In 2012, a separate IT recruitment watchdog group, Bright Future Jobs, published an analysis of one hundred IT ads on Dice.com restricting applicants by national origin. The group reported that 37 percent of the ads "made no mention of IT job terms or skills in the ad title. Instead, they contained only references to visa types."[84] In other words: Foreign workers only need apply. "The public is led to believe that companies can't find Americans to fill high-tech jobs when, in fact, they are not searching for Americans— as these ads show," Bright Future Jobs founder Donna Conroy warned.[85]

Conroy's activism forced Dice.com to crack down on H-1B-only jobs. Unfortunately, the H-1B-only recruitment has just moved elsewhere. In fact, there are entire websites devoted to posting jobs in which companies scout out foreign workers.

But hey, let's not let reality intrude on the White House press secretary and the White House press corps. In response to the social justice reporter who asked whether President Obama was concerned that Jennifer Wedel's questions about H-1B were "xenophobic," Carney reverted to trite tech industry mumbo-jumbo. Like his boss, Carney dismissed the facts and evidence before him. Here's the word salad he tossed at the press briefing:

> I think that the President's position, which you state clearly, is that we need to make it more possible for highly qualified people who are being educated here, or coming from abroad to work here, build businesses here, grow the economy here, create jobs here—that is a message that you hear from business leaders across the country, especially in the fields of technology and engineering and the like, so—which doesn't take away from this individual's experience at all, but the broader picture is one of a need for more engineers, a need for more highly skilled, highly educated workers to help us grow those industries in the United States that will be the foundation for our economic future.[86]

In short: unemployed American engineers? What unemployed American engineers?

While the White House prattles on about the need for more engineers, according to the Bureau of Labor Statistics, the number of engineering jobs has declined from 2,506,000 in 1990 to 2,381,000 in 2013. American engineers are getting a double whammy: fewer jobs and more foreign workers.

In April 2012, three months after the Hope and Change president turned personal job placement officer so ostentatiously offered to help Darin find a job, the *Fort Worth Star Telegram* reported: "Texas engineer, whose wife sent Obama his résumé, still unemployed."[87] Jennifer told the paper that after an initial flurry of interest, the phone calls and emails died down without any results.

"I did feel we got our hopes up a little," Jennifer reflected. "I mean, he's the POTUS. But it seems not even the leader of our country can get [Darin] a job."[88]

•   •   •

"Why'd you favor foreigners over Americans?!"

Reporter Neil Munro of the conservative *Daily Caller* was standing in the Rose Garden behind a long cordon. It was a bright and muggy Beltway afternoon in mid-June 2012. Journalists and cameramen had been summoned to listen to President Obama announce a radical set of executive actions "to mend our nation's immigration policy, to make it more fair, more efficient, and more just."[89] The media representatives jostled for position.

Unfortunately for the Wedels and thousands of other unemployed American engineers and their families, the new "reforms" had nothing to do with their concerns. Obama was unilaterally granting deportation relief and employment documents to an estimated eight hundred thousand illegal immigrants who call themselves "DREAMers."

"Effective immediately, the Department of Homeland Security is taking steps to lift the shadow of deportation from these young people," Obama proclaimed. "Over the next few months, eligible individuals who do not present a risk to national security or public safety will be able to request temporary relief from deportation proceedings and apply for work authorization."[90]

Impatient with the dog-and-pony show, Munro shouted out his question, Sam Donaldson style: "Why'd you favor foreigners over Americans?!"

The imperious president insisted: "It was the right thing to do."

With rising irritation in his voice, he admonished the journalist: "It's not time for questions, sir."

It never is. Obama plowed ahead with his statement stocked with platitudes about America being a "nation of immigrants." Again, he asserted that granting mass amnesty "was the right thing to do for the

American people," and then called on Congress (over which he had just steamrolled) to "get behind this effort."

Munro shouted out one last time: "What about American workers who are unemployed while you import foreigners?"

President Obama stalked off without responding.

In one fell swoop, he had officially opened the floodgates to nearly one million illegal aliens now eligible to come "out of the shadows" to apply for college scholarships, student loans, state and federal grants, and jobs. From entry-level to high-skilled work, unemployed Americans faced increasing competition from cheap foreign labor—all at the hands of their own president. The jobless rate stood at a whopping 8.2 percent that summer, with 12.7 million Americans out of work.[91] But instead of pressing Obama on the rhetoric versus the reality of his economic policies, Beltway pundits fretted that Munro was rude, unprofessional, and, yes, racist for daring to challenge the president.[92]

"Would the right-wing press be doing this if we had a white president there?" asked a Democratic hack on MSNBC.[93]

Munro's questions were "discourteous," complained Reuters correspondent and White House Correspondents Association president Caren Bohan. "It's not the way reporters who cover the White House conduct themselves.[94]

Perhaps if more members of the White House press corps refused to swallow Obama's Big Business/Big Government propaganda, it wouldn't be left to ordinary young moms from the heartland like Jennifer Wedel to do their jobs for them.

When President Obama's job search help failed, Wedel took a temporary gig at Alcon Laboratories in Fort Worth. The good news: He finally secured full-time employment in June 2012 and has worked the past three years for the manufacturer of eye care products doing quality control and assurance. The bad news: With rare exceptions, Democrats and Republicans alike are pressing forward with their plans to drive more American high-tech workers out of their jobs and out of their fields.

Jennifer told reporters she has no regrets about seizing the moment in her few minutes with President Obama. "We didn't do the interview with the president to get a job. We did it to get a voice for so many Americans who, like my husband, are in the very same situation." [95]

Sen. Charles Grassley (R-Iowa) gets it.

He knows how the H-1B game is played. For years, he has pushed for real reform of foreign guest worker programs that punish American workers and reward Big Business donors. After Jennifer Wedel confronted President Obama with the plight of her unemployed American engineer husband, Sen. Grassley fired off his own reality check to the White House.

Reiterating his longstanding call for legislative changes to protect American workers first, Grassley wrote:

> Your response to Ms. Wedel leads me to believe that you don't understand the plight of many unemployed high-skill Americans. Mr. Wedel's situation is all too common. Thousands of qualified Americans remain out of work while companies are incentivized to import foreign workers. I'm concerned that you're hearing only one side of the story—from businesses who claim that there are better and brighter people abroad.
>
> Despite your online chat and interest in investigating the problem, just last week, your administration proposed rules to "attract and retain highly skilled immigrants.". . . Your

administration will also provide work authorizations to spouses of H-1B visa holders, thus increasing the competition for many Americans who are looking for work.

It's astonishing that, at this time of record unemployment, your administration's solution is to grant more work authorizations to foreign workers. These initiatives will do very little to boost our economy or increase our competitiveness.[96]

A-freaking-men.

At a time of perilous unemployment and underemployment, politicians and voters have no excuse for remaining ignorant of H-1B's catastrophic impact on American workers and their wages. Congress has expanded the number of foreign workers on the H-1B program three times since 1998 and allowed H-1B workers to extend their "temporary" employment indefinitely to pursue permanent residency.

These politicians pay lip service to the American Dream, but not once have they acted to counter the systemic displacement of American workers. Instead, Congress responded to H-1B abuses in 1998 by explicitly making it legal for employers to replace Americans with lower-paid H-1B workers in nearly all cases. Despite politicians' endless encomiums to middle-class workers, they're at the bottom of Capitol Hill's priority list.

2

Debunking the Big Fat Lie

There Is No American STEM Worker Shortage

The H-1B swindle employs more spinners than SoulCycle. Sellout politicians employ activist lawyers who write industry-backed loopholes, exemptions, protections, and other assorted goodies into "immigration reform" legislation. Revolving-door lobbyists supply talking points to gullible, lazy, or ideologically sympathetic journalists, op-ed writers, and think tank analysts, who author phony Chicken Little studies funded by the industry groups, whose officials turn up on cable TV or open-borders editorial pages to regurgitate the marketing points and myths cooked up behind closed doors.

Then, like Heather Locklear in that old Fabergé Organic Shampoo commercial from the eighties, they tell two friends, who tell two more cronies, and so on and so on and so on.

The fiction of a perilous U.S. STEM worker shortage has been at the center of the push for H-1B visas. The 1998 and 2000 visa increases in the H-1B program came just as the dot-com bust hit Silicon Valley. As unemployment among U.S. technology workers soared, Big Tech's claims of a worker shortage grew more and more absurd—yet the propagandists still cling bitterly to their talking points today. Let's put the biggest, fattest lie of the H-1B debate to rest.

THE MANUFACTURING OF A "CRISIS"

There is no STEM shortage. We repeat: There is no STEM shortage.

You see the claim made everywhere by local education officials,[1] magazine writers,[2] tech lobbyists,[3] and the White House.[4]

A good example can be found in the slick document sent by industry lobbyists to the Senate Judiciary Committee in advance of the panel's hearing on H-1B harm to American workers in March 2015. It boldly declared in the face of grim reality:

> MYTH: Foreign workers displace American workers in the science, technology, engineering, and math (STEM) fields.
>
> FACT: Employment data show that there are not enough native-born STEM workers to fill available STEM jobs and foreign STEM workers are not displacing their native-born counterparts.[5]

Tell that to the Americans who worked at Southern California Edison until they were fired and replaced with H-1B workers. If that was all a "myth," can they go back to work now?

Here are the organizations who produced this document:

American Immigration Lawyers Association
BSA (The Software Alliance)
Compete America Coalition
Computer & Communications Industry Association
Consumer Electronics Association
Council for Global Immigration
FWD.us

HR Policy Association
Information Technology Industry Council
National Association of Home Builders
National Association of Manufacturers
National Venture Capital Association
Partnership for a New American Economy
Semiconductor Industry Association
Silicon Valley Leadership Group
Society for Human Resource Management
Tech CEO Council
TechNet
U.S. Chamber of Commerce

A Senate staffer who asked not to be named told us that these "tech cronies"—who promote every last tall tale of woe by business execs wailing about a nonexistent STEM worker shortage—dismissed the real-life testimonies of American workers as mere "anecdotes."

The truth is that the U.S. boasts a huge and healthy supply of gifted American scientists, mathematicians, engineers, computer programmers, and other technology workers. Objective analyses—that is, analyses by researchers with no vested corporate, political, or governmental conflicts of interest in promoting cheap foreign labor—have all determined that no evidence of a STEM shortage has existed for decades.

Here are just a few of the myriad studies and independent assessments debunking the tech lobbyist–driven panic:

- In 1999, Princeton University sociologist Thomas J. Espenshade concluded while at the U.S. Office of Population Research: "Apart from spot shortages that exist in any production process, longer-term labor shortages can only exist if there is some artificial mechanism that prevents wages from rising to a market-clearing wage. None of these mechanisms seems to be present in today's competitive labor markets. . . ." Perhaps the view of one labor economist comes closest to the heart of the matter: "If computer companies' response to difficulty in hiring *at the existing wage* is just to put out ads and not to raise salaries, then it is not surprising that they perceive some sort of shortage."[6] [Emphasis added.]

- A 2006 study published in the National Bureau of Economic Research by distinguished Harvard University labor economist Richard B. Freeman found that "labor market measures show no evidence of shortages of S&E [science and engineering] workers."[7]
- In 2007, addressing panic about the STEM education pipeline and industry claims of American students "falling behind," Lindsay Lowell and Hal Salzman of the Urban Institute reported that "our review of the data leads us to conclude that, while the educational pipeline would benefit from improvements, it is not as dysfunctional as believed. Today's American high school students actually test as well or better than students two decades ago. Further, today's students take more science and math classes, and a large number of students with strong science and math backgrounds graduate from U.S. high schools and start college in S&E fields of study. The pool of S&E-qualified secondary and postsecondary graduates is several times larger than the number of annual job openings. The flow of secondary school students up through the S&E pipeline, when it reaches the labor market, supplies occupations that make up only about a twentieth of all workers. So even if there were deficiencies in students' *average* science and math performance, such deficiencies would not necessarily deplete the requisite supply of S&E college majors."[8]
- In 2008, a RAND Corporation study for the Department of Defense concluded: "Judging by recent versus past wage and

unemployment trends, there is no evidence of a current shortage of S&E workers. At any given time, a firm or set of firms within an industry may be unable to fill their S&E job openings, but that is true for non-S&E positions as well."[9]

- Claire Brown and Greg Linden published a paper in the University of California, Berkeley, Institute for Research and Employment's working paper series that noted: "When companies claim they face a shortage of engineers, they usually mean that they face a shortage of young, relatively inexpensive engineers with the latest skills, even when they have a queue of experienced engineers who want retraining."[10]

- In 2013, a report by the Economic Policy Institute found that there was actually a *surplus* of technology workers in America.[11]

- In a rare departure from conventional unwisdom, an enlightened *Chronicle of Higher Education* writer summarized the state of STEM shortage research in late 2013: "Most researchers who have looked into the issue—those who don't receive their money from technology companies or their private foundations, anyway—say no. They cite figures showing that the STEM-worker shortage is not only a meme but a myth."[12]

- In May 2014, four prominent independent scholars—Rutgers University public policy professor Hal Salzman, University of California at Davis computer science professor Norman Matloff, Harvard Law senior research associate Michael Teitelbaum, and Howard University public policy professor Ron Hira—held a joint conference call organized with Sen. Jeff Sessions (R-Ala.). The quartet of academics rejected and refuted all the shortage shouting with blunt reality checks. The majority of H-1B visas are being used to import cheap foreign workers, they pointed out, and average wages, adjusted, have remained flat since the 1990s.[13]

- In July 2014, Hira, Salzman, Teitelbaum, Matloff, and Paula Stephan, a professor of economics at Georgia State University, jointly declared in *USA Today*: "The facts are that, excluding advocacy studies by those with industry funding, there is a remarkable concurrence among a wide range of researchers that there is an ample supply of American workers (native and immigrant, citizen and permanent resident) who are willing and qualified to fill the high-skill jobs in this country. The only real disagreement is whether supply is two or three times larger than the demand." [14]

Karen Ziegler and Steve Camarota of the Center for Immigration Studies summarized their own findings in 2014, which were "consistent with research from Georgetown University, the Economic Policy Institute (EPI), the Rand Corporation, the Urban Institute, and the National Research Council that have also found no evidence that America has a shortage of high-tech workers:" [15]

- Only one-third of native-born Americans with an undergraduate STEM degree holding a job actually work in a STEM occupation.
- There are more than five million native-born Americans with STEM undergraduate degrees working in non-STEM occupations: 1.5 million with engineering degrees, half a million with technology degrees, four hundred thousand with math degrees, and 2.6 million with science degrees.
- An additional 1.2 million natives with STEM degrees are not working—unemployed or out of the labor force in 2012.
- The supply of STEM workers is not just limited to those with STEM degrees. Nearly one-third of the nation's STEM workers do not have an undergraduate STEM degree.

- Real hourly wages (adjusted for inflation) grew on average just 0.7 percent a year from 2000 to 2012 for STEM workers, and annual wages grew even less—0.4 percent a year. Wage growth is very modest for most subcategories of engineers and technology workers.

The only persistent tech worker shortage in America is a shortage of workers *at the wage employers want to pay.* One business exec candidly described how H-1B aids companies that don't want to pay market wages: "[H-1B is] an incredible source for bringing in cost-effective labor that we have a shortage for."[16] Another CEO gets to the heart of the matter that the STEM shortage panic industry pretends away: "If you're willing to pay market rate, you can find people. The issue is if you're budget-constrained, you can't get the people you want."[17]

As Professor Michael Teitelbaum has thoroughly documented, the "alarm/boom/bust cycle" of STEM worker panics dates back to at least World War II. His invaluable book on the subject, *Falling Behind? Boom, Bust, and the Global Race for Scientific Talent,* traces how the U.S. has gone through five major cycles in which industry and universities hit the panic button; the government responded with visa increases for foreign workers and students; "and then after a booming period of growth," he explained, "the system sort of busts and we have large numbers of people in these fields laid off and a lot of prospective students turned off from going into these fields."[18]

"REALLY NO BASIS TO PREDICT A SHORTAGE"

The myth of a STEM worker shortage got a boost in 1984, when Erich Bloch became head of the National Science Foundation.[19] One of his goals was to double the NSF budget.[20] Part of the marketing effort for the budget increase was to hype a huge shortage of scientists and engineers. Between 1986 and 1991, the NSF produced a series of widely circulated draft reports (*never published* and not peer-reviewed) predicting imminent scientist and engineer shortfalls. NSF leaders, including Bloch, made repeated claims that there would be a deficit of 675,000 scientists and engineers in the United States by 2010. The internal research came from an "insular unit" at NSF known as the Policy Research and Analysis division.[21] Disturbingly, these unpublished NSF documents spawned technology worker shortage claims that persist to this day.

The press frequently repeated these shortage figures.[22] Science leaders bemoaned the STEM vacuum. Richard Atkinson, chancellor of the University of California, San Diego, delivered a typically alarmist speech to the American Association for the Advancement of Science in 1990 on the "National Crisis in the Making." A news story covering the speech lamented: "Who Will Do Science in the 1990s?"[23]

In the wake of the manufactured crisis created by the shortage claims, funding at the NSF soared.[24] But after Bloch departed NSF in 1990, the year the H-1B program was born, the alarmist claims fell apart. In 1992, the House Science Committee's Oversight and Investigations Subcommittee held hearings to investigate the NSF's fabrication of a worker shortage to encourage greater funding.[25] The projections "proved so erroneous," researcher Eric Weinstein recounted, "that the current NSF director, Neal Lane, has since repudiated the projections claiming that the shortage alarm was groundless."[26]

Lane testified to Congress in July 1995:

[The NSF scarcity study] went on to project the Ph.D. replacement needs would double between the years 1988 and 2006. Based on a number of assumptions, these data were pretty widely interpreted as predictions of a shortage, while there was really no basis to predict a shortage.[27]

Alas, like herpes, technology worker shortage claims always come back with a vengeance. After the Information Technology Association of America (ITAA) produced its own scare-mongering report, *America's New Deficit: The Shortage of Information Technology Workers*,[28] the U.S. Commerce Department hyped its findings and produced a similar study.[29] Once again, Congress uncovered junk science at the heart of the H-1B racket. The Government Accountability Office (GAO) investigated the Commerce Department's work at Capitol Hill's request and concluded:

> The Commerce report cited four pieces of evidence that an inadequate supply of IT workers is emerging—rising salaries for IT workers, reports of unfilled vacancies for IT workers, offshore sourcing and recruiting, and the fact that the estimated supply of IT workers (based on students graduating with bachelor's degrees in computer and information sciences) is less than its estimate of the demand. However, the report fails to provide clear, complete, and compelling evidence for a shortage or a potential shortage of IT workers with the four sources of evidence presented.[30]

Although some data showed rising salaries for IT workers—these reports were published in the late 1990s, near the height of the dot-com bubble—other data indicated that those increases in earnings were commensurate with rising earnings in all professional specialty occupations. Second, while the ITAA study gave some indication of a shortage of IT workers by providing information on unfilled IT jobs, "ITAA's survey response rate of 14 percent is inadequate to form a basis for a nationwide estimate of unfilled IT jobs," the GAO determined. "Finally, while the report discusses various sources of potential supply of IT workers, it used only the number of students earning bachelor's degrees in computer and information sciences when it compared the potential supply of workers with the magnitude of IT worker demand."[31]

The GAO also torpedoed the ITAA's "unfilled IT jobs" statistics:

ITAA's estimate of the number of unfilled IT jobs is based on reported vacancies, and adequate information about those vacancies is not provided, such as how long positions have been vacant, whether wages offered are sufficient to attract qualified applicants, and whether companies consider jobs filled by contractors as vacancies. These weaknesses tend to undermine the reliability of ITAA's survey findings.[32]

You'd think that at some point the tech industry would abandon these faulty methods. But in 2012, Microsoft, an ITAA member, was at it again, with a report that revived the "unfilled jobs" methodology that the GAO had debunked more than a decade earlier.[33] Microsoft's report cried wolf over the "urgent demand"[34] to import massive numbers of H-1Bs because America did "not have enough people with the necessary skills to meet that demand and drive innovation."[35]

Bad timing highlighted Microsoft's hypocrisy. Just two years later, Bill Gates and his open-borders billionaire buddies Warren Buffett and Sheldon Adelson brayed for more H-1B visas in the op-ed pages of the *New York Times*.[36] That same week, Microsoft was handing pink slips to eighteen thousand people.[37]

THE MIRACLE OF SELF-CORRECTION

A shortage of STEM workers as a whole does not exist, but it is possible for temporary shortages in certain subfields to arise. This can happen when, for example, a change in technology creates a new industry. The strong demand for web programmers in the 1990s is an example, although as Michael Teitelbaum notes, the boom lasted for less than a decade.[38]

Another example: petroleum engineers. For a variety of reasons, demand for petroleum engineers increased sharply in the mid-2000s. As oil companies struggled to fill their job openings, petroleum engineers' wages rose 71 percent during a period of five years.[39]

What happened next is no surprise to anyone familiar with Adam Smith's invisible hand.

By 2013, there were almost 35,000 petroleum engineers recorded in the BLS Occupational Employment Statistics, up from just 11,600 ten years earlier and fewer than 9,000 in 1997. . . .

Enrollments at U.S. universities in graduate and postgraduate engineering programs with a petroleum focus have more than doubled since hitting a low point in the late 1990s.[40]

Alas, the good times didn't last long:

When Daniel Forero left home in California to pursue a petroleum engineering degree at Texas A&M University, he thought his career prospects were strong.

As the energy sector flourished, many around him pointed to a petroleum engineering degree as a surefire ticket to success in the age of the American oil boom.

But as oil prices continue to plummet—they reached five-year lows last week—Forero, now a senior, is quickly getting a harsh lesson in the cyclical nature of the energy business.

"What I kept hearing was 'there's plenty of jobs in this industry,'" Forero said. "Now that I've gotten to this point, it doesn't seem that way.". . .

At the University of Houston, petroleum engineering enrollment has nearly doubled over the last two years to 932 students as the school expanded the program. That's made the hunt for jobs and internships more competitive, said Aziz Rajan, a junior and president of the university's Society of Petroleum Engineers chapter.

"The market is becoming saturated," Rajan said. "I can't imagine, if all of them were to graduate in four years, there would be enough jobs for all these people."[41]

When shortages or surpluses in particular niches arise, they eventually self-correct if market forces are allowed to operate.

UNINTENDED CONSEQUENCES

Despite sparse evidence in support of a persistent STEM worker shortage, the hysteria continues. As a result, students are being encouraged to enter fields that often have limited job opportunities.

As Professor Michael Teitelbaum has noted, the STEM worker shortage alarmists have "produced large unintended costs for those talented students who devoted many years of advanced education to prepare for careers that turned out to be unattractive by the time they graduated, or who later experienced massive layoffs in mid-career with few prospects to be rehired."[42]

Of course, the importation of H-1Bs and other low-cost foreign guest workers makes careers in technology less attractive than would otherwise be the case. The forecast of a shortage of American technology workers could turn into a self-fulfilling prophecy if the guest worker programs said to be justified by those forecasts continue apace.

Yet many Americans continue to believe, as President Obama told Jennifer Wedel, that "somebody in that kind of high-tech field, that kind of engineer, should be able to find something, uh, right right away."

Do you need more examples of how disingenuous the Big Tech shortage shills are?

In October 2014, Professor Teitelbaum shared a story with U.C. Davis engineering students about "how a Microsoft official had told him privately that the firm has tons of applicants." Most of them were rejected, the corporate official said, not by vigilant recruiters in a desperate search for the best and brightest, but "by applying an automatic computer algorithm, with no human involvement at all."[43]

Along the same lines, Google CEO Eric Schmidt bragged in the fall of 2014: "For every opening, Google receives at least 1,000 applications." The good news, he told a Cleveland audience, "is that we have computers to do the initial vetting."[44] A year later, Schmidt was in Washington, sounding the tech work shortage alarm.[45] "Everyone actually agrees that there should be more H-1B visas in order to create more tech, more science, more analytical jobs. Everyone agrees, in both parties," Schmidt said.[46]

Everyone?

Somehow, we don't think U.S. workers being replaced by H-1B workers would agree.

Marketing, Media, and Myths

More Big Fat Lies of the Cheap Foreign Labor Lobby

Where there's smoke, there's fire. And where there are Chicken Little lobbyists clucking about a nonexistent American tech worker shortage, there are plenty more lies and liars. We've selected six of the most glaring H-1B marketing gimmicks, media misperceptions, and persistent myths to debunk for you, but our list is by no means "comprehensive." The Cheap Foreign Labor Lobby's propagandists are, after all, indefatigable masters of deception.

The first step in curing Truth Deficit Disorder is sunshine. Lots of it.

CLAIM

Employers have to show they cannot find Americans before hiring foreign guest workers on H-1B visas.

H-1B expansionists often assert that U.S. firms can't hire an H-1B until they have first attempted to find an American. As President Obama said to Jennifer Wedel, "[T]he H-1B should be reserved only for those companies who say they cannot find somebody in that particular field."

The myth is spread by gullible mainstream media reporters:

- "Before an employer can hire a noncitizen in a specialized field, it must obtain an H-1B visa from the U.S. Citizenship and Immigration Services. The employer must prove that it searched far and wide for qualified Americans or permanent residents and the noncitizen is the best candidate."[1]
- "There is always controversy surrounding the H-1B visa program that allows U.S. companies to employ foreign nationals when American workers with equivalent skills are not available."[2]
- "To obtain an H-1B visa, companies must first convince the federal government that they cannot find qualified workers in the United States."[3]
- "The H-1B visa program lets businesses bring in foreign workers with specialized skills when they cannot find American citizens capable of doing the jobs."[4]
- "Employers can hire foreign workers under H-1B visas after proving there are no qualified candidates available in the U.S. Each year about 85,000 are issued, mostly in tech firms."[5]

Once one newspaper prints such misinformation, other newspapers use that article as a source and repeat it. False information gets passed from one publication to the next like a sexually transmitted disease.

REALITY CHECK

The truth is that only a small number of firms—so-called "H-1B-dependent" companies—are required to certify that they tried to recruit and hire an American before making a visa petition for *certain* foreign workers.[6] For the vast majority of companies, there is no requirement whatsoever that they show they could not find an American before hiring a foreign H-1B worker.

Many commentators and journalists confuse the labor certification process required for companies applying to obtain *green cards* (lawful permanent residency status) for H-1B workers with the Labor Condition Application (LCA) process for H-1Bs.[7] Labor certification in the green card process "exists to protect U.S. workers and the U.S. labor market by ensuring that foreign workers seeking immigrant visa classifications are not displacing equally qualified U.S. workers."[8] Only in extremely narrow and exceptional circumstances do these nominal protections exist in the H-1B LCA process.

In his 2013 report on H-1B, National Public Radio's Martin Kaste asserted that "the law does require an employer to show that it can't find Americans."[9] Two days later, however, NPR was forced to issue a correction after H-1B watchdogs hounded the network for its blatant error.[10] "In fact," a chastened NPR's Kaste admitted in a 180-degree turnaround, "most prospective employers can avoid having to show they've recruited Americans, as long as they meet certain guidelines."

Ding, ding, ding! Now, here are the nitty-gritty details that every American needs to know and that the vast majority of reporters who cover H-1B (not to mention most of the politicians who crusade to expand it) fail to tell you.

The closest that H-1B law comes to requiring any steps that even remotely resemble a prioritization of American workers involve just a few, very narrow categories of employers. One set of "good-faith" stipulations only affect companies classified by the government as "H-1B dependent"—defined as companies with 25 or fewer workers and more than 7 H-1B workers; between 26 to 50 workers and more than 12 H-1B workers; or more than 50 workers with 15 percent or more of them being H-1B foreign nationals (not counting those earning more than sixty thousand dollars or who have a graduate degree—even if it is from an Indian diploma mill).

Another set of "good-faith" stipulations only affected certain

H-1B-employing banks and other financial institutions that accepted federal bailout money from the Troubled Asset Relief Program (TARP). The "Employ American Workers Act," sponsored by Sens. Charles Grassley (R-Iowa) and Bernie Sanders (I-Vt.), was included in the federal stimulus law signed in February 2009 by President Obama. It prevented TARP recipients from displacing and replacing American workers with H-1B workers by requiring the companies to "take good-faith steps to recruit U.S. workers" and offer them wages "at least as high" as those offered to H-1B workers. In addition, the targeted employers "must not have laid off, and will not lay off, any U.S. worker in a job essentially equivalent to the H-1B position in the area of intended employment of the H-1B worker" within a narrow time frame.[11] These token measures merely required that TARP recipients *certify*, not *prove*, that they met the conditions that H-1B-dependent companies must meet. The law, vociferously opposed by the tech industry and universities, expired in 2011.[12]

As part of the LCA process, H-1B-dependent[13] firms sometimes must state that they have "taken good faith steps to recruit in the United States using procedures that meet industry-wide standards" and have "offered the job to any United States worker who applies and is equally or better qualified for the job for which the nonimmigrant or nonimmigrants is or are sought." The certification requirement only applies when three conditions occur together: 1) The employer is classified as H-1B-dependent or has been found to have committed a willful failure of misrepresentation in LCA compliance within five years; 2) The H-1B worker is paid less than sixty thousand dollars; and 3) The H-1B worker does not have a master's degree or higher.

If any of those conditions are not met, the employer (even if it has been found to be a "willful violator" in the past) has *no recruitment obligation* whatsoever.

In those few situations where the employer is supposed to at least look for an American, what does the employer have to do to satisfy that requirements? Simply check the box shown in Figure 3.1. No proof of any kind is required.

FIGURE 3.1

If you marked "Yes" to questions I.1 and/or I.2 and "No" to question I.3, you <u>MUST</u> read Section I – Subsection 2 of the Labor Condition Application – General Instructions Form ETA 9035CP under the heading "Additional Employer Labor Condition Statements" and indicate your agreement to all three (3) additional statements summarized below.

b. Subsection 2

   A. **Displacement:** Non-displacement of the U.S. workers in the employer's workforce
   B. **Secondary Displacement:** Non-displacement of U.S. workers in another employer's workforce; and
   C. **Recruitment and Hiring:** Recruitment of U.S. workers and hiring of U.S. workers applicant(s) who are equally or better qualified than the H-1B nonimmigrant(s).

4. <u>I have read and agree</u> to Additional Employer Labor Condition Statements A, B, and C above and as fully explained in Section I – Subsections 1 and 2 of the Labor Condition Application – General Instructions Form ETA 9035CP. §	❏ Yes ❏ No

The Labor Department itself spelled out the lack of U.S. worker protections in the clearest way possible in a document found on its website that has now been deleted: "H-1B workers may be hired even when a qualified U.S. worker wants the job, and a U.S. worker can be displaced from the job in favor of the foreign worker." [14]

CLAIM

H-1B workers must be paid "prevailing wage" or higher, so American workers' wages are protected.

The American public has been led to believe that employers must pay H-1B workers as much as their American counterparts:

- "One of the common misconceptions about foreign national workers is that employers hire them and pay below-market wages. While this certainly may happen for undocumented workers, employers that lawfully hire H-1B workers must pay the higher of the actual or the prevailing wage." [15]
- "By law, H-1B visa holders must be paid the same as Americans doing the same work." [16]

- "The most widely held misconception is that H-1B workers drive down U.S. salaries. However, in order to get an H-1B, employers must show the Department of Labor they are paying H-1B workers either the prevailing wage or the actual wage (the same as other employees at the same company)."[17]
- "H-1B workers are paid on the same level as the U.S. citizens and the company has to prove that they are paying the prevailing wage in that geographical area for the same job position."[18]

REALITY CHECK

The 1990 Immigration Act set up multiple recipes for determining the "prevailing wage." Under these approaches, employers are allowed to liberally stretch the meaning of "prevailing wage" and exploit gaping loopholes to underpay H-1B workers. The toothless Labor Department has little authority to stop them.

First, a little background about the process: To secure an H-1B visa, the employer must submit an LCA (as described previously). The Labor Department is supposed to ensure that the hiring of foreign workers will not adversely affect the wages and working conditions of U.S. workers and the LCA is the ostensible tool for ascertaining this. The Immigration Act of 1990 originally required the employer to file an LCA that attests:

(A) The employer—
   (i) is offering and will offer during the period of authorized employment to aliens and to other individuals employed in the occupational classification and in the area of employment wages that are at least—
   (I) the actual wage level for the occupational classification at the place of employment, or

(II) the prevailing wage level for the occupational classification in the area of employment, whichever is greater, determined as of the time of filing the application.[19]

The key question: What is the "prevailing wage"?
Under the first "prevailing wage" definition, employers can either
request a prevailing wage determination from the government or they
can make the determination for themselves. Those who make the
determination themselves can use effectively any source. More than
seventy-five different data sources, many of which use entry-level
wage surveys to conjure up extremely low prevailing wages, appear
each year in LCAs.[20]

The Labor Department is required to approve LCAs within seven
days of their filing and can only review them "for completeness and
obvious accuracies"[21] so whatever the employer puts down becomes
the prevailing wage. Got it? The objective is to push paper, not protect
workers. Remember: When the employer submits the prevailing wage
claim to the Labor Department, the law specifically limits the approval
process to perfunctorily checking that the form is filled out correctly.

In 2006, GAO investigators "found 3,229 applications that were
certified" by the rubber-stampers at the Labor Department, "even
though the wage rate on the application was lower than the prevailing wage for that occupation."[22] A prescient DHS inspector general's
report in 2003 had warned that the Labor Department needed "statutory authority to ensure the integrity of that process, including the
ability to verify the accuracy of information provided on labor condition applications." The IG told Congress: "Our concern with the Department's limited ability to ensure the integrity of the certification
process is heightened by the results of OIG analysis and investigations
that show the program is susceptible to significant fraud and abuse,
particularly by employers and attorneys."[23]

But wait, there are more loopholes. Buried in the law is a special sweetheart deal for universities, nonprofits, and government research agencies for which "the prevailing wage level shall only take into account employees at such institutions and organizations in the area of employment."[24]

Cheap labor-hungry universities only have to pay the prevailing wage in academia, not in a given industry at large. In a university town, its wage effectively becomes the prevailing wage. In high-wage areas of the country, the law allows universities to maintain submarket wage rates.

It gets worse. In 2004, Congress explicitly authorized employers to pay H-1B workers less by creating a second scheme for determining the "prevailing wage"—a complex scheme that assigns H-1B workers to four separate categories.[25] Here are the four categories and how they correspond to U.S. wages for the occupation and location:

- Level I (entry) wage rates are at the seventeenth percentile of U.S. wage and are assigned to job offers for beginning-level employees who have only a basic understanding of the occupation. These employees perform routine tasks that require limited, if any, exercise of judgment.
- Level II (qualified) wage rates are at the thirty-fourth percentile and assigned to job offers for qualified employees who have attained, either through education or experience, a good understanding of the occupation. . . .
- Level III (experienced) wage rates are at the fiftieth percentile and are assigned to job offers for experienced employees who have a sound understanding of the occupation and have attained, either through education or experience, special skills or knowledge. . . . Words such as "lead" (lead analyst), "senior" (senior programmer), "head" (head nurse), "chief" (crew chief), or "journeyman"

(journeyman plumber) would be indicators that a Level III wage should be considered.

- Level IV (fully competent) wage rates are at the sixty-seventh percentile and are assigned to job offers for competent employees who have sufficient experience in the occupation to plan and conduct work requiring judgment and the independent evaluation, selection, modification, and application of standard procedures and techniques.[26]

While Congress requires the Department of Labor to provide four skill-based prevailing wages, there is no requirement that the H-1B worker be classified according to his actual skill. Even if such a requirement existed, it would be unenforceable because skill is a subjective measurement.

The GAO found that more than half of H-1B workers with approved LCAs between June 2009 and July 2010 were categorized as Level 1 workers.[27] These H-1B workers are in the U.S. earning bargain-basement wages to perform "routine tasks" that require only "limited judgment." Meanwhile, employers braying about losing the world's "best and the brightest" laugh all the way to the bank. H-1B workers are only "high-skilled" when employers want more of them. When it comes time to determine what these same workers have to be paid, they suddenly become low skilled.

And it's all perfectly legal.

Either most H-1B computer workers are entry-level workers who make no special contribution to the American economy or employers are deliberately understating workers' skills in order to justify paying them lower salaries.[28]

Here's a real-world application to illustrate the book-cooking scam and its cost savings. In Charlotte, North Carolina, the Level 3 wage is about $80,000—the actual prevailing wage. But an employer, unlikely to be caught by the DOL rubber-stampers, could claim the Level 1 prevailing wage of $51,000 and save $29,000 a year. Alternatively, a university (which enjoys special treatment, as we noted above) could claim the Level 1 academic prevailing wage of $44,000 and save $36,000 annually.[29]

It gets still worse. Employers are even allowed to use their own internal wage surveys or other surveys as a data source. When they do so—surprise!—prevailing wages are much lower than if the median wage is calculated using Bureau of Labor Statistics data.[30] One wage survey that appears regularly in LCAs comes from the National Association of Colleges and Employers (NACE). This is a *national* survey of wages paid to recent college graduates. Because the NACE survey does not give geographic breakdowns, it is not valid for use on an LCA—but employers use it anyway. As we just mentioned, the DoL must approve all correctly filled out LCAs within seven days, so even those using improper wage surveys get approved. By using the national NACE survey in higher-than-average wage locations, an employer can get an even bigger H-1B wage saving. In Chicago, the average wage for an architect is $77,000 a year. Under the four-tier prevailing-wage system, an H-1B worker can be paid just $49,000. An approved LCA for an H-1B architect using the NACE survey in 2014 gave the prevailing wage and wage to be paid to the H-1B worker as $38,000.

If the DoL is required to approve LCAs like this, you may wonder why it does not go back and review them later to check for compliance. The answer to that is quite simple: The DoL is explicitly prohibited from doing that under 8 U.S.C. § 1182(n)(2)(G)(v). H-1B abuse is routine *because Congress has designed the system to be abused with impunity.*

Democratic Rep. Zoe Lofgren, an H-1B advocate who represents Silicon Valley, acknowledged that computer systems analysts working on H-1B visas in her district could be paid a legal "prevailing wage" of $52,000 a year—versus the local average computer analyst wage of $92,000.[31]

Professor Ron Hira told Congress about one large offshoring firm that hired H-1B visa-holding computer programmers at $12.25 an hour. "That's hardly the best and the brightest," he bluntly testified.[32] The end result, as Lofgren admits, is depressed American workers' wages. "Small wonder there's a problem here," Lofgren observed. "We can't have people coming in and undercutting the American educated workforce."[33]

And yet, the practice continues virtually unabated.

H-1B defenders might point to federal data showing that the median IT worker in the U.S. earns $70,000 per year versus $61,000 for H-1B IT workers. The difference is only $9,000, or a little more than 10 percent. But bear in mind that a disproportionate number of H-1Bs work in expensive metropolitan areas such as New York City, Silicon Valley, and the Washington, D.C., area—meaning the pay gap between U.S. IT workers and their H-1B counterparts in those locations is much larger than $9,000.

In Rosemead, California, where Southern California Edison sacked four hundred Americans and replaced them with H-1B workers from Infosys and Tata in February 2015,[34] Labor Department data show that the annual average wage for a computer systems analyst is $91,990. By comparison, Professor Ron Hira reported that the average wage for an H-1B employee at Infosys in FY13 was $70,882 and $65,565 for Tata. "That means Infosys and Tata save well over $20,000 per worker per year, by hiring an H-1B instead of a local U.S. worker earning the average wage," Hira noted. Actually that probably understates the wage gap. At Southern California Edison, IT specialists were earning an average annual base pay of $110,446—meaning Tata and Infosys likely saved about $40,000 to $45,000 per worker per year.[35]

A March 2015 study by economists Kirk Doran of the University of Notre Dame, Alexander Gelber of the University of California at Berkeley, and Adam Isen of the U.S. Department of Treasury used a clever design to examine the effect of H-1Bs on employees' wages and other outcomes, comparing firms that won H-1Bs in the H-1B visa lottery to firms that lost in the H-1B lottery.[36] This is what is known in social science as a "natural experiment"—a study in which subjects (in this case, firms) are exposed to experimental and control conditions (in this case receiving an H-1B visa or not) mimicking a randomized controlled trial. The researchers found that in the firms that won H-1B visas, average employees' wages shrank relative to firms that didn't win in the H-1B lottery.[37]

"Our results are consistent with the narrative about the effects of H-1Bs on firms in which H-1Bs are paid less than alternative workers whom they replace, thus increasing the firm's profits," the authors conclude.[38]

New York Times correspondent Josh Barro is one of the few H-1B expansionists who admits the truth about the wage-lowering effects of the H-1B program. He tweeted: "Ugh the whining of U.S. citizen high-skill workers who complain that H1-B [*sic*] visas drive down their wages. Cry me a river."[39]

A reader asked for clarification: "Don't believe it or don't care?"[40]

Barro retorted: "I do care. I think it's a good thing! Lower consumer prices for the rest of us, and less income inequality."[41] For Americans sacked in favor of cheaper labor, "less income inequality" means no income. Somehow, we doubt Barro would be so callous about the "whining" if *he* were the one being replaced by an H-1B worker.

CLAIM

U.S. companies cannot function without an unlimited injection of the most "highly skilled" and "highly educated" H-1B foreign workers, who are smarter, more inventive, and more entrepreneurial than Americans!

Writing in the *Wall Street Journal*, H-1B advocate Gary Beach approvingly cites Vivek Wadhwa, a Stanford University Fellow who "says unreasonable visa policies could lead to a 'reverse brain-drain' where talented non-immigrant foreign nationals choose home, rather than the United States, to start their companies."[42] But we are talking about *nonimmigrant* visas, such as H-1B guest workers and F-1 students. These temporary-visa-holding aliens are *supposed* to go home.

Echoing Beach as well as prominent Big Tech leaders such as Bill Gates and Mark Zuckerberg, misguided theoretical physicist Michio Kaku dubbed H-1B the "genius visa" and breathlessly claimed that without the program the entire scientific establishment, Silicon Valley, and the American economy would collapse.[43] Kaku may know physics, but his understanding of the H-1B racket is an astronomic black hole. The "best and brightest" deception embedded itself into tech lobbyist talking points twenty-five years ago and won't go away.

REALITY CHECK

Genius entrepreneurs? Forty-five percent of H-1B visa holders in 2014 had nothing more than a bachelor's degree.[44] As noted above, a majority of H-1Bs are classified by their own employers as "beginning level employees who have only a basic understanding of the occupation."

A majority of the H-1Bs granted in 2013 went to offshoring firms like Infosys, Tata, and Wipro. Such firms are not known for technological innovation and have received very few patents (see Table 3.1). In fact, the research paper by Kirk Doran and his colleagues found that H-1Bs have no effect on patenting within eight years. These results held even when the researchers excluded offshoring firms from the analysis.[45]

TABLE 3.1 [46] H-1BS AND PATENTS RECEIVED

Company	Offshorer?	H-1Bs FY 2007–09	Patents since 2009
Infosys	Yes	9,625	54
Wipro	Yes	7,216	30
Satyam	Yes	3,557	20
Microsoft	Yes	3,318	11,544
Tata	Yes	2,368	19
Deloitte	Yes	1,896	6
Cognizant	Yes	1,669	0
IBM	Yes	1,550	22,893
Intel	No	1,454	5,630
Accenture	Yes	1,396	372

Despite all the paeans to entrepreneurialism, very few H-1B workers are creating new businesses. In fact, almost all of them are *forbidden* from being entrepreneurs because their corporate-sponsored visas restrict them from self-employing and starting their own businesses.

The H-1B hype artists engage in distracting non sequiturs by extolling the virtue of any foreign-born immigrant entrepreneurs, whether they came over as children (as Google's Sergey Brin and Yahoo's Jerry Yang did), college students (as Instagram's Mike Krieger did), or guest workers. And they discount the plain fact that despite all the sound and fury, America's most successful technology companies—Apple, Google, Microsoft, Facebook, Amazon.com, Cisco Systems, IBM, Intel, Oracle, Qualcomm, Intuit, Yahoo, eBay, Priceline, Adobe, and Twitter—were founded by native-born talents and, in a few cases, by immigrants who came to the U.S. as children with their families. Not one of these companies was founded by an H-1B worker.

The concept that America should turn universities into the gatekeepers of the immigration system by allowing foreign students to remain permanently because some of them will otherwise return home and *might* start start a new company is patently absurd.

CLAIM

"H-1B doesn't take American jobs. H-1B creates jobs."

It's an article of faith among the open-borders crowd that H-1B workers don't take Americans' jobs:

- "[F]oreign-born STEM workers complement the American workforce, they don't take American jobs."[47]
- "The myth of H-1B visa holders taking American jobs is preposterous on its surface."[48]
- "H-1B visas for high-skill employees are not allocated in sufficient numbers to meet the labor force demands of U.S. companies . . . Foreign-born high-skilled workers do not take jobs away from Americans."[49]

Some open-borders billionaires and their front groups have gone one step further. Like Vegas stage magicians, they have conjured up numbers to "prove" H-1B guest workers create additional American jobs:

- The Heritage Foundation, citing the National Foundation for American Policy, claims that "research shows that technology companies hire five new workers for each H-1B visa for which they apply" and, with no citation included, "that on average, the skills of each highly skilled H-1B worker support the jobs [of] four Americans."[50]
- Facebook CEO Mark Zuckerberg's FWD.us lamented: "Why do we offer so few H[-]1B visas for talented specialists that the supply runs out within days of becoming available each year, even though we know each of these jobs will create two or three more American jobs in return?"[51]
- "Every additional 100 foreign-born workers in science and technology fields is associated with 262 additional jobs for

US natives," *New York Times* op-ed columnist David Brooks declared, citing "a study by Madeline Zavodny, an economics professor at Agnes Scott College."[52]

- The National Foundation for American Policy claims each H-1B visa creates 7.5 jobs in small- to medium-sized companies.[53]

- Bill Gates, citing National Foundation for American Policy (NFAP) research by Beltway operative Stuart Anderson, testified before Congress that "a recent study shows for every H-1B holder that technology companies hire, five additional jobs are created around that person."[54]

- In response to the massive replacements of American by H-1B workers that made in the news in early 2015, the Senate Judiciary Committee held a hearing on March 17, 2015, on the issue. A number of groups, including the American Immigration Lawyers Association, Mark Zuckerberg's FWD.us, and the U.S. Chamber of Commerce submitted a statement.[55] That statement, citing the Zavodny study asserts: "2.62 MORE JOBS are created for U.S.-born workers for each foreign-born worker in the U.S. with a U.S. STEM graduate degree."[56]

REALITY CHECK

The very first thing to notice about these "studies" and the people who cite them is how dizzyingly circular and self-referential they are. Take the NFAP 2008 study, which was published as a "policy brief" by the NFAP (not, say, in a peer-reviewed economics journal). It was recirculated by like-minded advocacy front groups such as the Council for Global Immigration,[57] the American Immigration Council,[58] and, as noted above, Bill Gates.

Or look more closely at the Zavodny study cited by David Brooks.

It was published by the American Enterprise Institute, sponsored by open-borders billionaire Michael Bloomberg's Partnership for a New American Economy,[59] and touted by the open-borders U.S. Chamber of Commerce,[60] the pro-H-1B FWD.us, and American Action Forum.[61]

We're not saying advocacy groups never produce quality research. But always consider the source—as well as the often unstated conflicts of interest and bias that may affect a study's results. That goes for *all* sides of the debate. Anyone can write a study. For a study to have any value, its results must be *reproducible*. A reader should be able to understand what the author did and other researchers should be able to get the same results.

The next thing to ask when open-borders billionaires and their advocacy groups are citing each other's work is: What are they *not* telling me? If you've ever read a peer-reviewed study in a respectable social science journal, you know that responsible researchers *always* acknowledge the limitations of the study and spell out inevitable caveats and shortcoming of their data. In the sloppy, frenetic world of 24/7 cable television, however, these nuances disappear.

The H-1B advocacy racket's omissions and distortions are so egregious that even the reliably open-borders *Wall Street Journal* had to call out Bill Gates on his misleading testimony to Congress regarding the oft-cited NFAP job-creation study. Carl Bialik, the newspaper's self-proclaimed "Numbers Guy," reported:

> Mr. Gates interpreted the study . . . as finding that "for every H-1B holder that technology companies hire, five additional jobs are created around that person." But the study shows nothing of the kind. Instead, it finds a positive correlation between these visas and job growth. These visas could be an indicator of broader hiring at the company, rather than the cause.[62]

- Professor Norman Matloff, a founding member of the Statistics Department at the University of California, Davis, explained the common analytical error, known as "Simpson's Paradox, in which the relation between two variables is very misleading, due to their mutual relation to a third variable."[63]
- After surveying academics across the country, Bialik identified several other flaws and limitations with the study. The data set was confined to S&P 500 technology companies, which "excludes the leading users" of H-1B visas—those offshoring companies we've told you about, such as Infosys, Wipro, and Tata. Moreover, Bialik noted, the analysis was based on "changes in global employment, rather than just domestic employment."

Let's apply a sanity check: Between 2001 and 2013, the average yearly job growth in the U.S. has been 540,000. The average new number of H-1B visas has been 118,000 a year during that same time period. If each H-1B visa creates five additional jobs, it would mean H-1B visas are responsible for more than 100 percent of job creation in the entire U.S. economy—590,000 jobs a year. That raises several questions: (1) How does an H-1B visa create a job—or rather why would an H-1B worker in a particular field create more jobs than an American in the same field? (2) How did America create jobs before H-1B existed? And (3) where are the 590,000 jobs a year H-1B is supposed to create? The claim that every H-1B visa creates five jobs for Americans is absurd on its face.

The most widely touted H-1B job-creation study is the Zavodny report cited by the *New York Times'* David Brooks, the U.S. Chamber of Commerce, the American Immigration Lawyers Association, FWD.us, and many others. Citing Zavodny, Brooks calls the "evidence" of the benefits of "increased immigration" of foreign-born workers "overwhelming."[64]

Zavodny, whose results have not been published in a peer-reviewed journal, initially examined data from the years 2000 to 2010. She hypothesized that states with more foreign-born workers would have higher rates of employment among native-born Americans. She ran her regression and concluded: "None of the estimates are significantly different from zero."[65] In other words, she was unable to find a significant effect of foreign-born workers on U.S. jobs. Clearly, that wasn't the "overwhelming" evidence H-1B expansionists were hoping for.

In correspondence with us, Zavodny revealed that she showed her initial results to the study sponsor, who we imagine must have been disappointed. The sponsor came up with the idea of discarding the last three years of data (2008–10) and trying again. "The guys at Partnership for a New American Economy [sponsor of the study] pointed out that the Great Recession might be leading to anomalous results and suggested I look at 2000–2007," Zavodny told us. "This seemed like a reasonable idea to me given that the recession led to huge job losses for immigrants and for natives (and also to changes in immigration patterns)."

Mirabile dictu, Zavodny found the effect the study sponsor was hoping for.

Standard research practice is to formulate a research hypothesis and specify a study sample *before* the analysis has been completed. The practice of "data dredging"—that is, tweaking the sample data until one gets rid of "anomalous results"—is frowned upon.

To her credit, Zavodny provided her data to R. Davis, a software developer in Silicon Valley who is interested in immigration policy. Davis doesn't have any deep-pocketed financial backers, but he is proficient at analyzing data. He discovered a number of serious methodological deficiencies in Zavodny's work.[66]

Most important, he documented that Zavodny's results are highly sensitive to the date range selected. When she studied the years 2000–2007, she found 100 foreign-born workers in STEM fields with advanced degrees from U.S. universities were associated with 262 additional jobs for native-born Americans. But change the date range a little bit to 2002–2007 and the exact same regression model shows the *destruction* of 110 jobs for natives, according to Davis.

Remember, this is the evidence in support of increased immigration that David Brooks calls "overwhelming."

Also, Zavodny's "262 additional jobs" factoid deals not with H-1B visa holders but with foreign-born workers in STEM fields who have advanced degrees (that is, a master's or doctorate) from U.S. universities. About 45 percent of H-1B visa holders do not have advanced degrees (as noted above), let alone advanced degrees from U.S. universities. According to Professor Ron Hira, only one in 206 of H-1B workers at Infosys holds an advanced degree from a U.S. university. Even fewer of Tata's H-1B workers do—just one in 222.[67] So there is almost no overlap between the highly educated workers in Zavodny's "262 additional jobs" analysis and the mostly entry-level workers who actually come to the U.S. on H-1B visas in the real world.

When Zavodny looked at H-1B Labor Condition Applications specifically, she found only a weak association with U.S. jobs. To obtain this result she used a regression technique that, by her own admission, can only identify a correlation, not a cause-effect relationship. In other words, she can't rule out the possibility that strong local labor markets led to requests for H-1B visas, rather than the other way around. Somehow that caveat wasn't mentioned by H-1B advocates who cited the study, such as FWD.us[68] and the *New York Daily News.*[69] There is a big difference between association (correlation) and causation. Roosters crowing are *associated* with sunrise, but do roosters cause the sun to rise?

Normally, when a researcher finds that a regression model produces conflicting results, depending upon the data range chosen, he would conclude that the model does not fit the data. Such a model cannot show H-1B is creating (or destroying) jobs. As before, Davis found that changing the date range used gives the result that each H-1B destroys additional American jobs, the number depending upon the range chosen.

Another researcher, seeing that the model produces conflicting results depending upon the date range chosen, could conclude that the observed correlations are probably spurious and would not claim that it shows H-1B creating (or destroying) jobs. The March 2015 study by Kirk Doran and his colleagues concluded that "H-1Bs cause no significant increase in firm employment" and that "[n]ew H-1Bs substantially and statistically significantly crowd out median employment of other workers."[70]

Comparing and contrasting coverage of the Doran study and the Zavodny study illustrates that media bias is as much about sins of omission as it is about sins of commission. A search for "Kirk Doran H-1B" turns up only four hits in Google News, of which three mention Doran's March 2015 research paper. All three are in obscure publications. By contrast, "Madeline Zavodny H-1B" yields thirty-one hits, including coverage in major MSM outlets such as the *Washington Post*, *New York Times*, and *Boston Globe*.

We asked AEI's president, Arthur Brooks, to comment on Davis's critique of Zavodny's study. Brooks, a highly regarded researcher who has a PhD from the RAND Graduate School in Santa Monica, California, referred us to AEI's chief economist, Kevin Hassett. Hassett replied: "I am not deep enough in the weeds on this paper to be able to respond to the specific points." He referred us to Zavodny.

That is how the numbers game is played. Have someone write a paper, creating a factoid that you want; twist the factoid to match your message; get the factoid out in the media; and hope no one in the media checks the factoid (usually a good bet). While industry lobbyists have to employ dubious means to show H-1B creates jobs, it is easy to show that H-1B workers take American jobs—just ask the folks who trained their H-1B replacements at Disney and Southern California Edison.

CLAIM

Low unemployment rates for STEM workers show that there is a shortage.

This is an apples-to-oranges comparison that lobbyists use regularly. "In 2011, while the national unemployment rate hovered at about 8 percent nationwide," the American Immigration Lawyers Association claims, "U.S. citizens with PhDs in STEM had an unemployment rate of 3.15 percent. Those with Master's level degrees in STEM fields had one of 3.4 percent."[71]

REALITY CHECK

The unemployment rates of most professional occupations are almost always much lower than the national unemployment rate. The fact that industry lobbyists compare the employment rate of STEM PhDs to that of ditch diggers is telling.

Compare the lobbyist depiction of the STEM job market to that of a law professor commenting on the state of the legal job market:

According to U.S. Department of Labor data, the unemployment rate for lawyers was 1.5 percent in 2010—more than six times lower than the overall rate of 9.6 percent. Since 2009, while the overall unemployment rate has remained above 9 percent, the rate for lawyers has exceeded 2 percent only once. It is true that unemployment among lawyers has increased significantly over the last few years (it was barely 1 percent in 2007), but the increase pales when compared to other occupations.[72]

Think about it: If a 3.15 percent unemployment rate for STEM PhDs indicates a shortage, then America has a critical shortage of lawyers. Does anyone want to argue there is shortage of lawyers in America?

CLAIM

If H-1B caps are not lifted, offshoring of U.S. jobs will accelerate.

Some companies say they will move overseas if they cannot get more H-1B visas. Microsoft, a heavy H-1B user, has been at the center of this marketing campaign. The company opened a facility in Vancouver, B.C., in 2014, and its existence has been held out as a reason America needs more H-1B visas.[73] A self-serving statement asserted that the move "allows the company to recruit and retain highly skilled people affected by immigration issues in the U.S."[74] A news report on the software giant's plans similarly reported: "Microsoft will open a software development office in Vancouver, Canada, later this year, *in part* as a way to retain talented workers who can't stay in the U.S. because of immigration laws."[75]

REALITY CHECK

It turns out there were other reasons Microsoft moved north, which had nothing to do with H-1B politics on Capitol Hill.

> Microsoft spokesman Lou Gellos said this morning that the Vancouver office has been in the works for some time and immigration issues weren't the primary factor in creating the facility. He said the company would be opening the center even if the H-1B challenge didn't exist.[76]

Soon after the original Vancouver announcement, Microsoft hired Don Mattrick to be the head of its games division.[77] Mattrick had previously been the head of the gaming company Electronic Arts. Mattrick is also a lifelong resident of . . . Vancouver. Most of Microsoft's three hundred employees in Vancouver work in its game and entertainment division.[78]

Microsoft's Vancouver facility is instructive, not as an example of how desperate American companies need H-1Bs in order to keep jobs at home, but as a telling example of how some double-talking tech execs prefer training foreign workers across the border to investing in retraining high-skilled, laid-off American workers right here at home.

The GAO, it should be noted, found that the lack of H-1B workers was not a significant factor for most companies deciding whether to move operations overseas.[79] The only exception was offshoring companies, some of which said their ability to provide IT services to U.S. customers depends in part on being able to hire H-1B workers. Of course, when these firms talk about "providing IT services" they often mean "offshoring IT jobs." In other words, reducing the size of the H-1B program would make it harder for the offshorers to do their thing. That, of course, would be bad news for the offshorers, but it would be great news for American workers.

Ironically, the tech industry's constant threats to pick up their marbles and leave home continue, even as many sobered-up companies are realizing the value of bringing jobs back to American shores. "After decades of sending work across the world, companies are rethinking their offshoring strategies," the *Economist* magazine reported in 2013.[80] Wages in developing countries have increased dramatically during the last fifteen years. In U.S. dollars, wages in China are five times what they were in 2000—and they are expected to continue rising.[81] Moreover, with companies making greater use of automation, the *Economist* notes, "labor's share of total costs is shrinking anyway."[82]

The difference in quality between American and offshore computer code is like the difference in quality between the Cleveland Orchestra and a high school orchestra. In the end, you get what you pay for. Fed up with subpar code, communication problems, and security breaches, companies such as Ford Motor, Caterpillar, Bank of America, Delta Airlines, Brooks Brothers, Whirlpool, 3M, and even offshoring giant General Electric have been "reshoring" the past few years.

Unfortunately, these corporate epiphanies about the shortcomings of offshoring came too late for thousands of American workers forced to train their own foreign replacements before losing their jobs.

To sum up: Employers do not have to look for Americans before hiring H-1Bs. Nor do they have to pay H-1B workers the same as Americans. Most H-1B workers are neither geniuses nor the best nor the brightest. Most are described by their own employers (mainly Indian offshorers) as entry-level workers. The number of large technology businesses in the U.S. started by H-1B workers is vanishingly small. There is no reliable evidence that the H-1B program creates jobs for Americans, nor is there any reason to presume that failure to expand the program will lead to an increase in offshoring. In other words, pretty much everything we've been told about H-1Bs is a big fat lie.

4

Dig Your Own Grave

H-1B's Devastating Impact on American Workers
Forced to Train Their Own Replacements

It's demoralizing enough for talented, skilled American workers to lose their jobs to cheap foreign competitors—who can now bring their spouses over to compete with American workers, too, thanks to President Obama's regulations in February 2015.[1]

Even worse is the fate of soon-to-be-jobless Americans who are forced by their employers to train their own foreign replacements before being tossed to the streets—or else lose all of their severance and unemployment benefits.

When large-scale replacements of U.S. workers with H-1B guest workers began in the 1990s, it jolted the national media into paying attention. Both CBS's *60 Minutes* and ABC's *20/20* devoted news segments to the issue. Over the years, however, the practice has become so commonplace that it rarely receives page-one or prime-time coverage in the national American news media anymore. Unless you read the computer trade press, local news outlets, or Indian newspapers, you are unlikely to hear about it. The concentration of news into the hands of just a few companies has exacerbated the problem. Do you think you are going to see a hard-hitting ABC News segment on Americans being replaced by H-1B workers at Disney . . . now that Disney owns ABC?

If you look hard enough, the impact of these localized, specialized stories of suffering is overwhelming. Yes, companies hire and fire workers all the time. But only in the case of H-1B and related foreign guest worker programs are American corporations and offshore outsourcing rackets explicitly aided and abetted by the U.S. government— and routinely in violation of the basic principles of these programs. With no well-financed, high-powered interest group in Washington, D.C., to advocate on their behalf, American technology workers have endured this systemic displacement and humiliation for at least two decades.

As we noted in our introduction, the mass layoffs and replacements of Southern California Edison workers with H-1B workers in early 2015 prompted a group of U.S. senators to demand federal investigations. Investigate what? What Southern California Edison did was perfectly legal, because Capitol Hill and its immigration lawyers and lobbyists codified it. Here is the law that applies when companies like Tata and Infosys supply H-1B workers to a company like Southern California Edison. A company making a Labor Condition Application must certify that it "will not place the nonimmigrant with another employer (regardless of whether or not such other employer is an H-1B-dependent employer)." The nonimmigrant must perform duties "in whole or in part at one or more worksites owned, operated, or controlled by such other employer" and there must be "indicia of an employment relationship between the nonimmigrant and such other employer"—unless the employer "has inquired of the other employer as to whether, and has no knowledge that, within the period beginning 90 days before and ending 90 days after the date of the placement of the nonimmigrant with the other employer, the other employer has displaced or intends to displace a United States worker employed by the other employer."[2]

To the casual reader this might appear to prohibit replacing Americans with H-1B workers. The trick here is that this restriction only applies in very narrow, specific circumstances buried in the federal immigration code when an application has been filed "on or after the date final regulations are first promulgated to carry out this subparagraph, and before by an H-1B-dependent employer (as defined in paragraph (3)) or by an employer that has been found, on or after October 21, 1998, under paragraph (2)(C) or (5) to have committed a willful failure or misrepresentation during the 5-year period preceding the filing of the application. An application is not described in this clause if the only H–1B nonimmigrants sought in the application are exempt H–1B nonimmigrants."[3] Say what?

The lobbyists who wrote that hope you won't understand. You have to follow the paths of indirection in the code to figure it out. First, the nondisplacement of Americans only applies to certain foreign workers. An "exempt H-1B nonimmigrant" means one who "receives wages (including cash bonuses and similar compensation) at an annual rate equal to at least $60,000; or who "has attained a master's or higher degree (or its equivalent)" in a specialty related to the intended employment. Second, preventing nondisplacement of Americans only applies to certain employers who are either "H-1B-dependent" or have been found to be willful violators of the H-1B program within the past five years. Here again, the code employs more misdirection. An H-1B-dependent employer is one with more than 15 percent of its total U.S. workforce who are H-1B workers paid less than $60,000 and who do not have a graduate degree. In other words, if you pay the H-1B worker more than $60,000 or the H-1B worker has a graduate degree from a foreign diploma mill, you can replace Americans at will.

That hurdle is easily overcome. In Los Angeles, the average wage for a computer programmer is $91,624. The lowest an employer is allowed to pay an H-1B programmer in Los Angeles is $55,245. Jack that up a bit to $60,000 and Americans can be replaced. Or simply hire someone with one of the notorious master's degrees in computer applications dished out by Indian diploma mills. Either method makes it perfectly legal to replace Americans.

This garbage has been going on since at least 1994. Members of Congress can feign outrage and call for "investigations," but they have done nothing about H-1B abuse other than make it easier. The American workers at Southern California Edison and Disney are just the latest example of roadkill from our immigration system.

The bottom line here is that Congress has gone to a lot of effort to ensure that Americans can be replaced by foreign workers. The replacement of Americans by foreign workers at Disney and Southern California is not an accident. It is the result of calculated design by lobbyists and Congress. As you will see, the result has been devastating.

AIG REPLACES AMERICANS WITH "HIGHLY SKILLED" H-1B PROGRAMMERS

In 1994, the insurance giant AIG was very profitable. In September of that year, computer workers at the company received a mysterious memo. They were all ordered to report to mandatory meetings at three hotels in New Jersey, New York, and New Hampshire. The memo gave no other details about the meetings.

Upon arrival at the hotel, the AIG workers were herded into one of two conference rooms. A smaller group of employees was told that their jobs were safe (for the time being). The larger group, sent to the other holding pen, received grim news.

AIG had prepared a document detailing their severance packages. Senior managers announced that the workers in that room were being fired and replaced by foreign guest workers. AIG had contracted with an offshoring company called Syntel Inc. to import foreign workers to run their computer operations. Syntel would hire the workers in India and bring them into the U.S. on H-1B guest worker visas. AIG management callously boasted to their soon-to-be former employees that they expected to save $11 million by replacing them with cheap foreign labor. That's not much consolation to American breadwinners trying to put food on their families' tables.

AIG heaped another insult on these workers. They would get sixty days of severance—but only if they trained their foreign replacements. Linda Kilcrease was one of the unlucky ones. She lost her job, health benefits, and accumulated pension.[4] "After we were seated," she told the *Daily Record* of Morris County, New Jersey, "an executive stood in front of the room and coldly told us that the computer systems were outsourced. We were each handed a folder of papers that detailed our 60-day notice and severance."[5]

A total of 249 full-time AIG employees, plus additional contract workers, lost their jobs to cheap, foreign workers imported into the United States.[6] Was it really worth it? A couple of years after the bloodletting John had an opportunity to do computer consulting at AIG. He became part of the cleanup crew for the resulting H-1B disaster. Rather than being "highly skilled," the workers supplied by Syntel were blithering incompetents. The programming work John and his team had to wade though and clean up looked like the work of high school–age programmers—and that might very well be an insult to high school students!

About a decade later, AIG had become functionally bankrupt, unable to make insurance payments to those it owed. In one of the largest federal bailouts in U.S. history, the Federal Reserve and U.S. Department of Treasury made $182 billion available to AIG so that it could meet its obligations. Needless to say, no equivalent bailout was given to the American workers laid off by AIG.

BANK OF AMERICA EMPLOYEE: "IT COULD BE ME. IT COULD BE ANYBODY"

In the spring of 2003, tech workers at Bank of America's Concord Technology Center in California felt like they were on "death row."[7] BofA was laying off workers left and right, sending jobs overseas, and contracting out work to offshore outsourcing companies Tata and Infosys. Kevin Flanagan, a forty-one-year-old software programmer, survived for months as the company slashed his friends' and colleagues' positions. He prepared for the worst by researching law school and applying for other bank positions.

Like his coworkers, Flanagan was forced to train his replacements. Unable to cope with the stress and humiliation, he killed himself in his office parking lot on the day he got his official pink slip. "This final blow was so devastating. He couldn't deal with it," his father said.[8] IT workers in Concord and across the country mourned Flanagan as they called attention to their collective plight. "It could be me," one anonymous BofA employee told the *Contra Costa Times*. "It could be anybody."[9]

Just three years later, BofA was at it again. As the company prepared to slash one hundred internal tech support workers, insiders told the *San Francisco Chronicle* about being subjected to Indian culture "team huddles," along with the unspoken grave-digging mandate. "If people want their severance packages, they have to train their replacements," a senior engineer at one of BofA's Bay Area facilities told the *Chronicle*'s David Lazarus. "There's nothing in writing that says this—the bank's been careful about that. But it's made clear at meetings what we're supposed to do."[10] BofA refused to comment about its outsourcing contracts, but the Indian replacement workers were plenty transparent.

BoA was "very open" about replacing Americans, the BofA engineer told the Chronicle. The H-1B workers are "here to learn our jobs then leave."[11]

PFIZER EMPLOYEE: "WE'RE TRAINING THEM"

In 2005, Pfizer executives circulated an internal memo saying they hoped to reduce the company's annual operating costs by $4 billion, in part by moving IT operations overseas. The memo described a plan to shift a large portion of the company's IT operations to two Indian contractors: Infosys and Satyam Computer Systems.[12]

Pfizer soon made good on its promise. According to sources cited by the *Day*, a local newspaper based in Groton, Connecticut, American contractors at two local Pfizer plants (one in New London, the other in nearby Groton) were headed for the chopping block:

> At the same time that local contractors are facing the anxiety of possible job losses, sources said, Pfizer is ratcheting up the number of foreign workers, mostly from India, who are arriving at the company's global R&D headquarters on controversial H-1B visas.
>
> These special visas were created to allow foreign workers to take jobs in the United States that could not be filled by Americans, but Pfizer—like other U.S. companies in the past— essentially has been using them to replace American workers, the sources said.
>
> "We're training them," said one source, who worries about being out of a job by the end of the year.[13]

The *Day*'s sources said that "scores" of foreign workers were present at the two Pfizer sites. Many were H-1B visa–holders employed by Infosys and Satyam.[14]

When former Sen. Chris Dodd (D-Conn.) and Rep. Joe Courtney, (D-Conn.) wrote Pfizer's CEO to find out what was going on, the company distanced itself from its H-1B contract workers:

In Pfizer's IT division, we have historically utilized third-party IT vendors for software development and applications support, and for daily IT-related functions. These vendors comprise both U.S. companies and companies that are based outside of the U.S. These vendors do employ foreign nationals, some of whom have been granted B1 non-immigrant visas to work in the U.S. for a limited period of time. That said, the third-party vendor would have petitioned for these visas, and Pfizer would have had no involvement in these petitions.

So Pfizer knew nothing about the foreign workers' visa petitions. Pfizer did, however, choose to contract IT work to Infosys and Satyam—two of the largest users of H-1B visas at the time—and required such workers to be hired only through such approved, preferred vendors.[15] As *Saturday Night Live*'s Church Lady might say, "Well, isn't that *conveeeenient!*"

Shortly after the *Day* published its exposé, Pfizer shut down its New London site. The site had opened just eight years earlier after local officials cleared out the neighborhood using the power of eminent domain to seize local residents' homes. Pfizer went on to announce a downsizing that it said would cut the local workforce from 4,500 to fewer than 3,400. By February of 2013, the number of Pfizer employees in the area had dropped to 3,150.[16]

Meanwhile, in a scandal that some called "India's Enron,"[17] Satyam chairman Ramalinga Raju revealed that more than 90 percent of the company's purported $1.1 billion in assets did not exist.[18] Around the same time, Fox News reported that Satyam had covertly installed spy software on some of the World Bank's computers.

Satyam was no fly-by-night operator. At the time, it was the fourth-largest IT firm in India based on revenue, with a workforce of fifty-three thousand[19] and more than one hundred Fortune 500 clients.[20]

DUN & BRADSTREET: "THESE DECISIONS WILL NOT BE MADE LIGHTLY"

Elahe Hessamfar was executive vice president of financial services giant Dun & Bradstreet's Global Technology Organization in March 2000. As Congress debated another huge expansion of the H-1B program and the usual corporate suspects brayed about tech worker shortages, Hessamfar prepared a company memo to her employees with this ominous subject line:

"Offshore development."

Hessamfar started off by informing the staff that large companies such as D&B needed to "find new ways to become more nimble and flexible to be able to respond more quickly to the competitive environment." She babbled about "core competencies," then cut to the chase: The firm was moving "to outsource work that can be done more efficiently by others." [21]

Translation: Brace for layoffs.

Hessamfar invoked the need for a "more flexible organization" again—by which she meant bouncing D&B's American tech workers out of their offices and bending over backwards to shift their duties to two of the world's largest employers of H-1Bs, India-based Wipro Infotech and Cognizant Technology Solutions. She explained:

These vendors have established Off-shore Development Centers (ODCs) in India where they build and support software for many large corporations such as ours. Over the course of the next year, these two organizations will become extensions to the GTO organization [Dun & Bradstreet's Global Technology Organization]. We've asked them to assist us in determining the priority in which systems will be moved off-shore. In order to facilitate this prioritization, representatives of both companies are meeting with application development and support teams to understand our applications. I ask that you consider them as members of our team and give them your full cooperation during this analysis. In the future, project teams will be composed of a mix of D&B resources [and] on-shore resources from these firms, as well as off-shore resources in India.[22]

With a rather clinical tone of detachment, Hessamfar promised that the new offshore program would "address the 'people' elements" of the transition. To those wondering whether their jobs would be transferred to India, the D&B executive offered tepid assurance "that these decisions will not be made lightly."[23]

Asked by a reporter how many American employees out of its fourteen-hundred-person workforce would be affected and how much money the company would save, D&B refused to comment.[24]

WATCHMARK-COMNITEL EMPLOYEE: "I FELT SUCKER PUNCHED"

At WatchMark-Comnitel, a telecommunications software company in Bellevue, Washington, seventeen quality-assurance employees got their pink slips in 2003. Despite repeated insistence by corporations that American workers "voluntarily" participate in prepping their own replacements, one whistleblower shed light on the truth. WatchMark-Comnitel software developer Myra Bronstein described to *USA Today* how she was told by managers that she had been laid off and was expected to retrain her new Indian successors—who would be making a sixteenth[25] of what she had been paid:

Bronstein felt trapped. She says she believes that if she refused, she would have probably been fired without severance and would have been ineligible for unemployment benefits. If she quit, she says, she wouldn't have received severance or been eligible for unemployment. . . .

"I was staring hard at my shoes and trying not to cry. It was hideously awkward. I felt forced," says Bronstein, forty-eight, of Mercer Island, Washington. She is still unemployed. "It was very deflating and dehumanizing to train your replacement. I felt sucker-punched. It was as if they handed us a shovel and said, 'Here, dig your own grave.' "[26]

FEAR, UNCERTAINTY, AND DOUBT AT NSTAR/EVERSOURCE ENERGY

In 2011, the Massachusetts-based utility company NSTAR merged with the Connecticut-based Northeast Utilities. The merged entities, which became New England's largest energy delivery system, operated under the Northeast Utilities name and then later Eversource Energy. Senior management positions were divided between people from both companies, with the chief information officer (CIO) coming from NSTAR.

The process of merging two companies created personnel turmoil. The two companies had different cultures. NSTAR had outsourced its computer operations to IBM. Northeast Utilities had tested outsourcing in the past, but found that it was cheaper to do the work in-house.

The year 2012 was one of misery for the employees as the company bled through constant layoffs. By the end of 2012, the newly created entity had laid off 750 employees. The old outsourcing contract that NSTAR had with IBM was set to expire in 2012; the new CIO told employees that she looked forward to bringing the work back in-house.

The year 2013 looked like it would be a better one for the computer workers at Northeast Utilities. The layoffs had ended and things looked as if they were getting back to normal. But as the year progressed, Northeast Utility employees noticed that a lot of people from India dressed in suits were meeting with senior management and collecting data. By September, *Computerworld* had caught wind of worker discord as the company signaled to its IT department that offshoring was imminent. Many experienced analysts noted that keeping employees in the dark about the actual dates and details was a "deliberate and calculated" move to destabilize the workforce.[27]

"Employees will begin job hunts and contact recruiters," Christine Santacroce, business development manager at Modis IT Staffing in Hartford, Connecticut, explained to *Computerworld*. Santacroce said some NU developers had already reached out to her. "As IT workers leave in advance of the outsourcing threat," the website reported, "it may reduce the number of severance packages that NU has to offer people, saving the company some money."[28]

There's even a name for the tactic of creating this artificial attrition: "FUD," which stands for fear, uncertainty, and doubt.

In the third week of October that year, the CIO came from Boston to hold a meeting with the computer group in Berlin, Connecticut. The CIO started out by making jokes and laughing. Then she swung the axe and announced they were all being fired. The company was replacing computer infrastructure employees with H-1B workers from the Indian company Infosys, and application development employees with H-1B workers from the Indian company Tata. The CIO explained that this change was necessary because Northeast Utilities needed global workers who could adapt to change faster than American workers.

The company swapped 223 Americans with workers imported from India. They were offered severance packages. But they had to train their Indian replacements to collect it. State lawmakers in Connecticut who had approved the utilities' merger decried the move. But they had no power to stop it.

As Yogi Berra quipped: It was déjà vu all over again.

As *Computerworld*'s Patrick Thibodeau, who included a photo of a Connecticut IT worker holding a sign that read "WILL CODE FOR FOOD" with his story on NU's layoffs, observed:

> I took that photograph about 10 years ago at a protest. . . . The sign was made by a Connecticut IT worker who was protesting the offshoring of jobs. This offshoring story, especially in Connecticut's manufacturing and financial services industries, has a very long history. What has changed is that the wave of offshoring has reached an employer, NU, long considered among its most stable.[29]

Not everyone at NSTAR (now called Eversource Energy) felt pain. CEO Thomas May received a $1.3 million pay raise to $9 million.[30] The Americans who got replaced can take consolation that a significant part of the paper savings from their sacrifice went straight into May's pocket.

AMERICAN WORKERS "HAVE BEEN MUZZLED"

If the Dig Your Own Grave phenomenon is common, why don't even more fired workers speak out? Often, they can't get their severance packages until and unless they sign on to nondisparagement and confidentiality provisions. Such provisions are standard to protect proprietary information. But these particularly insidious stipulations are intended to squelch free speech and prevent workers from talking about their plight. They're ruthless gag orders stapled to Dig Your Own Grave death sentences. If an American is brave enough to forgo a severance package and says, "Shove it, I'm not training any foreign replacements," he risks termination with cause and denial of unemployment benefits as well because then the employer can fire the American and report to the state unemployment agency that it was for cause.

At a Senate Judiciary Committee hearing on H-1B's displacement of American workers in March 2015, lawmakers heard from Jay Palmer, the former Infosys worker whose federal lawsuit over abuse of the H-1B and B-1 programs resulted in the largest work-visa program settlement of its kind—$34 million.[31] Palmer faced harassment, retaliation, blacklisting, and death threats for exposing the Infosys racket.[32] He knows firsthand what American workers who speak out about their predicament face: "They have been threatened, muzzled, and asked to train less qualified individuals as their replacements."[33] Palmer described how in January 2009 he "personally witnessed more than 7,000 American jobs cut at Home Depot in Atlanta. Months before these American employees trained their replacements from Infosys and other Indian based companies. The only reason was cheap labor."

The next summer, while doing Infosys work at Heidrick and Struggles (an executive search firm in Chicago), he watched HCL Technologies (an Indian offshoring company) take over Heidrick's IT department. "Heidrick employees were forced to train HCL employees in order to receive their compensation package. This situation turned hostile due to the fact that the American workers were blindsided." HCL is the same company bringing in H-1Bs to replace thousands of workers laid off at Disney,[34] which inked a $200 million IT outsourcing contract with the Indian firm in 2012.[35]

Palmer (whose battle you'll learn more about in Chapter 6) urged Congress to tell their stories and take up their cause. "We are their voice. We are the only one they have left because they were FORCED to sign non-disparaging remark clauses in order to get their benefits. They have been muzzled."[36] In his oral testimony, he noted, "That's why they're not here today!"

Indeed, Sen. Jeff Sessions (R-Ala.) noted that several victims had submitted confidential statements. One worker laid off from Southern California Edison wrote the committee:

> I started working at Southern California Edison several decades ago. SCE was a company that many people started with at a young age, could work there through their lifetimes, and retire with a good pension and benefits. That was my plan. And I would have been able to do exactly that—until an executive announced a couple years ago that my department was going to be outsourced.
>
> We were forced to train the less qualified foreign workers hired to take our jobs.
>
> Over 400 hardworking, intelligent people have lost their jobs due to the H-1B visa program. Many of us, and countless more like us, face enormous hurdles to find new jobs—why would companies want to hire us when they can hire cheaper workers on the H-1B visa to do our jobs for us?[37]

POURING MORE SALT IN AMERICAN WORKERS' WOUNDS: ANTI-AMERICAN DISCRIMINATION AT INFOSYS

Forcing U.S. workers to dig their own graves is only the most egregious part of the H-1B nightmare. As we told you in recounting laid-off Texas Instruments engineer Darin Wedel's story, age discrimination against tech workers thirty-five and older runs rampant. In addition to older workers, minorities and women have suffered as a result of importation of H-1B workers. Immigration policy scholar David North notes that "selections within the H-1B program—made by males, often Indian males—tend to be disproportionately of other males, despite the fact that the number of women attending Indian high-tech training institutions is steadily rising."[38] The broad access to foreign labor under our current law has undermined the incentive for technology companies to hire women and minority U.S. citizens.

While Indian government officials and tech industry lobbyists frequently invoke the race and ethnic cards to protest immigration enforcement measures as "discriminatory," they have little to say about explicitly anti-American practices and sentiments from Indian offshore outsourcing executives.

Apple, which claims to promote ethnic and racial "diversity" as a way to inspire "creativity and innovation," employed 509 contract workers from Infosys at its Cupertino, California, headquarters in 2013. *Computerworld* reported that government records show "499 are listed as Asian"—that's a whopping 98 percent—"with the remaining 10 identified as either white or black."[39]

Infosys whistleblower Jay Palmer's former colleague Brenda Koehler blew her own whistle on the "systematic, company-wide discrimination" she witnessed at the company.[40] In August 2013, she filed a class-action lawsuit detailing how managers at the Indian outsourcing giant directly discriminated against non–South Asian employees, abused H-1B to bring workers of South Asian descent into the country rather than hiring qualified individuals already in the United States, and abused the B-1 short-term business visa system "to bring workers of South Asian descent into the United States to perform work not allowed by their visa status rather than hiring individuals already in the United States to perform the work."[41] Infosys failed to convince a federal judge to dismiss the case in May 2015, greenlighting it for the discovery phase in preparation for trial.[42]

Koehler described applying for an administrative position in VMware, an area of expertise for Koehler—who holds a BS and MS in information systems, along with seventeen years of experience in the business. The job went to a worker of Bangladeshi national origin after a curious interview in which Infosys representatives misstated Koehler's work experience. She asserted that lower standards for South Asian hires at Infosys were routine and that, while 1 to 2 percent of the U.S. population is of South Asian descent, 90 percent of Infosys's workforce is. Backing up her claims, three other Infosys workers joined the class-action suit, which is currently pending.

Layla Bolten revealed how she was harassed because she didn't speak Hindi and also lost out on a job opportunity that she was qualified for in favor of a Bangladeshi applicant. Bolten, an experienced tester in Maryland, had been employed by Infosys to work on its $50 million contract overseeing the District of Columbia's Obamacare exchange. She described being forced to train less-experienced and less-knowledgeable foreign workers, including H-1Bs.[43]

Greg Handloser, a Florida-based senior sales manager at Infosys from 2004 to 2012, exposed a "purge" of non–South Asian employees "in the sales force and other areas that had comparatively large numbers of non–South Asian employees." Like Bolten, Handloser was excluded from work-related conversations by Hindi-speaking supervisors.[44]

Kelly Parker was an Infosys contractor employee who did IT work at motorcycle manufacturer Harley Davidson's plants in Wisconsin. It had been her "dream job" and her excellent performance earned her positive reviews. But she, too, was laid off after training her foreign replacement from India in 2013.[45]

Brenda Koehler and her coplaintiffs cited bigoted comments witnessed by Infosys whistleblower Jay Palmer, including multiple references to "stupid Americans" and this one: "While working on the assignment at Vinings, Georgia, in December 2008, Infosys employee-whistleblower Jay Palmer claims that another Infosys employee wrote 'Americans cost $,' and 'No Americans/Christians' on a whiteboard."[46]

Don't believe them? Then take it from Indian Infosys hiring

manager Ramesh Elumali, who acknowledged to an Indian media outlet that "[t]here does exist an element of discrimination. We are advised to hire Indians because they will work off the clock without murmur and they can always be transferred across the nation without hesitation unlike [the] local workforce."[47]

Another former recruiter at Infosys (who is not a party to the lawsuit) submitted an affidavit in the American workers' case. When he complained about qualified Americans not being hired, an Infosys senior manager responded: "Americans don't know s#$t."[48]

"THIS IS WHY I DON'T LIKE DEALING WITH AMERICANS"

In April 2015, as the Senate stepped up scrutiny of H-1B's displacement of U.S. workers at Southern California Edison and other companies, American IT worker Steven Heldt hit offshore outsourcing giant Tata Consultancy Services with a class-action employment discrimination lawsuit under Title VII of the Civil Rights Act. Heldt had earned a BA in economics from the University of North Carolina at Chapel Hill, held multiple technical certifications, served in the U.S. Army's 101st Airborne Division, and worked in positions in project management, business analysis, software development, networking, IT operations, IT governance, IT security, IT risk management, IT auditing, IT compliance, and business continuity and disaster recovery.

While working as a project manager to service Tata client Kaiser Permanente in Pleasanton, California, Heldt (who was one of only three non–South Asians on the Kaiser contract) witnessed repeated anti-American bias by Indian supervisors. During his twenty-month employment with Tata, according to the pending lawsuit filed in federal court in San Francisco, Heldt:

• Was intermittently placed in five different positions that often involved only menial responsibilities (no position lasting more than three months) servicing large client organizations that hired Tata to perform IT services;

- Spent approximately thirteen months "benched" with no substantive work to perform even while Tata continued to service the client organizations to which Mr. Heldt had been assigned, using approximately 99 percent South Asian workers;
- Routinely applied for new positions within Tata (for U.S. clients including Genentech, Apple, and Cisco) and was denied by South Asian management within Tata;
- Was passed over and not hired in favor of South Asians preferred by Tata;
- Experienced substantial anti-American sentiment—e.g., being told by Tata management: "This is why I don't like dealing with Americans," being told that he would have difficulty finding work within Tata because he is American, and being told that Tata was not even looking for Americans to hire; and
- Ultimately was terminated.[49]

The complaint outlined the many methods by which Tata allegedly achieved its discriminatory goals, foremost of which was the use of temporary guest worker visas to hire mostly, if not exclusively, South Asians. Tata is consistently one of the top three H-1B sponsors in the United States, having sponsored 8,701 new H-1B visas in 2013, 6,692 new H-1B visas in 2012, and 5,365 new H-1B visas in 2011, as well as 25,908 L-1 intracompany transfer visas between 2002 and 2011.[50]

When Heldt objected to his treatment, he says a Tata human resources manager criticized Americans for trying to "exercise their rights.[51]

Pesky things, those rights.

H-1B ADVOCATES: FAIR WEATHER FRIENDS OF THE FREE MARKET

The pro-H-1B lobby likes to accuse its opponents of opposing the "free market" flow of people across borders. In the pages of the open-borders *Wall Street Journal* (of course), immigration lawyers Martin J. Lawler and Margaret Stock bemoaned: "In a country that supposedly values the free market, why are companies like Apple, Google, Intel and scores of others being denied the workers they need to compete in the global economy?"[52] With a complete lack of self-awareness, an *American Spectator* writer decried the short-lived, American-worker-first requirements for TARP government bailout recipients as "anti–free market."[53]

Many of Silicon Valley's most celebrated technology companies, including Apple, Intel, Adobe, Intuit, Lucasfilm, Pixar, and Google, demonstrated their commitment to free market principles by engaging in a conspiracy not to hire each other's workers in order to suppress wages and restrict employee mobility.[54] A class-action lawsuit filed by sixty-four thousand tech workers alleged that the illegal antipoaching pact, in place from 2005 to 2009, kept salaries down in violation of federal antitrust law. An infamous email exchange between Google chairman Eric Schmidt (net worth: $9 billion) and the late Apple founder and CEO Steve Jobs (net worth at the time of his death: $11 billion) over a rogue recruiter's termination was punctuated with a smiley-face emoticon sent from Jobs to Schmidt. (See Appendix B.) In March 2015, the Big Tech cartel operators agreed to a settlement worth $415 million—an amount that still falls well short of the affected workers' potential lost wages, according to several of the plaintiffs.[55]

So much for the phony-baloney arguments of K Street operator Grover Norquist and company who accuse H-1B critics of betraying "free market" principles.[56] Conservative journalist W. James Antle has it exactly right: "If the government has discretion in how it exercises its legitimate authority over who comes and who goes, a prerequisite for national sovereignty, then shouldn't it exercise such discretion in a way that minimizes the impoverishment of Americans?"[57]

The H-1B program has had precisely the effect employers desired. During the 1990s, inflation-adjusted wages for computer workers rose about 3 percent annually. Since Congress expanded the H-1B program in 2000 and 2004, programmer wages have been flat.[58]

These workers, however, have fared better than workers in the U.S. economy as a whole. Most Americans have seen their real wages decline during the past ten years. A report circulated by industry lobbyists calling for more H-1B visas spins that grim reality this way: "Over the past decade, the earnings of STEM workers have risen *relative to all other* U.S. occupations by 3% to 6% [emphasis added]."[59]

In other words, America needs more H-1B guest workers so U.S. computer programmers can be as bad off as everyone else—excluding tech billionaires and their lobbyists, that is.

"I WAS STUNNED": NORTH CAROLINA SUBSIDIZES OFFSHORE OUTSOURCING

Many critics of the H-1B program liken it to a government subsidy for corporations. Nobel economist and free-market godfather Milton Friedman reportedly acknowledged that H-1B visas are "a benefit to their employers, enabling them to get workers at a lower wage, and to that extent, it is a subsidy."[60] In North Carolina, this is literally true. North Carolina's GOP governor Pat McCrory and Commerce Secretary Sharon Decker proudly announced in November 2014 that the state had offered taxpayer-subsidized incentives worth up to $5 million to lure H-1B offshore outsourcing giant Cognizant to a new office in Charlotte and to "create 500 jobs" for residents.[61] The governor's office touted the company's nearly fifteen hundred employees already working in North Carolina, and Secretary Decker promised that "as

Cognizant expands, these new jobs will be added all across North Carolina."[62]

Of course, Cognizant is in the well-publicized business of moving American jobs overseas; 40 percent of its business comes from financial companies outsourcing their IT departments. Charlotte is the nation's second-largest banking center, home to the headquarters of Bank of America[63] and East Coast headquarters of Wells Fargo.[64] It also happens to be a top requestor of H-1B visas in the state of North Carolina. Professor Ron Hira drew the obvious conclusions: "If I was a North Carolina taxpayer I would be really baffled and shocked that we would be taking our tax dollars and subsidizing a firm that's actually going to be a net negative for the economy."[65] Hira pointed out to the local National Public Radio station that from mid-2009 to mid-2013, Cognizant received twenty-three thousand H-1B visas. That's 75 percent of its North American workforce of about thirty thousand employees—and doesn't include another large chunk of guest workers on L-1 intracompany transfers. Clueless North Carolina officials, however, didn't connect the dots. Only after being informed by a local news outlet of Cognizant's primary business agenda did one Democratic lawmaker respond: "I was stunned." According to WFAE, "nothing in its contract with North Carolina prevents Cognizant from filling the new jobs with more temporary guest workers."

State officials, asleep at the wheel, earmarked $5 million in the name of job creation and economic development to a company infamous for obliterating American jobs. As the *International Business Times* concluded, "The Cognizant corporate incentive deal in North Carolina underscores a lack of due diligence by local officials too eager to jump at any opportunity to throw taxpayer money at companies whose business models are built around pushing labor costs as low as possible."[66] Sold out and screwed over again.

"THEY ARE NOT LOOKING AT AMERICANS"

As we explained in Chapter 3, most employers do not have to check the box on the LCA form certifying that they tried to recruit and hire an American before making an offer to an H-1B visa holder. However, separate from the H-1B program, discrimination against Americans based upon immigration status is illegal—if you can prove it. But that is exactly what IBM did, according to an employee who reached out to John.

John's source was working on a software development project that had recently ended. He needed to find another project to avoid being laid off. One of the methods he used to find an internal job was a mailing list for employees who were available for a new project. Through this mailing list, he received a timely email from IBM HR that began:

> We are *urgently* seeking Business Analyst resources with Test experience for two positions on the Alcatel-Lucent account.

A lengthy job description and instructions on how to apply followed this introduction. The job was located in the United States and John's source lived close to the project. IBM uses the term "resource" to refer to employees.

John's source responded to the job posting with a cover letter explaining how his qualifications matched the posted job requirements. He included the additional information requested in the job posting and a résumé.

This is the IBM hiring manager's complete response:

> Thank you for your interest in the eBusiness Analyst position on the Alcatel-Lucent account. We are in the process of gathering résumés for this position and will send you a follow-up response once we have had an opportunity to review your qualifications.

> Please understand the client[']s first preference is IGSI [IBM Global Services India] landed resource, then local US candidates, then remote, so these candidates will be in the second group to be considered.

This hiring manager openly admitted that Americans must get in line for jobs behind "landed resources" from IBM India. John's source forwarded the emails to IBM HR and attached the following complaint:

> You included these two positions—below—again into today's email to "Available." Per below, they are NOT looking at Americans. Pretty clear.

American workers are a protected class under the law and discrimination against them based upon immigration status is unlawful.[67] So what IBM was doing here (giving preference to foreign workers) was not kosher.

One would think that IBM's HR office, upon learning of blatant discrimination against Americans, would disavow the actions of its hiring manager and take decisive corrective action. Instead, IBM HR responded by explaining to the American employee *why* IBM prefers foreign workers to Americans:

> There are often US Reg [U.S. Regular] seats that also have landed GR [Global Resource] seats open—sometimes the customer will take either as long as they are working onsite—and the cost difference is too great for the business not to look for landed GRs or to use them if they are a skills match.

Straight from the IBM HR department: Foreign workers supplied by IBM India are paid so much less than Americans that it is worth it to

IBM to take the chance of explicitly excluding Americans, and hope they do not get caught. The "cost difference is too great" for them not to do so.

Companies such as IBM make a gamble when they discriminate against Americans. Under the current law it is illegal to do so, but this is generally a safe bet to make.

Employers have several things going for them when making the wager. First, an American applying for a job is unlikely to know that he has been discriminated against. Even if the employer sends a rejection letter to an applicant, it is not likely to say that it was looking for a foreign worker instead. Usually companies are more careful than IBM was here. Second, even if the applicant suspected discrimination, he would have to prove that the reason he was not hired was that he was an American. Third, even when discrimination is proven, the penalties are small. In September 2013, IBM reached a settlement agreement with the Department of Justice over allegations that the company discriminated against U.S. developers by favoring foreign job applicants who held H-1B visas or foreign student visas. Under the settlement agreement, IBM agreed to pay a piddly $44,400 in civil penalties.[68] For perspective, IBM's CEO earned $19,345,125 in 2014.[69]

Keep in mind that immigration-related discrimination and H-1B visas are enforced separately. So, even after getting caught and paying a fine, IBM can still get cheap foreign workers on H-1B visas. In fact, IBM remains one of the biggest users of H-1B visas.

Up against the massive legal resources of IBM, John's source decided to accept a severance package (contingent upon waiving legal action) instead of challenging the company in court.

Judging from one immigration law firm's survey of employers seeking H-1B workers, discrimination against U.S. workers is common. The survey found that 17 percent of employers admitted they would not have hired an American even if one had been available.[70] Those results certainly jibe with an infamous video posted to YouTube in 2007 by the law firm of Cohen & Grigsby in Pittsburgh, Pennsylvania, to promote its immigration services. The video provided an inside look at how lawyers help employers game the immigration system. The result was a public relations debacle.

Attorney and then–vice president of marketing Lawrence Lebowitz, describing the process for an employer to go through the recruitment process, boldly stated:

> Our goal is clearly *not* to find a qualified and interested U.S. worker. In a sense that sounds funny, but it is what we're trying to do here. . . . We are complying with the law fully, but our objective is to get this person a green card and to get through the labor certification process. So certainly we are not going to try and find a place where the applicants are going to be numerous. We're going to try to find a place where again we're complying with the law and hoping and likely not to find qualified and interested worker applicants.[71]

If a highly qualified American worker does happen to apply, one of Lebowitz's colleagues explained how the law firm would step in: "If necessary, schedule an interview. Go through the whole process to find a legal basis to disqualify them for this particular position. In most cases that doesn't seem to be a problem."[72]

The reaction to the video was overwhelmingly negative. *Business-Week*, for example, wrote about the video in an article that led with, "Want to hire cheaper foreign workers instead of Americans? A lawyer tells you how to game the immigration system—and it's all on YouTube."[73]

The law firm pulled the video from YouTube and referred inquiries to a public relations firm. The PR firm said, "It is unfortunate that these statements have been commandeered and misused, which runs contrary to our intent." Fortunately, many people made copies of the video before it was taken down and it remains widely available on the Internet.[74] Lebowitz is still at the firm, but after this marketing debacle, he is no longer the VP of Marketing at Cohen & Grigsby. The good news? If you are in the market for American worker-evasion services, there's a firm in Pittsburgh that fits the bill.

ADDICTION TO FOREIGN WORKERS

If we go back to the contemporaneous legislative history, it's clear to see that the Immigration Act of 1990 has been an abject failure.

In its report on the original bill creating the H-1B visa program, the House Judiciary Committee made clear: "[Immigration policy can fill] the need of American business for highly skilled, specially trained personnel to fill increasingly sophisticated jobs for which domestic personnel cannot be found and the need for other workers to meet specific labor shortages."[75] The same report asserted: "The Committee believes that increased immigration levels should not lead to a dependence on foreign workers, nor should they place training of unemployed U.S. citizens at risk."[76] The panel also noted: "Employers seeking foreign workers have a special obligation to ensure that obtaining workers from abroad is a last resort."[77] The incessant demand to bust the H-1B cap and the mad rush for H-1B visas every April show that cheap foreign workers are a first resort, not the last. Ask yourself: How much of a U.S. worker shortage can there be when U.S. companies can fire thousands of technology workers they already have after forcing them to train their H-1B substitutes? The irony here, of course, is that the driving purpose of H-1B visa is to solve a U.S. technology worker vacuum that doesn't exist.

Desperate for their fix, billionaires now demand that Congress give them even more cheap foreign labor on H-1B visas.[78] Google goes even further, claiming complete addiction to H-1B workers:

> It is no stretch to say that without these employees, we might not be able to develop future revolutionary products like the next Gmail or the next Google Earth.[79]

It is long past time for Congress to admit that H-1B has been a spectacular failure in all regards. It is time to cut the foreign labor junkies off. Not only are they a menace to America's best and brightest, they are also serial abusers of the indentured foreign guest workers they can't get enough of, as well.

⊣ 5 ⊢

50 Shades of H-1B Abuse

Binding, Bodyshopping, and Benching

Binding. Bodyshopping. Benching. No, this is not a lurid sequel to *50 Shades of Gray.* But be forewarned: you are about to enter a chamber of H-1B perversities involving the guest worker trafficking scam perpetrated by IT firms engaged in offshore outsourcing, as well as their corporate clients in the U.S.

The primary business of the largest H-1B employers is to move U.S. work to offshore locations. These IT services companies use H-1B visas to bring foreign workers onsite to (1) learn the jobs of Americans and ship the knowledge, work, and the workers abroad and (2) fuel the booming business of undercutting and replacing American workers here on American soil. Although many of the IT offshoring companies are based in India, it's important to recognize that this is not just an "Indian" problem. American companies such as IBM and Deloitte have joined their Indian competitors in the business of moving jobs overseas. Moreover, the offshoring companies can't do their thing without the cooperation of their U.S. clients, including Adobe, Best Buy, Cisco, Hewlett-Packard, Microsoft, Pfizer, and Xerox.

Of course, the Americans displaced by H-1B workers here represent just the tip of the iceberg of U.S. job losses. In addition to the direct losses of U.S. jobs to H-1B workers, there are the additional jobs being moved overseas that the H-1B workers facilitate.

Ron Hira, professor of political science at Howard University and coauthor of *Outsourcing America*, boils down the rotten impact: "Rather than keeping jobs from leaving our shores, the H-1B does the opposite, by facilitating offshoring and providing employers with cheap, temporary labor—while reducing job opportunities for American high-tech workers in the process."[1]

BINDING H-1B WORKERS TO THEIR EMPLOYER

The H-1B visa program has often been criticized for creating a system of indentured servitude that permanently binds the foreign worker to the employer.[2] In 2008, Congress enacted a provision that purported to address this problem:

> (vi)(I) It is a violation of this clause for an employer who has filed an application under this subsection to require an H–1B nonimmigrant to pay a penalty for ceasing employment with the employer prior to a date agreed to by the non-immigrant and the employer.[3]

The language is designed to make it appear at quick glance that employers cannot force H-1B workers to sign contracts that force them to pay penalties if they change jobs. But right after that section, the code adds:

> The Secretary shall determine whether a required payment is a penalty (and not liquidated damages) pursuant to relevant State law.

"Liquidated damages" are used in contracts to specify the compensation a party must pay for a breach when the underlying damages cannot be quantified at the time of the agreement. An employer can require, as a condition of employment, that the H-1B worker sign a contract in which he agrees to pay a fixed sum for liquidated damages if he changes jobs. But just don't call it a "penalty" (wink, wink, nudge, nudge).

The upshot: An H-1B worker can have thousands of dollars in potential liability hanging over his head if he quits.[4] Tata's standard employment agreement contained a provision requiring an employee to pay thirty thousand dollars for leaving.[5] A company spokesman explained: "We require our employees to sign a contract with us that states they will return to India upon completion of the work and that they won't leave TCS and take a job in the U.S."[6] Tata also required its H-1B workers to sign a power of attorney allowing a company-designated tax preparer to do their income taxes.[7] The employer then required H-1Bs to endorse and sign over their tax refunds back to the company.

Many other employers of H-1B guest workers, such as Softech, CompSys, and Vensoft, routinely require guest workers to pay the company if they change jobs.[8]

"You can pretty much see a leash on my neck with my employer," Saravanan Ranganathan, a Washington, D.C.–area computer security expert here on an H-1B visa, told the Center for Investigative Reporting (CIR) in 2014. "It's kind of like a hidden chain . . . and you'd better shut up, or you'll lose everything."[9] Noting that Labor Department documents showed "from 2000 through 2013, at least $29.7 million was illegally withheld from about 4,400 tech workers here on H-1B visas," the CIR team spotlighted a web of unscrupulous "labor brokers"—both small and large—who wield restrictive employment contracts and intimidation lawsuits to create an "ecosystem of fear" among foreign guest workers. Asked why the Labor Department refused to intervene when H-1B workers for Indian-run Softech blew the whistle on its unlawful bonding and serial fraudulent practices, an official drily responded: "We need to be strategic with our resources."[10]

The binding phenomenon is not just limited to companies that specialize in offshoring. "Handcuffing," as U.C. Davis professor Norm Matloff calls it, also occurs among Big Tech companies in Silicon Valley. "If the employer sponsors the H-1B for a green card," he explains, "the H-1B is basically immobile . . . Silicon Valley firms hugely value this, even more than having cheap labor."[11] Indeed, immigration lawyers openly encourage companies to exploit such green-card-based handcuffing. "By far the most important advantage of [green card sponsorship]," immigration attorney David Swaim informed readers of his employers' guide to immigration law, "is the fact that the employee is tied to a particular position with one company and must remain with the company in most cases for more than four years."[12]

BODYSHOP TILL YOU DROP

Another sordid side effect of the H-1B program: the shady enterprise of foreign guest worker "bodyshopping." In theory, H-1B workers are only supposed to be brought here when Americans are not available to fill a specific job opening. In reality, however, "placement companies" import workers on H-1B visas for the purpose of contracting them out to other companies that have the actual jobs. This system of importing workers and pimping them out puts H-1B workers in direct competition with Americans for the same jobs.

Companies that supply H-1B contract labor are known in the tech industry as "bodyshops." This term refers to firms that sponsor large numbers of H-1B workers who then perform IT or back-office tasks for U.S. companies on a contract basis. Their business is to provide bodies by the hour. The worker gets paid by the bodyshop, but works in the facilities of and at the direction of another company contracting with the bodyshop for the labor. Often the contract worker is performing tasks that were once done by a regular U.S. employee.

The increasingly common practice of bodyshopping seems to have emerged as a direct result of the availability of H-1B workers as a low-cost alternative to U.S. workers.[13] Bodyshops may sponsor large numbers of H-1B workers who have no actual assignment when they arrive in the U.S.

Sometimes, the employer-employee relationship between the bodyshop and H-1B worker is suspect. Some companies advertise on the Internet for H-1B workers and after sponsoring them keep a percentage of the worker's earnings. In a number of cases, companies obtained H-1B visas for individuals who then disappeared upon arrival.[14]

One of the earliest government reports on the H-1B program came from the Department of Labor's Office of Inspector General. The report found that 6 percent of H-1B workers were being contracted out to other employers. The report concluded: "[I]n our opinion, the H-1B program was not intended for an employer to establish a business of H-1B aliens to contract out to U.S. employers."[15] That was in 1996. By 2013, the majority of H-1B visas were being used for bodyshopping.[16]

The system of bodyshopping creates a hidden labor market in which Americans are excluded.[17] Companies seeking contract labor will only let their preferred vendors know about the opening, often bodyshops that only supply H-1B workers (see Pfizer above). If the preferred vendors do not have a worker available, they often circulate job openings among themselves, rather than advertising the position to Americans. The firm making the original request may not be aware that the H-1B worker it gets may actually be an employee of a second bodyshop, with two different companies taking a cut of the wages paid.

Many H-1B bodyshops are public companies, and some of their

shares trade on U.S. stock exchanges. The extent of their reliance on the H-1B program is documented in filings with the SEC. For example, the Indian company Wipro warns investors:

> Our employees who work onsite at client facilities or at our facilities in the U.S. on temporary or extended assignments typically must obtain visas. If U.S. immigration laws change and make it more difficult for us to obtain H1B and L-1 visas for our employees, our ability to compete for and provide services to our clients in the U.S. could be impaired.[18]

KForce presents a similar warning to investors:

> Our Tech business utilizes a significant number of foreign nationals employed by us on work visas, primarily under the H-1B visa classification. . . . Current and future restrictions on the availability of such visas could restrain our ability to employ the skilled professionals we need to meet our clients' needs, which could have a material adverse effect on our business.[19]

Cognizant Technology Solutions warns investors:

> On August 13, 2010, President Barack Obama signed legislation which imposed additional fees of $2,000 for certain H-1B petitions and $2,250 for certain L-1A and L1B petitions beginning in August 2010 through September 20, 2014. . . . Given the ongoing debate over outsourcing, the introduction and consideration of other restrictive legislation or regulations is possible. . . . In the event that any of these measures become law, our business, results of operations and financial condition could be adversely

affected and our ability to provide services to our customers could be impaired.[20]

Remember: Congress originally asserted when it established H-1B that "[e]mployers seeking foreign workers have a special obligation to ensure that obtaining workers from abroad is a last resort."[21] These financial disclosure documents of H-1B visa users operating in the U.S. demonstrate the Grand Canyon–sized gulf between past intent and present reality.

WHO'S LURKING IN HIDDEN H-1B BASEMENTS?

The huge number of H-1B visas going to a few, largely Indian companies has attracted considerable attention—and with good reason, of course. After years of abuse, some of the big names in offshore outsourcing are finally being held accountable. Six years after confessing to having engaged in Bernie Madoff–style accounting, Satyam's founder was convicted by a trial court and will be sentenced to seven years in prison.[22] As we'll show you in depth in Chapter 7, Infosys paid a record $34 million to settle a visa fraud case after it committed systemic visa fraud and abuse of immigration processes. And in 2013, Tata forked over $30 million to settle a wage theft dispute in a class-action lawsuit brought by Indian workers—though the company admitted no wrongdoing.[23]

But what has largely escaped notice are a plethora of smaller companies in the same business of H-1B bodyshopping. An audit by USCIS found a violation rate of 54 percent for companies with twenty-five or fewer employees.[24] At companies with more than twenty-five employees, the violation rate was 11 percent.

Table 5.1 contains a list of companies in one small city—Edison, New Jersey—that obtained H-1B workers in fiscal year 2009 using a residential address on their Labor Condition Applications.[25] These employers are apparently hiring H-1B workers—the best and brightest the world has to offer, remember—out of their basements. If H-1B workers are needed so badly to fill vacant positions at world-beating firms like Apple and Facebook, why are so many of them working out of home offices and basements in small towns like Edison, New Jersey?

TABLE 5.1 COMPANIES WITH APPROVED H-1B PETITIONS HAVING RESIDENTIAL ADDRESSES IN EDISON, NEW JERSEY

Company	Number of H-1B workers	Address
Sigma Group Inc.	2	1080 Amboy Ave.
Ramps International Inc.	4	18 Beech St.
Sofia Technology LLC	4	16 Cactus Ct.
Techwave Consulting Inc.	7	2 Carnwarth Ct.
1 Global Solutions Inc.	1	732 Denver Blvd.
Prudent Source LLC	7	608 Forest Haven Blvd.
M&M Hotbreads LLC	1	490 Grove Ave.
Waltz Solutions LLC	2	86 Hana Rd.
Avignah Systems Inc.	1	131 Hillcrest Ave.
Medha Consulting Group LLC	4	27 Judson St., Suite 6B
Valleysoft Solutions LLC	1	1801 Merrywood Dr.
Tekplant Inc.	3	2801 Merrywood Dr.
Source Info Tech Inc.	10	2804 Merrywood Dr.
Clemac Technology Services LLC	4	16 Palm Ct.
Techno Marketing Group LLC	2	385 Pierson Ave.
Promag Systems Inc.	1	712 Rivendell Ave.
Thapovan Infosystems Inc.	1	67 Spring St.
Hudson Data LLC	1	42 Utica Rd.
JB Tech Systems LLC	1	135 Waterford Dr.
Prudent Professionals Inc.	1	42 Westwood Circle

Another company, Astron Consulting LLC, obtained an H-1B visa using a UPS mailbox store address. Still another, Venkateshwara Computers, located in a modest home in Livingston, New Jersey, applied for two H-1B programmers.[26] These tiny bodyshops get passed over by overburdened, understaffed regulators and enforcement officers, so they can routinely exploit foreign workers and disadvantage American workers with impunity.

Even when they do get caught, the charges and punishment are often bargained down to wrist-slaps. In 2009, for example, federal prosecutors charged small H-1B bodyshop Vision Systems Group with ten counts of criminal conspiracy over its scheme to bring foreign guest workers from India using phony documents and its fraudulent use of wage rates from Iowa to determine the "prevailing wage" for their H-1B aliens working in New Jersey.[27] Vision Systems Group also made H-1Bs sign bondage contracts[28] and benched the workers. Two years later, the case ended "quietly," *Computerworld* reported, with the company's owners agreeing to a plea bargain on a single count— and paying less than $240,000 of the $7.4 million in restitution the feds had originally sought.[29]

Why has bodyshopping of H-1B workers not been eliminated since the Labor Department exposed the problem nearly two decades ago? Connect the dots and follow the money: The large bodyshops have lobbyists;[30] big U.S. companies want access to cheap labor through bodyshops large and small;[31] and lawyers want to keep the bodyshop H-1B visa stream flowing to collect the legal fees.[32] Surely it is reasonable to expect Americans to sacrifice their jobs so that immigration lawyers can maintain their yachts?

ALL BENCHED UP AND NOWHERE TO GO

What happens when the bodyshop does not have actual work for the H-1B guest worker? By law, an H-1B worker is supposed to be continuously employed and paid to maintain his visa status. When he loses his job, he's supposed to go home. This makes perfect sense because the H-1B worker is purportedly here for the sole purpose of filling a job that no American can or will do.

In practice, bodyshops like Infosys stockpile H-1B visas for jobs that don't exist yet to be meted out as their salesmen book business. An H-1B visa is good for six years *in the United States*, so large H-1B employers can delay bringing aliens with visas into the country until there is actual work. Otherwise, the foreign guest workers sit on the "bench," confined to a company "guest house"—a small apartment often crammed with eight to ten other foreign workers—until project work materializes.[33] If they're lucky, they'll get paid at a reduced rate while they wait. Or not at all.

One company in the bodyshop business, Upani Consultants Ltd. in Pennsylvania, charged potential employees four thousand dollars upfront, but when the H-1B workers arrived in the U.S., they found they had no jobs.[34] In December 2014, the company's founder, Sudhakar Majety, pleaded guilty to four counts of visa fraud involving 50 H-1B workers, whom he imported here with false promises of employment at his false company.[35] His scheme involved creating doctored résumés, phony shell companies, and fake contracts purporting to pay fifty thousand to seventy thousand dollars a year. When the H-1B aliens finally found employment on their own, Majety snatched 20 percent of their wages off the top.[36] Federal prosecutors reported that one worker "actually had to pay Upani her own salary [of which Majety kept 20 percent] for a few months in order to generate the appropriate paperwork to renew her H1-B [*sic*] visa."

Once again, an H-1B worker finds himself in a bind. If he reports the employer to the feds, the employer will undoubtedly respond by reporting his termination to the USCIS and he will have to leave the country immediately. Doing so is just as pragmatic on the part of the employer as it is vindictive. If the complaint results in the Labor Department assessing back pay, that amount is limited to the date of termination.

Benching is supposed to be illegal. H-1B workers are supposed to be paid their full wage while in the U.S. An employer who benches H-1B workers is supposed to incur liability for back pay and penalties. An H-1B guest worker who accepts being on the bench is not supposed to be in valid H-1B status, which can jeopardize future immigration prospects. Yet, the phenomenon is so common that websites with names like "Benchfolks.com" and "Benchfolks.org" have sprung up to help the H-1B workers find jobs. The lobbyist spin is that we need H-1Bs because there are jobs that cannot be filled by Americans. The reality is the system of bodyshoping aliens is designed to put foreign workers in competition with American for jobs. The push for H-1Bs is motivated by a desire to reduce wages. For big corporations, the more H-1Bs, the better—even if there are not enough jobs for all of them. Indeed, we bring so many workers in on H-1B visas that often the foreign workers cannot find real work either.

No one knows how many H-1B workers in the United States do not have actual jobs. But the number is clearly large enough for employers to target them openly for recruitment. One job posting[37] on Dice.com read:

> Have H1B, but still NO JOB?
>   Employer is not marketing your profile?
>   You have not even selected for an interview?
>   No interview offers?
>   Feeling of getting wasted in the employer's guesthouse?
>   Pl contact us, we will help you train, market and place it throughout USA. You can transfer your H1B to our company and we will file your Green Card

Nearly every Internet forum on H-1B is flooded with complaints about benching and pleas for help like this one:

I am in US from 1.5 months, i got an opportunity to work in comp X, but comp X is asking 3 paystubs to transfer my H1

My current employer had not generated any paystubs till now as I am not into project till now.

Please suggest what I need to do if my employer refuses to give paystubs for the last 1.5 month's period.

Your suggestions are highly appreciated.

Thanks[38]

When an H-1B worker tries to transfer out of a benching predicament, the bureaucratic hurdles are high. Here's what happened to one guest worker after he was benched without pay for a month:

I was working for company A till April 2011 and since the project was completed by mar 2011, I was in bench and not paid for april 2011. Hence I was moved to new employer B in May 2011 and they filed H1B transfer in May 2011 through normal H1B processing and started working after receiving the h1b receipt notice. I got the [Request for Evidence] RFE in July asking for my april month pay stub, employer and client details. Since old employer has not paid me, he is not generated the pay stub for april, i was unable to submit the april pay stub for RFE. . . . After 4 months from the RFE submission, we got the H1B denial status on 12/23/2011. . . . Please do advise me what can be done on this situation to be in legal work status.[39]

Here's another poor worker in the torturous position of being on the bench at a company that is also sponsoring his green card:

Hi I'm currently on H1, i have [received] my labour approval, and want to proceed with I-140, but i have another offer from

an India based company, now i'm in a fix, i have roughly a yr
and half left on my H1, and the new company does not sponsor
GC's, I'm currently on bench and don't want to leave gc process
if possible, so i was wondering if any of you experts out here
can tell me if there are any signals as to when the economy will
improve, so that i can hope that i won't be on bench longer and
proceed with GC, else i will have to give up the dream of set-
tling in US.[40]

If the guest worker quits or complains to the Labor Department, he has
no hope of getting a green card. If USCIS figures out that he is on the
bench, the green card petition will likely be denied. Benching forces
employers and H-1B guest workers into gambling. The wager employers make is whether consequences to the H-1B worker for complaining
(i.e., being forced to go home) outweigh the risk of being forced to pay
a fine and back pay. The wager H-1B guest workers take is whether the
consequences of not being paid (lack of income, possibility of being
caught) outweigh being forced to leave the country.

Once again, the odds are stacked against foreign guest workers
even if their abusers get caught. A case involving a small H-1B bodyshop, Texas-based Dibon Solutions, made a few headlines in early 2013
when the feds indicted a half-dozen of the company's Indian executives on charges of benching its workers, misleading the U.S. government, and perpetrating both visa fraud and wire fraud.[41] According
to the indictment, Dibon required eight H-1B workers between 2008
and 2010 to provide consulting services to third-party companies located elsewhere, and only paid them an hourly wage for the times they
worked: "The conspirators earned a substantial profit margin when
a consultant was assigned to a project and incurred few costs when a
worker was without billable work."[42]

The case was supposed to go to trial in the fall of 2014. But for unexplained reasons, the trial was delayed and was rescheduled for June 2015. The company refused to comment.[43]

"Even without fraud, the H-1B program is, of course, a disgrace in its design, its operation, and because of the way it depresses the high-tech labor market," Center for Immigration Studies analyst David North observed. "It is too bad that cases like that of Dibon do not secure more press attention."[44]

CRIMINAL ENTERPRISE: PAYROLL-RUNNERS AND TEEN SEX-TRAFFICKERS

Foreign guest worker traffickers have inevitably turned H-1B into an illicit immigrant travel agency.

Cygate Software & Consulting of Edison, New Jersey, operated a scam to bring a half-dozen tech workers here from India.[45] After arriving in the country, the H-1B workers discovered they had no jobs. Cygate CEO Nilesh Dasondi turned them loose and told them to find their own employment. But there was a cruel catch: Dasondi made the H-1B orphans pay the company a monthly fee to appear on the books—a practice called "running the payroll"—so they could maintain their legal status. Cygate created fake pay stubs to keep up the ruse. Dasondi collected more than five hundred thousand dollars before getting caught.[46] He served six months in jail in 2011; just three years later, he was back in respectable public life, raising money for Democratic Edison, New Jersey, mayor Thomas Lankey.[47]

The city seems to breed these H-1B hucksters. In September 2014, Sandip Patel, also of Edison, New Jersey, pleaded guilty to a similar "running the payroll" scheme. From 2001 to 2009, Patel brought over a dozen phony H-1B workers who he claimed would be employed in tech jobs. The Indian nationals paid Patel tens of thousands of dollars for their fake credentials and fake pay stubs. They also had to re-imburse Patel for payroll tax expenses that he incurred."[48] Patel, like fellow Edison resident and H-1B crook Dasondi, was active in Democratic politics in central New Jersey; he was former mayor Antonia Ricigliano's running mate in 2013.[49]

In 2014, Phani Raju Bhima Raju, president of iFuturistics in Pineville, North Carolina, was sentenced to four years in prison for the exact same type of scheme.[50] He had collected a whopping $13.2 million as payment from various unnamed staffing companies in the U.S., where he dispatched H-1B workers who he falsely claimed were working at the nonexistent iFuturistics headquarters.[51] Before a rare government inspection visit, Raju set up furniture and computer workstations to build a Potemkin office; iFuturistics recruited people to act as employees of the company for the visit. Inspectors returned a week later and found the office in its original condition: empty and deserted.[52]

You might think that foreign-born, convicted H-1B con artists are sent home after serving their sentences. Think again.

In 1994, Dnyanoba "Ken" Kendre came to the U.S. from India to work for Atlanta-based Software Technical Service.[53] He moved to Harrisburg, Pennsylvania, and earned an MBA from Lebanon Valley College. Kendre founded a medical staffing, home care, and government contracting firm called Global Healthcare Company (aka Fortune 500 and Global Empire) in 2001. The high-flying businessman bragged about earning an Ernst & Young Entrepreneur of the Year finalist recognition in 2002, the "Forty Under 40 Award" from the *Central Penn Business Journal*, and a "Top 50 Fastest Growing Company" recognition from the *Central Penn Business Journal* in 2004.[54]

But behind the scenes, Kendre was operating a fast-growing bodyshop, ripping off H-1B workers, and illegally undercutting the Americans who welcomed him to their shores. In September 2011, the U.S. Attorney's Office for the Middle District of Pennsylvania announced Kendre had been sentenced to twenty-one months' imprisonment and ordered to pay $100,112 in restitution following his guilty plea to visa fraud and money-laundering charges. Kendre operated a scheme between 2003 and 2007 that will sound very familiar to you by now:[55] He accepted cash payments from unemployed foreign tech workers in order to produce false payroll checks and W-2 wage and tax statements.

The fake payroll checks and W-2 wage and tax statements were submitted in support of H-1B Visa renewals or for adjustments of alien status by way of the Permanent Labor Certification Program," the feds explained. "Foreign workers also paid Kendre a $5,000 "Annual Maintenance Fee" for keeping a visa active with the company, as well as a 25 percent fee for each payroll check processed by the company.[56]

He lied. He defrauded. He money-laundered. So, where is Kendre now? His LinkedIn page is silent about his conviction and his H-1B bodyshop fraud, of course. Instead, the H-1B convict boasts that "Global became one of the fastest growing company in central Pennsylvania. I sold it in 2011."[57] After serving nineteen months out of his original twenty-one-month sentence, Kendre walked out of prison in April 2013. He's back in Pennsylvania—and now owner and operator of "Rent-to-Own Properties, Inc" in Mechanicsburg. The motto of his new business? "Rent To Own Properties making the American Dream come true! We say yes when banks say no."[58] Sounds like another winner.

In an even more extreme case, a calculating sleazeball used the H-1B program to import teenage sex slaves from India.[59] Multimillionaire landlord Lakireddy Bali Reddy was the largest owner of residential rental property in Berkeley, California, in the 1990s. He used his son Vijay Kumar Lakireddy's software consulting company, Active Tech Solutions, as a front to import two young girls for sexual exploitation.

Reddy had bought the children, seventeen-year-old Seetha and fifteen-year-old Lilitha, from their parents in India. Reddy then obtained an H-1B visa for an acquaintance, Venkateshwara Vemireddy, as a computer software consultant on an H-1B visa. Vemireddy's sister posed as his wife, and the two slaves became their "daughters." The happy "family" accompanied Vemireddy into the United States on H-4 dependent visas to make "a better life for themselves," as the manufactured story goes.[60] Once inside the country, the "family" split up. The parents went to work in a restaurant Reddy owned. The underage girls joined another young slave, eighteen-year-old Laxmi Patati, in an apartment where Reddy used them for sexual favors.

The sick scheme unraveled in November 1999 when a motorist driving by the Berkeley residence witnessed a group of Indian men loading a woman rolled up in a carpet into the back of a van. The men were also trying to shove another young girl, who screamed in resistance, into the vehicle. The passerby, Marcia Poole, heroically intervened and called law enforcement while the suspicious men around her refused to help. She noted that the man who claimed to be the girls' father (Vemireddy) showed no concern for their health and well-being. In addition to the screaming girl (Laxmi, who did not speak English), paramedics discovered an unconscious girl (Lilitha) wrapped in carpet in the back of the van. Someone exiting the building pointed out the door to the right of the main entrance. This area led to a stairwell where a third girl (Seetha) lay critically injured and would shortly be pronounced dead at the hospital.

In an alternate universe, one might expect that a dead girl in the stairwell, an unconscious girl wrapped in a carpet loaded into the back of a van, and a crowd of men trying to load a third, screaming girl who did not speak English into the back of the same van to be suspicious— but this was Berkeley.

Reddy cunningly assured the politically correct Berkeley police that nothing criminal had occurred; the cops took his word over Poole's. So did local media outlets, which reported that Laxmi had discovered Seetha and Lilitha poisoned by carbon monoxide from a broken heater in the apartment. Reporters framed the story as an American Dream destroyed by a bad-luck mechanical tragedy. But very little of what the media had published about the Vemireddy sisters had been true—not even their names.[61]

Troubling questions haunted the case but went unasked and unanswered:

- Why was a programmer on an H-1B visa working in a restaurant?
- Why were his children not living with their parents?
- Why were the teenage girls not in school?

But media outlets tiptoed around tough questions of noncitizens from another culture.[62]

It took the Berkeley High School newspaper, of all places, to piece together the inconsistencies in the story.[63] "Every other Bay Area newspaper just had the story of the tragic death, but we were finding out [the girl who died] wasn't even going to school and she was 17," said high school journalist Megan Greenwell. "That made me think there was something bigger."[64] Student journalists figured out that the girls being loaded into the van were, in fact, sex slaves. When she died, Sita Vemireddy (Seetha's real name) was pregnant, apparently with Reddy's child.[65]

Putting aside the more salacious aspects of this case, Reddy was able to:

- Get an H-1B visa for a nonexistent programming job for a man who had never been a programmer;

- Get a labor certification approved claiming that forty-two thousand dollars was the prevailing wage in the Bay area;
- Import three people on H-4 visas (for dependents of H-1B) who were not dependents; and
- Employ an H-1B "programmer" to work in a restaurant.

An audit at the time found that claims on 45 percent of H-1B visa applications from India could not be verified.[66] The U.S. government gets pressure from the Indian government not to reject H-1B visa petitions in spite of the high level of fraud coming from that country.[67] If you follow their press, you find that India regards H-1B visas as a God-given entitlement. In such an environment, it is no wonder that the range of abuse has extended to importing sex slaves. Meanwhile, the practice of getting H-1B visas for nonexistent jobs and creating phony families to import people as dependents goes on unabated.[68]

The chance discovery of Reddy's scheme in no way shows the system of enforcement. Reddy was not defeated by government vigilance, but by one brave passerby and a few inquisitive teen journalists. A local INS spokesman stated that in the forty-nine-county district where the Reddy incident occurred, this was the only case of criminal H-1B fraud investigated.[69] One has to conclude either Reddy was the only abuser in the area or that there is no enforcement to speak of in the H-1B program.

Reddy was sentenced to eight years in prison.[70] He was released on April 2, 2008.[71] While he was in prison he had a new mansion built. There is now even a college named after him in India.

You might think that using the H-1B program to import teenage sex slaves would spur Congress to reform. But you'd be wrong. Congress responded to the Reddy scandal by *expanding* the H-1B program a few months later. In Washington campaign cash speaks louder than dead teenage sex slaves.

ADAM UNIVERSITY: SCAMMING FILIPINO NURSES

The federal case of Nigerian-born, naturalized U.S. citizen Kizzy Kalu shows the extreme lengths fraudsters will go to in exploiting cheap foreign labor. Kalu, the Denver area owner of an outfit called the "Foreign Healthcare Professional Group," was sentenced to eleven years in federal prison in February 2014 after a grand jury indicted him on nearly ninety charges of mail fraud, visa fraud, human trafficking, and money laundering. Codefendant Philip Langerman of Georgia was sentenced to three years' probation for his role in the scheme. Both must pay nearly $3.8 million in restitution.

Kalu and Langerman manufactured a nonexistent school, "Adam University," which trafficked in foreign nurses from the Philippines. Kalu bamboozled incompetent federal officials into granting H-1B visas to twenty-five nurses, who he claimed would be helping remedy a "specialty occupation" labor shortage of nursing instructors and supervisors at his make-believe campus. Kalu lured the foreign nurses to Colorado with a promise of seventy-two-thousand-dollar-a-year jobs. But when they arrived in the Rocky Mountain State, the indentured nurses were pimped out to work low-wage jobs at long-term care facilities and nursing homes.[72] "Those facilities paid Kalu's company, Foreign Healthcare Professionals Group, for the hours the foreign nationals worked," federal prosecutors showed. "Kalu retained approximately 40 percent of the money earned from the labor of the foreign nationals" and threatened to deport the duped nurses if they didn't comply.[73]

Kalu bound the nurses in other ways: 1) by illegally forcing the trapped Filipinas to go into debt as they paid him five-thousand-dollar fees to obtain their H-1B visas and 2) by including a twenty-five-thousand-dollar termination fee in their employment contracts if they attempted to leave.

No federal officials lost their jobs for allowing the "Adam

University" scam to slip past their radar. But the brave nurse whose refusal to participate in Kalu's kickback scheme led to its unraveling lost her job, her visa, and her American Dream.[74]

GREEN CARD BINDING AND THE FOREIGN TEACHER SHAKEDOWN

One of the simplest ways the employer controls H-1B guest workers is through immigration status. The employer has total control over whether the H-1B guest worker has legal status to be in the United States.[75] When a company fires an H-1B worker, it must notify USCIS and the H-1B worker must leave the country. There is no grace period for an H-1B worker to remain in the U.S. and look for a job.

The law now allows H-1B workers with pending green card applications to remain in the U.S. until a decision is made. The green card system binds such workers to the employer for a long period of time. Imagine the power the employer has over an Indian worker who has been in the green card queue for ten years. A guide for employers describes how this traps the H-1B worker:

> Advantages [of H-1B]: This forces the recent graduate to commit to a company for at least five years in order to complete the green card process. There is no obligation on behalf of the employer to continue the H-1 employment. Subject to other employment law requirements, the H-1 employee can be dismissed at any time as with any other employee.[76]

The enticement of green cards is a powerful lure—and subject to systemic abuse. For the past decade, foreign teachers in the Garland, Texas, school district fell victim to the H-1B-to-green-card hustle. The Garland schools had a growing Spanish-speaking student body, but few Spanish-speaking teachers.[77] The school system applied for more than six hundred H-1B visas to recruit foreign teachers from the

Philippines, Colombia, Mexico, and other countries and successfully imported 280 to America.

The human resources director of the Garland school system, Victor Leos, seized the opportunity to enrich himself.[78] He charged potential foreign teachers a one-thousand-dollar fee for a job interview and a four-thousand-dollar kickback to be hired.[79] Leos also required the job-seekers to rent rooms from his stepson[80] and required them to use a law firm that employed another relative.[81] More than two dozen foreign teachers were required to fork over their visa fees to the law firm.[82] In addition, the Garland school district underpaid the foreign teachers.[83] In 2012, the Labor Department ordered the district to pay back more than $250,000 to 153 H-1B teachers who were illegally charged bogus fees.[84]

The teachers were falsely promised green cards.[85] But that is a promise an employer cannot guarantee because immigration comes through federal government action, not as an employer fringe benefit. Of the 280 foreign teachers hired, only 80 got green cards. The rest are subject to deportation, but with President Obama's continuing series of executive amnesty orders and a de facto deportation freeze, those teachers are effectively here to stay.

The foreign teacher trafficking business has stretched from the Prince George's County, Maryland, school district (which was ordered to pay $5.9 million in back wages and penalties for H-1B abuses in 2011)[86] to the East Baton Rouge, Louisiana, school system (which required H-1B teachers to pay a $50 interview fee, $5,000 job application fee, and a $7,500 additional fee to a recruitment agency)[87] and beyond. While a few violators have received fines, lackluster enforcement is once again the norm. A foreign teacher trafficking outfit called the Teachers Placement Group (TPG) in Newark, New Jersey, for example, illegally required recruits to pay the group 25 percent of its wages and threatened to revoke H-1B visas if teachers did not comply.[88] An

AFL-CIO report noted that while the Labor Department initially required TPG to pay $187,546 in back wages and a $120,000 fine, the charges were eventually dropped and "in the end, TPG paid a reduced fine of $3,050 per teacher." [89]

CIS analyst David North analyzed Labor Department data on applications for foreign kindergarten, elementary, and high school teachers in 2010.[90] He found a total of 13,157 new K–12 jobs, mostly bilingual and special education positions, filled by H-1B workers. The top employers were concentrated in New York City, Texas, and Maryland. North took his analysis much further and deeper than any of the mainstream media coverage of the *Washington Post* and other outlets reporting on the foreign teacher trafficking scandal. Yes, the abuse of foreign H-1B visa holders is deeply troubling, and the plight of these exploited workers merits public attention.

But what about the effects of such criminal operations on American teachers and American students? North observed:

The most troubling set of apparent by-products of the H-1B/K-12 mix is what it does to the U.S. labor market. To what extent does it harm unemployed legally resident U.S. teachers, including Anglos, Blacks, and Hispanics, native-born and naturalized citizens, and lawful permanent residents (green card holders)?

... These H-1B hirings were taking place just as school systems across the country were preparing to lay off tens of thousands of public school teachers. Couldn't Houston and Dallas, for example, have looked to adjacent states for teachers rather than to distant nations? Aren't there plenty of laid-off teachers within commuting distance of, say, Baltimore? [91]

The foreign guest worker trafficking network subjugates H-1B visa holders, enriches unscrupulous racketeers, and cheats law-abiding

American workers. Now, the corrupt practices of binding, bodyshopping, benching, and payroll-running have seeped into K-12 education, exposing American schoolchildren to the seamy consequences of *50 Shades of H-1B Abuse*.

But these abuses and perversities are just the tip of the iceberg. What's happening in the H-1B program is happening in America's other major temporary visa and green card programs for tourists, business people, investors, and post-secondary students. It's much worse, far worse, than you could possibly imagine.

PART II: AN ALPHABET SOUP OF VISA FRAUD, ABUSE, AND CORRUPTION

⊢ 6 ⊢

"BILOH": The B Visa Boondoggle

Several years ago, Michelle received an anonymous tip from a reader who worked as a Customs and Border Protection officer. He described how U.S. consulate workers in Chennai, India, were exploiting visas for businessmen and tourists to get around H-1B limitations. The information came from a document posted in the tipster's break room.

"It was not marked as 'law-enforcement sensitive' or 'classified' in any way—and in any case is in full view of the cleaning staff," the CBP officer wrote. "Apparently, the U.S. consulate in Chennai [India] is issuing B1/B2 visas that can be used in lieu of H-1B visas for legitimate H-1B classified work so long as the recipient is 1) paid abroad and 2) shows conclusively that he/she will return abroad at the end of his/her authorized admission."

"You can see where this is going," the agent continued. Companies could "set up a dummy subsidiary in India and avoid the hassle of petitioning for H-1B workers; avoid numerical limitations on H1B workers; and avoid the (nominally enforced) requirements that a job be posted in the U.S. and have pay comparable to that of a U.S. worker.

This also guarantees that not one dime of tax revenue for this high-tech work will go to U.S. coffers."

The officer concluded: "It is sad and outrageous that this is now incorporated into State Department policy and I thought you would be interested in this information."[1]

"B" visitor visas are nonimmigrant visas meant for foreigners on short-term stays for business (visa category B-1), tourism, pleasure or visiting (visa category B-2), or a combination of both (B-1/B-2).[2] There is no cap on the number of B visas available. The approval process is relatively quick and cheap.[3] Initial periods of stay on B-1s and B-2s are between one and six months. Validity periods for multiple-entry B-1/B-2 visas vary by country; it's ten years for China, India, Israel, Japan, Mexico, many South American countries, and most European countries.

These visas are *not* supposed to be used for paid performances or gainful employment of any kind. That includes both skilled and un-skilled labor. Foreigners conducting short-term business in the U.S. (attending conferences or meetings, for example, or scouting out lo-cations for new offices) must be paid in their home countries, not by any U.S. entity. All B visa applicants must "overcome the presumption of immigrant intent," required by law, by sufficiently demonstrating to consular officials abroad that they have strong ties to their home country that will compel them to leave the U.S. at the end of their tem-porary stay.[4] Are your fraud detectors going off, yet?

The Internet is filled with "tips" and advice from lawyers and "in-siders" on how to clear this hurdle.[5] Exploiting the B-1 program to get around H-1B has become so commonplace, it has earned its own acronym in the immigration lawyer and diplomatic community: "BILOH" or "B-1 visa in lieu of H-1B." The U.S. consulate in Chen-nai[6] and the State Department's Foreign Affairs Manual[7] helpfully laid out the scheme that Michelle's tipster described. As long as the B visa holder had the "equivalent of a U.S. bachelor's degree," claimed he or she planned to perform "H-1B caliber work or training," received payment only from a foreign employer, and promised to return to his or her home country, this visa-hopping game was acceptable to the U.S.

In 2009, classified cables from the U.S. Embassy in India turned up on the Wikileaks website. Diplomats reported that "B1/B2 travelers/tourists" were one of the "most targeted" visa classes for fraud and that "B1/B2 visa fraud is the most commonplace." In Chennai, the same Indian town that Michelle's correspondent from U.S. Customs and Border Patrol mentioned, the U.S. Embassy confirmed fraud in 1,214 cases.[8]

When John worked at Digital Equipment Corporation in the early 1990s, he, too, saw the company using B visas to import foreign workers. The scheme he witnessed allowed the company and the foreign contract workers, who were paid overseas, to dodge U.S. income taxes. When a B visa expired, the foreign workers took a vacation to Bermuda or the Bahamas, obtained a new B visa, and returned to the United States for more work. A decade later, while John worked as a computer consultant, he encountered foreign outsourcing companies using B visas to circumvent H-1B visa limits and prevailing wage regulations.

Sneaking foreign workers into America through visitor visas actually predates H-1B. In the 1980s, in Lake County, California, the International Union of Bricklayers and Allied Craftsmen discovered ten West German B-1 business visitor visa holders illegally performing bricklaying work. The scheme, sanctioned by internal rules and guidelines crafted by the then-INS, circumvented the normal Labor Condition Application process that would have required the employer to apply for H-2 temporary worker visas on behalf of the West German foreign laborers. H-2 employers must show that importing foreign workers will not adversely affect wages and working conditions of American workers.[9] The union won a preliminary injunction in district court in California ordering the then-INS to change the aliens' visa status from "B-1" short-term business visitors to "B-2" tourists.[10] A federal court then permanently enjoined the feds from issuing B-1 visas to foreign construction workers and awarded summary judgment to the plaintiffs.

Immigration enforcement officials saw it. U.S. embassy workers saw it. Tech workers saw it. Union workers saw it. So to those in the know and those paying attention, it was no surprise when the bombshell B-1 abuse case against Infosys, the Indian offshore outsourcing company and top H-1B user,[11] exploded in 2011. It has dominated tech news and captured the attention of pro–American worker advocates on Capitol Hill. But the continuing nightmares of U.S. whistleblowers at Infosys are still unknown to most of their fellow citizens.

This is their story.

"DO NOT TELL THEM YOUR [SIC] WORKING" [12]

From August 2008 through 2013, Jack "Jay" Palmer worked as a principal consultant in the Enterprise Solutions Practice of Infosys. He was based in Alabama. A graduate of Auburn University and the U.S. Army School of Computer Science with extensive public administration, business, and technical training, Palmer managed "hundreds if not thousands" of workers at the multinational IT company, which was founded and based in Bangalore, India.

Infosys employs more than fifteen thousand foreign nationals working in the U.S., 90 percent of whom are of South Asian descent.[13] An estimated ten thousand of those foreign workers are here in America on H-1B visas.[14] We've previously explained that, like most of the top offshore outsourcing conglomerates doing business in the U.S., Infosys is classified as an "H-1B-dependent" firm because of the high ratio of its H-1B workers to its total workforce.

As a result of his excellent work with Infosys client Baker Hughes

Oil on technology to prevent oil spills, Infosys flew him to Bangalore in March 2010. But it wasn't a celebration party. At the time, Infosys faced new restrictions as a result of its "H-1B-dependent" status, along with higher application fees. The company needed its managers to think "creatively" about how to circumvent these pro–American worker protections "to fulfill the high demand for its customers at lower cost." Palmer found himself smack dab in the middle of a tremendous pressure campaign to betray his country and subvert U.S. laws.

Infosys brass sought to exploit the B-1 visa program as an expedient pipeline to sneak cheap foreign labor into the U.S. "There was no monitoring of the B-1 system and it was understood that 'no one would ever know,' " Palmer recounted. The company flooded the consulate with applications "in order to get as many approved as possible no matter the level of an individual's skill." In blatant violation of the law, Infosys employees were applying for and fraudulently obtaining B-1 visas for the specific purpose of gainful employment by American clients. Infosys misrepresented payments to these business travelers as "stipends," instead of what they really were: salaries to full-time employees doing full-time work in violation of B-1 law.

According to Palmer, during the meetings in India, his bosses also discussed fraudulent methods of ensuring that the true intent and purpose of B-1 employees went "undetected" while transiting through the port of entry. Infosys disseminated internal memos and a company website of "dos and don'ts" on how to address U.S. immigration officials. "Do not mention activities like implementation, design & testing, consulting, etc., which sound like work," Infosys B-1 visa holders were told. "Please do not mention anything about contract rates as you're on a B-1 visa," the memo instructed.

In case their B-1 conspirators needed even more clarification, Infosys deceivers spelled it out in all-caps, albeit ungrammatically:

"DO NOT TELL THEM YOUR [sic] WORKING. Speak little English."[15]

In May 2010, after U.S. consular officials in India instructed Infosys to bolster its B-1 visa applications with visitation proof from U.S.-based hosts, the company turned up the heat on Palmer.

"My Indian managers in the U.S. and India started asking me to write these 'welcome letters' and were very insistent," he recalled. "They would state if I did not do this it would drastically affect the company's profit because we did not have people in the U.S. to complete the work. Also, they threatened it would affect my salary and standing in the company. Basically, what these letters do is falsely claim that the foreign employee is coming for a 'visit' rather than to 'work.' I was very concerned about these letters and contacted Infosys [human resources] because the content of the template of the letter was false." (See Appendix C for one of the letter templates.)

In response to his objections, Infosys admonished Palmer for "not being a team player." His bosses shifted him to a new division and different project. There, Palmer spotted even more illegal behavior. The contract he was working on was a "time and material" (T&M) contract, as opposed to a "fixed price" (FP) contract. Palmer explained the difference between the two arrangements and the reason his superiors wanted him to alter the contract:

In order for Infosys' scheme to work, the U.S. contracts had to be written as FP contracts and not as T&M contracts. The reasoning is that on a FP contract, a customer is charged a lump sum for labor. The people who are actually doing the "work" do not have to be named to the customer, but they are named on internal labor spreadsheets in order to come up with a cost and price. There were some customers such as Baker Hughes that wanted to see the names of the staff and Infosys did furnish these names—and some of the people named were illegal. On a T&M contract, the people doing the actual work must be named along with their hourly rate. This is when the proverbial cat came out of the bag.

Put simply, Infosys was revising contracts for clients in order to conceal the fact that the company was providing B-1 visa holders to illegally perform jobs that involved skilled or unskilled labor that were otherwise required to be performed by United States citizens or required legitimate H-1B visa holders.

Palmer refused to participate in a cover-up of the B-1 ruse. He was told to "keep quiet." He couldn't and he didn't.

"JUST LEAVE YOUR NOT WANTED HERE HOPE YOUR JOURNEY BRINGS YOU DEATH STUPID AMERICAN" [SIC]

"At Infosys, I witnessed and received emails, screen-shots and other documents proving that Infosys intentionally violated our visa and tax laws for the purpose of increasing revenues," Palmer testified. He discovered that some of the illegal B-1 workers were being paid an average of $2.00 an hour, while clients of Infosys were paying the company upward of $150.00 an hour. In an all-too-familiar narrative, the B-1 employees "have no rights and are being paid their salary in India which is about $5,000.00 a year" in U.S. dollars, Palmer reported. "The living conditions of the workers are horrific. Many times 6–8 people are living in a hotel room or 1-bed apartment."

Palmer filed an internal whistleblower complaint. It went nowhere. He turned to the State Department, Department of Homeland Security (DHS), Justice Department, and Internal Revenue Service, among other agencies. Finally, his whistleblowing led to a federal criminal grand jury investigation. He also filed a civil suit in Lowndes County, Alabama, against Infosys in February 2011.

Meanwhile, despite repeated pleas from Palmer to the company's top legal counsel, Infosys failed to initiate its own internal investigation of the systemic illegal conduct he had extensively documented. Other inside Infosys employees had provided Palmer with information of illegal B-1 workers at Wal-Mart, Goldman Sachs, American Express, and other customers. One employee provided Palmer a spreadsheet with a list of illegal B-1 workers at Johnson Controls, Inc. (JCI), an energy company, who were "working full time testing software code and writing scripts but were paid their salaries by Infosys depositing money into . . . cash card accounts without withhold or paying any income tax."

While Infosys officials publicly tried to marginalize Palmer as an untrustworthy lone wolf,[16] more whistleblowers came forward to corroborate and extend Palmer's findings.

A former Infosys manager based in India who spoke anonymously to journalist Don Tennant shared his own description of the "briefing sessions" that Infosys held for its fraudulent B-1 workers:

[T]hey would basically tell you very clearly that a B-1 visa is only intended for sales professionals to attend meetings and things like that, and you can't actually be working. So what you need to do when you reach the United States is you need to lie to the official at the airport about the purpose of your visit. You can't tell them that you're there to work or to do any kind of programming or anything like that. They even advise you not to take any kind of programming books in your bags, just in case you're searched. You can't tell them you're there for a sales meeting when your bag is packed with six books on Java.[17]

Infosys human resources employee Linda Manning confirmed the illegal B-1 circumvention and tax evasion schemes. She also warned of irregularities in the company's H-1B Labor Condition Application filings and complained to her superiors about systemic failures to file I-1 employment verification documents with the IRS. "When I started working for Infosys in April 2008," she informed higher-ups, "I was immediately aware that there were problems with I-9 compliance. When I continued to bring up the issue to my manager I was told 'don't worry, this is the responsibility of the immigration department' (which takes direction out of India) and 'what we don't know won't hurt us.' " [18]

Marti Harrington, an Infosys project manager, filed her own whistleblower report detailing knowledge of visa abuse and discriminatory behavior involving workers at Infosys client Johnson Controls, Inc. "In February of 2011, I became fully aware of issues with the visa fraud. I began getting phone calls from various [Infosys] legal counselors, wanting to know what I knew about the visa usage," she asserted in a sworn affidavit.

"While I was in fear of company retaliation, I sent an email to our whistleblower account and immediately started getting phone calls from Infosys lawyers." Palmer's lawyer asked Harrington for permission to put her in contact with the federal agents investigating Infosys. She consented, but the agents stopped contacting her. Under immense pressure, Harrington left the company. She found out later that the federal agents "were not allowed to discuss issues with me without an Infosys attorney present. This large consulting company was illegally using U.S. visas for their own corporate gain and they were forbidding direct contact with me by the U.S. government because I (a U.S. citizen) worked for a company based in India."

Said Harrington: "Infosys employees harassed Jay in my presence, discriminated against me, conducted business in the U.S. illegally and I'm still worried they will seek retaliation against me for being honest."[19]

Infosys continued to violate its own whistleblower policies and ignore his complaints, Palmer testified. According to testimony, the company even hired a criminal defense attorney, posing as an "independent Infosys whistleblower counsel," who tried to pressure Palmer into handing over his laptop computer, which contained copious files of the firm's wrongdoing. He refused. After DHS served a warrant on the laptop, Palmer put it in the hands of the feds.

As Palmer and his lawyer Kenneth Mendelsohn pushed forward with their civil lawsuit, the American whistleblower came under fire by his own colleagues and their sympathizers. He enumerated the threats to his family and his life in court documents:

- On October 27, 2010, at 12:37 a.m., Palmer's wife answered their home phone and a man with an Indian accent asked to speak with him. His wife said he was unavailable, and the caller mumbled something and hung up. A similar incident occurred that same night at 2:27 a.m.
- Palmer has received other threatening calls along the lines of "Why are you doing this, you stupid American, we have been good to you."
- On February 28, 2011, Palmer reported to work to find a note on his keyboard stating that, "Jack: Just leave your not wanted here hope your journey brings you death stupid American." When Palmer turned on his computer, a Word document displayed the same message.
- On April 21, 2011, Palmer received an email stating that, "if you make cause for us to sent back to india we will destroy you and yuor [sic] family."
- On May 25, 2011, Palmer received a threat through his LinkedIn account from an Indian national and self-professed "advocate" of Infosys: "you still working at infy? they should have fired you

long back . . . . . after you stabbed their back by falsely implicating them on the misuse of visa. unfortunately infy is an indian company and indian's don't stab . . . . . even in the front. that's what hypocrites like you take advantage of. Hope they learn the rule of Tit for Tat. I just wish you were here in India. we would have taken *good* care of you." [20]

Benched, blacklisted, and isolated by Infosys, Palmer suffered through the threats and retaliation. He fought depression, feared for his family, and started carrying a concealed weapon. His lawsuit was originally filed in Alabama state court, but Infosys had the case removed to federal court under something called diversity jurisdiction (Infosys is a corporate citizen of a different state than Palmer, who calls Alabama home). Palmer's lawsuit was dismissed in federal court in August 2012. Under diversity jurisdiction, a federal court interprets and applies the applicable state law. Judge Myron Thompson found, "without question," that the allegations of harassment and retaliation were "deeply troubling." The judge acknowledged that "an argument could be made" the whistleblower retaliation by Infosys against Palmer "should be illegal," but that he was bound by Alabama state law and statutes, not federal law. [21]

Infosys, which had opposed Palmer's claims on jurisdictional basis, crowed over the legal victory and claimed that the judge had found "no basis" for Palmer's charges. The company patted itself on the back for its "integrity" and "transparency," then said, "We are pleased to consider this matter completely closed." [22]

Not so fast.

A RECORD SETTLEMENT

In October 2013, Palmer received bittersweet vindication. The U.S. Attorney's Office in the Eastern District of Texas, where the Infosys office that handles the company's immigration practices and procedures is located, made a milestone announcement. Its press release read: "Indian Corporation Pays Record Amount to Settle Allegations of Systemic Visa Fraud and Abuse of Immigration Processes" [23]

The $34 million civil settlement, [24] U.S. Attorney John Bales noted, "represents the largest payment ever levied in an immigration case." Bales declared: "The H-1B and B-1 visa programs are designed and intended to protect the American worker; and we will vigorously enforce the requirements of those programs." Of the $34 million, $24 million went to the U.S. Attorney's Office in the Eastern District of Texas, $5 million went to the State Department for civil or administrative forfeiture, and $5 million went to the Department of Homeland Security's Homeland Security Investigations office. Palmer received an undisclosed portion of recovered damages as a result of the False Claims Act, which awards whistleblowers in successful cases.

The findings of federal investigators tracked everything Jay Palmer and the other whistleblowers had uncovered, documented, and complained about to Infosys. In addition to the false invitation letters, the fraudulent use of B-1 visas to circumvent H-1B, the "do's and don'ts" memo advising B-1 visaholders to deceive immigration officials, and the contract-rewriting cover-ups, agents also found that Infosys had "failed to maintain I-9 [identity and work authorization] records for many of its foreign nationals in the United States in 2010 and 2011 as required by law, including a widespread failure to update and re-verify the employment authorization status of a large percentage of its foreign national employees." [25]

In the settlement document, the feds also listed numerous examples of H-1B workers whose labor condition applications provided false representations:

- On or about November 26, 2008, Infosys directed an individual known as ST to tell U.S. consular officials that he was destined for Seattle, Washington, consistent with the Labor Condition Application; however, his true destination was Henrico, Virginia.
- On or about October 28, 2009, Infosys directed an individual known as VG to tell U.S. consular officials that he was destined for Seattle, Washington, consistent with the Labor Condition Application; however, his true destination was Bentonville, Arkansas.
- On or about October 29, 2010, Infosys directed an individual known as SK to tell U.S. consular officials that he was destined for Beaverton, Oregon, consistent with the Labor Condition Application; however, his true destination was Sunnyvale, California.[26]

David M. Marwell, special agent in charge of Homeland Security investigations in Dallas, added: "This settlement against Infosys is the largest immigration fine on record. The investigation indicated that Infosys manipulated the visa process and circumvented the requirements, limitations, and governmental oversight of the visa programs. The investigation also showed that more than 80 percent of Infosys's I-9 forms for 2010 and 2011 contained substantive violations. Ultimately, these actions by Infosys cost American jobs and simultaneously financially hurt companies that sought to follow the laws of this nation. Companies that misuse the visa process can expect to be scrutinized and held accountable."[27]

But despite finding "systemic visa fraud and abuse,"[28] the feds dropped civil and criminal charges against the company in exchange for the settlement money and admission of paperwork violations. The feds also agreed not to use any of the evidence it uncovered in its investigations to revoke any visas fraudulently obtained by Infosys workers; not to debar or suspend Infosys from any B-1 or H-1B program; and not to make any referrals to any agencies for debarment or suspension of Infosys from visa programs.

It was disappointing, but not surprising. As we've shown you time and again, wrist-slaps and watered-down settlements are the norm in federal immigration enforcement. In addition, Infosys had a savvy and powerful advocate at the negotiating table: Michael Chertoff, who just two years earlier had stepped down as secretary of the Department of Homeland Security. Chertoff joined the "white collar defense and investigations group" of the influential law firm of Covington & Burling in 2009[29] and also served as a consultant to the lead law firm representing Infosys, Wilmer Hale.[30]

Journalist Don Tennant reported that the lead federal prosecutor in the Infosys case, Eastern District of Texas assistant U.S. attorney Shamoil Shipchandler, insisted he wasn't swayed by Chertoff's presence. Shipchandler told Tennant:

> I'll be 100 percent honest with you, if they had not introduced me to him, I would not have been able to recognize him. . . . Give me the people who lived with this on a day-to-day basis, and I will trust their judgment. But I'm not going to take the judgment of someone who has left the employ of the government, and now is being paid to offer information that is to the benefit of a corporate client.[31]

We certainly commend the diligent and vigilant agents and prosecutors who pursued the case and got as far as they did. But in the Beltway, money and power do matter. Corporations pay revolving-door hired guns such as Chertoff top dollar to influence immigration officials in their favor. As Jay Palmer observed, "the political backing from large companies" is an effective deterrent against prosecution. "Even though the law is clear, consultants such as Michael Chertoff are telling AUSAs [assistant U.S. attorneys] they will never win because of the arguable loopholes in the law. . . . I was informed by a high ranking Special Agent that [Chertoff] 'threw the American people under the bus' by contradicting his prior policy and rulings. This was a 'sad day for America.'"

Arrogant Infosys honchos insisted to its employees that no illegal visa abuses had taken place and that no systemic violations had occurred. But in a company call to spin the settlement, head of Infosys's American operations Prasad Thrikutam encountered skepticism from his workforce.

"You've mentioned that we have found that it was not a systemic problem," one employee challenged Thrikutam, according to tech journalist Don Tennant. "I signed a fairly significant code of ethics with the company, as I'm imagining everybody did. Has anything been done to deal with the non-systemic individuals that may have violated our policies, that caused a lot of this?"

Thrikutam suddenly had auditory problems: "I'm sorry, I'm really having a hard time hearing."[32]

Infosys fired Jay Palmer not long after the settlement was announced. Why? The company's staying mum on the termination. But not Palmer. His old employer "was embarrassed and angered by Mr. Palmer's revelations of Infosys' conduct," Palmer's lawyer Maurice Mitt noted in a retaliation complaint filed in October 2014. "Infosys punished Mr. Palmer by blacklisting him, putting him on leave, denying him work, denying him promotions and bonuses, eventually demanding his resignation and denying him rehire."[33]

Vowed Palmer: "I am not going away in this matter."[34]

THE B AND H-1B VISA BATTLES RAGE ON

In the aftermath of the Infosys whistleblowers' exposés, the State Department quietly put its "BILOH" (B-1 in lieu of H-1B) visa policy "under review." The phrase no longer appears in the Foreign Affairs Manual. Pressed by Sen. Grassley, a State Department official revealed that the consular officials had incorporated additional screening measures in India to "probe for specific details" of purported short-term business trips.[35] Cables issued to all State Department personnel in June 2012 and October 2012 informed them that the BILOH policy "is under review," but "is still in effect until further notice."[36]

But India isn't the only country that companies have imported labor from under this B-1/H-1B circumvention scheme—and Indian outsourcing firms aren't the only ones exploiting the system. In the fall of 2011, the *Seattle Times* reported that eighteen engineers on B-1 visas from Russia had been stopped at Sea-Tac airport by alert U.S. customs and Border Patrol agents. The entire group worked as third-party contract employees for Boeing's engineering design center in Moscow; several members had traveled to the giant defense contractor's Seattle area headquarters up to seven times during the previous four years.

The foreign business "tourists" carried letters of invitation similar to the ones Infosys whistleblower Jay Palmer flagged in his lawsuit. Upon questioning, several engineers admitted they had been "coached" and "instructed" to lie about the true purpose of their visits.[37] They hadn't come to do "training," but to do ordinary work for Boeing in violation of B-1 rules. One of the contractors candidly volunteered the truth: He was there because it "was cheaper to hire Russian engineers than American."[38]

Though the unlucky eighteen were turned back, Boeing remained undeterred and unpunished. Six months after the incident, the white-collar union at Boeing, the Society of Engineering Employees in Aerospace, found that about 250 Russian contract engineers had entered the country at Boeing's invitation. The company refused to comment, and an ICE official chalked up the initial airport confrontation to a "communications error" and "cultural differences."[39] Sen. Grassley's request for an investigation went ignored by both DHS and the Department of State.[40]

Meanwhile, a year after the feds settled with Infosys, Jay Palmer launched a new campaign for justice. In October 2014, he filed suit in a U.S. district court in New Jersey seeking reappointment and compensation for wrongful termination.[41] Separately, as we noted in Chapter 4, four Infosys workers hit the company with a class-action lawsuit alleging intentional employment discrimination against American workers who are not of South Asian descent in hiring by abusing the H-1B visa process and B-1 visa systems.[42]

Palmer says despite the personal and professional toll his whistleblowing battles have taken, he "would do it again." He is a voice for other American workers who've been gagged and bullied into silence. And he continues to bear witness to the ravages of temporary guest worker visa program fraud and criminality.

"The abuse of the B1 and H1 visa laws as well as the income tax laws is widespread in this country. Americans are being displaced and foreigners are working full time jobs in the U.S. without paying income taxes," Palmer told Congress. The solution is simple: "We need to tighten the visa law and enforce the law. Until a major company is disbarred from the visa program or someone is indicted from a major company, this behavior will continue."

7

EB-5: America's Disastrous
Cash-for-Citizenship Racket

What could go wrong with putting citizenship up for sale to attract overseas investment for struggling American businesses?

In a word: *Everything.*

Corrupt government officials have been selling citizenship for favors since the days of the Roman Empire. And we all know how that self-doomed civilization turned out.

Under the reign of Claudius, the once-precious privilege of citizenry became a cheaply auctioned trinket. Messalina, the emperor's scheming wife, enlisted senior members of the imperial court known as the Palatium freedmen to collect payments in exchange for citizenship (not to mention governorships, procuratorships, and military commands).[1] At first, Messalina charged "great sums."[2] But as the practice became commonplace and indiscriminate, the price plummeted. According to ancient historian Cassius Dio, "a man could become a citizen by giving the right person some bits of broken glass.[3]

In America, the modern-day equivalent of Messalina's cash-for-citizenship scheme is known as the EB-5 immigrant investor program. Like the Palatium freedmen of ancient Rome, an entire legion of middlemen, lawyers, lobbyists, bureaucrats, book cookers, and promoters has formed a cottage industry around the U.S. government racket. The "EB" stands for employment-based immigration; the "5" signifies that it was the fifth preference category of its kind created by Congress under an obscure section of the 1990 Immigration Act.[4]

On paper, it sounded reasonable and manageable: The law allows ten thousand alien entrepreneurs a year to obtain green cards by investing between five hundred thousand dollars and $1 million in new commercial enterprises or troubled businesses. After two years, foreign investors, their spouses, and their children can receive "conditional permanent resident" status for two years and a gateway to permanent U.S. citizenship. Originally, the law required individual investments in commercial enterprises to directly generate at least ten new full-time jobs. Investors were expected to manage the businesses themselves and dedicate some of the newly created jobs to exports.[5] Failure would mean loss of their money and their business.[6]

In 1992, Congress created the "Immigrant Investor Pilot Program" and established government-approved EB-5 "regional centers"—specially selected business groups and corporate entities designated to administer EB-5 investments and oversee a much more relaxed definition of job creation.[7] The idea was to pool investor funds in a defined industry and targeted region to promote economic growth. Under this loan model, the regional center would recruit and collect funding from a group of foreign investors, then turn around and lend the money to selected projects at a low interest rate. The project would then pay off the loan over an agreed period of time. In targeted areas of high unemployment, the threshold for investment was lowered.

As of March 2015, there were 614 such regional centers approved by the feds.[8] Participation in the program has risen from 5,748 visa winners in 2008 to 22,444 in 2014.[9] EB-5 participants in these joint ventures can fulfill job-creation requirements if they "create or preserve" either direct jobs or "indirect" jobs shown to be "created collaterally or as a result of capital invested in a commercial enterprise affiliated with a regional center by an EB-5 investor."[10] The five-year "pilot program," which has been reauthorized routinely since its inception, was set to expire in September 2015.

Early EB-5 boosters used various theoretical multipliers to hype the program's benefits, predicting that "4 million millionaire investors along with family members, would sign up, bringing in $4 billion in new investments and creating 40,000 jobs [annually]."[11] In 2011, President Obama's Council on Job Competitiveness regurgitated the same old figures in its call to "radically expand" the program:[12]

> If the EB-5 program reaches maximum capacity, it could result annually in the creation of approximately 4,000 new businesses, $2 billion to $4 billion of foreign investment capital, and create 40,000 jobs.

But in practice, like so many of the Beltway's immigration programs, EB-5's ever-evolving regulations are Byzantine and arbitrary. Fraud and abuse are rampant. (As Michelle reported in *Invasion* in 2002, former Immigration and Naturalization Services official-turned-lobbyist Paul Virtue lobbied for loosened financial requirements.[13]) Unsurprisingly, the purported economic benefits of EB-5 are woefully dubious. One sensible journalist, Charles Lane, put the EB-5 promoters' claims in proper perspective: "Sounds impressive," he explained, "until you realize that foreign investment in the United States totals $2.5 trillion and that the program's fuzzy job-creation count includes jobs 'indirectly' attributable to the investment. EB-5 would be dubious policy even if it could claim five times that impact. Simply put, it is corporate welfare—yet another attempt to subsidize the flow of capital into politically favored channels."[14]

Center for Immigration Studies analyst David North added that "foreign investment comes to the United States routinely, in large volume, with minuscule help from EB-5." In 2010, he observed, total foreign investment in the United States increased by $1.9 trillion, according to the U.S. Department of Commerce. Based on the investors' green card applications filed two years after the first investment, North estimated that "EB-5 investment that year was about $191 million, and that was a well above-average year for the program. So, for every $100 of increased foreign investment that year, the EB-5 program contributed about one penny."[15]

Now-retired Sen. Tom Coburn (R-Okla.) asked DHS in 2014 for more information to verify the job creation claims of 430 EB-5 regional centers. After supplying a mealy-mouthed excuse about how "legal restrictions" prevented them from answering, the department then explained that "while USCIS requires information about the job-creating company where the investment funds will ultimately be used to generate economic activity and create jobs, that information is not currently captured in any system of record." The beleaguered DHS whined that a "thorough and complete list of investments would require the physical review of tens or hundreds of thousands of pages."

In a move that immigration lawyers attacked as "saucy" and "disturbing," Sen. Coburn and his staff then took it upon themselves to do the job DHS refused to do—track down every one of the federally approved regional centers and ask for:[16]

- Any approval from USCIS to participate in the EB-5 program regarding the regional center and its business plan, including any subsequent recertification;
- The total annual amount of investment and the number of individuals by country of origin making investments through the regional center since it has been in operation;

- The name, address, and a description of each business in which the regional center has made an investment of funds and the number of jobs created by each investment;
- Any fees charged to EB-5 applicants or received by the regional center, including amount and description;
- A list of any current or former corporate officers of the regional center, including title, position, and dates of employment; and
- The name and address of any individual or entity—either foreign or domestic—that the regional center has an agreement with to provide legal, accounting, recruiting, or consulting services, as well as a description of the service provided.

More than half of the 430 regional centers surveyed failed to respond to Sen. Coburn. Roughly half reported receiving no EB-5 investments since their creation. Fewer than sixty of the centers said they had received an investment or were awaiting approval of EB-5 visas. Ten centers responded to the letter, but supplied no answers to Sen. Coburn's questions. "Given the absence of compelling information or government oversight into how the EB-5 program is being used," Sen. Coburn sensibly concluded, "it is unclear whether any economic benefit of the program justifies the criminal and national security risks associated with the program."[17] Despite the unanswered questions, a bipartisan group of congressmen led by Colorado tech mogul Jared Polis of Colorado (net worth: $68 million) is pushing forward with a bill to make EB-5 permanent.[18] In August 2015, the GAO released a report spotlighting the program's persistent failure to collect and maintain basic electronic data on EB-5 participants (including their names and birthdates!), as well as the pathetic state of its job creation estimates. Its "methodology for reporting program outcomes and overall economic benefits is not valid and reliable because it may understate or overstate program benefits," the GAO found. In other words: totally worthless.[19]

Let's face it: The government has had a perpetually lousy record of picking economic winners and losers. See, most infamously: federal green loan recipient–gone–bankrupt Solyndra. President Obama's make-believe math on "shovel-ready" stimulus jobs saved or created—coupled with the snowballing $535 million, stimulus-funded Solyndra solar company bankruptcy scandal—tells you all you need to know about Washington's credibility in picking economic winners and losers.

If the feds can't be trusted to invest government subsidies wisely in *American* companies, how can they possibly determine which overseas investors will be successful here?

And if top U.S. loan officials have demonstrated such sloppy, politically driven disregard for financial due diligence on risky half-billion-dollar enterprises, how can immigration officials be entrusted to better protect the national interest?

A BIPARTISAN BOONDOGGLE

Key supporters of the original immigrant investor visa program included Democratic Sens. Ted Kennedy (D-Mass.) and Paul Simon (D-Ill.). Big Government Republicans embraced it, too. Prescott Bush, George W. Bush's uncle, was on the board of American Immigration Services, one of the leading EB-5 visa vendors. So was former president Bush's INS commissioner, Gene McNary. GOP Sen. Mitch McConnell worked closely with the woman who was instrumental in drafting the EB-5 law: Maria Hsia.

The name should ring a bell. Hsia was a Simon and McConnell donor identified by the House Governmental Affairs Committee as "an agent of the Chinese government."[20] In 2000, she was found guilty by a federal jury of laundering more than one hundred thousand dollars in illegal donations to the Democratic National Committee through the infamous I Lai Buddhist temple in California.[21] At the time Funny Money Honey Hsia was working for McConnell and others on the 1990 immigration bill, she also worked for a campaign fund-raising group called the Pacific Leadership Council. Hsia co-founded the PLC with Lippo Bank officials John Huang and James Riady, the chief figures in the Clinton-Gore Donorgate scandal convicted of campaign-finance crimes.[22] At least six Lippo Bank officials reportedly benefited from the EB-5 law.[23]

Hsia partnered with former Democratic Rep. Bruce A. Morrison of Connecticut, an immigration lawyer, author of the 1990 Immigration Act in the House, and main sponsor of EB-5. After leaving Congress to run (unsuccessfully) for governor in Connecticut, Morrison formed a business to market the investor visa program. The *Baltimore Sun* reported that his 1991 contract with Hsia outlined "payments of $10,000 per month for six months."[24] Morrison's former press secretary, Paul Donnelly, set up his own company, Investment Immigration Consulting Co., "to provide consulting and other services related to the investor visa program."[25] Asked whether he saw any ethical conflict in cashing in on a program he helped create, Morrison scoffed: "What was I supposed to do for a living?"[26]

The benefits of the EB-5 economic development plan have long redounded primarily to the benefit of former federal immigration officials who have formed lucrative limited partnerships to cash in on their access, and to shady foreign fraudsters. Here's how their racket worked in the early 1990s: Immigrant investors paid token fees to these partnerships. The partnerships secured promissory notes for the remainder of the foreign investments, which were forgiven after investors received their permanent green cards. Former Immigration and Naturalization Service employees, working for these partnerships, aggressively lobbied their old colleagues to accept such bogus financial arrangements. As a result, according to an internal U.S. Justice Department investigative report, "aliens were paying $125K" instead of the required five-hundred-thousand-dollar to $1 million minimum, and "almost all of the monies went to the General Partners and the companies who set up the limited partners."

A ground-breaking *Baltimore Sun* investigation published in 2000 found "only a tiny fraction of the money ever made it to the companies seeking assistance."[27] Many of the distressed U.S. firms that the program intended to help have closed because they never received promised funding. Elnor Bailey's clothing factory in Alabama "received only $50,000," the paper reported. That was a fraction of the six figures promised her—and "not enough to keep the factory from closing." She was never told she was entitled to substantially more money."

"It makes me angry," she said. "It really does."[28]

Small businesses crumbled, but well-connected bureaucrats made out like bandits. The biggest beneficiaries of the visa-vending business in its first decade included:

- Gene McNary, who was INS commissioner from October 1989 to January 1993. As the *Sun* reported: "By his estimate, after leaving the federal government, McNary acted as the attorney on 200 to 250 applications for the program"; and
- Former INS general counsel Maurice Inman and Diego Asencio, the former U.S. ambassador to Colombia and Brazil, "who had extraordinary access to and incessantly lobbied former colleagues in the government for preferential treatment and obtained a series of highly favorable but questionable rulings on the requirements for the program that only years later were reversed."[29]

In 2007, the *Seattle Post-Intelligencer* reported that the "program between 1995 and 1998 was fequently abused when would-be immigrants were allowed to pay a small amount in cash for a green card, signing a promissory note for the balance. The note didn't come due for several years—long after the two-year conditional period built into the EB-5 visa had ended and permanent residency had been granted."[30]

A 2011 *Los Angeles Times* report on the program noted: "U.S. Citizenship and Immigration Services, the federal agency that administers the program, can't say how many net new jobs have been created. Under USCIS rules, the projects don't even have to hire 10 workers. Instead, an investor's money can be used to preserve 10 jobs that economic models show, and the government concludes, would otherwise disappear without such funding."[31]

A December 2013 study by the Department of Homeland Security's inspector general concluded that the laws and regulations governing the program prevent the feds from terminating any EB-5 regional center based on fraud or national security concerns and that the feds were "unable to demonstrate the benefits of foreign investment into the U.S. economy."[32] In fact, the DHS inspector general found, USCIS "cannot demonstrate that the program is improving the U.S. economy and creating jobs for U.S. citizens as intended by Congress."[33]

Instead, investigators found EB-5 visa holders gaining permanent residency without any proof of U.S. job creation. In one case, an EB-5 project received 82 percent of its funding from U.S. investors through a regional center. The regional center then applied 100 percent of the projected job growth from the project to its foreign investors—even though foreign investment was only 18 percent of the total investment in the project. In other words, while nearly all the money came from U.S. investors, the EB-5 program was getting the credit for it. "Every foreign investor was able to fulfill the job creation requirement even though the project was primarily funded with U.S. capital," the DHS inspector general's office reported. "When we questioned USCIS about this practice, the officials explained that the EB-5 project would not exist if not for the foreign investment."[34]

Another typical scam involved construction of a hotel that had opened in 2009. The next year, a foreign national invested five hundred thousand dollars to pay off an existing loan on the project. "Total project costs for the hotel were about $28 million, in which foreign investments totaled $4.5 million. Four million of the foreign investments were used to pay off existing loans, and $500,000 was used to purchase existing equity," investigators found. But "[a]lthough 84 percent of the funds were contributed by U.S. investors, the foreign investor was subsequently granted permanent U.S. residency based upon an investment in a project that had already been completed."[35]

In 2014, *Fortune* magazine dubbed EB-5 a "magnet for amateurs, pipe-dreamers, and charlatans, who see it as an easy way to score funding for ventures that banks would never touch."[36] That same year, the Brookings-Rockefeller Project on State and Metropolitan Innovation determined that "all in all, the program has underperformed since its inception." Moreover, the report determined, "The regional center program has never been evaluated by Congress, despite its 20-year lifetime and multiple temporary reauthorizations, and against recommendations by the Government Accountability Office to do so." The "true economic impact" of EB-5, despite its cheerleaders' hype, "is elusive at best" and "practitioners are hard-pressed to evaluate the efficacy of regional centers for wise investment or to find successful investment models."[37]

The Securities and Exchange Commission launched a series of investigations into the program's misuse "as a means to carry about fraudulent security offerings." In 2014, one probe led to the indictment of Chicago businessman Anshoo Sethi, accused of defrauding nearly three hundred Chinese investors in a sham $160 million convention center complex.[38] Another case involved EB-5 abusers who siphoned foreign investments "for personal use such as funding their Cajun-themed restaurant."[39] Yet another case involved a trio of accused con artists who raised $11.5 million from Korean and Chinese EB-5 applicants and told them the money would be invested in an ethanol production plant they would build and operate in Ulysses, Kansas. No plant was built. No jobs were created. Instead, some of the money was sent to the Philippines to fund an iron ore development.[40]

Another novel EB-5 racket perpetrated by two Chinese nationals used embezzled funds from a Chinese grain warehouse, which they told U.S. officials were cash advances from Chinese flour companies the wife owned. They laundered $2.2 million in funds, some of which they used to buy a $525,000 home in Newcastle, Washington.[41]

To our north, Canadian immigration officials finally wised up to the international cash-for-visas scam. In 2014, the country ended its foreign investor program that put residency up for sale to the highest bidder. Canada's Immigrant Investor Program had granted permanent residency to wealthy foreigners who forked over eight hundred thousand Canadian dollars for a five-year, zero-interest loan to one of the country's provinces. The scheme turned out to be a magnet for tens of thousands of millionaires from Hong Kong and China. But as the Canadian Ministry of Finance concluded in its annual budget report, the program "undervalued Canadian permanent residence" and showed "little evidence that immigrant investors as a class are maintaining ties to Canada or making a positive economic contribution to the country."[42]

In several provinces, the foreign investor racket was riddled, from top to bottom, with fraud. Whistleblowers in the Prince Edward Island immigration office exposed rampant bribery among bureaucrats and consultants, who helped their clients jump the queue. The government failed to monitor immigrant investors or verify the promised economic benefits of the "investments." The program didn't just fast-track supposed businesspeople with dubious business backgrounds, but their entire extended families as well, who walled themselves up in segregated neighborhoods.

Ads in Dubai bragged that investors didn't even need to live in Canada to take advantage of the citizenship-for-sale deal—and that their dependents could avail themselves of full health care and education benefits.

In 1999, a prescient independent auditor hired by the Canadian government had warned that he had "found that in many cases there was no investment at all or that the amount of that investment was grossly inflated."[43] The auditor nailed the expedient commodification of citizenship: "Canadians gave up something of real value—a visa or passport—and received very little in return." He concluded: "A lot of people made a lot of money, mostly lawyers and immigration consultants who set up these bogus investments. It's a massive sham. The middlemen made hundreds of millions of dollars."[44]

Undaunted by reality, open-borders billionaires Sheldon Adelson, Warren Buffett, and Bill Gates grudgingly acknowledged "reports of fraud" related to EB-5, but united in July 2014 to push for its expansion instead of calling for investigations or a moratorium.[45] Rather than pause or sunset the corruption-plagued program, former Obama Department of Homeland Security secretary Janet Napolitano "streamlined" the EB-5 immigrant investor green card process—guaranteeing processing within fifteen calendar days for foreign business "projects that are fully developed and ready to be implemented."[46]

In April 2015, ABC News reported that the FBI had launched an investigation into former military aide and retired Air Force colonel Tim Milbraith over allegations that his firm had bilked EB-5 investors in his purported hotel complex out of at least $16 million. The name of Milbraith's crony venture: "Noble Outreach."[47] This investigation is pending.

Twenty years ago, when the program's failures were first exposed, Rep. John W. Bryant, a Texas Democrat, protested on the House floor:

"This provision is an unbelievable departure from our tradition of cherishing our most precious birthright as Americans."[48]

As the case studies in this chapter show, both Democratic and Republican politicians have recklessly sold out that birthright in foreign investor pay-for-play schemes that make a mockery of the American Dream. EB-5 cronyism and corruption are bipartisan diseases.

GREENTECH: STARRING DIRTY HARRY REID, ALEJANDRO MAYORKAS, TERRY McCAULIFFE, BOBBY JINDAL, HALEY BARBOUR & HILLARY'S SHADY BRO

In December 2013, just days before Christmas, the Senate hurriedly confirmed the nomination of Alejandro Mayorkas (who was, at the time, USCIS director) to helm the number-two position at the Department of Homeland Security.[49] These last-minute maneuvers right before the holidays are typical from Beltway swamp creatures trying to minimize public scrutiny of their dirty business.

It spoke volumes about the ethics-challenged Obama White House that the most qualified person it could find for this important post was a DHS hack and Democratic campaign finance bundler under investigation by other DHS hacks, who themselves were under investigation. As Sen. Tom Coburn (R-Okla.) pointed out in a valiant attempt to slow the speeding train carrying Mayorkas into office: "Holding this vote in light of an active investigation into serious, relevant allegations of professional misconduct by the nominee, and over objections of the Ranking Member and others, appears to be virtually without precedent."[50]

The nomination vote would not have been possible without a huge assist from then-Senate majority leader Harry Reid, who had nuked the sixty-vote threshold for filibusters.[51] Fifty-three Democrats and two Independents voted to end Senate debate on the nomination, five short of the traditional hurdle, craftily torpedoed by Reid,[52] and Mayorkas moved up the DHS ladder.

Behind the scenes, Dirty Harry Reid had pressured Mayorkas, in his prior role of USCIS director, to overturn his agency's rejection of EB-5 visa applications for Chinese investors in a Las Vegas casino hotel,[53] which just happened to be represented by Reid's lawyer son, Rory.[54] The meddling "was so intense," the *Washington Times* reported, that one Homeland Security official detailed a phone meltdown between his agency and Reid's thugs. "This one is going to be a major headache for us all because Sen. Reid's office/staff is pushing hard and I just had a long yelling match on the phone," USCIS Legislative Affairs official Miguel "Mike" Rodriguez warned in a December 5, 2012, email to Homeland Security Department officials.[55] (We'll return to the Vegas strip shortly.)

At the time of Mayorkas's nomination to deputy secretary of Homeland Security, the DHS inspector general had been probing a *separate* visas-for-sale scheme tied to this big Obama donor turned Homeland Security bureaucrat. The Mayorkas investigation had dragged on for fifteen months, in large part because the IG's office itself was under investigation for unethical behavior and favoritism.[56] Mayorkas and other higher-ups were being investigated for their alleged roles in intervening on behalf of GreenTech Automotive, a crony company with intimate ties to Democratic Virginia Gov. Terry McAuliffe and Hillary Clinton's brother, Anthony Rodham. Mayorkas testified that he had "never, ever in my career exercised undue influence to influence the outcome of a case."[57] But in the words of one USCIS official, Mayorkas "absolutely gave special treatment"[58] to the company, which zealously sought EB-5 visas for deep-pocketed Chinese investors.

McAuliffe, the prolific Clinton/Democratic National Committee fund-raiser who pioneered the Lincoln Bedroom sleepovers-for-sale scheme[59] and made millions off his Beltway revolving-door access,[60] joined GreenTech in 2009. The firm billed itself as a U.S.-based automotive manufacturer of supposedly affordable, energy-efficient "low-speed electric vehicles."[61] The company website describes McAuliffe's cofounder, Charles X. Wang, as an "accomplished entrepreneur" and "experienced capital markets attorney who has raised billions of dollars for financial transactions on Wall Street and abroad."[62]

But alert auto industry reporters immediately smelled a big, fat rat or two. In 2011, the Truth About Cars, an automotive news and opinion website, spotlighted photos of McAuliffe and Wang celebrating GreenTech's ground-breaking in remote Inner Mongolia. Reporter Bertel Schmitt identified Wang as the former business partner of a shady Chinese operator with multiple names who had established his own green-car company, Hybrid Kinetic Automotive Holdings, from which GreenTech spun off.[63] Wang bragged about getting help from Bill Clinton, who had been "traveling to Hong Kong and introducing company representatives to heads of state at his recent global initiative," according to the Chinese tycoon.[64]

Schmitt noted that both Wang's former partner and Wang were operating parallel schemes to attract foreign investors through EB-5 to open plants in Alabama and, in GreenTech's case, Mississippi.

Enter Tony Rodham. In 2009–10, the favor-trading, nepotism-mooching youngest brother of Hillary Rodham Clinton became president of Gulf Coast Funds Management. The company won designation as an EB-5 regional center, certified to invest foreign capital in federally approved commercial ventures in Louisiana and Mississippi, including GreenTech. Before Rodham's hiring, Louisiana GOP Gov. Bobby Jindal and former Mississippi GOP Gov. Haley Barbour both signed letters urging DHS to approve Gulf Coast as a regional center.[65] As we told you, EB-5 cronyism is a bipartisan disease.

McAuliffe had introduced his partner Charles Wang to Rodham, who traveled with Wang to China to help open doors with investors.[66]

Gulf Coast, the *Washington Post* reported, "is based in the same Tysons Corner [Virginia] complex that houses GreenTech's corporate offices."[67] At some point, Wang then bought Gulf Coast—yes, the very regional center in charge of channeling foreign investments into his auto company—through a separate front called the American Immigration Center, also based in Virginia.[68] In March 2011, Rodham registered as the agent for a second EB-5 regional center in his home state, known as the Virginia Center for Foreign Investment and Job Creation. It, too, shares the same address as GreenTech and Gulf Coast.

As McAuliffe stepped up his public relations campaign for the company, more auto industry veterans called bull. A reporter for the trade website Hybrid Cars voiced skepticism about the Democratic bagman's hyperbolic green jobs claims and lofty one-hundred-thousand-unit sales goal. GreenTech had boasted at its ground-breaking in Tunica County, Mississippi, in 2009 that it had already raised closed to $1 billion and was poised to create five thousand jobs in the area by 2014.[69] Then-Mississippi Gov. Haley Barbour's administration agreed to loan GreenTech and Tunica County $5 million in taxpayer funds. But by 2011, nothing had been built yet on the site. "Too good to be true?" the trade publication mused. Another industry newsletter bluntly pronounced the enterprise "dead on arrival."[70] The *Memphis Daily News,* a Tennessee business journal, raised its eyebrows, too, calling GreenTech's funding mechanisms "murky."[71]

Virginia economic development officials were also raising questions. Before Mississippi promised to pony up public subsidies, GreenTech had sought government funding from McAuliffe's and Rodham's home state of Virginia. The *Washington Post* reported in 2013 that after reviewing the Gulf Coast pitch in 2009, Liz Povar, vice president of the Virginia Economic Development Partnership, told colleagues: "I maintain serious concerns about the establishment of an EB-5 center in general, and most specifically, based on this company." Povar criticized the venture's lack of management expertise and a marketing plan, and she confided that she "also still can't get my head around this being anything other than a visa-for-sale scheme with potential national security implications that we have no way to confirm or discount." [72]

Another official wrote: "We are concerned that the financing plan does not fit the rules for the EB-5 program." Investors would not receive the visas they thought they would receive, he noted, and this would give Virginia a "black eye." The analysts harbored "grave doubts" about GreenTech's business plan. [73]

In the spring of 2012, the conservative Franklin Center's investigative website, Watchdog.org, published a devastating, multipart series on GreenTech's efforts to drum up cash. Mississippi officials told Watchdog.org's Kenric Ward that up to $20 million supposedly raised by Gulf Coast had yet to reach the green car venture. The company and the regional center refused to answer Ward's questions or disclose any information on how many vehicles it had actually manufactured. [74] Watchdog.org's Tori Richards also reported that McAuliffe, Green-Tech finance director Gary Yi Tang, immigration and EB-5 attorney Steve Yale-Loehr (on retainer for Gulf Coast) and Northwestern University economist Michael K. Evans (a professional consultant who generates EB-5 job growth reports [75]) met with White House top economic aide Greg Nelson—"the key White House aide responsible for helping bankrupt solar-panel maker Solyndra win federal loans and high-profile presidential support." [76]

Despite the looming clouds of scandal overhead, McAuliffe announced he was running for governor in Virginia in November 2012. He quietly resigned from GreenTech a month later, [77] but remained the majority owner and continued to turn up the heat on the feds on behalf of the company.

A nonpartisan government watchdog, Cause of Action, released a lengthy report in September 2013 detailing GreenTech's "abuse of political influence." The group discovered that:

- McAuliffe, while GreenTech chairman, emailed then–Mississippi governor Haley Barbour, seeking his assistance in pressuring Alejandro Mayorkas (then United States Citizenship and Immigration Services [USCIS] director) into fast-tracking EB-5 visa applications by GreenTech's Chinese investors;[78]
- In 2009, then-governor Barbour contacted Barbara Velarde, the head of the USCIS office that oversees the Regional Center program, to lobby on behalf of Gulf Coast;[79]
- GreenTech may have violated USCIS regulations in every one of its four rounds of financing by impermissibly structuring each investment as "risk-free;"[80]
- GreenTech made misleading statements to investors that potentially violated Section 17(a) of the 1933 Securities Act by inflating job-creation estimates; and
- GreenTech submitted exaggerated projections about its manufacturing output and job creation prospects in its funding applications to both Mississippi and Virginia. Unlike Virginia, Mississippi state officials failed to conduct proper due diligence on GreenTech and ultimately gave the company millions in loans and tax incentives to locate its manufacturing facility within the state.[81]

Finally, in late March 2015, fifteen months after Alejandro Mayorkas won confirmation to the number-two post at DHS (deputy secretary of Homeland Security), the department's inspector general released its own report on GreenTech and other related EB-5 shenanigans. Investigators interviewed more than fifteen whistleblowers ranging from rank-and-file employees to several senior managers in California and at the D.C. headquarters who accused Mayorkas of bestowing both preferential access and preferential treatment to politically connected EB-5 applicants and stakeholders. "Their allegations were unequivocal," the inspector general reported, and the corruption was systemic. Mayorkas "created special processes and revised existing policies in the EB-5 program to accommodate specific parties." According to the employees, "but for Mr. Mayorkas' actions, the career staff would have decided these matters differently. Employees felt uncomfortable and pressured to comply with managers' instructions that appeared to have come from Mr. Mayorkas or those working directly for him."[82]

The report emphasized: "Again, these comments were not from one or even a couple of disgruntled employees with axes to grind; rather, these were individuals throughout the ranks of USCIS, in different locations, engaged in different functions, with different experience levels."[83]

"I'LL WRITE THE F—ING THING MYSELF"

The DHS inspector general's office found that Mayorkas intervened on GreenTech's behalf after USCIS denied the Gulf Coast EB-5 regional center's multiple applications to extend its geographic reach into Virginia, expand its investment reach into GreenTech, and construct facilities in Mississippi, Virginia, and Tennessee. Adjudicators dismissed the company's job claims as "ridiculous," "flawed," and "not approvable." McAuliffe personally leaned on then-DHS secretary Janet Napolitano, "complaining about the denial of the Gulf Coast amendment and requesting her assistance to get the amendment approved and to expedite more than 200 investor petitions."[84]

In violation of record-keeping and disclosure rules, Mayorkas met with McAuliffe in February 2011 after USCIS had denied GreenTech's requests. Napolitano's office would not tell the inspector general's office who else from DHS attended the meeting. Mayorkas mysteriously took no notes and could not recall just exactly how many phone calls he took from McAuliffe and what exactly they discussed (though he did remember the "caustic" Democratic bagman yelling "expletives at high volume" on one occasion).[85] The IG reported its agents "were unsuccessful in our attempts to interview McAuliffe."[86]

On July 21, 2011, Mayorkas met personally with senior staff to force the agency to reverse its denials and give McAuliffe and company what they wanted. Mayorkas repeatedly referred to "people with money" and "people of influence." Staff members "froze," as the IG described it, when Mayorkas made the highly suspect suggestion that he take the decision "home and rewrite the report" himself—you know, to "lighten" the appeals officer's "load." How generous.[87]

Another staffer recalled Mayorkas's demand this way: "Give it to me . . . I'll write the f—ing thing myself."[88]

(Such untoward behavior and conflict of interest were nothing new for Mayorkas. As a U.S. attorney in 2001, Mayorkas phoned the Clinton White House on behalf of convicted drug dealer Carlos Vignali.[89] Mayorkas joined other high-profile California liberals in the dialing-for-pardons campaign.[90] Vignali's father, also suspected of drug trafficking, had dumped two hundred thousand dollars in the coffers of Hillary Clinton's brother, Hugh, to secure his son's commutation. Mayorkas pleaded ignorance of Vignali senior's suspected criminal activity and admitted failure to do his "due diligence." The House Committee on Government Reform concluded: "U.S. Attorney Alejandro Mayorkas provided critical support for the Vignali commutation, which was inappropriate, given his position.")[91]

Over the next eighteen months, Mayorkas continued to meddle as Tony Rodham's Virginia and Gulf Coast regional centers separately sought and won approval for individual foreign investor petitions. The IG report spared no adjectives for Mayorkas's behavior and its impact on staff who objected: "corrosive," "destabilizing," "chilling," and "muzzled."[92]

But in the immediate aftermath of the report, Mayorkas didn't even warrant a slap on the wrist. DHS secretary Jeh Johnson asserted "full confidence" in his bullying, meddling, unethical deputy.[93] His "impatience" with adjudicators who refused to immediately cave in to McAuliffe's demand was turned into an asset by Johnson. And his disturbing and unprecedented personal intervention morphed into, as Johnson spun it, a "hands-on" management style that Johnson deemed "honest and patriotic."[94] Instead of focusing on all the protocols Mayorkas violated, Johnson disingenuously announced "creation of a new protocol to ensure that the EB-5 program is free from the reality or perception of improper outside influence."

As for the thousands of jobs and millions of cars this crony-fueled operation was supposed to have produced by now, the company refused to "put a number or goal on GreenTech's manufacturing capacity or employee numbers" at its long-delayed "grand opening" in Tunica, Mississippi, in the fall of 2014.[95]

"Power lawyer" A. B. Culvahouse, who worked with Mayorkas at O'Melveny and Myers[96] and is a famed political campaign vetter, vigorously defended his scandal-tainted friend and former colleague. The disgust of fifteen DHS staffers, the outrage of independent watchdogs, and the hijacking of a foreign investor program by graft-seekers and political back-scratchers was, Mayorkas's old pal shrugged, "much ado about nothing."[97]

The day after the DHS IG report became public, White House spokesman Josh Earnest agreed. He took the podium to defend Mayorkas as an "effective leader."[98]

Terry McAuliffe, Charles Wang, Tony Rodham, and friends no doubt agree.

A SIDE TRIP TO THE VEGAS STRIP

Now, let's revisit Vegas. As we noted, while Mayorkas awaited Senate confirmation to his number-two DHS post, Dirty Harry Reid's office aggressively harangued him to reverse his agency's rejection of EB-5 petitions for Chinese investors in the SLS Hotel & Casino. The company employed Reid's son, Rory, and his law firm as corporate legal counsel; the firm, in turn, showered Reid's with individual and PAC donations totaling more than forty thousand dollars.[99] Papa Reid has a long and infamous track record of using his influence to enrich his large brood. Between 1998 and 2002 alone, the *Los Angeles Times* reported, firms tied to Reid's family of lawyers and lobbyists earned more than $2 million "from special interests that were represented by the kids and helped by the senator in Washington."[100] Rory Reid also represented Chinese solar energy company ENN, which Sen. Reid has championed despite dubious job-creation claims and the high-profile combustion of several federally backed green energy projects. Bloomberg News reported that ENN's founder, Wang Yuso, one of China's richest men, joined with Reid "to win incentives including land 113 miles southeast of Las Vegas that ENN is buying for $4.5 million, or less than one-eighth of the $38.6 million assessors say it is worth."[101]

The nonpartisan government watchdog Cause of Action filed an ethics complaint in December 2013 on Reid's intervention in the SLS matter, charging Reid with violating the Senate's Code of Official Conduct by using his influence to help the hotel/casino obtain visas for two dozen Chinese investors.

SLS was a project of the Las Vegas Regional Center, which received federal EB-5 approval in 2010 to channel foreign investments into "10 industry economic clusters" in the region, including hotels, retail shops, and casinos. Two years later, more than 230 individual foreign investors filed their EB-5 petitions with USCIS. Reid's office contacted the agency requesting "expedited" processing. An adjudicator objected to Reid's office's circumventing the usual procedures for making such a request and questioned whether the petitions actually met the criteria for expedited review, which is rarely granted and only in cases of "extreme hardship."[102]

SLS wanted to jump in front of the line as part of a financing deal with J.P. Morgan Chase. Top Reid aide Michael Vannozzi urged USCIS officials in a missive: "As you can imagine this project is pretty important to Southern Nevada. It will probably be the only 'new' property opening up on the Strip for some time, and if their $300 million senior lending facility from JP Morgan Chase expires because these visas aren't processed expeditiously, it will be a huge setback for the project and the 8,600 jobs associated with it."[103]

Chiming in for the home team, Nevada GOP Sen. Dean Heller also wrote an alarmist letter on behalf of SLS: "I strongly encourage you to consider this request and the impact the project will have on Nevada's economy," he told EB-5 reviewers. "Time is of the essence."[104]

USCIS wisely ignored the hype and denied the Nevada contingent's demand—er, "request"—in December 2012.

Then the excrement hit the fan.

"A NEW PHASE OF YUCK"

After receiving a personal phone call from Reid during the first week of January 2013, Mayorkas ordered his underlings to take a "fresh look" at the case.[105] No promises, of course. Nudge nudge, wink wink. But the staff again denied the request.[106]

Hammered by Reid and pressured by Mayorkas, skeptical EB-5 staffers who wanted more evidence from SLS of their claims received a mysterious missive out of the blue from a Commerce Department official named Steve Olson. He served as executive director for something called SelectUSA, a little-noticed initiative established by President

Obama in 2011 through executive order "to attract and retain investment in the American economy."[107]

Olson, it turns out, was an old O'Melveney & Myers law firm
buddy of Mayorkas who had also worked as an assistant U.S. attorney under his command in California.[108] Olson informed USCIS that
SLS had a "track record of past successes" and that rejecting its EB-5
petitions at that moment would put its "capital at risk and derail the
project."[109] Olson did not, however, explain why USCIS bore responsibility for the risky financing arrangements and timing chosen by SLS
and its regional center. The arrival of the letter from a Mayorkas-tied
official at an entity that had never weighed in on EB-5-related matters
reeked of outside influence. Whistleblowers told Sen. Charles Grassley
that despite Mayorkas's claim of impartiality, he had actually *solicited*
the letter from Olson.[110]

"I fear we are entering a whole new level of yuck," one staffer
lamented.[111] EB-5 officials were in near-revolt, but Mayorkas overruled
the critics. The SLS petitions proceeded to a fast track.[112]

While the DHS inspector general responded to government whistleblowers, the Senate Ethics Committee was not so responsive to
civilian watchdogs. After the nonpartisan group Cause of Action
alerted the committee to Reid's dirty deeds in December 2013, Democratic members on the panel claimed ten months later that they had
"never received the complaint" and did not know of its existence.[113]
The phony-baloney excuse was contradicted by a signed certified mail
receipt, direct press inquiries to the panel about the complaint, and
Google analytical data showing that several Senate employees had
visited the group's website, where the complaint was posted for the
public.[114]

Cause of Action executive director Daniel Epstein re-sent the full
complaint to the Senate Ethics Committee in October 2014 a second
time.[115] As of April 2015, no action had been taken. The group also

urged the chief public integrity officer at the Department of Justice to immediately investigate Mayorkas, Sen. Reid, Terry McAuliffe, and others for their undue influence in playing favorites with government resources.[116]

As of April 2015, no action had been taken.

ATLANTIC YARDS: STARRING CHUCK SCHUMER, BRUCE RATNER, FRANK GEHRY, THE SHANGHAI GOVERNMENT, ACORN, JAY-Z, BEYONCE, THE BROOKLYN NETS, AND A RUSSIAN OLIGARCH FOR GOOD MEASURE

The EB-5 racket is bad enough on its own, but fold it into a gargantuan, multi-billion-dollar urban redevelopment scheme in the heart of the Big Apple and you're talking the Mother of All Corrupt-a-paloozas.

Welcome to the twelve-year-long festival of Big Business and Big Government fraud, graft, greed, land confiscation, and foreign intrigue known as "Atlantic Yards." The site is located at the intersection of Atlantic and Flatbush avenues in the Prospect Heights neighborhood of northwest Brooklyn, where an entire network of commuter rail lines and subway routes converge. Thriving small businesses, warehouses, and handsome nineteenth-century brownstones lined the streets of the multiethnic community without disturbance until the early 2000s, when developers seized on construction opportunities for luxury condos and other commercial opportunities.

Democratic bigwig Bruce Ratner, a former official in the Ed Koch administration and dynastic real estate mogul, embarked on an epic crusade in 2003 to build a sprawling, $5 billion, twenty-two-acre public-private project encompassing a sports arena, high-rise office towers designed by famed architect Frank Gehry, and thousands of residential units.[117] Ratner's company, Forest City Ratner, marketed the slick plan as a magical recipe for "Jobs, Housing, and Hoops."[118]

In a pie-in-the-sky pitch that should quite familiar to you by now,

Ratner lured supporters with the lofty promise of creating ten thousand permanent jobs, fifteen thousand temporary construction jobs, $6 billion in tax revenue,[119] and endless benefits to the community, including thousands of office spaces, a public park, and thousands of affordable housing units.[120]

What Ratner didn't have, he bought (e.g., the New Jersey Nets basketball team, which he purchased for $300 million and relocated to Brooklyn).[121] What he couldn't buy, he seized (with the help of land-grabbers in government who redefined "blight" in order to clear out families and store owners in the way).[122] Ownership of the Nets helped ensure eminent domain as a "redevelopment" tool to raze the occupied homes and buildings in his way, because government condemnation of private property could be justified as a "public use" if it was snatched to build a sports stadium.[123] To provide cover and bolster public support for this dirty business, Ratner enlisted the power and influence of celebrities (such as music magnate Jay-Z, who purchased a small stake in the Nets). Then, he paid off the community activists of scandal-plagued ACORN with a $1 million loan and five-hundred-thousand-dollar grant in exchange for their support of the project and its phony promise of affordable housing.[124]

About half the financing for Atlantic Yards came from the sale of tax-exempt bonds for the sports arena, underwritten by Goldman Sachs and Barclays Capital (which paid $10 million for twenty years for naming rights on the stadium). The other half came from a hodgepodge of state and city tax subsidies (including a nearly $200 million subsidy from the former Bloomberg administration) and private investment. Hit hard by the 2008 economic recession and court battles challenging his land-grab tactics, cash-strapped Ratner replaced planned office space and low-cost housing units with luxury apartments and condos—and then sold his majority stake in the Nets to Russia's wealthiest playboy billionaire, Mikhail Prokhorov, for $200 million.[125]

As writer Malcolm Gladwell described the deal: "Prokhorov helped Ratner out by buying a controlling interest in the Nets. But he also paid off some of Ratner's debts, lent him $75 million, picked up some of his debt service, acquired a small stake in the arena, and bought an option on 20 percent of the entire Atlantic Yards project. This wasn't a fire sale of a distressed basketball franchise. It was a general-purpose real estate bailout."[126]

But this *still* wasn't enough—and that's where EB-5 comes in.

"CULTURE OF CHEATING"

"Ratner Mulls Visa Financing," a curious *Wall Street Journal* item in September 2010 reported.[127]

The article disclosed the real estate scion's plans to fly to China to entice EB-5 investors to pitch in $250 million for the Atlantic Yards project. He was urged by New York City officials to seek the funding after their successful experience exploiting the below-market-rate EB-5 loan scheme for the city's Brooklyn Navy Yard redevelopment project.[128]

"It was like a gift from the gods,"[129] the lead official exulted.

Taking a page from the Navy Yard playbook, EB-5 funds for Atlantic Yards would be used to finance the construction of a new rail yard with new, low-cost capital and "help pay off land loans on the project," a Ratner executive told the paper.[130]

Doing the investigative journalism no other media outlet would do, New York citizen watchdog Norman Oder dug deep into the "culture of cheating" at the heart of the Atlantic Yards EB-5 racket involving Forest City Ratner and the New York City Regional Center. He exposed how:

- The redevelopment partners' promotional materials to Chinese investors featured "the already-funded arena, and the basketball

team, using the glitz of NBA basketball as the lure." [131] This
deceptive marketing obscured the true risks of the project
elements the Atlantic Yards officials sought to fund: the troubled
residential towers and railyard;

- The EB-5 plan inflated dubious job-creation numbers by
  redefining the scope of the project to include the already-built
  arena, the railyard, and related infrastructure; [132]
- The New York City Regional Center and its salesmen, who
  brought Brooklyn Nets players with them to wine and dine
  Chinese investors, steered clear of informing the wealthy
  foreigners that Russian oligarch Mikhail Prokhorov already
  owned 80 percent of the team and nearly half the basketball
  arena; [133]
- Ratner sold 70 percent of his stake in Atlantic Yards [134] to the
  Shanghai government–owned property developer Greenland
  Group, [135] which will handle construction of fifteen of the sixteen
  towers in the renamed "Pacific Park" project; and
- The developers and the regional center snagged $228 million from
  Chinese investors for their first injection of EB-5 cash, raised
  $245 million for a second round of EB-5 funding, and launched
  a third, $100 million round in the fall of 2014 with promotional
  materials improperly featuring a purported endorsement from
  active State Department official Charles Rivkin. [136]

The scandal here lies not in what's illegal, but what remains perfectly
legal: A foreign government (a communist one no less) "profiting by
marketing a scarce U.S. public resource—green card slots under the
EB-5 program—to its own citizens," Oder explained. "And that, as far
as I know, is unprecedented." [137]

Center for Immigration Studies analyst David North marveled:
"So the administration allows an entity controlled by the Chinese

government to accept investments from (and perhaps take fees from) rich Chinese who make those payments in order to secure American green cards. Who says our government is not in bed with Beijing?"[138]

Watchdog Cause of Action's independent, eighteen-month investigation of the Chinese conglomerate's American bedmates found that:

- Between 2002 and 2012, Ratner's Forest City Enterprises (FCE), its subsidiaries, and employees "spent $23 million on campaign contributions and lobbying at the federal, state, and local level. In return it received 52 direct and indirect government subsidies or financial benefits totaling at least $2.6 billion. These subsidies amounted to 23% of FCE's $11.4 billion revenue during that time";[139]
- FCE engaged in a repeated pattern of promising inflated job creation, then reneging on the economic benefits. "In short, FCE lobbies, profits, and then bilks taxpayers by breaching its promises to the community";[140] and
- FCE "manipulated census data" to qualify as a "targeted employment area" under EB-5 by improperly aggregating unemployment rates.[141]

This last practice of gerrymandering development zones to create the illusion that they are economically distressed has become so commonplace that even the *New York Times* (a former business partner of Ratner's) decried its excesses. One project, a $750 million office tower in mid-Manhattan's diamond district, raised 20 percent of its financing through EB-5 "through a trick of mapmaking in which state officials counted the number of unemployed people in the census tract next door, which includes Times Square, to justify calling the whole area a high-unemployment zone."[142] Another development zone in Lower Manhattan near Wall Street folded in a Brooklyn public-housing project to score EB-5 funds. "Visa-seekers have used this district in three separate projects to qualify." [143]

Instead of raising questions, however, U.S. politicians jumped aboard the gravy train and won't let go. Sen. Charles Schumer (D-N.Y.) has pushed to make the EB-5 regional centers permanent and championed widespread adoption of similar EB-5 investment schemes across his state, including:

- Steiner Studios, which received $65 million of EB-5 funding to assist with the expansion of a film production studio project in Brooklyn;
- Global Vascular Institute on the Buffalo Niagara Medical Campus, where EB-5 funding was used to help the Buffalo Niagara Medical Campus support Kaleida Health's development of the new institute;
- Acadia Realty Trust, which received $200 million of EB-5 funding to assist with the construction of the City Point project in Downtown Brooklyn;
- SJM Company, which received $72 million in EB-5 funding to assist with the redevelopment of the George Washington Bridge Bus Station; and
- Dermot Company and Harry's Restaurant, which received $96 million of EB-5 funding to assist with the redevelopment of the Battery Maritime Building and Pier A in Lower Manhattan. [144]

Singing the same Chicken Little hymn that Harry Reid and Terry McAuliffe belted out in their pressure campaigns to help their cronies secure EB-5 visas, Schumer warned of the dire impact that failure to renew and make permanent EB-5 would have on "attracting foreign investment." [145]

The Chinese bureaucrats of Greenland pushed forward with the sordid business of wiping out the few remaining American businesses in the path of the Atlantic Yards/Pacific Park site. In February 2015, after the state supreme court ruled against them, the last property owners to hold out were ordered to evacuate. New York's Empire State Development Corporation, the government enforcer of eminent domain, oversaw the proceedings—and lowballed compensation to the land-grab victims.

One condemnee was Aaron Piller, whose immigrant father survived the Holocaust and established the Atlantic Wool company in 1954. The second-generation Brooklyn business will now be demolished by Shanghai-based developers dispensing green cards to wealthy Chinese investors under the guise of promoting job growth and the American Dream. Piller's father died in 2013.

"I don't want to trivialize what happened by comparing this to the Holocaust," Piller told the *New York Times*, "but in the end, he felt like here was the government again, coming to take everything from him."[146]

BOWING TO HOLLYWOOD: STARRING SONY PICTURES, TIME WARNER, ED RENDELL, EB-5 KINGPIN TOM ROSENFELD & MORE MAYORKAS CRONIES

Tom Rosenfeld is also the son of Holocaust survivors. But unlike EB-5 victim Aaron Piller, the Israeli-born business tycoon made a fortune cashing in on the EB-5 frenzy. Rosenfeld is president of CanAm, one of the country's leading immigrant investment sponsors. CanAm is the exclusive overseer of seven USCIS-designated regional centers, including those located in the city of Philadelphia; the states of Pennsylvania, Florida, and Hawaii; metropolitan New York; Plattsburgh, New York; and Los Angeles County.[147]

CanAm's venture in Los Angeles targeted the film industry. In the spring and summer of 2011, the firm submitted more than two hundred EB-5 petitions proposing to invest money in Sony Pictures. But the shady plan did not obligate Sony to accept any of the foreigners' investments. Moreover, DHS officials could not verify whether the proposed investments would actually be spent in the designated "targeted employment area." EB-5 officials in California prepared a draft denial, but once again, staffers committed to following the law were about to get an earful from Obama DHS deputy secretary Alejandro Mayorkas and his cronies.

Mayorkas, you'll recall, was a prominent law partner at O'Melveny & Myers in Los Angeles and former U.S. attorney in southern California. In June 2011, a top economics aide in the L.A. mayor's office contacted him about progress on approving the Sony EB-5 petitions. The official, Katherine Hennigan, noted in an email to Mayorkas that "she had met a mutual acquaintance from O'Melveny & Myers," according to the DHS inspector general. Over the course of several weeks, Hennigan continued to email Mayorkas—who told his staff the Sony petitions "have an urgency" because of the "sensitive" timing of the project's investment vehicles.[148]

Yes, that old line.

Once again, staffers tried to resist the pressure and prepared to issue denials of the crappy EB-5 petitions. But after former Democratic mayor Ed Rendell—a consultant to CanAm and zealous EB-5 promoter—personally lobbied Mayorkas, the California office in charge of reviewing the petitions entered "crisis mode." Mayorkas had ordered the workers to stop denying any film-related EB-5 petitions and to reopen any cases in which denial had been issued.

Rosenfeld followed up with a barrage of phone calls, emails, and letters—as well as a pressure campaign on Mayorkas through intermediaries. Rosenfeld's lawyer, Ronald Klasko, had also represented EB-5 investors in the SLS hotel/casino case, which Mayorkas fast-tracked for Harry Reid and friends. The DHS inspector general noted that Mayorkas and Klasko, chair of the EB-5 committee of the American Immigration Lawyers Association, were in direct contact more than twenty times between 2011 and 2013. Investigators also found several emails to Mayorkas from his "career adviser" John Emerson, who forwarded emails from Rosenfeld and pestered his protégé about the Sony case.[149] By November 2011, after Rosenfeld had pulled out all the lobbying stops, Mayorkas forced a reversal and approved the two-hundred-plus EB-5 petitions.

But Rosenfeld was just getting started.

Flexing his muscle, the EB-5 kingpin teamed with Rendell and other pals to pressure Mayorkas to grant approval for another 240 foreign visa applications to invest in Time Warner. Underlings in California opposed the plan, which had failed to source its job creation estimates, contained problematic escrow agreements, and failed to include commitments from Time Warner on using the proposed EB-5 investment funds.

Amid the conflict, the DHS inspector general's office learned, one petition was "inadvertently approved when a staff member mistakenly believed an economist had reviewed the file as required when in fact it had not been reviewed."[150]

Savvy lawyer Rosenfeld seized on the error to demand that all of the 240 petitions be rubber-stamped based on a policy of "deference." A week later, Mayorkas indulged Rosenfeld by establishing a "deference review board" (DRB) to allow unspecified affected parties to appeal their denials in person. Mayorkas claimed not to remember why exactly he created the radical and unprecedented panel. In March 2013, the DRB met with Rosenfeld, two attorneys from AILA (one of whom had dealt extensively with Mayorkas in the Gulf Coast/GreenTech case), and a private economist. No actual investors were present. No notes or recordings of the hearing were kept. Afterward, adjudicators were ordered to approve all 249 of the Time Warner EB-5 petitions in a "mad rush" of two weeks.[151]

To date, according to investigators, the "deference review board"— or rather, the Bow Down to Hollywood board—has not held any other hearings on any other matters for any other petitioners.

THE SOUTH DAKOTA SCAM: STARRING FORMER GOP GOV. (AND NOW SEN.) MIKE ROUNDS, BEEF PACKERS, A BRITISH VIRGIN ISLANDS BUSINESS FRONT, AND A MYSTERIOUS SUICIDE

If Hollywood studios weren't so entangled in their own EB-5 fiascos, they might have seen the cinematic potential of a made-for-TV immigrant investor scandal that unfolded in the heartland. South Dakota Republicans and agricultural special interests sought to lure Asian investors to the Mount Rushmore state through aggressive pursuit of EB-5—only to see their grand schemes produce bankruptcies, lawsuits, an FBI investigation, and one dead body.

Mike Rounds, an insurance and real estate businessman, grew up in Pierre and climbed the political ladder from the state Senate to state Senate majority leader to the governor's mansion for two terms from 2003 to 2010. Seeking to attract capital to his state, Rounds first signed on to use of EB-5 for dairy development. He was not involved in the day-to-day "transactional details" of pursuing the investments, but he was "aware and supportive" of the efforts.[152]

Under Rounds's administration, South Dakota operated its EB-5 program through an unusual arrangement. A special agency called the South Dakota International Business Institute, created under the South Dakota Board of Regents and based at Northern State University in Aberdeen, received funding from the Governor's Office of Economic Development to chase visas-for-dollars projects. USCIS certified the entity as an EB-5 regional center in 2004, making it one of the first and oldest centers in the country. EB-5 experts called it a "showcase example of what State governments could do with the promise of capital investment from foreigners through the EB-5 visa program." [153]

Ambitious Dutch immigrant investment banker Joop Bollen helmed the institute. From a few tiny dairy investments involving fewer than five foreign investors, Bollen expanded the state's reach into meatpacking, casino gambling, petroleum, coal projects, electricity production, and even a turkey plant. [154] In 2008, Bollen scored a lucrative deal with about seventy Chinese EB-5 investors, who committed five hundred thousand dollars each to loan money to construct a state-of-the-art processing plant for Northern Beef in Aberdeen.

A year later, Bollen's efforts resulted in the state's abandoning the South Dakota International Business Institute and instead awarding his newly formed private company, SDRC, Inc., the exclusive, no-bid monopoly contract to manage and promote South Dakota's EB-5 investments. The contract was signed on behalf of the state by Richard Benda, Governor Rounds's jet-setting secretary of tourism and state development. The hard-driving Benda had been a zealous champion of EB-5, traveling frequently to China to conduct investment seminars and ferrying foreign visitors around the state to drum up funds for Northern Beef.

As the *Argus Leader* reported, not long after he authorized Bollen's racket, Benda quit his job and went to work for the Bollen as a "loan monitor" overseeing the funds administered to Northern Beef. [155] By this time, the meatpacking firm had received an estimated $100 million of its total $115 million cost from EB-5 funders. In 2013, a year after the much-hyped plant opened, Northern Beef went bankrupt.

According to investigators, Bollen was cashing in on the side. He charged EB-5 investors each an annual fee of ten thousand dollars or more, "plus extra money collected for expenses and a consulting agreement each group of investors had to sign." [156] While the beef plant was going belly up, Bollen was allegedly milking his EB-5 monopoly for untold millions. The *Argus Leader* estimated that at the high end, Bollen's arrangements with his vast array of EB-5 investors could have amounted to "as much as $8 million in yearly revenue." [157]

Benda, meanwhile, allegedly attempted to siphon five hundred thousand dollars from a $1 million state grant for the Northern Beef plant.[158] He reportedly threatened to withhold the remaining amount from the company unless the meatpackers paid up. As the state attorney general prepared to bring a felony theft indictment against him, Benda drove out to a shelter belt on his sister's farm near the tiny town of Lake Andes and shot himself in the head.[159]

The apparent suicide didn't end the scandal. Bollen, who has since clammed up, was also at the center of a shady funding scheme for Northern Beef involving a British Virgin Islands–incorporated company called "Epoch Star." It provided a $30 million high-interest loan to Northern Beef, the *Argus Leader* reported, "which then used lower-interest EB-5 funds to buy out the Epoch Star loan by purchasing the company." [160]

It all stinks worse than a football field's worth of open-air manure lagoons on a South Dakota dairy farm. Yet, national Republicans rallied to Gov. Rounds's side and helped him win his Senate bid in 2014. An FBI investigation has gone nowhere. The GOP-controlled state legislature won't subpoena Bollen. And while the state quietly canceled its contract with Bollen's private EB-5 venture, it has yet to recoup $1 million in lost taxpayer funds.[161]

Now-senator Rounds remained outspoken in his defense of EB-5 during his campaign.[162] But in the aftermath of the DHS inspector general's report on rampant EB-5 corruption and influence-peddling in the Obama White House in March 2015, Sen. Rounds was quieter than a church mouse in a barn full of cats.

A THREAT TO NATIONAL SECURITY

The sellouts on Capitol Hill and inside the highest echelons of the federal government have sold America's birthright to enrich themselves and their corporate cronies. They've bilked taxpayers, destroyed successful American businesses, grabbed the homes of hard-working families, steamrolled over conscientious adjudicators, and polluted the landscape with phony promises and bogus studies projecting nonexistent "job growth" over the past twenty-five years.

Even more troubling, bipartisan champions of EB-5 are demanding expansion of the program despite continued warnings of the national security threat the program poses. Rank-and-file workers in Laguna Niguel, California, under pressure from their bosses and facing retaliation, "often rushed or skipped altogether economic reviews of applicants to the EB-5 visa program." [163] They did so under orders from senior managers pandering to wealthy and politically connected foreign applicants. "In essence," Sen. Charles Grassley (R-Iowa), noted in a public letter, "high-level officials in the [U.S. Citizenship and Immigration Services] are accused of creating an environment hostile to those who insist on following the law." [164]

Sen. Grassley and Sen. Tom Coburn learned in 2013 that the White House and National Security Staff (NSS) had launched an interagency review of EB-5's vulnerabilities. They obtained a draft document apparently written by or on behalf of the NSS titled "Forensic Assessment of Financial Flows Related to EB-5 Regional Centers" that raised flags about the regional centers' potential for "investor fraud," violations of U.S. securities law," and risks of money laundering, tax evasion, or other illicit financial conduct." The report also warned: "Vulnerabilities relating to possible infiltration by terrorist groups or foreign operatives are also before the NSS and being addressed separately by the interagency." [165] Top Obama National Security adviser Susan Rice refused to respond to Sen. Coburn's request for information about the interagency review and any resulting changes or outcomes.

A disturbing memo from Homeland Security Investigations (HSI), the investigative arm of ICE, sounded a similar alarm in December 2013 on one of the most nightmarish EB-5 scams to date. Agents reported that EB-5 was apparently "abused by Iranian operatives to infiltrate the United States," "facilitate terrorism," and illegally procure items exported to Iran "for use by 'secret' Iranian government agencies."[166] How could this happen? EB-5 beneficiaries, the HSI memo pointed, out "do not need to establish a significant and verifiable background for program eligibility."[167] As so many other internal and external watchdogs have pointed out, the investigators reported that EB-5 regional centers use "problematic" job growth projections, "which inherently creates an opportunity for fraud."[168]

HSI forcefully recommended freezing the regional center programs, substantially raising the minimum EB-5 investment threshold, prohibiting participation by passive investors, and ending the inclusion of "indirect" or "induced" jobs as measurements of job creation.

The calls went unheeded. As with Rome, our downfall is being hastened faster from within than from without.

The L Visa: A Secretive "Back Door to Cheap Labor"

Indian media outlets from Chennai to Mumbai to New Delhi bubbled with excitement in March 2015. Word had just come down that the president would be taking action to protect and defend Indian workers. No, not the president of India. The president of the United States:

> "*Obama to ease norms for L-1B work visas.*"[1]
> "*Obama vows L-1B visa reform to attract global business.*"[2]
> "*Indian IT cos rejoice as Obama promises to ease L1 visa process.*"[3]
> "*Boost for Indian IT workers as US L-1B visas now easier to get.*"[4]
> "*In boost to Indian companies, US to ease L-1B visas.*"[5]
> "*L-1B visas to become easier to get: Barack Obama;*
> *Huge influx of foreign IT workers expected.*"[6]

Demonstrating arrogant disregard for the deliberative process and in defiance of rising public discontent with lax immigration policies, the White House announced unilateral action to loosen restrictions on the fraud-friendly L-1B business visa program. President Obama claimed the move "could benefit hundreds of thousands of nonimmigrant workers and their employers." Welcoming all these supposedly "temporary" foreigners "will benefit our entire economy and spur additional investment," he insisted.[7]

Uh-huh. Is your BS detector off the charts yet?

The usual suspects clamored for the liberalization of L visas, which allow multinationals to transfer their foreign employees into the United States: Indian offshore outsourcing companies, the U.S. Chamber of Commerce, and immigration expansionists on both sides of the political aisle. The National Association for Software and Services Companies, the trade group for leading Indian outsourcing companies such as Infosys, Wipro, and Tata, spearheaded the lobbying campaign, blasting American immigration enforcement of L-1 rules as "discriminatory."[8]

Stuart Anderson's National Foundation for American Policy decried high rejection rates of L-1 applications from India, claiming that the crackdown "harmed innovation and job creation in the United States."[9] NFAP executive director and militant open-borders advocate Stuart Anderson griped about "the difficulties of the US immigration system."[10] The American Council on International Personnel (ACIP) asserted that L visas were "essential to international investment and the economic expansion in the United States."[11]

Now, do you remember SelectUSA? That's President Obama's government initiative, housed at the U.S. Department of Commerce, "to attract and retain investment in the American economy."[12] We told you in Chapter 7 about how SelectUSA's former executive director, Steve Olson, an old lawyer chum of DHS number-two official Alejandro Mayorkas, meddled in the EB-5 case of Harry Reid, Reid's son, and the SLS casino project. Olson quietly left SelectUSA in 2013 and returned to the O'Melveny & Myers law firm in Los Angeles.[13] Indian-born businessman Vinai Thummalapally took his place.[14]

Thummalapally hails from Hyderabad—a hotbed of H-1B visa

fraud.[15] During an eighteen-month period, according to State Department cables leaked in 2011, U.S. consular officials in India discovered that 77 percent of H-1B applications submitted by 150 companies in Hyderabad "turned out to be fraudulent or highly suspect."[16] The cable also called Thummalapally's hometown a "hub for fraudulent document vendors in India."[17] He immigrated to the U.S. as a young man, was a friend and roommate of President Obama's at Occidental College, attended Obama's wedding, and became one of his wealthy campaign finance bundlers. Before taking over SelectUSA, Thummalapally was appointed by his pal to a cushy post as ambassador to Belize.[18]

Thummalapally describes SelectUSA's role as that of an "ombudsman"—not for American companies and workers, but for Indian businesses in need of help to "resolve visa issues."[19]

As he told reporters, "We highlight the specific situation so that the agencies responsible come into the picture and make a resolution." (Or change a determination that corporate and foreign special interests don't like.) "When it is highlighted, it gets the attention," Thummalapally bragged.[20] (And we've seen exactly how that works under the reign of Mayorkas and his political cronies.)

In an announcement of Thummalapally's trip to Hyderabad and other cities in his home country in 2014, the State Department made clear: "India is an important focus country for SelectUSA."[21] Southeast Asian media touted Thummalapally's invitations to Indian companies for the 2015 SelectUSA Investment summit. It was at this very meeting in March that President Obama unveiled, to roaring applause, the L-1 visa "reforms" demanded by Big Tech and foreign lobbyists.[22]

Who spoke up for American workers in the backroom negotiations and summit forums? No one.

Where were the public hearings to debate the matter before Obama acted? There were none.

"WHAT IS HAPPENING HERE?"

Like the B visa program, L visas for foreign guest workers are uncapped, require no Labor Condition Applications or prevailing-wage protections, and are subject to laughable oversight and little transparency. As an added bonus, the spouse of an L-1 alien can work as well with no restrictions.[23]

Like the EB-5 program, attempts by government adjudicators to protect the original congressional intent of the L visa program have come under fire from partisan and politicized bureaucrats.

As with the H-1B program, the end result of liberalized L visa issuances has been shoddy enforcement, unchecked fraud, and displacement of American workers. "It's a back door to cheap labor," Rep. John Mica (R-Fla.) warned a dozen years ago.[24] But despite pledges from Rep. Mica and others on Capitol Hill to rein in abuse and damage, it appears there's no end in sight.

Congress created L visas in 1970 to allow multinational companies to transfer certain types of employees from their overseas offices to a U.S.-based operation. L-1 visas are dispensed to the foreign workers; L-2 visas are available for spouses and dependent children of L-1 visa holders. Legislation at the time explained that the program was intended to "help eliminate problems [then] faced by American companies having offices abroad in transferring key personnel freely within the organization."[25]

As Big Tech's appetite for cheap foreign workers grew, so did the demand for more guest worker pipelines. Along with creation of the H-1B and EB-5 programs, the Immigration Act of 1990 significantly broadened the L visa program.

Congress split the "L-1" into two subcategories: L-1A visas are for executives and managers transferring to existing offices in the U.S. or seeking to establish new ones. L-1B visas are for professional employees with "specialized knowledge" of a company's "product, service, research, equipment, techniques, management, or other interests and its application in international markets, or an advanced level of knowledge or expertise in the organization's processes and procedures."[26]

Certain large multinational companies are eligible to apply for L-1 "blanket petitions" to transfer employees en masse without having to file individual paperwork. The corporations' need for "flexibility" trumped our country's duty to carefully and deliberately scrutinize who enters and conducts business here. There are no centralized databases on how long L-1 visa holders have stayed or how much they've been paid, or how many are actually here at any given time. One immigration lawyer exulted that the L visa was "really a dream visa."[27]

Or a nightmare visa, depending on your perspective.

By 2003, Bloomberg News had dubbed the L visa program a "mainframe-size visa loophole."[28] It's important to emphasize that Indian outsourcing companies aren't the only exploiters here. Their L-1 visa holders are doing contract work for multinational corporations and American companies such as Bank of America, Dell Computer, General Electric, and Merrill Lynch (now part of Bank of America).[29] Inevitably, con artists and opportunists flocked to L-1 visas as a shortcut around H-1B requirements. As with displaced American workers forced to train their H-1B replacements, Americans displaced by L-1 workers found themselves digging their own graves.

During the Y2K frenzy, an IT firm in Ohio called Manifest sacked American programmers. Contractor Kevin Sherman "taught several dozen Indian workers how to build and maintain computer databases in 1999 and 2000," *USA Today* reported. "He quit rather than take on his next assignment: fixing the newly trained foreigners' broken PCs."[30]

Whistleblower Patricia Fluno, a computer programmer and senior systems analyst in Orlando, Florida, exposed how the scam worked at multinational engineering corporation Siemens—where she and eleven other workers were being forced to train their replacements from one of India's offshore outsourcing giants and top H-1B-dependent users, Tata Consultancy Services, as a condition of their severance packages.

"We are employees in the data processing department (IT) of Siemens ICN at both the Lake Mary and Boca Raton sites," she first wrote Florida GOP Rep. John Mica in 2002 and later testified before the Senate Judiciary Committee in 2003.[31] Her team consisted of fifteen American full-time, salaried programmers and analysts ranging in age from thirties to fifties. After receiving layoff notices, Fluno and her coworkers were ordered by Siemens to show the Tata foreign workers how to do their jobs.[32]

"This was the most humiliating experience of my life," Fluno recalled. The foreign substitutes were paid one-third of the Americans' salaries and circumvented tax laws. More disturbingly, Fluno discovered that Tata was importing the Indian programmers through the L-1 program.[33] "They are not working on Tata's computer systems, but on those of Siemens. In our particular case, Tata knew Americans were being laid off," Fluno explained, "so they didn't use H-1B visas. Instead, they abused the L-1. There are no regulations regarding the misuse of L-1s and only limited penalties for H-1B abuse."[34]

U.S. corporations deny responsibility by shrugging at American workers' complaints as out of their hands. Siemens spokeswoman Paula Davis passed the buck on the company's Dig Your Own Grave treatment of employees replaced by the cheaper foreign replacements from India this way: "They don't work for us. They work for Tata."[35]

Fluno called on Washington to increase monitoring of L-1 visa holders, fine abusers, collect punitive damages for affected American workers, and "enforce the laws we already have." She asked a question that all American taxpayers and workers should be asking: *"What is happening here?"*

Mike Emmons, a Siemens contractor who had consulted for the company for six years, also stepped forward to expose how so-called specialized workers with L-1Bs were "just average [skilled] people."[36] Emmons witnessed one of his replacements "reading the introductory textbook to using the database language—a skill level well below what an L-1 visa purportedly requires."[37] He shared with Congress how one Tata employee told displaced American workers at Siemens that the L-1Bs made "$3,000 per month. Of that $2,000 is paid as expenses to work in the USA and $1,000 paid in Indian rupees. They get $24,000/year tax free to work in the USA while tax-paying Americans go to the unemployment line."[38] Emmons disclosed "knowledge transition" documents from Tata detailing how Americans trained their replacements—and he blasted grandstanding politicians who bemoaned American workers' lack of skills:

> Congress continues to spout out that Americans need to get retrained. We're training our competition to take our jobs. And our Congress allows this because Corporations want cheap labor and Congress wants corporate campaign donations.
>
> I've read in the news where [revolving-door immigration lobbyist] Harris Miller has stated Siemens is an isolated case. That is so very far from the truth. Siemens is in the news because I chose to not give up, because I chose to be blackballed from the industry, but I, Mike Emmons, am one proud American that has stood up for millions of Americans being shortchanged by our government's cheap labor policies.[39]

Peter Bennett, a former computer programmer in Northern California, started documenting the trend in his region. L-1s "seem to be sprouting up all over the Bay Area, and they're totally off the radar screen," he told the *San Francisco Chronicle*. Through his website tracking H-1B abuse, he reported receiving between fifty and five hundred emails a day from tech professionals, many of whom shared stories of L-1 workers turning up at their offices as layoffs and terminations loomed.[40]

Workers at the Indiana Department of Workforce Development got their own wake-up call in 2003 when the state job training agency announced plans to import sixty-five Indian IT workers through Tata on H-1Bs and L-1 visas.[41] The $15.2 million contract to build a new claims processing system in Java was canceled after word leaked of the questionable procurement process involving the project.[42]

Offended Indian government officials condemned the backlash and whined about American protectionism.[43] Then–Indian prime minister Atal Bihari Vajpayee bemoaned America's lack of a "more liberal regime for the free movement of businessmen and professionals from India to Europe and the U.S."[44] A cursory check of India's own strict requirements for foreign business and employment visa applicants seeking to enter its country[45] — conversion of business and employment visas to other visas is almost impossible, visa holders must register with local police upon arrival, and no change of employer is permitted during the currency of an employment visa, for example[46] — demonstrates how India zealously refuses to live by the liberal immigration policies it sanctimoniously demands of other countries.[47]

"PROJECT DELHI BELLY"

The common refrain from some open-borders expansionists that critics of H-1B, B-1, and L-1 are somehow racist against "brown" people[48] is belied by the testimony of naturalized Americans harmed by the massive foreign guest worker pipelines. Sona Shah immigrated to the U.S. with her parents when she was three; all became proud U.S. citizens. She earned degrees in physics from NYU and mechanical engineering from Stevens Institute of Technology. After graduating, she took a job in 1996 as a programmer with the New York City office of multinational software company Wilco Systems, a subsidiary of Automatic Data Processing, Inc. (cofounded by the late New Jersey Democratic Sen. Frank Lautenberg), which operated as an outsourcing bodyshop for financial service companies. She stepped forward in 2004 to tell Congress about the alphabet soup of visa schemes being used to import cheap foreign labor.

"From almost the day I was hired, I saw that most of Wilco's employees were non-immigrant guest workers on a bouquet of temporary visas including H1, L1, J1, F1 and even visitor and training visas," she reported. "I witnessed firsthand the degradation of the workforce, foreign and domestic, enabled by these unregulated visa programs."[49]

Shah was dispatched to London for training, then asked by her boss to travel to India to recruit Indians for the New York office because, as he told her, "Americans don't make quality workers, they are stupid, expensive and difficult to control." An appalled Shah refused and was stripped of her job opportunities.

"Around this time I also learned that Wilco had named this Indian recruitment program, 'Project Delhi Belly,'" she recounted. "Delhi Belly is a derogatory term coined by the British during their occupation of India. If a British officer arrived in India and got diarrhea it was called getting a 'Delhi Belly.' Wilco management thought calling their Indian recruitment effort the equivalent of 'Project Diarrhea' was appropriate. Management distributed memos entitled 'Project Delhi Belly Task List,' which detailed the systematic process of bringing Indian programmers to New York City."

Shah detailed how thirty to forty U.S. workers were kept on staff as "window dressing" so Wilco could meet domestic employment thresholds required of H-1B dependent companies. After being replaced by cheaper H-1Bs on three separate projects, Shah was fired in 1998. A colleague of hers, H-1B worker Kai Barrett (originally from Britain) joined her in filing a federal class-action lawsuit and a state lawsuit in New York, claiming discrimination based on citizenship and immigration status.[50]

Shah framed the issue with perfect clarity for the sellouts and the spin brigade working to preserve the status quo: "This is not an issue of Indians vs. Americans," she testified. "This is not about being anti-Indian or anti-immigration. This is about reforming corporate abuse of unregulated visa programs that are out of control."

Shah filed a lawsuit over this H-1B visa abuse. The case was dismissed in 2000 because the court held that Congress intended H-1B abuse to be policed by administrative agencies and that there was no legal cause of action to bring a suit for H-1B abuse in the federal courts.[51] Today the case of *Shah* v. *Wilco Systems*, which was dismissed in 2000, is widely cited for the proposition that Americans have no remedy in the courts when they are the victims of employer violations of the H-1B and L-1 programs.[52]

"TOOTHLESS" REFORM

Between 1995 and 2000, the number of approved L-1 petitions doubled to nearly sixty thousand per year.[53] The DHS inspector general reported that from 1999 to 2004, nine of the top ten L-1 petitioners were computer- and IT-related offshore outsourcing firms. (They were Tata Consultancy, Cognizant Technology Solutions, Wipro Technologies, Hewlett-Packard, I-FlexSolutions, IBM Global Services, Information Systems Technology, Syntel Incorporated, and Satyam Computer Services. Honda Motor Co. was the only non-IT-related company on the list.)[54]

The DHS IG analysis further reported that nearly 50 percent of L-1B "specialized knowledge" worker visa petitions submitted in 2005 named Indian beneficiaries—far outpacing any other nation.[55]

After individual workers, professional associations such as the

Programmers Guild, and some labor groups such as Seattle's WashTech all raised hell, Capitol Hill finally started paying attention. Congress passed and President George W. Bush signed the L-1 Visa Reform Act of 2004 to address (or rather, mute) their concerns.[56] The law prohibited L-1 visas if applicants were to be "controlled and supervised principally" by an "unaffiliated employer" and if the visa seeker was planning to enter an "arrangement to provide labor for hire" for an unaffiliated employer, "rather than a placement in connection with the provision of a product or service for which specialized knowledge specific to the petitioning employer is necessary."

But the restrictions on "third-party" L-1 workers and blanket petition abuse were watered down, beside the point, or easily bypassed. No cap on L-1 visas was imposed. Calls for more stringent application requirements were ignored.

Indian media outlets couldn't help but gloat that "Indian software circles" were scoffing at the reforms as "relatively toothless."[57] Smug Indian IT companies felt confident the new rules would not "cramp their style," the *Economic Times of India* reported.[58] "Given that the 'reform' is only 'skin deep,' big companies are not worried."[59]

It should be noted that Rep. Mica, whom the displaced Siemens workers in Florida had turned to, was one of the top recipients of Siemens campaign cash,[60] and that the Senate sponsor of the L-1 "reform" bill, Georgia GOP Rep. Saxby Chambliss, ultimately championed the program as an "important tool" for multinational businesses.[61]

In other words: It was back-stabbing, double-talking business as usual in the Beltway.

RETURN OF THE RUBBER-STAMPERS

A year after the Kabuki theater L-1 "reforms" were adopted, the DHS inspector general reviewed the program. Put on your shocked faces: Investigators found that it remained "vulnerable in several respects."[62]

As we've shown you time and again, that result is by design, not accident.

Adjudicators told the IG staff that it was difficult to verify whether L-1 transferees were truly being used in the capacity their corporate sponsors claimed. They had trouble substantiating the credibility of petitioning firms overseas. The blanket petition process was still ripe for abuse. Rank-and-file DHS staff also warned that "specialized knowledge" L-1B workers were defined so broadly that they believed they had "little choice but to approve almost all petitions," resulting in "displacement of American workers."

Translation: More of the same old rubber-stamping machine.

Sens. Charles Grassley and Dick Durbin continued to press for more disclosure of L-1 visa use by top H-1B-dependent firms. In 2007, they obtained and published an extensive list of the top L-1 visa users.[63] Their analysis found that of the top twenty L visa users, many were Indian IT outsourcers that also happened to be among the top H-1B users.[64]

"I find it hard to believe that any one company has that many individuals that are legitimately being transferred within a single year," Sen. Durbin said after releasing data. "I find it even harder to believe that these L visas are being used appropriately when many of the same companies are some of the largest employers of H-1B workers."[65]

It "certainly makes one wonder if companies are using the L visa to circumvent the worker protections required under the H-1B program," added Sen. Charles Grassley. "I'd like to know how many American workers these companies hire compared to the number of foreign workers they bring in."

The top user of combined H-1Bs and L-1s at that time? Tata with nearly 8,000 applications filed in 2006, 4,887 of which were L-1s.

From 2009 to 2014, the U.S. has handed out an average of 68,000 L-1 visas each year—up from about 20,000 per year in the early 1990s.[66]

Ron Hira estimates that the current "stock of L-1 workers is likely to be in the neighborhood of 300,000"—in addition to upward of 200,000 spouses on L-2 visas also working in the U.S. labor market.[67]

FIGURE 8.1 [68] **L-1 VISAS ISSUED**

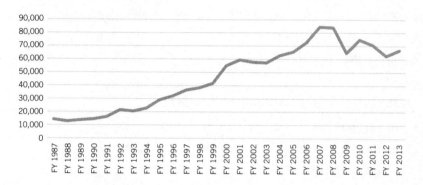

FOREIGN TECH WORKERS FOR $1.21 AN HOUR

In the fall of 2014, after fielding an anonymous tip, the U.S. Department of Labor announced the results of an investigation into Electronics for Imaging (EFI), a printing technology company in Fremont, California.[69] The agency found that the Silicon Valley employer had "paid as little as $1.21 per hour in Indian rupees to employees brought in temporarily from India to work at the company's U.S. headquarters"[70] to install computers. The employees came from Bangalore, India, through the L-1 program.[71] EFI failed to pay California minimum wage and overtime compensation to several employees, some of whom worked as many as 122 hours per week.[72] Shocked bureaucrats lectured that "business owners need to understand that when they bring employees here to the United States to work, they must pay them in accordance with U.S. labor laws."[73]

Once again, what's legal is as disturbing as what's illegal. The Employment Policy Institute's Daniel Costa pointed out[74] that even if EFI had paid the $8 an hour minimum wage, it "would have been compliant with immigration and labor laws, even though the average hourly wage in Fremont for a worker who installs or repairs computers is $19.[75] If that worker is configuring the network as well, it's $45."[76]

EFI paid piddly back wages of $40,000 to eight workers and dismissed its systemic importation of underpaid, average-skilled L-1 workers as an "administrative error."[77] In 2014, the publicly traded company pulled in total "record revenue" of nearly $800 million.[78]

"AMERICA IS PROUDLY OPEN FOR BUSINESS"

Unfortunately the EFI debacle did little to slow down Big Tech's L-1 expansion juggernaut. The U.S. Chamber of Commerce and Indian outsourcing companies wrote an open letter to the White House in 2012 whining about "delays," "denials," and "significant costs" due to increased scrutiny of L-1 applications from India.[79] Oh, the horrible inconvenience of immigration officials doing more than just rubber-stamping and fast-tracking every last guest worker application! The gall!

Among the signatories joining the Chamber in pressuring President Obama and then–USCIS director Alejandro Mayorkas to broaden, rather than restrict, the definition of what constitutes an L-1B "specialized worker": Accenture, the American Council on International Personnel, the American Immigration Lawyers Association, Boeing, Cargill, Caterpillar, Cognizant, Deloitte, eBay, GE, Hewlett-Packard, Intel, Intuit, Microsoft Corporation Oracle, Tata, Texas Instruments, and Wipro.[80]

Ignoring years of firsthand testimony by displaced American workers, these corporations, their front groups, and their immigration lawyers decried high denial rates of L-1B petitions from India.[81] The expansionist National Foundation for American Policy released widely disseminated statistics showing that about 35 percent of L-1 visa applications are rejected, and of that number, 56 percent of the applications from Indian nationals were denied.[82]

Rather than show alarm at high levels of rejection as red flags for the same kind of historic fraud that has riddled B-1, EB-5, and H-1B, Big Tech groups smugly challenged the "training, supervision, and procedures" of the career civil servants adjudicating petitions.[83] Then they pointed to upticks in "requests for evidence" as de facto evidence of wrongdoing without providing any of their own evidence that the decisions were unwarranted.

While the D.C. open-borders lobbyists brayed repeatedly about the need to protect U.S. "competitiveness," enhance foreign "investments," and head off the mythical American tech worker shortage, they could not cite specifics on the exact occupations in which L-1 and L-2 workers are employed. That's because, as the Employment Policy Institute observed, the State Department and USCIS do not release that data. The Department of Professional Employees division of the AFL-CIO accurately described L-1B as a "black box."[84] The program "is not a long-term investment in the U.S. economy since only a small fraction of L-1B visa beneficiaries will be sponsored by their employers to stay in the U.S. permanently." Moreover, the group summed up for lawmakers, the "L-1B visa is really about businesses having ready access to a powerless, low-wage workforce."

No matter. DHS brass plowed ahead with a fifteen-page "draft memo" offering "guidance" to out-of-line adjudicators who did not properly respect the need to indulge corporate "partners" demanding that government cater to the "fluid dynamics of the twenty-first-century business world."[85] The document laid out its broad criteria for how L-1B visa holders can qualify by possessing either "special" or "advanced" knowledge of a company's products and procedures—which doesn't need to be proprietary, unique, or narrowly held with the employer's organization.

The *Washington Examiner*'s Byron York further reported on the memo's lowered standards of judgment. "An applicant, or petitioner, does not have to prove that there is a need for an L-1B worker. Instead, he just has to make a case that an adjudicator can decide is 'probably' true."[86] Indeed, the new, backroom-crafted rules assert:

> Even if an officer has some doubt about a claim, the petitioner will have satisfied the standard of proof if it submits relevant, probative, and credible evidence . . . that leads to the conclusion that the claim is "more likely than not" or "probably" true.[87]

As the open-borders *Wall Street Journal* also explained, the March 2015 guidelines advised adjudicators to "be liberal in extending the tenure of existing L-1B visas. The USCIS should deny applications for extensions only if there was some sort of error when the visa was originally issued."[88] After a few months of a token "public feedback period," the memo was scheduled to go into effect in August 2015.

Once again, as we've shown you throughout the book, the guest worker visa liberalizers sold out both skilled American workers *and* dedicated, rank-and-file American immigration enforcement officials trying to police L visa applications.

"The bottom line is this," President Obama crowed upon announcing his latest foreign guest worker expansion by fiat, "America is proudly open for business." By which he means, of course, the entrenched dirty business of screwing over America's best and brightest skilled workers to satisfy the demands of insatiable cheap foreign labor gluttons.

⊶ 9 ⊶

F-1: The Foreign "Student" Visa Ruse (aka Yet Another Cheap Foreign Worker Pipeline)

The Internet is filled with advice for foreign students seeking educational opportunities in America.

"How to get your US student visa," the StudyUSA.com website beckons.[1]

"Easy ways To Get a Student (F-1) Visa for America," an online immigration guide advertises.[2]

"Student Visa Tips from Visa Officers,"[3] a Voice of America story offers.

Growth of the F-1 foreign student visa program has exploded (see Figure 9.1). By FY 2012, the feds estimated that there were nearly 1.2 million foreign students and their dependents living in the U.S.[4] (There are other types of foreign student visas, such as the J cultural exchange visa and M vocational studies visa, but F-1s comprise the vast majority of all foreign students—nearly 80 percent.[5])

FIGURE 9.1[6] **F-1 VISAS APPROVED**

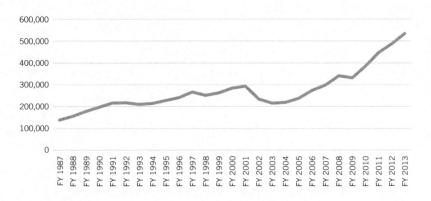

In FY 2013, the State Department reported that it had issued 534,320[7] new F-1 visas.[8] By comparison, in FY 2013 the State Department issued 153,223 new H-1B visas and 66,700 L-1 visas.

Despite requiring foreign students to demonstrate they intend to go home after their studies are complete,[9] you'll remember that America still has no way of tracking whether visa holders actually have gone home after their visas expire. Our government simply does not know how many illegal alien student visa overstayers are currently in the country.

The origins of the foreign student visa program[10] can be traced to the advocacy efforts of the Institute for International Education (IIE)—founded by Nobel Peace Prize laureates to foster cultural exchange—and its successor organizations, the National Association of Foreign Student Advisers/the Association of International Educators (NAFSA), and the Council on International Educational Exchange (CIEE). Among IIE's early activities: lobbying for establishment of the foreign student visa, designing the visa application form for the State Department,[11] founding the Fulbright Program, countering Axis propaganda, and reconstructing European universities destroyed by war.[12]

The noble idea of educating international students and exposing them to American culture to "foster understanding" and "peace" rested on those students' *returning* to their homelands after graduation to share their positive experiences and apply what they had learned to improve their own countries. But over the years, the F-1 program morphed into conduits that are entirely different from its original mission. It has become a massive cash cow for American higher ed and schlocky Internet consultants selling their tips and advice on getting in; a convenient avenue for illegal aliens; and yet another foreign worker pipeline for corporations. (Sen. Bob Menendez [D-N.J.] allegedly found yet another way to abuse the F-1 student visa program, according a federal indictment in April 2015—as a conduit for the Brazilian supermodel girlfriend of one of his high-flying donors. We like to call it the 36DD visa program.[13])

Immigration expansionists and Big Tech lobbyists often complain about how difficult it is for foreign students to work in the U.S. and become permanent residents and eventual citizens. A writer for the liberal *New Republic* called it "Kafka-esque" and bemoaned the plight of foreign students "who study in American universities and who are kicked out before they have a chance to work in or contribute to U.S. society."[14]

Pardon us for not breaking out a box of Kleenex. It's *supposed* to be difficult. We repeat: The original intent of the F-1 program was to invest in foreign students' education in order to benefit America by creating goodwill ambassadors who return to their home countries, not to create cheap workers for U.S. companies. The tech lobby argues that since we educate F-1 students, we shouldn't send them home.[15] Yet every foreign student is required to certify, as a condition of admission, that:

I seek to enter or remain in the United States temporarily, and solely for the purpose of pursuing a full course of study at the school named on page 1 of this form.[16]

Oblivious to the original purpose of the F-1 program, Salesforce CEO Marc Benioff (net worth: $3.6 billion) tweeted a chart contrasting explosive growth in F-1 visas with H-1B visas, which have not grown during the last decade. The title of the chart: "Hit the book, then the road."

"When will our government learn we need more [H-1B] visas?" Benioff asked. "@BarackObama this is holding our economy back! Amazing chart!"[17]

Benioff appears to be implying that a large percentage of foreign students are returning to their home countries after graduating because they are unable to obtain H-1B visas. But despite the sound and fury over heartless Americans ejecting foreign students from their shores, the *New York Times* reported in 2013 that the return rates for foreign students from China and India studying in U.S. graduate schools was "shockingly low." In fact, "approximately 92 percent of all Chinese who received a science or technology Ph.D. in the U.S. in 2002 were still in the U.S. in 2007. This rate was well above India's, which is in second place with 81 percent."[18]

So "temporarily" and "solely for the purpose" now effectively mean "permanently" and "tangentially for the purpose" of studying.

Both Democrats and Republicans in Washington, at the behest of Microsoft and other industry lobbyists, espouse a plan to "staple green cards" to the diplomas of foreign students. Mitt Romney promised during the 2012 presidential campaign: "I'd staple a green card to the diploma of someone who gets an advanced degree in America."[19] Not to be outdone by the GOP, the White House issued a position paper emphasizing that President Obama "supports . . . stapling a green card to the diplomas of science, technology, engineering and mathematics (STEM), PhDs and select STEM Masters."[20] Romney and Obama echoed a TechNet executive council member who asserted: "The issues are common sense. I haven't met anyone from either party who thought it was a bad idea to staple a green card to the diploma to a kid who graduates from the University of Illinois with a STEM diploma.[21]

So, Mr. Tech Lobbyist hasn't met anyone who disagrees? These people need to get out more.

Imagine if universities could confer automatic green cards along with diplomas. Foreign students would flood for-profit universities devising innumerable ways to exploit this bottomless source of tuition income.

Imagine quickie master's degrees and programs to convert foreign degrees into American degrees. Public universities would undoubtedly join in as well. The expectation of receiving a green card would attract more foreign students paying full tuition. The universities would have a financial incentive to pass over American students who need financial aid. Unrealistic, you say? The California State University system already created a storm of controversy when plans leaked in 2012 detailing how administrators intended to bar in-state graduate students in favor of full-tuition-paying foreign and out-of-state students.[22]

What type of students would be getting green cards stapled to their diplomas? Romney justified his stapling proposal with well-worn rhetoric: "We want the best and brightest to enrich the nation through the jobs and technologies they will help create."[23] If we are truly looking for the "best and brightest," a master's degree from a domestic university such as San Jose State should not necessarily receive preference over a PhD from a foreign university such as Oxford.

For that matter, why should an advanced degree be considered the sine qua non of technology prowess? PhDs are great, but many successful tech entrepreneurs, including the late Steve Jobs of Apple, Bill Gates of Microsoft, Larry Ellison of Oracle, Michael Dell of Dell Computer, Mark Zuckerberg of Facebook, Jack Dorsey of Twitter, and Evan Williams of Twitter were college dropouts. Other tech entrepreneurs, like Sean Parker of Napster and David Karp of Tumblr, never even attended college. Under the green-card-stapling plan, the best and brightest foreign wunderkinds who don't happen to have advanced degrees would be given lower standing than, say, a master's degree holder who finished at the bottom of his class at DeVry University.

There's another more basic problem with proposals to attach instant green cards to the diplomas of F-1 foreign students. The F-1 program in and of itself has become an unmanageable, fraud-riddled, and national-security-endangering mess.

THE ABCS OF F-1

There are about ten thousand educational institutions accredited by the federal government's Student and Exchange Visitor Program[24] (SEVP) to accept foreign students.[25] Oversight is lax. Incentives to police F-1 holders are weak, despite several high-profile terrorism cases involving student visa violators (including the 1993 World Trade Center bombing,[26] the Times Square bombing plot,[27] the Boston Marathon bombing,[28] and the 9/11 attacks[29]).

One immigration lawyer explained: "Usually, schools have only one person monitoring student visas. . . . There's also a conflict of interest. Schools are in the business of making money and by rounding up students and sending them back, they don't make any."[30] Indeed, universities and colleges raked in an estimated $21.8 billion in tuition in 2012 from foreign students, who must pay full price as a condition of their visas.[31] The F-1 magnet has also attracted unscrupulous operators who've formed illicit visa mills by creating sham universities.

To qualify for the F-1 visa program, an applicant must be a full-time student enrolled "at an accredited college, university, seminary, conservatory, academic high school, elementary school, or other academic institution or in a language training program" in a "program or course of study that culminates in a degree, diploma, or certificate."[32] How rigorous are federal accreditation standards? The *Wall Street*

Journal described it as a "useless process" in which "almost no institution misses the mark."[33] Approved schools include "beauty academies" and career training programs. F-1 visa applicants must demonstrate full, financial self-proficiency over the entire proposed course of their studies and convince consular officials that they have every intention of returning home.

After gaining admission to an accredited school, the institution issues an I-20 form certifying that the student is eligible for a foreign student visa. Critical data on students and schools is supposed to be entered and updated in the Student and Exchange Visitor Information System (SEVIS) database.[34]

There is no cap on the number of F-1s issued. There are no wage or labor protections because these "students" are not supposed to be guest workers. Moreover, F-1 visa holders are exempt from paying Federal Insurance Contributions Act (FICA) taxes for Social Security and Medicare.[35] These foreign students may not work off-campus during the first academic year, but after that, they have several off-campus employment options involving part-time or full-time work that are supposed to enhance their educational experiences with limited "practical training." F-1 holders can secure "Optional Practical Training" (OPT) for twelve months at the undergraduate, graduate, and postgraduate levels during and after graduation. Science, technology, engineering, and mathematics (STEM) students can apply for an additional seventeen-month, postcompletion work program.[36] (We'll go into further detail on this progam's expansion and abuse in Chapter 11.)

A 2014 analysis[37] of the foreign student visa program by Neil Ruiz of the Brookings Institution, who favors liberalization and expansion,[38] found that two-thirds of foreign students pursuing a bachelor's or higher degree are in STEM fields.[39] Ruiz reported that 45 percent of foreign students extended their visas through OPT to work in the same metropolitan areas as their colleges or universities. Of the top twenty foreign hometowns for F-1 students, six were located in China and five were in India.[40]

The top Indian city sending F-1s to America was the tech hub of Hyderabad. Yes, that's the same Hyderabad we've told you about that was identified by consulate officials as a hotbed of immigration-related fraud. Hyderabad was also the top source of all foreign STEM students to the U.S. (20,800). Of those, the Brookings study noted, "The vast majority were studying for computer and information sciences (9,100) and engineering (8,800) degrees."[41]

You'll never believe what happened next. Except, of course, you will.

F IS FOR FRAUD: THE VISA AND DIPLOMA MILL FRENZY

With thousands of schools across the country accepting hundreds of thousands of new foreign students every year, and usually just a few, but no more than ten, "designated school officials" (DSOs) at any one school overseeing enrollment, recordkeeping, and compliance,[42] slipping through the cracks isn't just a bug of the F-1 system. It's a feature.

Despite repeated warnings by the Department of Homeland Security's Counterterrorism and Criminal Exploitation Unit (CTCEU), which tracks, coordinates, and oversees school fraud investigations, U.S. Immigration and Customs Enforcement (ICE) officials in charge of the Student and Exchange Visitor Program (SEVP) have neglected to institute the most basic risk management measures and controls. A damning 2012 Government Accountability Office report documented repeated and systemic failures to verify schools' legitimacy and eligibility;[43] "consistently verify certain evidence initially submitted by schools in lieu of accreditation"; and maintain records to document SEVP-certified schools' continued compliance.

SEVP officials did not bother to evaluate program data on prior and suspected instances of school fraud and noncompliance. They showed little interest in obtaining or analyzing information gathered by CTCEU criminal investigators. The GAO also noted that DSOs are not subject to criminal background checks and that SEVP administrators had ignored repeated warnings about the security risks of granting DSOs access to the SEVIS database.

"According to investigators at three of the eight field offices we interviewed," the GAO team informed Congress, "SEVP allowed designated school officials to maintain SEVIS access and the ability to modify records in the system while being the subject of an ongoing criminal investigation, despite requests from CTCEU to terminate SEVIS access for these officials." [44]

Center for Immigration Studies analyst David North found that despite SEVP bureaucrats' complaints about lack of funding, the agency "consistently refuses to spend money allocated to it, and refuses to raise the fees that would solve its own funding problems." [45] The vast majority of the program's enforcement budget comes from SEVP fees paid by the foreign students. Yet, North pointed out, officials had used "only portions of it; at the end of FY 2012 it had an estimated $135 million in surplus, more than enough to fund a year's activities. Further, it can raise substantial additional funds without using a penny of taxpayer money." [46]

Several high-profile prosecutions of "visa mill" and "diploma mill" operators have garnered headlines during the past several years. But these cases undoubtedly represent the tip of the foreign student visa fraud iceberg. Given the intransigent apathy and negligence endemic in Washington, it's fair to conclude that any meaningful enforcement happens *in spite* of F-1 administrators, not because of them.

Florida Language Institute (FLI). At the federally certified Florida Language Institute (FLI), located in a Miami strip mall, foreign nationals who had been issued I-20 forms were not required to attend classes. Between 2007 and 2010, hundreds of the documents were issued fraudulently as FLI's owner Lydia Menocal raked in six hundred thousand dollars in fees. Menocal received a fifteen-month prison sentence and two years of supervised release, a five-hundred-thousand-dollar fine, and a forfeiture order of all the ill-gotten gains and property related to the scam. The scheme would not have been detected but for an informant who tipped off the feds.[47]

California Union University. At the federally certified California Union University, run by Korean pastor Samuel Chai Cho Oh in Fullerton, California, foreign students from twenty different nations (primarily from South Korea) paid Oh fees ranging from six hundred dollars to more than ten thousand dollars for documentation enabling the students to fraudulently obtain visas. Many received bogus degrees at staged graduation ceremonies, despite the fact that they never attended class. Oh laundered the money through a church and a Chinese restaurant. In 2011, Oh was sentenced to a year in prison and twelve months in home confinement. He forfeited $418,000 in proceeds from the racket and property and assets worth nearly $5 million.[48] The scheme would not have been detected but for an informant who tipped off the feds.

College Prep Academy. Here's an example of the literal prostitution of the F-1 program. In Duluth, Georgia, Dong Seok Yi headed up College Prep Academy (CPA), purportedly an English language school. In 2009, Yi filed an application with DHS/SEVP and obtained approval for his "academy" to enroll foreign students and issue I-20 forms. Along with two codefendants, Yi cooked up documents to facilitate F-1 visa issuances—not to students, but to bar girls. The "academy" conspired in the sex-trafficking scheme with a Korean businessman who owned "room salons"—notorious brothels popular in South Korea and the U.S.[49]

CPA's "academic director" arranged for another woman to supply fake transcripts, bank statements, and other false documents to the "students." Yi and CPA "profited by charging thousands in quarterly tuition payments for maintaining the immigrant on the student rolls," federal prosecutors showed. Yi was sentenced to one year and nine months in prison, and ordered to forfeit nearly thirty-seven thousand dollars from bank accounts associated with his criminal enterprise.[50]

Herguan University. This Sunnyvale, California, school, which claims to have enrolled 450 students, is headed by CEO Jerry Wang. In March 2011, a *Chronicle of Higher Education* reporter described a visit to the "eerily unoccupied" campus—a two-story office building with "mazelike hallways of unused classrooms, very little furniture, and a library with mostly empty shelves."[51] Unlike FLI and California Union, Herguan was not officially accredited to enroll F-1 students. Instead, Wang had successfully presented alternative credentials to the feds. Unaccredited schools can get on the SEVP list of acceptable programs if they provide testaments from three accredited schools that they have accepted or will accept the unaccredited school's academic credits. The *Chronicle of Higher Education*, however, interviewed representatives of two colleges who said Herguan had falsified letters from their schools claiming that they accepted Herguan's academic credits.

In August 2012, more than a year after the *Chronicle of Higher Education* and Northern California newspapers had raised questions about the educational institution's operations, accreditation, and CPT program,[52] ICE raided Herguan University's offices. Wang was indicted on fifteen fraud, identity theft, forgery, and conspiracy charges.[53] He is accused of providing phony visa documents in exchange for "tuition and other payments" from foreign students. He denies any wrongdoing and pleaded not guilty to all charges.

ICE officials initially served notice that the agency intended to withdraw the school's SEVP approval, but then immediately changed its mind as a result of a supposed legal snafu.[54] Meanwhile, Herguan officials have been quite busy trying to gain access, influence, and immunity. The *San Jose Mercury News* reported in February 2013 that the school sent campaign contributions "to state lawmakers Jim Beall, D-San Jose, and Paul Fong, D-Mountain View, as well as congressional Democrats Mike Honda, Zoe Lofgren, and Judy Chu, of Pasadena"—as well as paying former Santa Clara County supervisor George Shirakawa "between $1,000 and $10,000" for "consultant services" in the same eighteen-month time period that DHS was secretly investigating Herguan.[55]

As the case drags on, Herguan University remains open for business and Wang is free on bond awaiting trial.

Tri-Valley University. Mechanical engineer Susan Xiao-Ping Su stole a page from Herguan University, where she had served as an adjunct faculty member and lecturer. She founded Tri-Valley University just down the road from Herguan's "campus" and successfully presented alternative credentials to the feds in order to get her own ball rolling. Like Herguan's Wang, Su claimed that academic credits from her school had been accepted by three other accredited colleges. But as the *Chronicle of Higher Education* reported, "Federal officials did not find out until more than a year after it approved Tri-Valley in 2009 that two of those three colleges denied ever having had such agreements."[56]

Tri-Valley's website should have been a bright red flag to anyone not snoozing over at SEVP. Riddled with errors and misstatements about its faculty and professional associations, Tri-Valley claimed its mission "was to make Christian scientists, engineers, business leaders and lawyers for the glory of God."[57] In reality, Su oversaw an "elaborate fraud scheme"[58] in which she charged fifteen hundred students (mostly from India) millions of dollars for fraudulent, visa-related documents. All told, Su pulled in more than $5.6 million through her operation of Tri-Valley University and laundered the money to purchase "commercial real estate, a Mercedes Benz car, and multiple residences, including a mansion on the Ruby Hill Golf Club in Pleasanton."[59]

Prospective foreign students on Internet immigration forums had warned other visa-seekers in 2010 that Tri-Valley's accreditation claims were suspect and that the school was violating federal rules against offering its full course load online.[60] (F-1 rules require foreign students to attend class full-time and limit online classes to one per academic term.) But the scam went undetected until informants tipped off ICE.

A federal court found Su guilty on thirty-one counts of fraud arising from the Tri-Valley sham.[61] The school was finally shut down, and in November 2014 Su was sentenced to sixteen years in jail and ordered to forfeit $5.6 million and to pay more than nine hundred thousand dollars in restitution.[62] Tatum King, acting special agent in charge for ICE's Homeland Security Investigations (HSI) office in San Francisco, remarked after sentencing: "Our message is simple—America's legal immigration system is not for sale and HSI will move aggressively against those who compromise the integrity of that system and put our country's security at risk simply to turn a profit."[63]

What about the students? Were they victims or co-conspirators? The Indian government threw a public tantrum when law enforcement officials radio-tagged some of the "duped" F-1s with ankle bracelets to monitor their movements.[64] But there was plenty of evidence of complicity.[65] Investigators had discovered, for example, that more than 550 of the foreign "students" were all recorded in the university's data system as living in a two-bedroom apartment in Sunnyvale—"allegedly to conceal that most of the students did not actually live in California at all."[66]

Instead, the "students" worked across the country, from Maryland, Virginia, and Pennsylvania to Texas and Oklahoma under the "Curricular Practical Training" (CPT) program. Their supposed "career" training was taking place in low-wage retail jobs at dollar stores, 7-Elevens, and a tobacco shop. CPT, as we noted earlier, is supposed to relate to the F-1 students' majors and official programs of study.

Indian students were specifically attracted to Tri-Valley because of its law-breaking promise to allow students to go straight to work anywhere on CPT without having to relocate to the campus or take exams in person.

One recruiter promised on an immigration forum:

University name is Trivalley university, it is located at pleasanton, california. here classes are online so you don't have to relocate, university offers CPT so you can work legally 40 hours as full time. they charge only $100 (Rs. 4,700) for CPT . . . you don't have to worry about the course work, they will give you good grades. By using CPT you can work full time so we will help you in your desired software technology.[67]

Another Tri-Valley promoter exulted: "no tests, no mandatory online classes, a perfect way to bypass the visa process!"[68]

Many of the "students" also participated in what the *San Jose Mercury News* described as a "profit-sharing system that gave students who referred newcomers from abroad a 20 percent cut of the tuition."[69] The commission was "lucrative," the *Times of India* acknowledged. Knowledgeable Indian observers detected the odor of complicity upon learning that the vast majority of the sham school's "students" came from the Andhra Pradesh region. One honest Indian journalist concluded that "eager beavers looking for a short cut to emigrating to the US through a questionable academic route ignored the red flags."[70] "They knew what they were up to," wrote one commenter. "Many of them were aware of the fact that university was fake. They just wanted to land there to do jobs and not study," wrote another.[71]

According to Indian media, students from visa-scamming hotbed Hyderabad obtained phony I-20 forms from Tri-Valley and presented them to U.S. consular officials in both Hyderabad and Chennai who "failed to detect the fraud." [72] In addition, many Indians chose to transfer to Tri-Valley after entering legitimate universities and obtaining legal I-20 forms that would not risk raising eyebrows among SEVP officials (not that they were paying attention).

One Indian blogger based in Pleasanton, California, blasted the "whining" by the Indian government and phony students caught up in the prosecution:

> Do I sound unsympathetic? That's because I am. I have plenty of friends and relatives who all struggled to get here on F1 visas. They did it the right way. They scrimped and saved and took the GRE/GMAT and applied to Universities and got transcripts and recommendation letters and stood in line to meet unsympathetic Visa officers and sweated and waited till they got their F1s. . . .
>
> I know this because I also got here the hard way—the legal way . . . I have had to live hundreds of miles apart from my son because I was on a work visa with a completely unyielding employer, to whom I was more or less indentured due to the immigration process and my conviction that everything needed to be done the right way . . . I know that however hard I work, I will NEVER own a home in Ruby Hill. So I have no sympathy for either Susan Su or the students—both thought they could get away with it. [73]

International Technological University. The Brookings Institution study on international students found that Tri-Valley and Herguan were two of the top five destination schools of F-1 students from India's tech visa fraud hub, Hyderabad. The largest was San Jose's International Technological University, "a non-profit accredited Master's Medium-Sized College with no research activity." [74] According to the

San Jose Mercury News, ITU was initially unaccredited and submitted letters in the same manner that Tri-Valley and Herguan had, which claimed its credits were accepted at San Jose State, Santa Clara, Stanford University, and the University of California system. Those colleges all denied to the *Mercury News* that they had vouched for ITU.[75]

Another similarity between ITU, Herguan, and Tri-Valley University: the enticement of quick, easy Curricular Practical Training (CPT). The *Chronicle of Higher Education* reported in 2011 that ITU lifted itself out of near-bankruptcy by "promising foreign students that they could work full-time jobs off-campus as soon as they arrived. They also offered existing students a $500 tuition rebate for each new student they referred. Business took off."[76] Enrollment skyrocketed from eighteen students in 2006 to nearly fifteen hundred today—the vast majority from India. School officials' salaries appear to have skyrocketed, too. In 2009, ITU's provost earned $445,832, "more than was earned by the provosts of Yale, Brown, or Berkeley," the *Chronicle of Higher Education* reported.

Internet forums in 2012 featured foreign workers looking to obtain the employment benefits offered by ITU without having to attend classes or earn a degree. The school offered an "unusual schedule," the *Chronicle of Higher Education* noted, with classes held only three weekends per semester, all day Saturday and Sunday. "That allows some of them to work full-time jobs in New York, Ohio, and other states and fly back to California when needed. They earn academic credit for the jobs, as well as the classes, and ITU considers them full-time students."[77]

One foreigner seeking advice about the school wrote:

"I am considering, enrolling in ITU to get the CPT. Do they really give CPT right away, as they state? And should I get my

F1 visa from the university itself. I hear the university not accrediated [*sic*].

Does that really affect me as i am only interested in CPT, not any degree?"[78]

Another ITU student, Prasath Koinaka, was recorded as having attended class on the same day he was killed in a robbery at a convenience store where he worked in Oklahoma City (presumably on CPT)—fifteen hundred miles from ITU's "campus."[79]

Despite the negative publicity and suspicions raised by the *Chronicle of Higher Education* and *Mercury News*, the mainstream Western Association of Schools and Colleges granted ITU accreditation in February 2013,[80] which the school touts as "particularly prestigious."[81] WASC then curiously backdated the accreditation to December 2012.[82]

"Expert staff members" are standing by to ensure that applicants follow their "easy steps for acquiring a student visa."[83] Meanwhile, an anonymous Google reviewer warned in February 2015: "Greediness or quench for money never ends. . . . Overall, my experience with ITU was horrible. . . . It's [a] huge rip off and risky."[84]

University of Northern Virginia. This strip-mall school in the D.C. suburb of Annandale, Virginia, was founded in 1998 and quickly attracted the usual Indian student clientele. It became one of the top destination sites of F-1 visa beneficiaries from Hyderabad, along with Tri-Valley, Herguan, and ITU. From its inception, UNVA founder Daniel Ho and his shady venture ran into regulatory problems. Once again, however, it wasn't ICE/SEVP watchdogs who sniffed out the scam. This time, it was an independent accreditation group, the government of Singapore, and state officials in Virginia who did the heavy lifting.

The Accrediting Council for Independent Colleges and Schools

(ACICS), which is one of the oldest and largest independent national accrediting organizations of degree-granting institutions recognized by the U.S. Department of Education, had initially approved UNVA. But beginning in 2007, ACICS discovered a raft of irregularities at the school, including lack of evidence the administration reviewed its distance education faculty, evaluated staff members, and maintained proper student or faculty transcripts.[85] After failing audits and getting entangled in messy battles over its ownership, UNVA saw its ACICS accreditation revoked in 2008.

Soon after, the government of Singapore banned UNVA affiliates from offering degree courses in the country.[86] The State Council for Higher Education in Virginia followed with its own investigation. That agency gave UNVA three years to get its act together, investigative journalist Bre Payton of Watchdog.org reported, and then revoked its certificate to operate in Virginia in 2011 after the school failed four state audits.

Finally, in July 2011, ICE agents raided the university. Two years later, in October 2013, ICE/SEVP withdrew the school's approval for attendance of nonimmigrant students.[87] Information surfaced that UNVA had previously claimed accreditation from a bogus organization whose headquarters address was an auto-body repair shop owned by the chairman of the "school's" board.[88]

Nevertheless, the SEVP pushovers gave in and allowed UNVA to stay open for another two years and legally issue I-20 forms to foreign student visa-seekers.

Instead of concentrating on enhancing academic life, UNVA chancellor David Lee busied himself with a "sex dungeon" that made international headlines in August 2011.[89] He resigned after a gossip site published the "sadomasochistic, suburban sex-dungeon master's" website solicitations "seeking 'attractive submissive' women to 'be part of our poly family. Ideally you will consider yourself a slave or a sub with slave tendencies.'"[90] Indentured servitude, it seems, is quite the fetish with the exploiters of the F-1 program in more ways than one.

Grasping for a lifeline, UNVA owner and president Daniel Ho tried to move the business to South Dakota, but state officials there acted on the scam artists and sued to kick them out after Center for Immigration Studies analyst David North alerted them to UNVA's false claims that it was "authorized by the State of South Dakota" to offer classes."[91] The UNVA building in Minnehaha County had no signs, personnel, or classes. Moreover, South Dakota officials reported, the sham school's "advertisements and brochures display photographs that are implied to be scenes from its facility that are in fact stock photographs."[92]

North reports that UNVA continues to invite former foreign students to pay one hundred dollars to obtain highly coveted extension forms for the Optional Practical Training (OPT) program.[93]

So, what's the deal with this OPT program? How did it come about? Who benefits? And what could it mean for the American workforce and college-age population? If the fraud-fest wrought by H-1B, B-1, EB-5, L-1, and F-1 spiked your blood pressure, you ain't seen nothin' yet.

⊢ 10 ⊢

OPT: Open-Borders Bureaucrats Run Amok

Optional Practical Training (OPT) is entirely the creation of un-elected bureaucrats. This de facto guest worker program first came into existence under Republican president George H. W. Bush, ex-panded under his son George W., and ballooned again under Demo-cratic president Barack Obama. Lawmakers in Washington had no say. The American people had no say. Congress had authorized a brief pilot program allowing work under foreign student visas as part of the 1990 Immigration Act. But lawmakers let it lapse amid concerns that it ran "counter . . . to an affirmative policy of U.S. labor force development," "may have adverse consequences for some U.S. workers," and was "in-consistent with the statutory intent of the F-1 nonimmigrant visa."[1]

But that didn't stop government minions—goaded aggressively by Microsoft honchos and other Big Business lobbyists—from hijacking the F-1 student visa program and manufacturing an entire new pipe-line of cheap foreign labor. Our system of regulation in D.C. gives immigration lobbyists two bites at the apple. First, the open-borders insiders get access to the congressional backrooms where expansionist statutes are crafted. Then, they get to lobby the faceless bureaucrats who create new programs via regulatory fiat. As we showed you, industry lobbyists secured large H-1B visa increases in 1998, 2000, and 2004. By 2007, the national backlash against President Bush's massive amnesty had dampened Capitol Hill's enthusiasm for Big Tech visa giveaways. So when industry lobbyists could not get what they wanted from Congress fast enough, they simply turned to the bureaucrats instead.

And boy, did the bureaucrats deliver.

While the labor protections for American workers under the H-1B program are meager, there are none at all in OPT: no wage floor, no cap, no recruitment or nondisplacement requirements, and virtually no oversight.[2] Basic data collection is so abysmal, the Government Accountability Office found in 2014, that the feds "cannot determine whether students with employment authorization are working in jobs related to their studies and not exceeding regulatory limits on unemployment."[3] The GAO reported that the approval rate for OPT petitions between 2008 and 2013 was a whopping 96 percent.[4]

Unlike American workers, OPT workers are exempt from Social Security and Medicare taxes. Investigators have discovered them working in food services and retail in violation of the requirements that their "practical training" be related to their academic field of study.[5] Employers can pay workers on OPT the minimum wage—or in some cases even nothing.[6] Researchers B. Lindsay Lowell and Johanna Avato estimated that OPT workers are paid 40 percent less than equivalent U.S. workers.[7] And, as Professor Ron Hira observed, many OPT workers attended "obscure universities with dubious credentials"[8] (such as the sham University of Northern Virginia we mentioned above, which had secured 189 OPT extensions).

Professor Hira added that the ever-growing list of OPT-eligible STEM degrees carries "a dubious link to actual STEM occupations." The "STEM" fields included in the OPT program include livestock management, urban forestry, HVAC technician, welding, exercise physiology, digital communications, media/multimedia, animation, econometrics, archeology, developmental and child psychology, pharmacoeconomics, actuarial science, management science, paleontology, and environmental health.

More important, Hira says the list of OPT-eligible fields "does not link the availability of OPT to the real world conditions of the job market for graduates with the listed STEM degrees. Biological sciences are included on the list even though no one can argue that there is a shortage of graduates in biology."[9] Since the STEM worker shortage is a myth (see Chapter 2), it is likely that very few of the fields allowed to participate in OPT are experiencing genuine shortages.

The end result, largely unnoticed by the American public, has been a flood of low-wage F-1 "students" working on OPT (see Figure 10.1). These workers, of course, are in direct competition with Americans.

FIGURE 10.1   NUMBER OF OPT "STUDENTS" APPROVED TO WORK IN THE U.S.

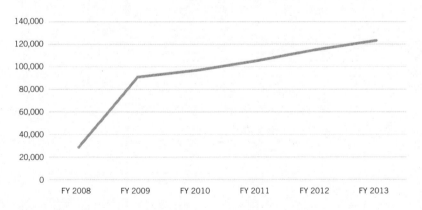

AMERICANS NEED NOT APPLY

U.S. tech companies have become so brazen in their pursuit of this new cheap foreign worker supply that they advertise for OPT workers while explicitly excluding American applicants. Here is a job advertisement posted on IBM's corporate recruiting site in August 2012 for a SAP software job in Boise, Idaho (Figure 10.2). The position was open only to SAP specialists on OPT with "India work authorization." Notice in the headers that the job was filed with the work location given as India, so that Americans searching by location would not find it.

FIGURE 10.2   IBM POSITION IN BOISE, IDAHO, OPEN ONLY TO INDIAN OPT PERMIT HOLDERS

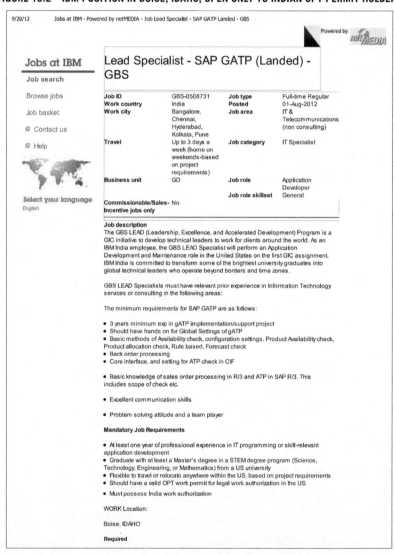

Usually, American companies seeking foreign workers hide behind third-party recruiting agencies to give them deniability. IBM has either grown sloppy or become so arrogant that it presumes no one will notice.

For the most part, companies that advertise that they are looking for foreign workers are little-known labor brokers. Big-name American companies that want cheap foreign labor use these little guys to do their dirty work. Figure 10.3 provides an example of an advertisement

FIGURE 10.3   ENTRY-LEVEL IT OPENINGS FOR OPT, CPT, AND TN WORKERS

Title:	ENTRY LEVEL IT OPENINGS for **OPT** CPT and TN
Skills:	C,C++,SQL
Date:	7-13-2010
Location:	Livonia, MI
Area code:	734
Tax term:	FULLTIME
Pay rate:	55K
Length:	full time
Position ID:	venkat115
Dice ID:	10116652

Job description:
Aim Computer Consulting is a professional IT services company, providing software consulting, development, support, maintenance and training services in a variety of industries. We assist clients in finding simple and timely solutions to business problems. Our Direct Client list includes several Fortune 500 companies like JP Morgan, Ebay, Chase bank, Fannie Mae, General Motors, Ford Motors and Chrysler Automotive.

Entry Level AND experienced candidates having good exposure in programming and database knowledge in any one of the below mentioned technologies.

REQUIREMENTS:

- Have knowledge in databases like in SQL, ORALCE, MYSQL, DB2 and Sybase.
- Have knowledge of any one Programming language like C, C++, C#, .NET... etc.
- Have Masters or Bachelors degree in IT/CS/MIS/Electrical Engg /Mechanical Engg.... etc.
- Be willing to relocate nationwide in the US for projects
- Good communication skills and openness for relocation.
-Willing to learn OR updated skills on any one of the below mentioned technologies.

1. Informatica
2. BizTalk
3. SAS BI

NOTE: We are an E-verified employer so if you are needed in **OPT** extension we would assist you.

If you are any one you know would be interested in making career with us email your updated resume along with write your experience and legal status to venkat@aim-cc.com

If you should have any queries,please feel free to contact me.

Thanks & Regards,

VENKAT
Resource Manager
Aim Computer Consulting
17197 N.Laurel Park Drive
Suite 513|Livonia|MI |48152
Phone: 734-956-9985 x 201
Fax: 734-418-2603
E mail: venkat@aim-cc.com
URL: www.aim-cc.com

Travel required:	100%
Telecommute:	no

Aim Computer Consulting	
Web:	http://www.aim-cc.com

on Dice.com in which a company seems to be looking for foreign IT workers knowledgeable in low-level programming languages C, C++, and SQL. The title of the listing specifies that the openings are for OPT, CPT, or TN workers. (TN visas allow citizens of Canada and Mexico, as NAFTA professionals, to work in the United States for U.S. or foreign employers.) The company placing the advertisement, Aim Computer Consulting, identifies JP Morgan Chase, eBay, Fannie Mae, General Motors, Ford, and Chrysler as end users of its services.

THE ROAD TO OPT HELL

How did good intentions fall prey to the cheap-labor gluttons? In the bowels of the immigration bureaucracy, rule-makers asserted their authority with no pushback from elected lawmakers. Then, they conspired to steamroll over the public comment process and perpetrate fraud in order to preserve and extend their H-1B-circumventing, American-worker-displacing scheme.

The name "Optional Practical Training" is a benign-sounding euphemism that purports to offer students on-the-job opportunities to enhance their educational experiences. Before OPT came into existence as we know it, the feds in 1947 allowed foreign students to take "practical training" gigs for six months if such work was required or recommended by their schools. Up to two more six-month periods could be authorized if the school and the training agency certified that the practical training could not be completed in a shorter period of time.[10] By the 1980s, the INS allowed aliens to work on student visas for a year after graduation if the school certified that a similar work experience was not available in the alien's home country.[11]

Along came the behemoth Immigration Act of 1990, which brought us H-1B, EB-5, and a slew of immigration expansionist measures. As the feds moved to implement regulations relating to all these other programs created by the 1990 law, they also granted authorization for student visa holders to work for up to a year after graduation in 1991.[12] INS tooled around again on their new vehicle and officially formulated the "Optional Practical Training" program,[13] offering either "pre-completion" OPT that took place while in school or during breaks or "post-completion" OPT that allowed up to a year of work after graduation.

The functions of the INS shifted to the newly created Department of Homeland Security in 2002. One of post-9/11 department's first regulations allowed aliens to work on OPT without being enrolled at a school.[14]

The description of valid F-1 student visa status straightforwardly required a student to be attending school.[15] But unknown, faceless regulators added the clause "or engaging in authorized practical training following completion of studies"[16] at the end of the statutory provision defining valid F-1 student visa status. Presto change-o! F-1 "student" visas effectively became guest work visas—with no messy, congressional debate or inconvenient public scrutiny.

DHS brass faced pressure from Big Business lobbyists at every turn. Instead of conducting public hearings, the transformation of F-1/ OPT into a new conduit for cheap foreigner workers occurred at insider D.C. cocktail parties and in corporate correspondence with the Bush administration.

COCKTAIL PARTY POLICY-MAKING ON THE POTOMAC

On November 15, 2007, Microsoft's managing director of government affairs and general counsel, Jack Krumholtz, wrote a chummy letter to then–DHS secretary Michael Chertoff. "I appreciated very much the chance to speak with you recently at the dinner that Ed and Debra Cohen hosted to discuss immigration reform issues," Krumholtz wrote. The Cohens are one of Washington's wealthy power couples. Husband Edward is a real estate lawyer; wife Debra is daughter of real estate mogul and Washington Nationals baseball team owner Ted Lerner.

Krumholtz reminded Chertoff of their private dinner discussion on "action that the Department of Homeland Security can take easily and immediately . . . to help address the H-1B visa shortage." How? By extending OPT from a maximum of one year to twenty-nine months by administrative fiat. Microsoft believed it was "wise" to "move forward on comprehensive immigration reform" after Congress rejected the Bush amnesty plan in 2006–7—and to enact Big Tech industry-supported measures "without congressional action." Invoking the "historic H-1B cap crisis" and the mythical STEM worker shortage, Microsoft's Krumholtz emphasized to Chertoff that "Today OPT exists solely by regulation; no statutory change is necessary to make this needed adjustment." On behalf of Microsoft, whose founder Bill Gates had sounded the H-1B alarm eight months earlier,[17] Krumholtz urged that the change "be in place no later than next spring." (See Appendix D for the full letter.)[18]

DHS received similarly worded, lockstep ultimatums from Compete America[19] and the U.S. Chamber of Commerce.[20] Entitled business leaders at Intel, Autodesk, and Qualcomm whined that it was "increasingly difficult for U.S. employers to secure the services of those who do study here"—as if the F-1 student visa was created solely for their corporate benefit.[21] While the D.C. lobbyist social circuit negotiations continued from the fall of 2007 through the spring of 2008, DHS gave no public notice that it was considering changing OPT under the guise of "fixing" an alleged shortage of American workers.[22]

What Microsoft and Big Tech demanded, Microsoft and Big Tech received. On April 8, 2008, the *Federal Register* published a new DHS rule transforming OPT into a full-fledged guest worker program designed to supply cheap labor to American industry.[23] The new regulation also allowed aliens on OPT to remain in the U.S. while they were unemployed to look for work, further increasing the supply of foreign labor.

By what definition are such people "students"? Only in the Beltway regulatory swamp does this make any sense.

The rule contained two distinct increases to OPT duration. The first applied to all foreign students working after graduation. It extended the OPT period from the time an H-1B petition is filed until a final decision is made. The second is the seventeen-month STEM OPT extension. DHS falsely asserted that the extension must be limited to fields where there is a shortage of workers in the United States. Depending upon when the foreign student graduated and on his or her degree field, the length of OPT could range from twelve to thirty-five months. DHS noted that these regulations would create a "significant expansion" in the number of skilled workers.[24] Under the new rule, the purpose of OPT explicitly became a means to supply low-cost labor to industry and circumvent the quotas on H-1B visas.

Here's how DHS justified the STEM OPT expansion:

U.S. high-tech employers are particularly concerned about the H–1B cap because of the critical shortage of domestic science and engineering talent and the degree to which high-tech employers are as a consequence necessarily far more dependent on foreign workers than other industries. See The National Science Foundation, Rising Above the Gathering Storm: Energizing and Employing America for a Brighter Economic Future (2007), pp. 78–83 (describing the critical shortages of science, math, and engineering talent in the United States).[25]

But if you actually turn to the referenced pages of the NSF report, you find a section titled "International Competition for Talent" that has nothing to do with a labor shortage. This is not a citation error. The phrase "critical shortage" does not occur anywhere in *Rising Above the Gathering Storm* nor does the report conclude there is a critical shortage of STEM workers. In fact, the report repeatedly *contradicted* DHS's characterization of the labor market.[26]

Nobody was around to unmask this fraud before the Bush DHS adopted its expansion of OPT because there were no congressional hearings, no public notice, and no comment period. Under the Administrative Procedure Act (APA), regulations are supposed to be subjected to a public notice and comment period. Chertoff and friends evaded these APA requirements by inserting their industry-indulging regulations into the *Federal Register* as an exempt "emergency measure."

For the ravenous cheap labor lobby, though, this regulatory giveaway *still* wasn't enough. It never is.

With a new administration and new political cronies to lobby, Big Tech went to work squeezing more favors out of the Obama White House. In 2011 and 2012, the Obama DHS announced expansion of the academic fields eligible for the STEM OPT extension from roughly three hundred to four hundred—without public notice, without public comment, and without even bothering to publish the new rule in the *Federal Register.* On November 20, 2014, as part of its package of administrative immigration expansions, the Obama White House signaled its plans to expand the eligible degree programs even further and "extend the time period and use of OPT for foreign STEM students."[27] The administration is now doubling down on OPT. DHS briefed Congress in the summer of 2015 on White House plans for executive regulations to allow aliens to work in the United States for up to *six years* on student visas after graduation.[28]

STANDING FOR AMERICAN WORKERS

One day after Obama's announcement in November 2014, a significant glimmer of hope for American workers broke through the D.C.

darkness. In a case that could have implications for all of President
Obama's executive actions on immigration, the U.S. District Court for
the District of Columbia ruled that the Washington Alliance of Technology Workers' (WashTech) court challenge to the OPT expansion
could move forward. Obama's DHS argued unsuccessfully that the
suit should be dismissed altogether.

John brought the case along with the Immigration Reform Law Institute on behalf of three displaced American workers who belong to
WashTech, a union of high-tech workers: Rennie Sawade, a contract
computer programmer with a degree in computer science; Douglas
Blatt, a computer programmer with an IT degree; and Ceasar Smith,
a computer systems and networking administrator with a degree in
business administration. All are high-skilled, experienced computer
specialists who had applied for STEM positions between 2008 and
2012, but were turned down repeatedly by companies that employed
F-1 student visa holders pursuing OPT STEM extensions.

An earlier court challenge to the OPT rules by programmers and
engineers from John's organization, the Programmers Guild, had failed
in 2008 over what's calling "standing." It's the federal law doctrine that
requires a plaintiff to have a personal stake in a controversy or conflict
in order to bring the issue to court seeking judicial redress. The Third
Circuit dismissed the 2008 lawsuit by asserting that the tech workers
had failed the "zone of interest test."[29] That's another legal invention
that requires a plaintiff's interest to be within the "zone of interests"
protected or regulated by the statute that he says was violated.[30]

Of course, the courts should ensure that the people who bring a
case have an actual interest in the outcome to bring the case. The problem is that the Supreme Court's definition of standing is so malleable
that its application has been inconsistent, incoherent, and inevitably
politicized.[31] When a government agency cannot defend a case on the
merits, it turns the case into a bloody, expensive battle over standing.

Plaintiffs challenging the feds rarely have the wherewithal to pursue and sustain these challenges. In many circuits, it's a crap shoot.

The consequences are often perverse, if not downright anti-American. Who deserves standing in a case about immigration measures that flood the U.S. with cheap foreign labor more than American tech workers harmed by those policies? Yet, while U.S. programmers challenging OPT in 2008 lost their case before it even started, the same Third Circuit court that ruled against them gave standing to illegal aliens in Hazelton, Pennsylvania, where the city had revoked business licenses of employers who hired illegal aliens and punished landlords who rented to them.[32]

In the Third Circuit, in other words, illegal aliens deserve standing in immigration cases, but American workers do not.

Fortunately, U.S. District Judge Ellen Segal Huvelle saw the matter differently in 2014. In response to the feds' argument that the WashTech workers did not have standing to challenge the OPT extension program, Huvelle noted the tax benefits of hiring OPT workers (who, remember, are exempt from Social Security and Medicare taxes) and the intentional flooding of the STEM worker market. "The seventeen-month extension to the OPT program swells the number of foreign nationals in the STEM labor market where WashTech members must compete. Indeed, the regulation was designed with this purpose in mind. . . . Plaintiff has sufficiently alleged that its named members face increased competition as a result of the 2008 interim final rule."

Huvelle concluded her opinion with a clear and blunt rebuttal to the government's argument (and the argument of all immigration expansionists) that massive visa expansions do not cause harm. On the contrary, the judge found, the American workers "were in direct and current competition with OPT students on STEM extension. . . . *This competition resulted in concrete and particularized injury.*"[33] (Emphasis added.)

When WashTech's lawsuit[34] successfully cleared the standing hurdle in November 2014, some astute observers realized its significance immediately. "Judge greenlights lawsuit against guest worker program expanded by executive amnesty," Tony Lee of Breitbart.com reported.[35] "Facebook's favorite party of amnesty already in trouble," Daniel Greenfield of FrontPageMag.com headlined his analysis of the ruling.[36] "Obama promised to expand and extend OPT just as tech workers are pushing back against it. In the tech industry, as in all other jobs, amnesty is based on repeating the lie that Americans don't want the jobs leading to a 'shortage,'" Greenfield correctly noted. "During a time of high unemployment, there is no employee shortage. The tech industry is outsourcing jobs on American soil. And now it's facing legal pushback." It won't be the last time.

In August 2015, the District of Columbia District Court struck down and vacated the 2008 OPT expansion. Judge Huvelle forcefully rejected Big Tech and Big Government's claims that it was necessary to circumvent the normal public comment process because of a "fiscal emergency."[37] However, taking into consideration the "substantial hardship for foreign students and a major labor disruption for the technology sector" that immediate implementation of the ruling would cause, the judge stayed the order until February 2016 to give time for a transition. The question is whether DHS will do the right thing and end this system of using student visas as a source of foreign labor or will try to double down and ram through new regulations doing the same thing.

The major long-term significance of the ruling is that it creates a path for American workers to challenge foreign worker regulations. In the past, industry groups have had an easy time in the federal courts on standing to challenge regulations that benefited or increased competitors. Now, finally, American workers have a route to get into the federal courts.

PART III: THE BIG GOVERNMENT–BIG BUSINESS BETRAYERS OF AMERICA'S BEST AND BRIGHTEST WORKERS

⊷ 11 ⊶

Legion of Doom

Open-Borders Billionaires, Phony Front Groups,
and Big Tech's D.C. Lobbyists

Who are the powerful special interests sabotaging the American Dream in pursuit of cheap foreign labor? As always, you've got to follow the money.

In 2000, while business credit reporting agency Dun & Bradstreet was replacing its American programming staff with imported workers,[1] a prankster employee with a grim sense of humor started posting a local newspaper article in all the break rooms. Each day, a human resources officer would take the article down. Each morning, the articles would go back up. The subversive educational effort continued for several weeks. The article contained this damning quote from Rep. Tom Davis (R-Va.), then-chairman of the Republican Congressional Campaign Committee:

This [H-1B] is a very important issue for the high-tech executives who give the money.[2]

On another occasion, Rep. Davis stated the obvious about Big Tech's push to eliminate H-1B caps altogether: "This is not a popular bill with the public. It's popular with the CEOs."[3] Rep. Davis told a reporter his constituent mail ran seven-to-one against H-1B and smugly described his support of the program as "an act of courage."[4]

Only in the Beltway can selling out be defined as valor with a straight face. And only in the Beltway can lemmings call themselves leaders. After the 2000 H-1B expansion legislation passed the Senate, then-Sen. Robert Bennett (R-Utah), a staunch immigration expansionist, described the campaign cash connection this way: "Once it's clear [H-1B] is going to get through, everybody signs up so nobody can be in the position of being accused of being against high tech. There were, in fact, a whole lot of folks against it, but because they are tapping the high-tech community for campaign contributions, they don't want to admit that in public."[5]

With a scathing dose of sarcasm, Sen. Jeff Sessions (R-Ala.), the Senate's most astute and vigilant voice in Washington, D.C., for American workers harmed by reckless immigration policies, dubbed the open-borders billionaires calling the shots the "Masters of the Universe." We prefer to call them the Legion of Doom. Like the cartoon villains, these deep-pocketed donors have banded together from remote galaxies to achieve their nefarious Big Business policy goals. They come from all parts of the political spectrum. A few, such as Facebook's Mark Zuckerberg and Microsoft's Bill Gates, are household names. But you've probably never heard of most of these movers and shakers who are "buying off" your congressional representatives with contributions, holding sway over the White House, and manipulating the media.

While money talks, American jobs walk. Big Tech's bigwigs lobby Congress for statutory changes, such as increasing the H-1B cap, and lobby government agencies for regulatory changes, such as loosening Labor Department requirements on labor certification and wages. According to economists at the International Monetary Fund, "a 10 percent increase in the size of lobbying expenditures by business groups per native worker is associated with a 2.9 percent larger number of visas per native worker."[6] Table 11.1 shows some of the largest domestic H-1B users' lobbying expenditures.[7] For each company, the chart lists the three bills for which it had the most lobbying activity. You might expect that technology issues, such as patents and communications, would be at the top of the tech industry's legislative agenda—but you would be wrong. The number-one priority of the tech industry is more cheap, foreign labor.

Companies can make direct contributions to politicians or political groups through their employees or Political Action Committee. Table 11.2 shows the amount of money that the six major U.S. technology companies listed above contributed in the 2012 election.

And it is not just American companies that lobby our government on behalf of cheap foreign labor. In 2009, the Indian government spent $5.6 million lobbying.[8] In addition, Indian firms spent at least $4.4 million lobbying in the U.S. that year.

Unlike the shady operators who lobby behind closed doors and the irresponsible lawmakers who pass their payoffs by voice vote in the dark of night, we believe sunlight is the best disinfectant. We've compiled a dossier for you of the most important players with the biggest bucks and widest influence. They've got the purse strings and the puppet strings. But as the defeat of Beltway insider and tech industry darling Eric Cantor (former GOP House majority leader) at the hands of American-worker-championing underdog Dave Brat in Virginia showed, they *can* be defeated.

TABLE 11.1   HEAVIEST LOBBIED ISSUES FOR TECHNOLOGY FIRMS IN 2013

Company	Amount Spent	Bill Number	Bill Title*
Microsoft	$10,490,000	S.169	*I-Squared Act of 2013*
		S.744	*Border Security, Economic Opportunity, and Immigration Modernization Act*
		H.R.2131	*SKILLS Visa Act*
Oracle	$7,190,000	S.744	*Border Security, Economic Opportunity, and Immigration Modernization Act*
		H.R.2131	*SKILLS Visa Act*
		H.R.624	Cyber Intelligence Sharing and Protection Act
Qualcomm	$7,090,000	H.R.624	Cyber Intelligence Sharing and Protection Act
		S.744	*Border Security, Economic Opportunity, and Immigration Modernization Act*
		S.866	Patent Quality Improvement Act of 2013
Facebook	$6,430,000	S.169	*I-Squared Act of 2013*
		S.744	*Border Security, Economic Opportunity, and Immigration Modernization Act*
		H.R.2131	*SKILLS Visa Act*
IBM	$5,950,000	H.R.1960	National Defense Authorization Act for Fiscal Year 2014
		H.R.624	Cyber Intelligence Sharing and Protection Act
		S.169	*I-Squared Act of 2013*
Intel	$4,393,750	H.R.527	Helium Stewardship Act of 2013
		S.744	*Border Security, Economic Opportunity, and Immigration Modernization Act*
		H.R.624	Cyber Intelligence Sharing and Protection Act

*H-1B-related bills are italicized.

TABLE 11.2 POLITICAL CONTRIBUTIONS, 2012 ELECTION

Company	Contributions
Microsoft	$4,962,918
Oracle	$5,159,534
Qualcomm	$614,793
Facebook	$760,733
IBM	$973,955
Intel	$542,056

TECHNET: SILICON VALLEY'S FIRST PAC

This is the granddaddy of the tech industry's political advocacy groups. Launched in 1997 during the Clinton administration, TechNet established Silicon Valley's first industrywide federal political action committee, which distributed an estimated $2 million to Democratic and Republican candidates in its first year.[9] Ever since, expanding H-1B visas has been job number one for TechNet founders John Doerr (a Democrat) and Jim Barksdale (a Republican).

The duo summoned what they called an "all-star"[10] team of corporate executives who shelled out a minimum ten-thousand-dollar fee for exclusive annual membership in TechNet. Charter members included Scott McNealy of Sun Microsystems, Scott Cook of Intuit, John Young of Hewlett-Packard, and Brian Halla of National Semiconductor. TechNet re-engineered the traditional way of doing lobbying business by making elected officials and candidates come to them instead of vice versa.

"We've learned that working with the government is far more productive than trying to ignore it," Barksdale explained.[11]

Before he was sidling up to Washington pols, Barksdale bounced from IBM to Federal Express and AT&T, then served as president and CEO of Netscape, the web browser company. Engineer Doerr worked for Intel, founded his own software company and broadband cable

Internet service, and then made his fortune as a venture capitalist for Kleiner Perkins (net worth: $3.4 billion[12]). Among his investment beneficiaries: Larry Page, Sergey Brin and Eric Schmidt of Google; Jeff Bezos of Amazon.com; and Scott Cook and Bill Campbell of Intuit.

Though billed as "bipartisan," TechNet leans left like most of Silicon Valley.[13] Doerr aggressively backed Democrat Al Gore for president in 2000, holding numerous TechNet fund-raisers and monthly meetings. The relationship was so tight that the venture capitalist called the TechNet team "Gore-Techs."[14]

Doerr bet on the wrong presidential horse, but the group had several ins with the new GOP administration. Founding TechNet member John Chambers of Cisco Systems supported Bush and had showered Republican candidates and causes with more than $300,000 in campaign contributions.[15] Another TechNet cofounder, semiconductor legend and Kleiner Perkins partner E. Floyd Kvamme, had backed George W. Bush and helped him raise $1 million in Silicon Valley—in addition to personally donating $145,000 with his wife to Bush.[16] Kvamme's reward? Appointment to the President's Council of Advisors on Science and Technology in 2001.[17] Kvamme also chaired Empower America, a conservative, corporatist think tank started by Bill Bennett and the late Jack Kemp, which supported H-1B expansion.

In 1998, President Clinton announced he was going to veto legislation to expand the H-1B program.[18] TechNet solved that problem by throwing him a fund-raiser at the home of Doerr.[19] Clinton reversed his veto threat two days before showing up in California to collect his bribe. In 2001, TechNet hired former GOP Rep. Rick White, who had represented Microsoft's congressional district in Washington state, to head the group. Job number one: raise the H-1B cap. In 2002, after intense lobbying led in Silicon Valley by TechNet and championed within the White House by TechNet's Kvamme, Congress voted to increase the number of H-1B visas to 195,000 and exempt all university-employed or nonprofit-employed foreign guest workers from the cap. President Bush signed another law that year that extended H-1B visa holders' status beyond the statutory six-year limit in one-year increments while they awaited green card approvals.

Meanwhile, the TechNet-Beltway revolving door spun smoothly for Lezlee Westine, who flitted from the Silicon Valley group straight into the Bush White House as a top aide to Karl Rove between 2001 and 2005—and then back to TechNet to helm its new D.C.-based office, where she returned to crusading for, you guessed it, loosened H-1B restrictions.

Founding TechNet political director and biofuels magnate Wade Randlett, who raised campaign cash for the Democratic National Committee and Al Gore on the side, split off from the group in 2007 to fund-raise for then-Sen. Barack Obama. Silicon Valley liberals were hungry for a fresh, new Democratic rock star who could deliver what they wanted faster and bigger. Campaign finance bundler Randlett and his wife, Lorna May Ho Randlett, raised between two hundred thousand and five hundred thousand dollars for Obama in 2007–8,[20] and a total of nearly $1.7 million by the fall of 2012.[21] Not long after, Mrs. Randlett won a plum appointment to a White House advisory commission on Asian-Americans.[22]

Doerr, like the vast majority of Silicon Valley CEOs and workers, backed Obama, too. Indeed, "individual contributions from employees among the Valley's top tech companies ran seven-to-one in favor of the president," the local *Peninsula Press* reported. "At Google the ratio was 31-to-one in favor of Obama, according to the U.S. Federal Election Commission data."[23] Obama named Doerr to the White House Economic Recovery Advisory Board in 2009. Doerr invited Obama to his home two years later to dine with Silicon Valley's Masters of the Universe. They raised their glasses while the *New York Times* drooled:[24]

> As documented on the White House Flickr account,[25] Steven P. Jobs of Apple and Mark Zuckerberg of Facebook enjoyed prime seats next to the commander in chief. Google's outgoing chief executive, Eric E. Schmidt, sat at the end of the long table, opposite Carol A. Bartz of Yahoo.
>
> Directly across from Mr. Obama sat the host and Larry Ellison of Oracle. With a guest list that included John Chambers of Cisco, Reed Hastings of Netflix and Dick Costolo of Twitter, however, a bad seat was hard to find.
>
> All told, the executives represent companies worth more than $938 billion.

And still, they clamored for more. By 2013, TechNet had stepped up its public pressure campaign on Obama to "enact high-skilled immigration reform" and "enable a more open and flexible U.S. immigration system to embrace highly-skilled workers"—that is, grant yet more H-1B visas to top-dollar corporate donors. An open letter signed by more than one hundred TechNet CEOs, plus the Association for Competitive Technology, Bay Area Council, Business Software Alliance, Consumer Electronics Association, Information Technology Industry Council, Internet Association, National Venture Capital Association, Silicon Valley Leadership Group, and TechAmerica, raised the usual alarm about STEM worker shortages while turning a blind eye to the Darin Wedels of America.

Industry leaders called for regulations allowing spouses of H-1B guest workers to work on H-4 dependent visas.[26] On May 6, 2014, the government gave them want they wanted. The very next day, President Obama jetted to Silicon Valley on a fund-raiser jaunt.[27] Among his stops: a $1,000- to $32,400-per-head dinner hosted by TechNet executive council member and Yahoo! CEO Marissa Mayer.[28] As is his imperial custom, the Decider-in-Chief circumvented Congress and the public to satisfy industry's demands through executive fiat. In February 2015, the Department of Homeland Security finalized work authorization benefits for spouses of H-1B visa holders while they awaited their green cards, acting with no authority whatsoever.[29]

Agencies can only promulgate regulation within the scope of authority granted by Congress. In the case of authorizing H-4 visa holders to work, there is no such authority. The grand bargain in the Immigration Reform and Control Act of 1986 (IRCA) was that those here illegally would be given an amnesty and be allowed to stay permanently in exchange for increased immigration enforcement—and we all know how that worked out. IRCA required the attorney general to authorize illegal aliens who had won amnesty to engage in employment.[30] (Those functions have since been taken over by the DHS secretary). For the first time, IRCA imposed penalties on employers who hired "unauthorized aliens"—those aliens who were not allowed to work in the United States. This is how 8 U.S.C. § 1324a defines an unauthorized alien:

(3) DEFINITION OF UNAUTHORIZED ALIEN.—As used in this section, the term 'unauthorized alien' means, with respect to the employment of an alien at a particular time, that the alien is not at that time either (A) an alien lawfully admitted for permanent residence, or (B) authorized to be so employed by this Act or by the Attorney General.

This definition makes it legal for employers to hire permanent residents, aliens on work visas, and those in the legalization process without visas that Congress directed the attorney general to engage in employment. The Obama administration has adopted an abusive interpretation of this provision. It now brazenly declares that the phrase "authorized . . . by the Attorney General" confers "unfettered" power to authorize *any* alien to work in the United States.[31] Clearly, that is not what was intended by the statute (note the qualifier "As used in this section" and that in its absence aliens in the legalization process could be authorized to work, but it would be unlawful for employers to hire them). But the law does not restrain a lawless president. The Obama administration now claims sweeping authority to allow aliens to work on H-4 visas and F-1 student visas, and illegal aliens to work under the Deferred Action for Childhood Arrivals and Deferred Action for Parents of Americans programs.

Promoted as a means to "to grow the U.S. economy and create jobs," the regulation authorizing H-1B spouses to work was mum about the hundreds of thousands of laid-off Americans looking for work. The Obama administration did, however, express its utmost compassion for the "economic burdens and personal stresses H-1B nonimmigrants and their families may experience during the transition from nonimmigrant to lawful permanent resident status."[32]

A group of laid-off Southern California Edison workers refused to lie down for the Obama steamroller. As we noted in the introduction, John and the Immigration Law Reform Institute filed a suit challenging the H-4 rule on the U.S. employees' behalf in April 2015 in the U.S. District Court for the District of Columbia. The case survived a motion to dismiss and is expected to conclude in October 2015, with a decision coming a few months afterward.

On top of their complaint alleging, in part, that DHS exceeded its statutory authority and ignored statutory labor protections when it issued the rule, the plaintiffs are requesting a preliminary injunction from the court against the program until a full trial on the merits of the case can be heard. In its response to the suit, the Obama Department of Homeland Security flippantly dismissed the effect of its expansive H-4 policy, concluding without evidence that the rule "will have minimal labor market impacts."[33] But as Dale L. Wilcox, IRLI's executive director, pointed out, "DHS admits its H-4 Rule will add as many as 179,600 new foreign workers in its first year and 55,000 annually in subsequent years. This is a slap in the face to the tens of millions of Americans suffering from unemployment and underemployment, especially those who are most vulnerable, such as students, seniors, single mothers and minorities." Despite repeated promises to support American workers, Wilcox said, "all we've seen during this administration is standards of living fall and outsized corporate profits continue to rise. We will continue the fight on behalf of the American worker and hold this administration accountable to the rule of law."[34]

The American CEOs of TechNet applauded the administration "for making good on a promise." They rejoiced that Obama's rule change "will materially change the professional and personal circumstances for nearly 180,000 spouses of high-skilled H-1B visa holders who are now eligible to work inside the United States.[35] But as usual, the tech gluttons remained unsatisfied. They demanded more, more, more foreign workers.

> While this is good news for high-skilled workers and their spouses, it underscores the dysfunctional immigration system that everyday permits the world's great minds to be educated at American universities, only to face a lack of visas, various restrictions, and lengthy processing delays, that force valuable talent to give up, move home and seek employment in their home countries to compete against American firms.[36]

TechNet needed reinforcements. Silicon Valley's next generation was ready to head to the front lines.

FWD.US: MARK ZUCKERBERG TAKES THE IMMIGRATION PLUNGE

As of March 2015, Facebook founder and CEO Mark Zuckerberg boasted a net worth of about $35 billion. In April 2013, the social media kingpin decided to spend a small chunk of that fortune on a new advocacy machine to push for mass illegal alien amnesty and foreign worker visa increases. With great fanfare, he announced the launch of "FWD.us"—pronounced "Forward Us"—that was "founded by leaders of our nation's technology community" to "advocate a bipartisan policy agenda to build the knowledge economy the United States needs to ensure more jobs, innovation and investment."[37] The new lobbying force raised nearly $37 million in its first year.[38]

As a 501(c)(4) organization, Zuckerberg's group is officially a "charity" organization focused on "social welfare," but can engage in political activity without having to disclose its individual donors or their contribution amounts to the public. IRS documents show that ten anonymous megadonors pitched in nearly 90 percent of its initial funding; one of the contributors gave $20 million.[39] To mollify transparency advocates, FWD.us named a few of its founding members, including Brian Chesky, CEO and cofounder of Airbnb; Reed Hastings, founder and CEO of Netflix; Max Levchin, cofounder of PayPal and chairman of Yelp; Andrew Mason, cofounder of Groupon; Hosain Rahman, CEO and founder of Jawbone; Eric Schmidt, executive chairman of Google; and Padmasree Warrior, chief technology and strategy officer at Cisco.

Zuckerberg enlisted his Harvard roommate Joe Green, an acolyte of Democratic community organizing guru Marshall Ganz,[40] to run the operation. A leaked prospectus authored by Green bragged that "our tactical assets" include "individuals with lots of money" who maintain "control" of "massive distribution channels, both as companies and individuals."[41] Touting support from Microsoft's Bill Gates and other millionaire and billionaire tech titans, Green emphasized: "We control the avenues of distribution."[42]

Green also turned to Hollywood. Among the group's millennial-pandering initiatives: a "Selfies4Reform" effort fronted by hipster actor/musician Jared Leto and comedian Chris Tucker, who sent FWD.us-branded photo postcards of themselves to their congressional representatives urging "immigration reform." Why? Because, as Leto insipidly put it, "immigrants enrich our American culture significantly."[43]

Well, Leto was right about one thing: There's been a whole lotta enrichment going on. According to campaign finance watchdogs at the Center for Responsive Politics, Facebook spent over $6.4 million lobbying the federal government in 2013. Its contributions to political candidates increased eightfold between 2008 and 2012.[44]

The company's top political focus: immigration liberalization. Mark Zuckerberg spent eight hundred thousand dollars in 2014 alone to expand the number of H-1B visas.[45]

Zuckerberg publicly sold his immigration push for the so-called "comprehensive immigration reform" package, carried by the U.S. Senate's bipartisan "Gang of Eight," as a "civil rights" and humanitarian cause.[46] But it was Beltway special interest business as usual behind the scenes. Facebook backed GOP-sponsored legislation to raise the annual cap on H-1B foreign guest workers from 65,000 to 180,000 and to eliminate the ceiling on green cards for foreign STEM workers.[47] The "Supplying Knowledge-based Immigrants and Lifting Levels of STEM Visas Act or SKILLS Visa Act" also gave tech companies "more flexibility when setting the wages for H-1B workers."[48] Pretending to care about illegal alien DREAMers and "best and brightest" foreigners gave Zuckerberg cover for the company's backdoor maneuvering to carve out a "Facebook loophole" in the mega–"immigration reform" bill before the Senate.[49] The "payoff" for Facebook would be "substantial," the *Washington Post* noted, allowing the company "to avoid a requirement that they make a 'good-faith' effort to recruit Americans for jobs before hiring from overseas" and to "sidestep proposed rules that would force it to pay much higher wages to many foreign workers."[50]

Facebook is classified under current law as an "H-1B dependent employer" because its workforce now exceeds 15 percent of workers on H-1B visas. To discourage offshore outsourcing, H-1B-dependent companies are required to pay higher fees and wages. Zuckerberg lobbied hard for an exemption covering a newly manufactured class of "intending immigrants" (H-1B workers that an employer sponsors for a green card) who "shall not be counted" by the government in determining the "H-1B-dependent" status of an employer.[51] As the *Washington Post* explained: "That means Facebook and other companies could file just enough applications to fall back below the 15 percent line."

Applications wouldn't have to be legit or approved—just "pending." No other industry that employs large numbers of foreign guest workers (such as agriculture or hospitality) would qualify for the carve-out. It's a paper-pushing ruse to protect Facebook from legal requirements that were passed to put American workers first.

To add insult to American worker injury, Facebook sought to undermine nominal federal protections that require H-1B-dependent firms to "attest" that they had taken "good faith" measures to recruit and hire qualified Americans before importing foreign workers that are easily circumvented and rarely enforced. Facebook pushed an amendment—sponsored by Sen. Orrin Hatch (R-Utah), a longtime immigration liberalization advocate—which removed these barest of American worker protections in the Gang of Eight bill. Marc Apter, president of the Institute of Electrical and Electronics Engineers–USA, which represents American engineers, blasted the Hatch-Facebook favors: "Every part of this package has the same purpose—to make it easier for employers to fire Americans and replace them with temporary foreign workers."[52]

Daniel Costa, director of the left-leaning Economic Policy Institute, which has long exposed H-1B's harm to American workers, accurately pegged the Gang of Eight's giveaway to Facebook and Big Tech: "It was pretty much a landslide," he concluded. "The industry got everything. They got way higher [guest worker visa] numbers with few protections in there."[53] Professor Ron Hira of the Rochester Institute of Technology didn't mince words: "Really, the tech industry wrote it."[54]

As Facebook turned up the heat on Congress to pass its goodie bag, FWD.us poured money into the coffers of political consultants and partisan operatives in both parties. Zuckerberg and Green spun off two FWD.us affiliates incorporated as separate LLCs—one GOP-leaning, the other Democrat-leaning—to run ads supporting politicians who supported Facebook's drive for cheap foreign labor.

The FWD.us liberal front group called itself the "Council for American Job Growth." Headed by Todd Schulte, former chief of staff of the Left's largest super PAC, the pro-Obama Priorities USA Action, its board includes former New York congressman Scott Murphy, former Clinton press secretary Joe Lockhart, and former Obama Latino voter organizer Alida Garcia.[55] As of March 2015, the group had poured more than seven hundred thousand dollars into independent expenditures.[56] Its ads supported Facebook-friendly Democratic Sens. Mark Begich of Alaska, Kay Hagan of North Carolina (both defeated in 2014), and Joe Manchin of West Virginia—in some cases, emphasizing their centrist voting records to provide them political cover, which alienated the group's more "progressive" supporters.[57] In 2014, the Council for

American Job Growth unveiled a five-hundred-thousand-dollar national ad campaign critical of House Republicans for not moving the Senate-approved Gang of Eight bill onto President Obama's desk.[58]

FWD.us's GOP subsidiary went by the phony name "Americans for a Conservative Direction." Its chief: Beltway GOP operative Rob Jesmer, who served as Texas Sen. John Cornyn's top aide at the National Republican Senatorial Committee; managed Cornyn's 2008 reelection campaign; and worked for the Republican National Committee, the National Republican Congressional Committee, and Arizona GOP Sen. John McCain's presidential campaign. Jesmer's former NRSC colleague Brian Walsh provided communications strategy to the group. Also riding the Facebook H-1B gravy train: a "blue-chip board of advisers," as Politico.com described the Americans for a Conservative Direction entourage, including "former Mississippi Gov. Haley Barbour; Sally Bradshaw, the former chief of staff to Jeb Bush; [and] Dan Senor and Joel Kaplan, the former George W. Bush advisers."[59]

Barbour was a paid, pro-amnesty lobbyist for the government of Mexico, which forked over thirty-five thousand dollars a month, plus expenses, for his services on behalf of "undocumented workers" in the U.S.[60] Kaplan, who heads Facebook's D.C. office, worked as a deputy chief of staff of the pro–illegal alien amnesty Bush White House. Politico.com called him "a driving force" in pressuring lawmakers to embed the "Facebook loophole" into the Gang of Eight plan.[61]

"Americans for a Conservative Direction" showered pro–illegal alien amnesty Sen. Lindsey Graham (R-S.C.) and flip-flopper Sen. Marco Rubio (R-Fla.) with millions of dollars in media ad buys. Both were leading members of the Gang of Eight in need of political air cover. The group also funded a deceptive, $150,000 ad campaign for immigration sellout Rep. Renee Ellmers (R-N.C.), which falsely claimed she opposed amnesty to help her fend off a primary challenge.[62] In all, FWD.us underwrote ad buys in more than one hundred Republican districts and spent an estimated $5 million on TV and radio spots before the Senate passed the Gang of Eight bill in June 2013.

Facebook's willingness to play both sides of the Beltway political aisle caused a minimutiny among some of its original, far Left supporters. Founding FWD.us board member Elon Musk of Tesla Motors resigned in protest over pro-GOP ads at odds with their liberal environmental views. So did investor David Sacks of the social network Yammer.[63] The Sierra Club pulled its ads off Facebook. Zuckerberg's pal Joe Green got the boot after House Republicans failed to pass the Gang of Eight package.

But the public relations stumble didn't deter Zuckerberg, who has continued full steam ahead with his FWD.us push for both a mass illegal alien amnesty and the legislative construction of a Facebook foreign guest worker pipeline. FWD.us shoveled $1 million into ads to help immigration liberalization ally Sen. Jeanne Shaheen (D-N.H.) successfully fend off a challenge from former GOP Sen. Scott Brown of Massachusetts in October 2014.[64] That fall, Zuckerberg also crusaded for immigration liberalization at a swanky gathering south of the border hosted by Mexican billionaire Carlos Slim (net worth: $76 billion).[65]

In March 2015, FWD.us kicked off a new, monthlong initiative to jumpstart congressional "immigration reform" under the pretense of creating "American jobs." The self-serving campaign was timed to climax with the opening date of the 2015 H-1B foreign guest worker visa filing season—which, fell, appropriately enough, on April Fools' Day. A few months later, FWD.us sponsored a *National Journal* forum on "Immigration and the Technology Sector." The host apologetically asked two CEO panelists about the Southern California Edison layoffs and stories of American workers being replaced by cheap foreign competitors. FWD.us contributor and business software mogul Lars Dalgaard smugly responded: "You know, I'm going to be rather crude about that. Nobody's going to hold you up and carry you around. . . . If you're not going to work hard enough to be qualified to get the job . . . well then, you don't deserve the job."[66] Does Dalgaard really believe SCE laid off high-skilled U.S. staffers because they didn't "work hard enough"? It's easy to adopt such arrogance and callousness when you can esconce yourself in an elitist Silicon Valley bubble and pretend that wages have absolutely nothing to do with the systematic sacking and replacement of America's best and brightest workers.

BILL GATES AND HIS BIPARTISAN BELTWAY MINIONS

Microsoft cofounder Bill Gates (net worth: $80 billion) may be "retired," but the liberal tech mogul has taken an aggressive role in crusading for expansive foreign guest worker programs. Lending his name to Zuckerberg's FWD.us initiative was just his most recent foray in the Beltway.

In 2007, Gates testified before the U.S. Senate Health, Education, Labor and Pensions Committee in favor of an "infinite number" of H-1B visas.[67] Gates spelled it out in response to a question from Sen. Judd Gregg (R-N.H.) about his preferred H-1B quota: "I don't think there should be any limit."[68] Instead of challenging Gates on the impact of such a radical and unprecedented policy on our American workforce, Senate committee members from both parties gushed over the billionaire. Sen. Patty Murray (D-Wash.) touted Gates's "leadership, vision, and eagerness to help us address the challenges that are facing our country." Then there was Beltway barnacle Sen. Orrin Hatch. Before he carried the legislative torch for Facebook, he was sucking up to Gates. Hatch spurned the opportunity to interrogate Gates and used his time during the congressional hearing to stroke the billionaire's ego: "You've done so much with your wealth that is so good for mankind that I don't think anyone should fail to recognize that. I usually don't lavish praise on anyone, but I think you deserve it."[69]

It was quite a change of tone for Hatch, who had joined the Clinton administration's antitrust jihad against Microsoft in the late 1990s, when he presided over a four-hour grilling of Gates.[70] What changed? For one thing, Utah-based Novell, a chief competitor of Microsoft's, faded into obscurity. Then there's the cold, hard cash. *Washington Examiner* reporter Tim Carney explained how money-grubbing Hatch forced Microsoft to play the K Street game after that hearing:

[Microsoft's] PAC increased spending fivefold in each of the next two elections. In the 2010 elections, Microsoft's PAC contributed $2.3 million to House and Senate candidates. The PAC has contributed the maximum $10,000 to each of Hatch's last two campaigns.

Back before the antitrust case, Microsoft's tiny lobbying contingent sat in the company's local sales office in Chevy Chase. Since the Hatch hearings, Gates' company has poured more than $100 million into K Street's economy, hiring up members of congress and Capitol Hill staff, many of whom then became top fund-raisers—such as Republican Jack Abramoff and Democrat Steve Elmendorf.[71]

Yes, *that* Jack Abramoff. He's the convicted influence peddler who bilked Indian tribes of millions of dollars, defrauded investors in a gambling boat venture, bribed countless public officials, and reveled in kickbacks with his cronies (can you "smell the money?!?!?!" he gloated).[72]

Like Zuckerberg, Gates doesn't mind employing open-borders Republicans to carry his water. During the heated battles over H-1B expansion between 1998 and 2000, Microsoft paid Abramoff $1.7 million.[73] The super-lobbyist once worked for the D.C. office of law and lobbying firm Preston, Gates & Ellis. The company's cofounder, William H. Gates II, is the Microsoft mogul's father. Another Preston,

Gates & Ellis lobbyist, Michael Scanlon, joined Abramoff's racket after serving as former House majority leader and Texas GOP Rep. Tom DeLay's press secretary. As the *Washington Post* reported, Rep. DeLay and Team Abramoff's "K Street project"[74] pressured corporations and trade associations "to hire more GOP-connected lobbyists in what at times became an almost seamless relationship between Capitol Hill lawmakers and some firms that sought to influence them." Scanlon later pleaded guilty to bribing a member of Congress and other public officials, including all-expense junkets to Europe and the Super Bowl in exchange for legislative favors.[75]

Microsoft also retained the lobbying services of Abramoff pals Grover Norquist (of Americans for Tax Reform) and Ralph Reed (formerly of the Christian Coalition).[76] The trio had known each other since all serving as College Republican National Committee leaders in the 1980s. After quitting the Christian Coalition, Reed collected a twenty-thousand-dollar monthly retainer fee from Microsoft for seven years.[77] Abramoff funneled more than $5.3 million to Reed from Indian gambling interests, which sought Reed's help enlisting Christian conservative activists to block the donors' competitors from opening or expanding casinos.[78]

Norquist is a longtime fanatic for both illegal alien amnesty and loosened immigration rules for foreign guest workers. He took twenty thousand dollars in seed money from pro–Islamic jihad agitator and Saudi government money-launderer Abdurahman Alamoudi to start the "Islamic Free Market Institute." Norquist and partner David Safavian founded Janus-Merritt, which acted as a registered lobbyist for Alamoudi—who was later convicted on al Qaeda terror financing, tax evasion, and immigration fraud charges.[79] Safavian, the former chief of the General Services Administration (GSA), was convicted on charges of obstruction of justice and making false statements. While Safavian assisted Abramoff in his attempts to acquire GSA-controlled properties, the lobbyist took the bureaucrat on a luxury golf trip to Scotland and a junket to London. He made false statements to numerous federal investigators "in an attempt to conceal the fact that around the time of the golf trip he aided Abramoff with business before the GSA."[80]

Corruptocrats of a soiled feather flock together.

The taint of the Abramoff scandals forced Microsoft to disassociate itself from the high-powered GOP lobbyists, but they had already reaped enormous legislative benefits. Team Abramoff successfully blocked a watershed H-1B reform bill sponsored by Sen. Alan Simpson (R-Wyo.) in 1995[81] and enlisted Sen. Spencer Abraham (R-Mich.) as sponsor of the radical 1998 bill (S.1723) that nearly tripled the H-1B yearly cap. In the fall of 2000, a bill sponsored by Sen. Orrin Hatch (R-Utah) and cosponsored by Sen. Abraham and twenty-three others to raise the H-1B cap yet again passed by voice vote in the House. Even Democratic Rep. Lloyd Dogget (D-Tex.), an H-1B champion, expressed his disgust by calling the stealth vote on S. 2045 in the wee hours of the morning in a nearly empty House chamber "underhanded."[82]

Now well-versed in Beltway games, Microsoft no longer needed GOP fraudsters to do its dirty work. Between 2008 and 2013, Microsoft hired nearly seventy other outside lobbyists to work on immigration issues.[83] In addition, the company's employees and political action committee forked over a combined $800,000 to President Obama in 2012 and another $2.7 million to mostly Democratic members of Congress. (By comparison, Microsoft employees donated about $213,000 to Romney.)

According to the Sunlight Foundation, the computer software giant filed for more than four thousand H-1B visas in 2010 and 2011.[84] While laying off thousands of American workers, the company's general counsel called on Congress to create a new supplemental visa category—call it MS Visa—"with 20,000 visas annually for STEM skills that are in short supply" and to "make a supplemental allocation of 20,000 new green card slots for workers with STEM skills."[85] In exchange, Microsoft promised to pay nearly four times the usual fees for H-1B applications. The estimated $500 million in funds raised would allegedly go to fund STEM education programs for American students. But duped supporters of the Microsoft-authored proposal led by the STEM Education Coalition, whose members include the nonprofit National Science Teachers Association and the Institute of Electrical and Electronics Engineers, soon realized it was a "bait-and-switch" scheme.[86]

Reporter Josh Harkinson of left-wing *Mother Jones* magazine unmasked the fox in the henhouse. The STEM Education Coalition was headed by executive director James Brown, who also lobbied legislators directly on behalf of, you guessed it, Microsoft. Harkinson laid out the strategy. Pressed by the software giant, the STEM Education Coalition signed a letter in support of the Microsoft visa bill. And then came the switch:

> With the coalition in its corner, Microsoft approached a bipartisan group of senators to craft what would become the Immigration Innovation, or "I-Squared" Act. And that's where the alleged "lobbying malpractice" came in. The act, as promised, would boost the caps on visas and green cards and use the fees to pay for STEM education. But in a crucial difference that has angered some of Microsoft's would-be allies, *the bill would nearly quintuple the number of available visas—raising the cap to 300,000—and charge companies far less for them: as little as $1,825 apiece.* [Emphasis added.][87]

That's just the tip of the iceberg. Working Americans should call the "I-Squared" Act the "I'm Screwed" Act. When you read the bill, it looks like industry lobbyists went through the entire immigration system, identified any possible place to increase the amount of foreign labor, and created the ultimate wish list.

Let's go through all the increases. First, Hatch would increase the H-1B quota from 65,000 to 115,000. In addition, the bill automatically adds up to 50,000 additional visas a year whenever the quota is reached, using a convoluted system similar to the Gang of Eight plan (the quota can be lowered by up to 20,000 if the quota is not reached). The effect is that the annual limit immediately rises to 165,000. The bill allows annual limits to rise up to 245,000 per year in the future.

The I'm Screwed Act exempts anyone with a masters' degree or higher from a U.S. school from the H-1B quota. It would give employers a twofer by allowing H-1B spouses to work. The irony here is that, for the H-1B worker, the employer would have to comply with minimal labor protections. However, the spouse could work without any American worker protections whatsoever. The bill also exempts 6,800 treaty visas set aside as a result of trade agreements with Singapore and Chile from the quota. This sets a precedent for future treaty visas to be exempt as well.

There are so many exemptions and quota increases in the bill that it is impossible to predict how many foreign guest workers Hatch's bill would add. It would be simpler to just say that the I'm Screwed Act effectively would remove any nominal limit on the H-1B visas. As usual with such bills, Hatch would provide Kabuki funding to train Americans for the jobs that won't exist because of the increases in foreign labor. In practice, these fees just provide a slush fund to dispense political favors.

What about enforcement? What about Americans being replaced by foreign workers? Nothing. Hatch gives Microsoft and other big donors everything they want and nothing they don't want. In fact, the I'm Screwed Act actually hinders enforcement by limiting the ability of DHS to reject a renewal petition for an H-1B or L visa.

The I'm Screwed Act does make it easier for H-1B aliens to change jobs by allowing them sixty days to find a new job after leaving their current job (quit or fired) before they have to return home. Fine for foreign H-1B workers. But what do working Americans get from the bill? Cue the chirping crickets.

In Orrin Hatch's world, working Americans rank lower than foreign guest workers. He's not alone. Hatch has five co-conspirators to make the I'm Screwed Act "bipartisan": Amy Klobuchar (from Minnesota, where Cargill recently offshored nine hundred U.S. IT jobs), Marco Rubio (from Florida, where Walt Disney World laid off hundreds of U.S. IT workers), Chris Coons of Delaware; Jeff Flake of Arizona; and Richard Blumenthal (from Connecticut, where Northeast Utilities recently laid off two hundred U.S. IT workers). Klobuchar received $10,000 from Microsoft's PAC and more than $14,000 from employees in 2012. Flake received $10,000 from Microsoft's PAC in 2012.

The I'm Screwed Act was waiting to be heard by the Senate Judiciary Committee in midsummer 2015, but its future has been clouded by the unexpected backlash resulting from the Disney and Southern California Edison layoffs. Industry lobbyists and political insiders are hoping for their guardian angel Sen. Hatch to slip the bill's provisions into other "must pass" legislation. Viva la transparency!

Another way in which Bill Gates and his Microsoft money perpetuate the manufactured STEM worker crisis is through the Gates Foundation's aggressive push for the federal "Common Core" standards. (See Glenn Beck and Kyle Olson's book, *Conform: Exposing the Truth About Common Core and Public Education* for a thorough debunking of the federal standards scheme.) In its 2012 manifesto decrying the tech worker "crisis," titled "A National Talent Strategy: Ideas for Securing U.S. Competitiveness and Economic Growth," Gates's company championed "strengthening America's STEM pipeline" by

"providing additional resources to recruit and train STEM teachers and implement Common Core State Standards." The standards,
Microsoft claims, will "better prepare students for college and work
in these disciplines."[88] The Gates Foundation has poured more than
$200 million into the Common Core marketing campaign, spreading
money across the politicial spectrum, from the conservative American
Legislative Exchange Council and the U.S. Chamber of Commerce,
to the liberal Center for American Progress, to the National Governors Association and the Council of Chief State School Officers.[89] The
Gates Foundation has donated at least $5 million to former Florida
GOP governor and fellow immigration expansionst Jeb Bush's nonprofit foundation, the Foundation for Educational Excellence, to promote Common Core.[90] Like much of the special-interest "immigration
reform" advocated by Gates and company, their "education reform"
was crafted by D.C. lobbyists in hidden backrooms.[91] The quality
of the so-called standards for both math and language arts has been
challenged by eminent academics who sat in on the validation panels.
Instead, they are a lucrative federal juggernaut for testing, textbook,
and technology companies. Microsoft peddled Common Core testing technology to schools, urging districts to "migrate to the new
Windows as soon as possible" and "upgrade all [computer] units."[92]
Bill Gates testily denied any payoff. "There's no connection between
Common Core and anything Microsoft," he told a *Washington Post*
reporter.[93]

While the Common Core advocates purport to care about the success and well-being of American workers and American STEM students, Microsoft's "National Talent Strategy" spells out the real agenda:
"Establish a new and supplemental allocation of 20,000 H-1B STEM
visas to meet employers' hiring needs" and "Recapture 20,000 unused
employment based green card numbers." The proposals include convoluted "investment" requirements that employers who obtain such

visas and green card numbers pay into a vaguely defined fund "for the development of future American STEM workers." Microsoft pompously declares in its "National Talent Strategy" that its "proposal is not simply a request for additional H-1B visas or green card numbers. It is also a call to action for employers to engage directly in efforts to solve the crisis in the American STEM pipeline."[94]

It's all gesture politics. Common Core is premised on an urgent need for "bridging the gap." But as you know now, the STEM worker shortage is a big lie of Big Tech. The Gates Foundation's Common Core window dressing is a grand marketing ploy—not to "solve" failures in American STEM education, but to solve corporate America's "problem" of not obtaining cheap foreign labor quickly enough. By foisting a "standards" racket on the nation's students that will, in practice, lower or stunt academic achievement, the Gates Foundation and its co-conspirators are actually helping to manufacture an American talent deficit with the world. And by continuing to push for a massive pipeline of wage-depressing foreign workers to cure a nonexistent STEM shortage, Gates and company are driving the considerable American talent that already exists away from pursuing tech careers.

One immigration lobbyist succinctly praised Microsoft's mastery of the lobbying world and legislative deceit: "They're not a multi-billion-dollar company for nothing."[95]

SPENCER ABRAHAM: THE SENATOR FROM SILICON VALLEY

Michigan's Spencer Abraham is the ultimate revolving-door political hack.[96] After stints as the Michigan Republican Party's chairman, former vice president Dan Quayle's chief of staff, and cochair of the National Republican Congressional Committee, he served one term in the U.S. Senate from 1994 to 2001. During that time he quickly became the H-1B program's most fervent supporter. In 1997, fellow open-borders GOP Sen. Orrin Hatch of Utah selected him to chair the Senate Immigration Committee. Abraham parlayed his prominent position into Big Tech campaign cash[97]—even announcing his chairmanship at the headquarters of Cypress Semiconductor Corporation in San Jose, California. He was so proficient at raising money from the tech industry that he became known in Washington as "the Senator from Silicon Valley."[98]

Abraham was responsible for removing the ban on replacing Americans with H-1B workers from the 1998 H-1B bill that passed the House Judiciary Committee.[99] Americans who lose their jobs to H-1B workers can thank Abraham—not fate—for their unemployment.

But while Abraham was shepherding the 2000 H-1B expansion through Congress, he faced rising opposition at home in Michigan. Grassroots conservatives and pro–American worker activists hammered the senator's zealous support for Big Tech. The Federation for American Immigration Reform, which opposes illegal alien amnesty and H-1B expansions, peppered Michigan airwaves with tough ads exposing Abraham's support for legislation that "killed the requirement that employers hire Americans first" and informing the public about how he "raised big political money from huge corporations that want cheap foreign labor."[100]

Initially, Abraham's plight generated little response from H-1B supporters, so Senate GOP leaders cracked the whip. Lobbyists from several technology companies who were seeking an expansion of the H-1B program, including Microsoft and Intel, received calls from the Republican National Committee because, collectively, they had only contributed twenty-five thousand dollars.[101] The corporate lobbyists were told to meet with then–Senate majority leader Trent Lott at a location outside Washington.[102] During the meeting, Sen. Lott suggested to the attendees that they contribute money to a front group called "Americans for Job Security" that was running ostensibly independent advertisements on Abraham's behalf.[103] While only the participants know what transpired during the meeting, the strength of Sen. Lott's suggestion can be gauged by an email an Intel lobbyist wrote to other H-1B lobbyists:

> I have heard that regardless of our "limitations," we need to do something for Abraham if we want to see something [H-1B] moved in the Senate.[104]

A Motorola lobbyist responded to that message:

> According to my calculations that has us at about $7,000 so far. Any chance other companies can kick in quickly so we can show our support for Abraham? I think the sooner the better! We really can't afford to lose this opportunity.[105]

In October 2000, Microsoft funded a soft-money advertisement campaign on Abraham's behalf; the money was funneled through the Michigan Chamber of Commerce.[106] One can debate how much influence these efforts had on the bill's process, but the results speak for themselves: Congress did indeed pass the legislation those companies sought.[107] The *Wall Street Journal* quoted insider sources who estimated that Microsoft's Rescue Abraham war chest totaled at least $250,000.[108] By that point, Microsoft had spent "nearly $16 million on lobbying, cash donations to candidates and unregulated soft-money gifts in state and federal races since it came under government antitrust scrutiny in 1997."

Abraham ended up losing his Senate re-election bid, but Beltway barnacles always land on their parasitic appendages. The Big Government Republican served one term as George W. Bush's energy secretary, then stepped down to become an executive at one of the contractors he oversaw.[109] He also opened a new consulting firm, the

Abraham Group, and companion law firm, Abraham & Roetzel, based in D.C. In 2013, he made a new splash with a Big Business GOP donor letter pressuring House Republicans to cave on the Gang of Eight amnesty/H-1B liberalization bill. Joining Abraham: former Bush commerce secretary Carlos Gutierrez, amnesty cheerleader Karl Rove, and soft-on-enforcement former DHS secretary Tom Ridge.

Abraham's legislative director during his Senate term, Cesar Conda, is another Beltway fixture who most recently served as chief of staff to immigration turncoat and Gang of Eight dupe Sen. Marco Rubio. Conda has bounced from the pro-amnesty/pro-H-1B expansionist halls of the U.S. Chamber of Commerce to the Senate Small Business Committee to the lobbying firm Navigators Global LLC, former vice president Dick Cheney's office, and presidential campaign adviser gigs with the 1996 Dole-Kemp and 2008 Romney-Ryan tickets. In fact, Conda mentored Paul Ryan from the age of nineteen and secured him a job at Jack Kemp's open-borders outfit, Empower America (Conda served on the think tank's board). Ryan, "whose ties to the pro-immigration mafia ran deep," according to *Wired* reporter John Heilemann, worked behind the scenes to kill key 1996 immigration enforcement and reduction measures as legislative director to former Sen. Sam Brownback (R-Kans.). Ryan went on to champion George W. Bush's illegal amnesty plan and the Gang of Eight's open-the-immigration floodgates plan.[110]

In her 2002 book *Invasion*, Michelle recounted one of Abraham's defining legacies in the Senate that demonstrates his reckless penchant for selling out. Carrying water for Big Business interests that wanted cross-border traffic to remain as fast and loose as possible, Sen. Abraham led efforts to block the implementation of two key homeland security tracking databases—one for foreign student visa holders and the other for all temporary visitors (which was mandated by Section 110 of the 1996 Illegal Immigration Reform and Immigrant Responsibility

Act). Abraham spearheaded the Capitol Hill campaign to starve the first database of funding and crusaded several times to kill Section 110 altogether.

On September 11, 2001, neither of those databases was in place. To this day, there exists no central database to track visa overstayers like four of the 9/11 hijackers who went undetected and undeported after their visas expired.[111]

Heckuva job, Spence-y.

STUART ANDERSON AND THE NATIONAL FOUNDATION FOR AMERICAN POLICY

Oh, what a tangled web the revolving-door lobbyists weave. Another of Sen. Abraham's top staffers, Stuart Anderson, has been a loud and longtime advocate for increased immigration and H-1B expansion policies on the libertarian right. Anderson wrote immigration papers for the open-borders Cato Institute before writing H-1B legislation on Capitol Hill first for Sen. Abraham and then for GOP amnesty cheerleader Sen. Brownback. Anderson was part of the toxic alliance between radical leftist lawyer Rick Swartz and libertarians, Big Business groups, and GOP immigration expansionists on the right. Next, he worked as powerful policy director of the Immigration and Naturalization Service between 2001 and 2003 under inexperienced Bush appointee James Ziglar.

Among other treacherous acts, Anderson played an instrumental role in killing a foreign student visa tracking database opposed by universities and immigration expansionists. Nicholas Confessore at *The Washington Monthly* reported how rank-and-file enforcement agents felt about the Beltway operative:

"The best analogy I can draw about Stuart Anderson is something that an INS agent said to me: If you were going to hire someone to run the DEA, you wouldn't pick somebody who favors legalizing drugs," says a top Republican aide on the Hill. "And by putting Stuart Anderson in a ranking position in the INS, you've essentially done the same thing—you've got somebody who favors open borders running the agency that regulates the borders."[112]

Following his INS stint, Anderson took a position as executive director of the National Foundation for American Policy, "a non-partisan public policy research organization" whose address is in Arlington, Virginia. It's a one-man band. Anderson is NFAP and NFAP is Anderson. Sen. Abraham serves on NFAP's advisory board, natch. Sen Abraham's former legislative director, Sen. Marco Rubio's former chief of staff, and Beltway open-borders fixture Cesar Conda also served on the NFAP board.[113] Team Abramoff crony Grover Norquist has participated in telephone conference calls hosted by NFAP.[114] Anderson and his group churn out endless papers[115] advocating for the same H-1B legislative goodie bags that Anderson himself wrote while working in Congress.

SAL RUSSO AND TEA PARTY EXPRESS

This longtime California GOP strategist and consultant made waves in May 2014 when he reversed his "Tea Party" group's position on immigration and endorsed the same principles that undergird the Gang of Eight's mega-amnesty and immigration expansion proposals. In addition to embracing "legal status" for illegal aliens, Russo parroted the STEM worker shortage propaganda of Big Tech lobbyists, repeatedly cited Michael Bloomberg's Partnership for a New Economy propaganda, and called for a "rational visa policy" that forks over more cheap foreign worker visas to U.S. corporations.

Conservatives who oppose radical immigration liberalization for

Big Business were not surprised to see Russo shilling for open borders.[116] He was a key consultant to soft-on-illegal-immigration Republican Jack Kemp, who cofounded Empower America, the H-1B expansionist think tank, which spawned H-1B champions Cesar Conda and GOP Rep. Paul Ryan. Russo joined Microsoft lobbyist and Jack Abramoff crony Grover Norquist at a press conference sponsored by gun-grabbing, amnesty-promoting liberal Michael Bloomberg's Partnership for a New Economy—all supposed "Tea Partyers" for "immigration reform." [117]

Dressing up in Tea Party drag has paid off for Russo. In June 2014, OpenSecrets.org reported on the group's spending. "Tea Party Express offloads money with ease—it has spent $8.6 million this cycle, more than the $8.5 million it has raised—and ranks 16th among the 20 biggest spending PACs this cycle (a list that includes super PACs)." Where did the money go? Most of it "went for fundraising, salaries and administrative costs—about $6.6 million. By far the biggest recipient was Russo's own consulting firm. In fact, so far this cycle, Tea Party Express has paid $2.7 million to his company. . . . In 2012, the group *raised $10.1 million* and *spent $8.3 million on fundraising and overhead*—including $3.1 million for Russo's firm, or about 85 percent of the total raised." [118]

Selling out pays.

HARRIS "THE SHILLER" MILLER

To veterans of the immigration wars on Capitol Hill, Beltway fixture Harris Miller seems as old and unmovable as the Washington Monument. He worked for the late Robert F. Kennedy when he was a teenager, served six years as chairman of the Fairfax County Democratic Committee, spent eight years as legislative director to Sen. John Durkin (D-N.H.), took a Carter administration gig as deputy director at the Office of Personnel Management, and ran unsuccessfully in Virginia for Congress in 1984 and Senate in 2006.

In between government stints, he fronted a pro-outsourcing group called the World Information Technology & Services Alliance. In 1995, he became president of WITSA's U.S. counterpart, the Information Technology Association of America (ITAA). ITAA contracted with Stuart Anderson to produce one of several Chicken Little reports on the IT workforce shortage, which despite significant analytical flaws and shortcomings became the basis of a similarly shoddy Commerce Department report used to justify a tripling of H-1B visas in 1998.[119]

Miller also served as president of Immigration Services Associates, a D.C. lobbying group, and as government relations director of Fragomen, Del Rey & Bernsen, P.C., a law firm cofounded by another decrepit Beltway swamp creature, immigration lawyer Austin Fragomen.[120] Miller next landed as chief operator of Harris Miller & Associates, his namesake lobbying group specializing in immigration.[121]

According to Center for Immigration Studies analyst David North, revolving-door lobbyist Miller "pioneered special arrangements for Irish immigrants (Irish illegals had not benefited much from the IRCA program)" and "helped expand the H-1B program to its new heights." [122]

He also earned a healthy paycheck. In 2006, when he ran unsuccessfully for a U.S. Senate seat in Virginia, Miller disclosed assets of between $2.8 million and $8.1 million.[123] He attempted to campaign as a Howard Dean–style progressive and Obama-esque community organizer, stressing his humble roots in coal and steel country in western Pennsylvania. Even his wife went out of her way to spin Miller's story. As the *Washington Post* reported upon the Miller Senate Democratic primary campaign's launch, "Harris's rise to Northern Virginia's booming technology corridors made him rich, a fact his wife, Deborah, seemed to want to play down when she told a reporter to write that the candidate lives in Fairfax County rather than the wealthy enclave of McLean."[124]

Fortunately, the voters of Virginia didn't fall for the phony make-over. IT workers and labor groups hammered the veteran lobbyist as an "antichrist of outsourcing"; rival Jim Webb beat him by seven points.[125] To Beltway insiders, his decades-long reputation as a corporate water-carrier was indelible. He earned his nickname: Harris "the Shiller" Miller.[126]

In 2009, the ITAA merged with the American Electronics Association to form TechAmerica.

Miller's former employer, fellow Beltway operator Austin Fragomen, is chair of the board of another powerhouse lobbying organization for employers seeking expansive immigration policies. The American Council on International Personnel, originally founded in 1972, is now known as the Council for Global Immigration. In 2014, the council's lobbying expenditures exceeded $530,000.[127] Paid membership with the group gives companies "access to a superior J-Visa Exchange Program for the integration of global workforces with American business practices" and a "bridge" to federal policymakers on "legislative and regulatory matters."[128]

REVOLVING-DOOR DUO: BRUCE MORRISON AND PAUL DONNELLY

Bruce Morrison, former Democratic congressman from Connecticut, served as chairman of the House subcommittee on immigration from 1989 to 1991. He was author of the Immigration Act of 1990, which created the disastrous H-1B program, the EB-5 investor visa program, and his own eponymous, ethnic visa carve-out. As *Irish America* magazine put it: "Bruce Morrison is best-known for pioneering the Immigration Reform Act of 1990, which increased the total visas granted by 200,000 and included 48,000 for Irish immigrants (now called the Morrison Visas)."[129] He served on the U.S. Commission on Immigration Reform from 1992 to 1995, then founded the immigration liberalization lobbying firm Morrison Public Affairs Advocacy Group in 2001. His clients include the American Hospital Association and the Institute of Electrical and Electronic Engineers (IEEE-USA).

Before Morrison and his underling Paul Donnelly came aboard, IEEE-USA was one of the few lobbying groups that vigorously opposed the tech industry's abuse of H-1B. The group released a "Misfortune 500" index spotlighting correspondence from displaced American engineers and debunking the STEM worker myth.[130] "These letters put a human face on the crisis in our profession—an epidemic of age discrimination that will worsen if Congress approves 150,000 additional indentured, high-tech guest-workers without even preventing U.S. companies from legally replacing U.S. workers with cheaper H-1B visa holders," then-IEEE-USA president John Reinert noted in 1998.[131] The campaign proved too effective for IEEE-USA's parent organization, the worldwide IEEE, which, as Professor Michael Teitelbaum observes, has "imposed restrictions on U.S. advocacy by IEEE-USA as contrary to the interests of IEEE as a global organization."[132]

IEEE-USA hired Donnelly, Morrison's former congressional press secretary, to help "wean the organization from its outright opposition to immigration," as *The New Republic*'s John Judis reported.[133]

Instead of crusading to put American engineers first, Donnelly and Morrison's signature immigration lobbying crusade involves "instant green cards" for foreign tech workers.[134] The InfluenceExplorer.com website, which tracks lobbyists, reported that the Morrison Public Affairs Group had earned total income of more than $8.1 million through the second quarter of 2014, including $395,000 from the IEEE-USA,[135] whose budget is overwhelmingly subsidized by member dues.

GEORGE SOROS AND THE NATIONAL IMMIGRATION FORUM

Hungarian-born financier George Soros (net worth: $23 billion) boasted in 2003 that he had dumped $100 million into proimmigration liberalization causes and groups through his Open Society Foundation.[136] The Soros-funded National Immigration Forum (NIF) lobbies for both illegal alien amnesty and expanded foreign guest worker programs.

NIF was founded by far-left attorney Dale Frederick "Rick" Swartz of the Lawyers Committee for Civil Rights,[137] who opposed tracking and deporting visa overstayers and opposed employer sanctions against companies that violated immigration laws. Swartz cozied up to conservative Wall Street whiz and philanthropist Richard Gilder, as well as H-1B expansionists Grover Norquist, the U.S. Chamber of Commerce, and the Cato Institute. Swartz also served as an adviser to Microsoft.[138] In the spring of 2013, GOP megabundler, Mitt Romney supporter, and hedge fund billionaire Paul Singer (net worth: $2 billion) forked over a "six-figure donation" to NIF.[139]

The NIF board brought the organizations together with the American Civil Liberties Union and the likes of former American Immigration Lawyers' Association head Jeanne Butterfield, "who used to be executive director of the Palestine Solidarity Committee, identified by the Anti-Defamation League as an alliance between members of the Popular Front for Liberation of Palestine and the Workers World party (the Trotskyites behind the Iraq War protests)," according to Mark Krikorian of the Center for Immigration Studies.[140]

Swartz's open-borders, left-right coalition helped sabotage the Immigration Act of 1990, which was intended to impose modest restrictions on immigration, and turned it into "one of the most expansionist immigration bills ever passed."[141] Swartz worked with Spencer

Abraham's legislative director Cesar Conda and Sam Brownback's legislative director Paul Ryan to kill 1996 immigration enforcement measures.

NIF propped up a faux grassroots initiative of religious conservatives, dubbed the Evangelical Immigration Table, to lobby for the Gang of Eight immigration expansion bill.[142] Another Soros acolyte, his "chief strategist" Stanley Druckenmiller, joined Mark Zuckerberg's FWD.us outfit in 2013.[143]

In February 2015, the Soros-funded NIF underwrote pro–immigration expansion ads during the Daytona 500 race starring none other than—you can't make this stuff up—

Team Abramoff crony and open-borders champion Grover Norquist.[144] The money-grubbing merry-go-round in Washington never stops.

MICHAEL BLOOMBERG'S PARTNERSHIP FOR A NEW AMERICAN ECONOMY

Former New York City mayor Michael Bloomberg (net worth: $35 billion) is best known for his witch hunts against Big Gulp drinkers and gun owners. But the financial news tycoon also spends considerable time and money pushing for the wholesale elimination of the H-1B visa cap. With an utter lack of self-awareness, Bloomberg has repeatedly condemned foreign guest worker restrictions as "national suicide."[145] During a speech to the U.S. Chamber of Commerce in 2011, Bloomberg whined: "This is just absurd to deny American companies access to the workers they need." Yet, as *Computerworld's* Patrick Thibodeau pointed out, Bloomberg's Chicken Little spiel came "at a time when demand for H-1B visas is relatively light—as is IT hiring overall."[146]

Bloomberg's propaganda machine has successfully planted its

talking points and agenda on Capitol Hill. *U.S. News & World Report* noted that "lawmakers in Washington have increasingly adopted the rhetoric of the Partnership for a New American Economy ... Republican Sen. Jerry Moran from Kansas said that 40 percent of Fortune 500 companies were founded by immigrants or their children, citing one of the coalition's talking points verbatim. . . . [W]hile remarking on the STEM Jobs Act, [former] House Majority Leader Eric Cantor repeated the same statistic."[147]

Bloomberg's front group, the Partnership for a New American Economy, is a coalition of mayors and CEOs who support radical liberalization of immigration laws. Founded in 2010, its founding cochairs and members include:

- Mark Hurd, chairman, CEO and president of Hewlett-Packard (now copresident of Oracle);
- Robert Iger, president and CEO, Walt Disney Co., one of the world's premier family entertainment and media companies;
- J. W. Marriott, Jr., chairman and CEO of Marriott International, Inc., one of the world's leading lodging companies;
- Jim McNerney, chairman, CEO and president of Boeing, the world's largest aerospace company;
- Rupert Murdoch, chairman and CEO of News Corp., one of the world's largest media companies;
- Julian Castro, elected in 2009, the mayor of San Antonio, Texas, the seventh-largest city in the U.S.;
- Phil Gordon, elected in 2003, the mayor of Phoenix, Arizona, the fifth-largest city in the U.S.;
- Michael Nutter, elected in 2007, the mayor of Philadelphia, Pennsylvania, the sixth-largest city in the U.S.;
- Ken Chenault, chairman and CEO, American Express, a leading global payments, network, and travel company;

- James P. Gorman, president and CEO, Morgan Stanley, one of the world's foremost financial institutions; and
- Mort Zuckerman, editor-in-chief of *US News & World Report*, publisher and owner of the *New York Daily News*, and chairman, director, CEO and cofounder of Boston Properties, a commercial real estate firm.[148]

The "partnership" also includes multiple events hosted by Grover Norquist, including a February 2015 powwow with "top national GOP donors" Spencer Zwick, founder and managing partner of Solamere Capital, and Romney for President National Finance chairman; Mike Fernandez, chairman of MBF Healthcare Partners, and a major Republican donor and fund-raiser; and Andrew Puzder, CEO of CKE Restaurants, and Romney for President economic adviser.[149]

RUPERT MURDOCH AND OBAMA'S BIG BIZ "STRANGE BEDFELLOWS"

The Australian-born News Corp. magnate (net worth: $14 billion) may be the Obama administration's public enemy number one in front of the cameras, but behind closed doors on immigration policy, it's all hugs and smooches. Murdoch dined privately with White House senior adviser Valerie Jarrett in June 2014 to strategize. As the *Washington Examiner* reported, Jarrett gushed that the meeting was "enjoyable" and that "good policy makes strange bedfellows."[150]

Or rather: Statist self-interest makes treacherous bedfellows.

The next morning, Murdoch published a calamity-filled op-ed[151] in his News Corp.–owned *Wall Street Journal* (the paper that infamously declared "There shall be open borders"[152]). Sounding more like an Oberlin College freshman than a CEO, Murdoch declared that "immigration reform can't wait" and demanded that Congress adopt both full amnesty for millions of illegal aliens and wholesale removal of the

H-1B cap for foreign guest workers. Dubbed "immigration reform's biggest booster,"[153] Murdoch had already joined fellow open-borders billionaire Michael Bloomberg on Capitol Hill in 2010 to push "a full path to legalization"[154] and signed on to Bloomberg's Partnership for a New American Economy.

Did Murdoch's views affect coverage of immigration on News Corp.–owned Fox News Channel? While Michelle never experienced any direct pressure to censor or alter her views on immigration enforcement during twelve years as a Fox News contributor, Murdoch's undeniable influence on the network was obvious. The *New Yorker*'s Ryan Lizza reported in 2013 that "Fox News has notably changed its tone since the election." GOP Gang of Eight immigration expansionists and Fox News regular guests John McCain and Lindsey Graham exulted over the shift:

> McCain told me, "Rupert Murdoch is a strong supporter of immigration reform, and Roger Ailes is, too." Murdoch is the chairman and C.E.O. of News Corp., which owns Fox, and Ailes is Fox News's president. McCain said that he, Graham, Rubio, and others also have talked privately to top hosts at Fox, including Bill O'Reilly, Sean Hannity, and Neil Cavuto, who are now relatively sympathetic to the Gang's proposed bill. Hannity voiced support for a pathway to citizenship for undocumented immigrants, which he previously dismissed as "amnesty," on the day after the 2012 election.
>
> "God bless Fox," Graham said. "Last time, it was 'amnesty' every fifteen seconds." He said that the change was important for his reëlection, because "eighty per cent of people in my primary get their news from Fox." He added that the network has "allowed critics to come forward, but it's been so much better."

In December 2014, Murdoch once again dined with Valerie Jarrett. They cuddled up next to each other at a *Wall Street Journal*–hosted CEO forum in Washington, D.C., as former Florida Gov. Jeb Bush extolled the benefits of mass immigration. Murdoch pronounced himself "pleased" with Bush.[155] A photo of the trio posted by *WSJ* associate editor John Bussey shows Jarrett leaning in, smiling broadly at her "strange bedfellows."[156]

SHELDON ADELSON: HIGH ROLLER FOR HIGH IMMIGRATION

Las Vegas gambling magnate Sheldon Adelson (net worth: $30 billion) has placed his bets on pro–illegal alien amnesty Republicans for years. The self-proclaimed "social liberal"[157] poured upward of $150 million into losing GOP causes and candidates in 2012 and he continues to fund efforts to remake the party in his Big Business/Big Government image.[158] In July 2014, Adelson joined fellow open-borders billionaires Warren Buffett and Bill Gates in penning a *New York Times* op-ed that demanded Congress give them more foreign worker visas.[159] Reality-based commenters of all political backgrounds mocked the trio.

"What we have here are three of the richest men in America telling us that no matter how many Americans are out of work or underemployed, it's still critically important to make it easier for employers to go over the heads of American workers and hire workers from other countries," one perceptive *Times* reader snarked. "And they must know what they are talking about, because even though none of them have any special expertise in immigration, they are, after all, billionaires. It's not like they would somehow confuse their own self-interest with the common good. Or that they would uncritically repeat the same old conventional wisdom on immigration that big business has been pushing for years, just because everyone they know thinks the same way."[160]

Another commenter wondered, as did hundreds of others in response to the tech titans' pleas: "How do these three privileged, insulated men believe that allowing current illegal residents to obtain citizenship is not rewarding law breaking and will somehow not lead to more? This is not 'America's self-interest.' It's only in the interest of those seeking cheaper labor and votes." The reader proposed a solution that simply does not exist in the worldview of the open-borders billionaires or their lobbyists: "How about hiring [our] own 'talented graduates' who by most accounts are woefully underemployed and in debt?"[161]

Put American workers first? Nah. That's not Adelson's style. Preoccupied with securing driver's licenses and work permits for illegal alien workers, the casino kingpin united with liberal media mogul Haim Saban at a November 2014 forum of the Israeli-America Council and "upbraided many in the GOP for their opposition to legalizing millions of undocumented immigrants."[162]

Priorities.

ABLI/COMPETE AMERICA: NEW NAME, SAME OLD AGENDA

During the epic battle over the 1996 immigration enforcement and reduction package, Big Tech giants Intel, Microsoft, and Sun Microsystems propped up a pressure group called American Business for Legal Immigration. Its aim, author Andrew Wroe recounted, was to "destabilize the effort to reform legal immigration"[163] and force Sen. Alan Simpson (R-Wyo.) to back down on his proposal to lower the total number of foreign guest worker admissions from 140,000 to 90,000.[164] ABLI's head, Jennifer Eisen, was a former official at the open-borders American Immigration Lawyers' Association and the daughter of veteran, pro–immigration expansion lobbyist Phyllis Eisen—a former vice president and cofounder of the Soros-funded National Immigration Forum with Beltway left-right coalition-builder Rick Swartz.[165]

ABLI morphed into a new corporate-funded group, Compete America, in 2004. The Fratelli Group, a D.C.-based public relations firm, recommended a makeover to try to separate itself from illegal alien amnesty special interests. In addition to the name change, Fratelli introduced "e-mail alerts bearing the title, 'It's About Innovation'" and "rebuilt the group's Web site to focus on higher education, offering up-to-date statistics on engineering and science graduates at U.S. universities."[166]

Despite the facelift, the organization continues to recycle the same old platitudes, non sequiturs, and propaganda factoids from other immigration expansion groups—along with a "Jobs Lost" countdown clock that bemoans lost job opportunities not for American workers, but for foreign ones.[167]

INDIAN LOBBYING MUSCLE: NASSCOM LEADS THE PACK

The National Association of Software and Services Companies (NASSCOM) is a New Delhi–based trade group of more than one thousand Indian IT tech companies, led by offshore outsourcing giants Tata, Infosys, and Wipro. Its primary mission: more guest worker and temporary visas for its $100 billion industry and fewer barriers to entry into the U.S. In 2013, NASSCOM hired former Mississippi GOP governor and longtime immigration expansionist Haley Barbour's lobbying firm, BGR Group, "to amplify their concerns about restrictive clauses" on H-1B-dependent firms in the Gang of Eight amnesty package.[168] Barbour's group also officially lobbies for the Indian government.

NASSCOM president Som Mittal disclosed that veteran K Street heavyweights at Patton Boggs were "also helping us."[169] Lobbying disclosure forms show that lobbyist Jeff Lande of the Lande Group raked in five hundred thousand dollars from NASSCOM to push its immigration liberalization agenda.[170] Through the first half of 2014,

NASSCOM had spent a total of nearly $3.6 million on lobbying activities.[171] Smaller Indian lobbying and industry trade groups include CII (Confederation of Indian Industry) and FICCI (Federation of Indian Chambers of Commerce and Industry), which coordinate on "backroom lobbying" with NASSCOM.[172] The groups are known for pulling the race card and crying "discrimination"[173] to protest American lawmakers' attempts to rein in outsourcing and corporate abuse of our visa policies.[174]

Both NASSCOM and CII have been welcomed to the Obama White House for meetings on protecting offshore outsourcing companies.[175] American workers harmed by H-1B don't get access to the White House. But foreign lobbyists do.

THE (NOT-SO-U.S.) CHAMBER OF COMMERCE

It's not your grandfather's U.S. Chamber of Commerce anymore. The powerful group no longer advocates for American businesses and American entrepreneurs, but represents a politically entrenched synod of special interests demanding cheap foreign labor.

In 2013, the Chamber channeled more than $52 million into K Street lobbying efforts—primarily on behalf of illegal alien amnesty and Big Business–supported, Bill Gates–spearheaded Common Core education programs to maintain the façade of an American worker shortage and American talent deficiency.[176]

The Chamber is one of the staunchest promoters of illegal alien amnesty and joined with the AFL-CIO and American Civil Liberties Union to oppose immigration enforcement measures, including E-verify and employer sanctions. At the start of 2014, U.S. Chamber president Tom Donohue declared he would "pull out the stops" on behalf of the Gang of Eight immigration plan[177] and protect open-borders GOP incumbents at all costs.

The militant vow echoed Beltway crony and Bush amnesty architect

Karl Rove's closely aligned campaign—via his American Crossroads SuperPAC—to crush Tea Party primary challengers who strayed from the Big-Business-as-usual agenda of the Republican establishment.[178] Rove's empire and the U.S. Chamber are intimately intertwined. Steven Law, who served as the Chamber's former general counsel and worked as a top aide to Senate majority leader Mitch McConnell (R-Ky.) before that, approached Rove pal and Beltway GOP fixture Ed Gillespie, then of the Republican National Committee, with the idea to form American Crossroads.[179] After the 2014 midterms, the Chamber claimed credit for GOP victories—and didn't wait long to demand repayment in the form of immigration expansion policies to benefit Big Business donors. Chamber president Tom Donohue issued his threat through Rupert Murdoch's *Wall Street Journal,* which reported that Donohue had given the new GOP majority "two years to 'enact a vigorous program aimed at meeting the needs of the American people' [translation: the needs of corporations seeking cheap foreign labor] or risk losing their majority."[180]

The business of the Chamber and its allies is the big business of the Beltway, not the business of mainstream America.

THE AMERICAN ACTION NETWORK/AMERICAN ACTION FORUM

The Chamber-Crossroads alliance spawned yet another lucrative GOP open-borders front group pushing the Gang of Eight plan called the "American Action Network." Led by former Sen. Norm Coleman (R-Minn.) and cofounded with McCain adviser and fund-raiser Fred Malek, AAN shares its offices with American Crossroads in D.C.[181] Haley Barbour (there he is again!) is a key adviser.[182] The group's "action tank," the American Action Forum (AAF), boasts well-heeled and well-connected board members such as former Homeland Security secretary Michael Chertoff and Vin Weber. 2016 presidential hopeful Jeb Bush was also a board member.

AAF was founded in February 2010 and proceeded to spend a whopping $25 million on elections that year.[183] Its "most notorious initiative," as *National Review* writer Ian Tuttle described it, was a four-hundred-thousand-dollar attack ad campaign against twelve congressional conservatives who objected to GOP House majority leader John Boehner's homeland security appropriations bill, which funded President Obama's executive amnesty program.[184] Boehner's former chief of staff, Barry Jackson, sits on the AAN board, too.

In 2013, the group dumped more than $750,000 into prime time, Fox News Channel ad buys pushing the Gang of Eight immigration bill, including $100,000 in ads to support leading GOP voices for amnesty, among them Sen. Marco Rubio, former Florida governor and 2016 presidential candidate Jeb Bush, and Wisconsin Rep. Paul Ryan.[185] AAN's affiliate, the Hispanic Leadership Network, has fashioned itself as a language watchdog and tone police monitor, rebuking conservative lawmakers who favor strict immigration enforcement for using the terms "illegal," "aliens," and "amnesty."[186]

ERIC CANTOR AND THE GRASSROOTS AMERICAN WORKER REVOLT

On June 9, 2014, Eric Cantor was a powerful "Young Gun" in the nation's capital—House majority leader, darling of Wall Street bankers, and seven-term representative of Virginia's affluent Seventh District. He had a massive campaign war chest and a virtual Rolodex full of deep-pocketed CEOs. Cantor had schmoozed with Silicon Valley bigwigs at Facebook, scooped up more than eighty thousand dollars in Big Tech campaign contributions in 2014, and embraced both a "pathway to citizenship" for millions of illegal aliens and generous H-1B expansions.

As he faced a swelling backlash back at home, Cantor showered his district with anti-amnesty flyers that fraudulently portrayed him as standing up to President Obama on amnesty.[187] Not mentioned:

his championing of the DREAM Act for illegal alien students and his lavish praise for the U.S. Chamber of Commerce/AFL-CIO collaboration on immigration expansion.[188]

On June 10, 2014, voters gave Eric Cantor the boot in a stunning rebuke to his Big Biz sellout and political fakery. Upstart challenger Dave Brat, an economics professor at Virginia's Randolph Macon College, pulled off "the biggest House primary upset in generations."[189] Outspent $5.5 million to two hundred thousand dollars,[190] the devout Christian called his victory "an unbelievable miracle."[191] Unlike the corporate and establishment special interests lined up against him, Brat was in tune with the concerns of ordinary American workers and small business people in the district. Cantor's biggest donors included New York financial conglomerates the Blackstone Group ($65,500) and Goldman Sachs ($26,000) and California tech company Oracle ($25,000).[192] Brat's biggest contributors were Virginia couple Gerry and Karen Baugh of Baugh Auto Body shop ($5,400), Michigan writer and artist Louis McAlpin ($5,200), and retired Virginia couple Martha and Kenneth Schwenzer ($5,200).[193]

One outside group, the American Chemistry Council, spent a whopping $300,000 on soft-money ads to protect Cantor—an amount that exceeded Brat's entire campaign funding.[194]

Stalwart conservative radio talk show host Laura Ingraham, who defied the GOP old boys' club and championed Brat's campaign, nailed the core reason for Cantor's stunning defeat. It was voters' "fury with the GOP establishment on fiscal issues and immigration" that sealed the political hack's fate. By contrast, Brat's "sense of integrity and duty is very appealing at a time when a lot of people dine out on incumbency status and yet they don't return real results for people," Ingraham told the *Wall Street Journal.* "Eric Cantor tried to be something he wasn't."[195]

Brat's no-nonsense and plainspoken advocacy of American workers and small business owners resonated in Virginia and across the country. On November 4, 2014, Brat won the general election in the Seventh District. Despite immense pressure to sell out, Brat has defied the open-borders powers that be. His message for Eric Cantor is the same message he carries on Capitol Hill to Cantor's cronies:

> Eric Cantor doesn't represent you, he represents large corporations seeking a never-ending supply of cheap foreign labor. He doesn't care about how this will affect your livelihood, your schools, your tax bills or your kids' chances of finding a job. I will fight to end crony capitalist programs that benefit the rich and powerful. The central policy issue in this race has become Cantor's absolute determination to pass an amnesty bill . . . this is not the Republican way to fix our economy and labor markets.[196]

Brat's victory sends a clear message that with faith, persistence, and clarity, grassroots activists fighting for American workers *can* defeat entrenched incumbents, their Beltway barnacles, and their money.

But this fight is just one battle in a long war. The Cheap Labor Lobby hasn't just sold out America's skilled workers on H-1B. They've managed to get their hooks into every other major temporary guest worker program, milked a corruption-friendly foreign investor visa program, and crafted a massive new pipeline for low-cost foreign workers on the D.C. cocktail party circuit—behind closed doors and beyond the reach of legislators and voters.

⊷ 12 ⊶

Exposed: How Beltway Crapweasels Cooked Up the Gang of Eight's "Comprehensive Immigration Reform"

As a general rule, wherever you find a large group of people who are baffled by complexity, you will find a smaller group of people making a good living screwing them.—Scott Adams[1]

Everyone in Washington pretends to agree: America's immigration system is "broken" and needs to be "fixed."

President Obama proclaimed, "If we want to keep attracting the best and the brightest from beyond our shores, we're going to have fix our immigration system, which is broken, and pass common-sense immigration reform."[2]

GOP House Speaker John Boehner declared, "[O]ur nation's immigration system is broken" and "must be solved."[3]

The House Democrats dedicated a website to "reforming our broken immigration system."[4]

The so-called bipartisan Gang of Eight in the Senate asserted in a joint statement: "Our immigration system is broken and it is time for a national conversation about how to fix it. We believe common sense immigration reform is vital in order to secure America's borders, advance our economic growth, and provide fuller access to the American dream."[5]

The problem, of course, is that for most bipartisan Beltway crap-weasels beholden to corporate special interests and open-borders lobbyists, the definitions of what's "broken" and how to "fix" it always translate into: more illegal immigration, more temporary guest worker visas, more complex and corrupt loopholes backed by Big Business, and more backroom regulatory schemes to undermine U.S. sovereignty and American workforce protections that are supposed to be at the foundations of our immigration and entrance policies.

When foreign guest worker expansionists moan about how "complex,"[6] "complicated,"[7] and "confusing"[8] our immigration laws are, it's all for show. As we've demonstrated for you time and again, our system is a mess *because* of the deliberate actions and advocacy of cheap labor gluttons, their influence-peddlers, immigration lawyers, and water-carriers in Washington.

That's why the Senate's Gang of Eight "comprehensive immigration reform" plan, or anything modeled on it (such as the House Speaker Boehner's "immigration reform" blueprint[9]) or spun off from it (such as Sen. Hatch's I-Squared green card expansion), is an absolute nonstarter. Period. This 180,000-word, 1,200-page legislative package, S.744, is a monster of deception. We're going to show you the fraudulent way to do "immigration reform" by dissecting some key, H-1B-related pieces of the Gang of Eight bill and showing you which special interests were in the driver's seat selling out America's skilled workers.[10]

"THEY SEE DOLLAR SIGNS"

The "comprehensive immigration reform" bill of 2013 was all about politics and profit—not about reform. "Comprehensive" is the open-borders weasel word for granting millions of illegal aliens the right to stay in the country without any meaningful consequences. "Reform" is the corporate weasel word for more guest worker visas for low-wage foreigners to replace Americans. Which leaves: "immigration." More immigration of future Democratic voters from south of the border. More importation of cheap labor, mostly from India and China. More visa overstayers from around the world slipping through the cracks.

Democrats wanted an amnesty for illegal aliens and held guest workers hostage to that goal. No amnesty would mean no guest workers for Big Business. Hardly anyone with political power wanted *real* immigration reforms, such as ending the practice of replacing Americans with H-1B workers, removing restrictions on enforcement, or removing the ability for employers to pay H-1B workers much less than Americans.

The entire process was corrupt to its core.

America *should* be having a national discussion on how much immigration we should allow. The question for a sovereign nation isn't whether, but *what* should our immigration limits be? Should that be a fixed number or should America have a target population and adjust immigration levels for that target? How would we allocate the annual immigration budget? Do we preserve our system of "diversity" in immigration? Do we want to emphasize skills or family ties?

But instead of having an open debate and transparent discussion with the public, the Gang of Eight (Democrats Michael Bennett, Dick Durbin, Bob Menendez, and Chuck Schumer and Republicans Jeff Flake, Lindsay Graham, John McCain, and Marco Rubio) worked in secret to create the bill. Durbin and Rubio plotted strategy during early morning workout sessions at the Senate gym; Schumer acted as a private emissary to the White House on behalf of his open-borders GOP gang members.

While the American people were locked out of the process, connected insiders owned prime seats at the discussion table. The Gang of

Eight senators allowed the AFL-CIO and the U.S. Chamber of Commerce to negotiate the provisions of a new guest worker program.[11] In fact, the *New Yorker* reported a year after the deal, "Schumer and Graham met privately with the leaders of the [AFL-CIO] and the Chamber of Commerce and told them to write that provision themselves."[12]

Meanwhile, Graham welcomed the insatiable appetite of Big Tech barons and their lobbyists. "They keep coming back for more," Graham told the magazine. "But he didn't mean it in a bad way," the reporter added. "You have the right to come back for more when you don't get what you want," Graham cheered on the lobbyists. "The country where you can ask for almost anything!"[13] With tech money pouring into their coffers, Gang of Eight members threw every inconvenient principle and stand out the window. Flake and Graham flip-flopped on border security measures they had previously supported. Durbin, who had teamed with vigilant Sen. Chuck Grassley on past bills, had to disavow his prior votes.

"I was sticking with the team and voting against things that I had supported in the past," Durbin shamelessly told the *New Yorker*.[14]

"Comprehensive immigration reform" *uber alles*. *Real* reform be damned!

For his part, Gang of Eight GOP leader Sen. Rubio, a 2016 GOP presidential contender,[15] wasn't consulting with American workers. Instead, he hired Enrique Gonzalez, a Democratic donor and partner from the prominent and politically connected global immigration law firm Fragomen Del Rey, to be his chief adviser on the bill.[16] Gonzalez specializes in obtaining H-1B and EB-5 visas for clients.[17]

Immigration lawyer-lobbyists are not interested in efficiency and efficacy. They need the system to be as complicated as possible to generate fees. When asked about the conflict of interest in Rubio's hiring of Gonzalez, a Fragomen partner insisted that his colleague had "cut his ties to the firm" and that it "was a clean break."[18] Yet, Gonzalez immediately returned to Fragomen after the Senate approved the bill he helped craft—and used the stint to enhance his business. His corporate biography brags:

> From January to August 2013, Enrique served as Special Counsel on Immigration to U.S. Senator Marco Rubio (R-FL) where he was the Senator's principal advisor/negotiator on the Border Security, Economic Opportunity, and Immigration Modernization Act (S. 744) that was approved by the U.S. Senate on June 27, 2013.

A "clean break"? Outside the Beltway, we call that a self-aggrandizing, pocket-lining revolving door.

In case you think we're being too harsh, take it from a *San Jose Mercury News* dispatch filed from the annual American Immigration Lawyers Association (AILA) conference in June 2013. New York attorney Sam Udani told a reporter that the Gang of Eight plan was like a "permanent pension plan for immigration lawyers."[19] Giddy AILA members salivated at the windfall. "Some are looking to ride the expansion of employment-based immigration," the *Mercury News* noted, "where attorney fees can range from $2,000 for a temporary tech worker's application to more than $20,000 for a wealthy investor trying to secure a green card." Still insistent on objectively describing the legislative behemoth as a "reform bill," the *Mercury News* acknowledged that it would be nothing but "a boon to thousands of immigration lawyers, especially those representing corporate clients."[20]

"Why are they supporting this? They see dollar signs," Kenneth Rinzler, an AILA member since 1992 and frequent critic of the group's leadership and lobbying, explained. "You're creating all these new regulations. The lawyers are going to benefit."[21]

A CHRISTMAS TREE OF GOODIES

The Gang of Eight's handiwork (or rather, their lobbyists', lawyers', and donors' handiwork) passed the Senate on June 27, 2013. The final bill, stuffed with favors and preferences for cronies and cheap-labor-craving corporations, exceeded 180,000 words and took up 1,198 pages. Thanks to profit-seeking immigration lawyers and obfuscation-minded lobbyists, the legislation is twelve times longer than the Immigration Act of 1952 that created the current immigration system. The roll call vote on S. 744 thoroughly debunks the stereotypes of Republicans as the Big Business party and Democrats as the working people's party. *Every* Democrat in the Senate voted for this goodie bag for corporate special interests, as did fourteen Big Business Republicans; thirty-two GOP Senators voted against it. The fourteen GOP sellouts: Alexander (R-Tenn.), Ayotte (R-N.H.), Chiesa (R-N.J.), Collins (R-Maine), Corker (R-Tenn.), Flake (R-Ariz.), Graham (R-S.C.), Hatch (R-Utah), Heller (R-Nev.), Hoeven (R-N.D.), Kirk (R-Ill.), McCain (R-Ariz.), Murkowski (R-Alaska), and Rubio (R-Fla.).

In addition to all the handouts written into the bill, the immigration gangsters tacked a laundry list of special backroom deals, buyoffs, and kickback amendments onto their vehicle. The proenforcement Federation for American Immigration Reform identified several of the Christmas surprises that most Americans have never heard about:[22]

- Sanders's Slush Fund. This carve-out for Sen. Bernie Sanders (I-VT) created a special "youth jobs" program at a cost of $1.5 billion from the U.S. Treasury. Until the Gang of Eight added the kickback, Sen. Sanders was an outspoken critic of the bill for taking jobs away from Americans. He has since been silent (Title V, p. 1169).
- Hotels for Harry and Heller. This kickback for Las Vegas hotel and casino chains permanently set aside $100 million annually to

the tourism industry under the Travel Promotion Fund, posing a win for Nevada senators Dean Heller (R-Nev.) and Harry Reid (D-Nev.). The funding was set to expire in 2015, but this provision would have extended it indefinitely (Sec. 1102(f), p. 66).

- Schumer's Skilled Worker Sellout. Sen. Chuck Schumer (D-N.Y.) obtained an exemption to allow public universities to displace U.S. workers with H-1B nonimmigrants.[23] The deal also exempted nonprofit education and research institutions from the higher fees and stricter requirements imposed on employers that rely heavily on H-1B workers.[24]

- Leahy's Celebrity Sweetener. Senate Judiciary Chairman Pat Leahy (D-Vt.) obtained a carve-out to grant special treatment to Hollywood by waiving fees for artist O and P visas if applications are not processed within fourteen days.[25]

- Marco Phones and Cruise Ships. S. 744 created a new nonimmigrant Z visa to admit individuals who possess "specialized knowledge" to perform maintenance on airlines and cruise ships—a big industry in Florida (Sec. 4606, p. 1034). The bill also included a two-year grant program for individuals living along the southern border "at greater risk of border violence" to purchase satellite telephones that can access 911 and are GPS-equipped.[26] TracPhone, a Florida-based company, makes these phones, and S. 744 appropriated "such sums as may be necessary" to fund the grant program.

- Hatch's High-Tech Hijack. To gain Sen. Orrin Hatch's (R-Utah) support for the Gang of Eight bill, the Judiciary Committee adopted an amendment to give tech companies greater access to cheap foreign labor, hijacking jobs from hardworking Americans. The deal Hatch struck with Sen. Schumer increased the number of H-1B visa holders admitted to the country annually, and admitted H-1B workers at a faster pace.[27] In addition, the Hatch Amendment eliminated the requirement placed on all H-1B employers in the original version of S. 744 that they attest they have not displaced and will not displace U.S. workers within a certain time frame.[28] It also eliminated the requirement on all H-1B employers in the original version of S. 744 that they attest they have offered the job to any U.S. worker who applied who was equally or better qualified.[29]

QUOTA QUACKERY

Section 4101 of the Gang of Eight bill would have put in place a so-called "market-based cap" system for H-1B visas. The system for calculating the cap was needlessly complicated to obscure the plain giveaway to Big Tech. The number of visas for the base quota of 65,000 would have been immediately raised by 50,000 to a minimum of 115,000 visas and would have been adjustable up to a maximum of 180,000 based on "market conditions."[30] The bill would have also raised the special H-1B allotment dedicated to foreign student graduates in master's or PhD programs from 20,000 to 25,000. In total, the base quota would have permanently risen to a range of 155,000 to 225,000 a year.

"Under the likely high-demand scenario," the Economic Policy Institute estimated, "we would have 120,000 more H-1Bs annually than we do now, and 58,800 of them would be in IT."[31] In other words: Nearly half of new IT jobs requiring a college degree could have been filled by foreign guest workers.[32]

To put the Gang of Eight's unwieldy new quota change in perspective, take a look at how the cap has morphed over time. When the law's limit was first created in 1991, it specified that the total number of aliens to be issued H-1B visas during any fiscal year "may not exceed 65,000."[33]

After twenty-three years of amendments, the loopholes have

proliferated like bunnies on Viagra. The iron-clad cap expanded from 65,000 to:

(ii) 115,000 in fiscal year 1999;
(iii) 115,000 in fiscal year 2000;
(iv) 195,000 in fiscal year 2001;
(v) 195,000 in fiscal year 2002;
(vi) 195,000 in fiscal year 2003; and
(vii) 65,000 in each succeeding fiscal year.

Cap exemptions were extended to any nonimmigrant visa holder who:

(A) is employed (or has received an offer of employment) at an institution of higher education (as defined in section 1001[a] of title 20), or a related or affiliated nonprofit entity;
(B) is employed (or has received an offer of employment) at a nonprofit research organization or a governmental research organization; or
(C) has earned a master's or higher degree from a United States institution of higher education (as defined in section 1001[a] of title 20), until the number of aliens who are exempted from such numerical limitation during such year exceeds 20,000.[34]

The Gang of Eight bill would have turned this already overly long section into a sprawling tangle that takes a law degree to understand. Appendix E provides the full text of the Gang of Eight's convoluted nonsense here. This is yet another example of what the Gang of Eight's "comprehensive immigration reform" bill—embraced by politicians who keep complaining about how "complex" and "complicated" our system is—proposed to satisfy Big Tech's demand for more H-1B workers.

Now you know why the bill was 1,198 pages long.

It would have been easier—and a hell of a lot more honest—to just remove the H-1B quotas altogether. That is what this part of the bill effectively did, anyway. The so-called market-based cap would not have been tied to any "market" force other than the bottomless demand for H-1B visas. The sole purpose of all this legislative diarrhea was to increase the cap when the cap is reached. Consistent with the rest of the bill, the authors felt a need to lard up the package with unwieldy language to conceal its true goals.

MORE EMPTY GESTURES FOR AMERICAN WORKERS

The Gang of Eight promised they would "prevent H-1B workers from undercutting the wages paid to American workers by requiring employers to pay significantly higher wages for H-1B workers than under current law."[35] Section 4211 purported to do this by altering the current prevailing wage system. Instead of giving employers the current four levels to choose from in H-1B law, the bill would have employed three prevailing wage levels with the lowest wage group no lower than 80 percent of mean wages. That's right. In the name of preventing H-1Bs from undercutting American workers, the law would have allowed employers to pay H-1B workers up to 20 percent *less* than the actual prevailing wage. (Also note: Spouses of H-1Bs who are granted work authorizations thanks to President Obama's 2015 administrative order would not have been subject to this thicket of prevailing wage rules.)

Making the H-1B prevailing wage no less than 80 percent of the actual prevailing wage and calling that a "strengthening" of the prevailing wage system is not "reform." It's a damning indictment of the politicians who pretended to care about U.S. workers.

The immigration gangsters' bill piled on even more complexity by creating new, separate prevailing wage rules for most employers and H-1B-dependent employers. FAIR noted that under this section, employers would have still been allowed "to pay H-1B workers discounted wages because the prevailing wage does not factor in 'hot skills' that command a premium in the open market." [36]

Professor Norman Matloff explained that "hot skills" such as Android programming "command a premium of 15–25% in the open market." The whole point of excluding them from the calculation was to ensure that the legal prevailing wage would typically be lower than the true market wage.

In addition, he wrote:

> The law also requires the employer to pay the "actual wage," a misnamed term that refers to the wage earned by other "similar" workers employed at the firm, in the same job. Clearly this is rife with loopholes too. The employer can claim the foreign worker is unique in terms of skills, experience and job, so the actual wage is actually his wage (Dept. of Labor written policy recognizes this). And of course if most or all of the "similar" workers are foreign too, the statute loses all meaning.
>
> Furthermore, [Labor Department data from] green card applications, which operate with the same wage rules as H-1B, show that most employers pay only the prevailing wage or very near it, NOT the actual wage. Since the legal prevailing wage is below market rates, it is clear that most employers are underpaying their H-1Bs. [37]

The "immigration reform" gangsters played the same obfuscation games with provisions allegedly protecting Americans from wholesale replacement with H-1B guest workers. A section of the bill addressed nondisplacement measures for "all employers" that would have required them to first seek out and hire "equally or better qualified Americans" before turning to H-1B.

Sounds good, right? But the very first provision in this section, which spelled out what employers must attest to before obtaining H-1Bs, featured *exemptions* to the rules. "All" meant . . . *not* all:

> (E)(i)(I) **In the case of an application filed by an employer that is an H–1B skilled worker dependent employer, and is not an H–1B dependent employer,** the employer did not displace and will not displace a United States worker employed by the employer during the period beginning 90 days before the date on which a visa petition supported by the application is filed and ending 90 days after such filing.[38]

Say *what*?

You'll recall that "H-1B-dependent employers" generally means companies of more than fifty-one full-time employees with 15 percent of workers on H-1B visas. These are the offshore outsourcing giants in India such as Infosys, Tata Consultancy, Wipro, and HCL. But what the heck is an "H-1B skilled worker dependent employer"? It was a new category manufactured by the Gang of Eight to mollify the complaints of American companies such as Facebook with burgeoning H-1Bs on their payrolls. The Gang of Eight bill would have divided employers into three categories:

- H-1B-dependent employers (more than 15 percent of workforce on H1B);
- H-1B skilled worker-dependent employers (more than 15 percent of professional workforce on H-1B) who are not H-1B-dependent employers;
- All other employers.

The newly-created SWDE ostensibly prevented H-1B-dependent employers from gaming the system by diluting the ratio of H-1B workers in their workforce by hiring relatively low-skilled employees.[39] As the Fragomen law firm (that's Sen. Rubio's immigration adviser's company) explained, the SWDE category was:

> ... defined as an employer whose skilled workforce—comprising full-time equivalent employees in occupations within Zones 4 and 5 of the Labor Department's O*NET database—is made up of 15 percent or more H-1B workers. . . . As a practical matter, the percentage of H-1B workers would be arrived at by measuring the number of H-1B workers against the H-1B-caliber U.S. workforce, rather than the entire workforce, and undoubtedly would yield a higher percentage.[40]

Confused? That's exactly how the Gang of Eight's bill-writers want you. The big, bad, Indian companies, which get the largest number of visas, became scapegoats and got one set of rules as H-1B-dependent employers. The sweet, innocent American companies that pretend to be fair and always do right by U.S. workers balked at being lumped in with their partners in crime, so they got a different set of rules. Thanks to Sen. Hatch's advocacy, however, the restrictions for H-1B-dependent employers were so watered down in the final bill that there was little practical difference, anyway.

In sum, the Hatch-Schumer deal gutted already-feeble American worker protections by significantly limiting the number of employers required to attest they hadn't displaced U.S. workers within certain time frames (90 or 180 days before and after filing a petition, depending on the category of employer)—and by excluding the vast majority of employers from a Kabuki requirement that all employers offer jobs to "equally or better qualified" American workers.[41]

As FAIR explained the provisions, H-1B "skilled worker dependent employers" had to offer a job to equally or better qualified U.S.

workers before considering an H-1B, while all other employers "merely [had] to advertise the position online; and take 'good faith steps' to recruit U.S. workers 'using procedures that meet industry-wide standards' and offer at least the wage rate offered to H-1B workers."[42]

The Gang of Eight bill also preserved a major, Grand Canyon–sized loophole. The nondisplacement requirement was restricted so that the employer "will not displace a United States worker *employed by the employer.*" The employer could still displace American workers employed by *other* employers—which left open the loophole of using third parties (Tata, Infosys, and all the other IT outsourcing companies) to replace American workers.

Translation: bipartisan Beltway crapweasel business as usual.

S.744 wasn't "comprehensive immigration reform"—it was *comprehensive fraud*. The lobbyists who wrote the bill deliberately made the bill overly long because they knew few reporters and voters would actually read it and expose the lies. If not for vigilant conservatives in the House of Representatives, this massive screw-over of working Americans would have become law.

Where Do the 2016 Candidates Stand?

Former presidential candidates Patrick Buchanan (1992, 1996, and 2000) and Tom Tancredo (2008) helped bring the issues of illegal immigration and border security to the forefront of the national debate in their respective bids. But when it comes to public officials who champion high-skilled American workers displaced by cheap foreign labor imported through ever-expanding temporary visa programs, the pickings on either side of the political aisle are like pop star Taylor Swift: impossibly slim and notoriously fickle.

Clinton Foundation donor and corporate mogul Donald Trump vaulted to the front of the GOP pack and the top of the polls in the summer of 2015 by spotlighting brutal crimes by illegal aliens against Americans. But while vowing to build a "Trump Wall" on the southern border, the *Celebrity Apprentice* star also espoused "a path" toward legalization for illegal aliens he deemed "outstanding"—a path to citizenship, in other words, that sounds a lot like the amnesty paths of his rivals.[1] In August, Trump distinguished himself again from the field by releasing a detailed immigration reform plan that addressed not only border security, but also reform of legal immigration levels and nonimmigrant visa programs. Most notably, Trump (after reportedly consulting with GOP Sen. Jeff Sessions) called for increasing the prevailing wage for H-1Bs and enforcing a real requirement "to hire American workers first" because "[t]oo many visas, like the H-1B, have no such requirement."[2] The campaign plan also rightly mocked Gang of Eight supporter Sen. Marco Rubio's Big Tech ties and zinged Rubio as the "personal senator" of Facebook CEO Mark Zuckerberg.

Trump's blueprint is a serious, impressive, and encouraging document. Whether he himself actually read and understood its proposals is another matter. Unfortunately, it took just a few days for schizophrenic Trump to undermine his own immigration reform plan by tweeting: "When foreigners attend our great colleges & want to stay in the U.S., they should not be thrown out of our country." He added: "I want talented people to come into this country—to work hard and to become citizens. Silicon Valley needs engineers, etc."[3] But the American technology worker shortage, as we've shown you, is a big fat lie. Moreover, as we've shown you, Trump's support for unlimited green cards to fraud-plagued foreign student visas (a proposal advocated aggressively by Big Tech CEOs like Mark Zuckerberg, as you now know) is fraught with peril for American workers and students. Veteran H-1B critic University of California Davis professor Norman Matloff initially cheered the Trump plan. But while it's "nice that Trump is shaking things up," Matloff warned: "If Congress creates special programs for the foreign students, e.g., fast-track green cards," as Trump unwittingly endorsed, "H-1B will become irrelevant. The big problem will be the green cards."[4] Once foreign students acquire work rights en masse, "the game is over."[5]

Trump's own companies have imported more than one thousand workers on guest worker visa programs for both low-skilled and high-skilled workers, including 250 foreign models on H-1B visas.[6] (Maybe that's why Trump donated to the campaign of New York Democratic congressman Anthony Weiner.)[7]

The good news is that American workers and taxpayers do have some serious and effective voices on Capitol Hill, including the House Republicans who blocked the Gang of Eight plan and stalwart watchdog GOP Sens. Sessions and Grassley.

The bad news is that almost every other major 2016 presidential hopeful in both parties, from Hillary Clinton on the corporatist left to former Florida Gov. Jeb Bush (R) and Sen. Marco Rubio (R-Fla.) on the Big Business right, to Sens. Ted Cruz (R-Tex.) and Rand Paul (R-Ky.) on the Tea Party right, favor more temporary guest worker visas and raising (or obliterating) visa caps originally established to protect the American workforce.

Here's our rundown:

Hillary Clinton. The Democrats' 2016 frontrunner campaigned in Silicon Valley on a pledge to increase H-1Bs during her failed 2008 presidential bid.[8] She devoted considerable time and energy to promoting offshore outsourcing during her Senate tenure. In 2003, then-Sen. Clinton celebrated the arrival of Indian IT outsourcer Tata Consultancy Services to upstate New York, where the company's research deal with the University of Buffalo yielded a measly ten U.S. jobs. During that time period, Indian outsourcer petitioned to import more than sixteen hundred temporary guest workers to the Empire State under H-1B.[9] Tata called the arrangement Hillary's "brainchild."[10] Two years later, she traveled to India, where she touted the economic benefits of offshore outsourcing giant Tata, endorsed "more of such partnerships," and assured Indian businesses and government officials, "There is no way to legislate reality. Outsourcing will continue."[11] (As we told you, Tata, whose U.S.-based workforce is 95 percent South Asian, is now the subject of an employment discrimination lawsuit by an American

IT whistleblower.) Internal White House emails released in 2010 show that her husband's administration caved to the cheap-labor lobby in the 1990s despite sharp awareness of the H-1B program's flaws and failures to protect American workers.[12] President Clinton later racked up three hundred thousand dollars in speaking fees from Cisco—an aggressive outsourcer that laid off thousands of American workers,[13] ranks thirty-fourth among the nation's top H-1B users,[14] and got caught in 2007 posting a fake job ad as part of a common ruse to hire H-1B workers.[15]

Sen. Clinton, who cochaired the Senate India Caucus, once joked about running "for the Senate seat in Punjab"[16]—a fact spotlighted by the campaign of then-rival Barack Obama, who apologized and threw his staff under the bus after Indian groups protested that highlighting her ties to offshoring companies was "nativist" and "racist."[17]

Bernie Sanders. The avowed socialist senator from Vermont and Democratic presidential contender, who officially announced his candidacy in April 2015, is an outspoken critic of H-1B abuses. He cosigned a Senate letter calling for federal investigations after the Disney and Southern California Edison layoffs in the spring of 2015. In a Senate floor speech, he attacked offshore outsourcing firms "responsible for shipping large numbers of American information technology jobs to India and other countries."[18] He loudly protested the Gang of Eight's H-1B expansion as "a massive effort to attract cheap labor" and "a great disservice to American workers."[19]

But when push came to shove, Sanders voted for the bill anyway after receiving a $1.5 billion jobs slush fund payoff[20] (and as we showed you, the Gang of Eight bill was stuffed with gobs of similar goodies for senators in both parties who sold out). Sellout actions speak louder than words.

Jim Webb. The decorated Vietnam War hero, former secretary of the navy, and former Democrat senator from Virginia is a long-shot candidate running to put "our American house in order."[21] A longtime critic of H-1B, Webb declared while in the Senate: "I do not support guest worker programs. This applies to H-1B visas, except in the most extraordinary circumstances. I do not believe the myth of the tech worker shortage."[22]

Martin O'Malley. The liberal former governor of Maryland is a staunch advocate of Gang of Eight–style immigration "reform," including expanded amnesty for illegal aliens and huge expansions in temporary visas for foreign skilled workers. His presidential campaign platform includes eliminating the "rigid visa caps," "promoting family unity" for both illegal aliens and skilled foreign workers, and "address[ing] barriers for high-skilled immigrant workers, such as credentialing and licensing requirements and policies."[23]

Jeb Bush. The former GOP Florida governor and flip-flopping advocate of a "path to citizenship"[24] for millions of illegal aliens is at least consistent on one thing: He's an unabashed champion of the H-1B program. In his book *Immigration Wars*, he blasted the cap on H-1B visas as "hopelessly inadequate to preserve America's leadership role in technology" and attacked a short-lived Senate attempt to ban the displacement of American workers by federal-stimulus-funded companies that hire H-1B workers.[25] Bush also supports automatic work visas to foreign STEM students with advanced degrees, plus "unlimited numbers" of visas to foreign business investors and work-based visas "vastly expanded beyond the current numbers."[26] In a speech at the Detroit Economic Club in February 2015, he snubbed the plight of thousands of laid-off American workers in favor of promoting the interests of "H-1B visa holders" who "don't get their status improved."[27]

Sen. Rand Paul. The libertarian GOP candidate proposes work visas for millions of low-skilled illegal aliens, along with "expanded" high-tech visas and "special entrepreneurial visas."[28] He would pile a new "economic freedom zone visa" program on top of the fraud-ridden, loophole H-1B racket.[29] Paul has aggressively courted donors in H-1B-hungry Silicon Valley.[30] In July 2014, he was spotted at a private meeting in Sun Valley, Idaho, with Facebook billionaire Mark Zuckerberg.[31]

Sen. Ted Cruz sponsored an amendment to the Senate's 2013 "comprehensive immigration reform" bill to "immediately increase the H-1B cap by 500 percent from 65,000 to 325,000" with no effective measures to address systemic displacement of American workers.[32] (That's actually a 400 percent increase, but never mind.) In support of his measure, Cruz cited a dubious American Enterprise Institute study, which as we'll show you cherry-picked data to manufacture the oft-repeated claim that H-1B creates jobs for Americans. During Senate debate on his amendment, Cruz argued that "imposing restrictions on the visa was unnecessary," *Computerworld* reported. As the publication noted, "Cruz is part of large group of politicians who will not acknowledge the H-1B visas' use in offshore outsourcing or the reality of U.S. workers who are forced to train their visa-holding replacements.[33]

Sen. Marco Rubio. The junior GOP Florida senator, once a Tea Party darling, set a record for going native in Washington. As we showed you, this "Gang of Eight" cheerleader and presidential hopeful is backed by exactly the kind of veteran Beltway immigration expansionists and encrusted lobbyists the Tea Party opposed. Rubio is cosponsor of another far-reaching bill,[34] spearheaded by veteran immigration expansionist Sen. Orrin Hatch (R-Utah), which would allow companies to hire unlimited numbers of foreign tech workers who graduate from U.S. colleges—even while government and independent watchdogs expose systemic fraud and lax enforcement of current foreign student visa and training programs, diploma mills, and for-profit sham schools. Rubio also supports creation of "startup visas" and "entrepreneur visas"[35]—even as federal investigators and insiders uncover fetid political corruption and book-cooking in the existing government-run investor visa program.

Dr. Ben Carson has criticized President Obama's executive orders on illegal alien amnesty, but as of August 2015, had made no public statements on H-1B abuse or any other foreign worker visa programs that adversely affected American workers.

Former Texas Gov. Rick Perry signed a letter along with governors of other tech-heavy states urging Congress to massively increase H-1Bs in 2007.[36]

Former Arkansas Gov. Mike Huckabee has a long record of immigration liberalization. In office, he crusaded for in-state tuition discounts and driver's licenses for illegal aliens and supported massive increases in foreign worker visas. Only in the summer of 2015 did he go on record questioning H-1B abuse and criticizing companies "undercutting an American worker just so they can increase their profits without regard to the people who made them profitable in the first place."[37]

New Jersey Gov. Chris Christie signed "DREAM" legislation to give young illegal alien students in-state tuition discount rates.[38] He only belatedly joined a multistate lawsuit against the Obama White House's executive amnesty orders[39] and as governor, he vetoed anti-offshoring legislation that aimed to protect American call service workers.[40] His position on H-1B and other temporary visa programs is harder to find than a wedding band lost in the sands of the Jersey Shore.

Carly Fiorina. The failed GOP Senate candidate from California and business executive with a reverse Midas touch[41] casts herself as the anti-Hillary. But she has more in common with her nemesis than she might care to admit. Both have held major positions of leadership without any material accomplishments—and both have cashed in big-time. In addition to running Hewlett-Packard into the ground and collecting $21 million to exit the debacle,[42] Fiorina, like Hillary, is a big supporter of H-1B visas.[43]

In June 2015, Fiorina seized a campaign opportunity to bash Disney for its "bad policy" of tech worker layoffs. But she was forced to admit to Boston conservative talk show host Howie Carr that HP benefited greatly from H-1B and defended the program with this non sequitur: "There is no reason for us to fear highly skilled immigrants who want to come to this country and stay here and live here and contribute to our nation. . . . After all, this is a nation built on immigration." H-1B, as you now well know, is supposed to be a program for temporary, *non*immigrant workers, most of whom are not highly skilled.[44]

Former Pennsylvania Sen. Rick Santorum, a long-shot candidate running his second presidential campaign, has a solid voting record on immigration enforcement and has forcefully opposed legislative efforts to expand H-1B. He champions U.S. worker protections[45] and has declared: "It's about time someone doesn't just bow to corporate America on the Republican side, or just play the ethnic politics that the left now plays."[46]

Wisconsin Gov. Scott Walker firmly backed the 2006 McCain-Kennedy immigration bill that would have granted blanket amnesty to illegal aliens and massive increases to the H-1B program.[47] But in April 2015, after flip-flopping on a "path to citizenship" for illegal aliens,[48] Walker told the Glenn Beck radio show that he believed in a legal immigration system "based on, first and foremost, on protecting American workers and American wages, because the more I've talked to folks, I've talked to Senator Sessions and others out there—but it is a fundamentally lost issue by many in elected positions today—is what is this doing for American workers looking for jobs, what is this doing to wages, and we need to have that be at the forefront of our discussion going forward."[49]

Trump's H-1B reforms, Santorum's focus on American workers, and Walker's acknowledgment of unfettered immigration's negative impact on the U.S. job market and wages (however tentative or temporary it may be) are all noteworthy among a GOP presidential field that has largely limited its discourse on the subject to simplistic "amnesty equals bad, everything else equals good" platitudes. The cluelessness of the rest of the GOP field is effectively summed up by Sen. Rubio's cognitive dissonance on the campaign trail. In Iowa, he decried America's "economic downturn" and warned that we are facing an "economic transformation"—oblivious to his own central role in radically undermining both low-skilled and high-skilled American workers through amnesty and expansive foreign worker visa programs.[50]

On the other side of the aisle, Democratic front-runner Hillary Clinton continues to bemoan the "wage gap" while kowtowing to Silicon Valley's cheap-labor H-1B addicts and scooping up their top-dollar campaign donations.[51] "Everyday Americans need a champion. I want to be that champion," Clinton says on her campaign website.[52] A search of Hillary's website for any mention of laid-off Disney workers, Southern California Edison workers, or any other American workers forced to train cheap foreign labor replacements before losing their jobs comes up empty.

It's no wonder the American public distrusts and despises the "leaders" in both major political parties. The fundamental question of whether our country's politicians should defend American workers and wages against Big Tech's foreign labor racket is one that should unite us all. Instead, the vast majority of presidential candidates actually support allowing the wholesale replacement of America's best and brightest with the world's cheapest and most mediocre. That is how low our political class has sunk.

Candidates in both parties and their staffers who are serious about "fixing" the American economy would do well to acquire more than an inch-deep understanding of H-1B abuse, the great technology worker shortage hoax, Big Tech front groups and their Big Government hand-maidens, and the alphabet soup of America's other fraud-friendly visa programs harming U.S. workers.

Putting America back to work starts with putting American work-ers first—in deeds, not just empty, election-year words.

Conclusion

Pro-American Immigration Reform

Now that you've had a mind-boggling look at "immigration reform" gone awry, let's cut to the chase. Unlike the Senate gangsters and their co-conspirators, we don't claim to be "comprehensive" in our plan to protect the American workforce and restore a controlled, orderly immigration and entrance system. These thirteen principles and recommendations are starting points focused on reform of temporary guest worker programs that affect high-skilled American workers, grounded in basic principles of law, order, and self-determination—with zero input from D.C. lobbyists, corporate donors, or political campaigns:

Comprehensively reform. If the immigration system is broken to the point that comprehensive reform is needed, such reform should truly be comprehensive. The first line of any real comprehensive reform would be: "The Immigration and Nationality Act of 1952 as amended is repealed." Without such a repeal, a reform bill is simply piling more complexity onto an already broken system. The Schumer/Rubio bill merely takes our current system and adds more than one thousand pages of complexity and political payoffs to it. That is not reform.

Establish rational immigration priorities. The immigration system needs to establish what skills and attributes the country needs from immigrants and select applicants based upon those criteria. The current immigration system is primarily family-based. A family-based system is out of date. A rational system needs to be predictable and workable. How do you create workable immigration system that creates immigration paths for people who violate the law? Amnesties for people who flout the immigration system create a system that is inherently irrational. How do you create a workable immigration path based upon something as unpredictable as entrepreneurship? It simply is not possible.

The process for creating a reform bill should take place in public. The Schumer/Rubio bill represented the worst of Washington incest. The public was completely excluded while Washington lobbyists wrote the bill. The needs of the American public should dictate the priorities of our immigration system. The public should have a say in what immigration reform looks like. This can only happen if the process is transparent and open to the public.

Get the congressionally mandated entry-exit database for all nonimmigrant visitors and workers up and running. There must be no exemptions from participation in the system. Full functionality means finally building the mandated exit tracking system, starting at airports using biometric data.

Deport visa overstayers. Nearly half of all illegal aliens in the country have violated the terms of their short-term visitor or work visas. Each and every one of these violators falsely told U.S. consular officials that he or she would return upon expiration of his or her visa. No consequences means continued mass law-breaking and systemic sabotage of the alphabet soup of visa programs we open up to the world.

Make guest workers be guest workers. Limit their admission to no more than two years, and start the clock as soon as the visa is approved (not when the worker arrives in the U.S.). Require guest workers to have an actual, identifiable job before they arrive. End the subcontracting out of H-1B workers.[1] Along the same lines, B-1 visas must be for short-term business trips (six months or less). The "B in Lieu of H-1B program" must be abolished. F-1 student visas must be for students, not cheap foreign workers. L-1 visas must be for legitimate business transfers. Scrap postcompletion Optional Practical Training. And no more work authorizations for H-1B spouses; make them apply and be evaluated on their own merits. The "fix" for these programs is simple: Enforce their original intent. End the fraud. Rein in the overreach of the White House and unaccountable bureaucrats creating guest worker expansions by fiat. Put the immigration lawyers out of work. Have people come to the U.S. for one purpose. Go back. Get another visa if they want to return. We'll know when the immigration system makes sense: No one would need a lawyer to complete a visa petition.

Abolish the concept of "dual intent." Nonimmigrants should come to the U.S. for a single purpose so that they know where they stand when they arrive on our shores and the system can be enforced. Though officially classified as nonimmigrants, H-1B workers are allowed to have dual intent status and can pursue permanent residence. Most other temporary visa holders are barred from doing so and can be turned away from a port of entry if they show any signs of intending to immigrate here permanently. Allowing massive numbers of nonimmigrants (who entered with minimum standards) to apply for highly coveted green cards produces an entirely predictable result: interminable backlogs, more confusion, and jacked-up immigration lawyer fees.

Kill the EB-5 program. The only practical way to "reform" the waste, fraud, abuse, and corruption wrought by this influence-peddling racket is to end it.

Eliminate employer-sponsored green cards. While employment-based categories have the theoretical appeal of ensuring that the immigrant has a job, they are unfair to those who want to live in this country. Employment-based immigration puts the potential immigrants at the mercy of their employer to process the visa application. The people of the United States through their government should confer immigration benefits. There should not be employment benefits granted by corporations. Immigrants should sponsor themselves and have control over their immigration process. Having a job offer can be part of the selection criteria. However, immigration should be for immigrants and should not be a corporate fringe benefit.

Centralize enforcement. Currently, enforcement of employment-based immigration is scattered across agencies and provisions. For example, an employer that abuses the system and gets barred from the H-1B program can still get foreign labor on student visas or other programs. Enforcement should apply across all immigration programs.

Require DHS to make all employment-based visa data available with only personally identifiable data removed. With the low cost of disk storage and the limitless facilities of the Internet, there is no reason comprehensive data about all guest worker programs should not be online and available for the public to monitor. Personally identifiable data can easily be removed.

Make employers pay for the truly "best and brightest." Require guest workers to be paid at least at the sixty-seventh percentile for their occupation within the geographical area in which they work. (Current law requires employers to pay only the seventeenth percentile.) If guest workers actually have special skills that cannot be found in the U.S., they should be paid a wage that is commensurate with their talent. Ensuring that all guest workers be paid the salary currently mandated for "fully competent" workers would allow corporations to import foreign workers who have unique skills, while protecting U.S. workers from low-cost entry-level indentured servants.

Put the best and brightest U.S. workers and U.S. students first. From the borders to our overseas consulates to our workplaces to our universities, American workers and students must be a top priority of politicians and public officials in deciding whom to let in, whom to let stay, and whom to kick out. Our immigration and entrance policies are first and foremost matters of national security and economic security for the citizens within our own borders.

It's time for Washington to stop selling out—and start protecting Americans' shot at the American Dream.

CITIZEN ACTIVIST RESOURCE KIT

Whether you identify yourself as liberal, conservative, or independent, it's important to make your voice heard by the bipartisan Beltway crapweasels selling out American workers. Here are some valuable resources from all parts of the political spectrum to get you started.

NumbersUSA.com, which supports "controlled immigration for the national interest," puts fear of the voters into Congress. Sign up for the free "Fax Congress" service, politician score coards, and email alerts on congressional action.

Federation for American Immigration Reform (FairUS.Org) fights "to improve border security, to stop illegal immigration, and to promote immigration levels consistent with the national interest." You can receive legislative updates, download the group's app, or join a local chapter. FAIR's legal affiliate, the Immigration Reform Law Institute, is the "only public interest non-profit law firm in the United States devoted exclusively to protecting the rights and interests of Americans in immigration-related matters."

ProgressivesForImmigrationReform.org "exists to protect low-skill, low wage American workers from unemployment and wage suppression caused by unfair labor and trade practices, including importation of large numbers of low wage foreign workers." The group runs a blog, weekly newsletter, internship program, and policy conferences.

If you work in a technology field, there are a number of professional groups fighting on these issues, including the **American Engineering Association** (AEA.org), the **Programmers Guild** (Programmers Guild.org), and **Bright Jobs Future** (BrightJobsFuture.com). The **Washington Alliance of Technology Workers Alliance** (Washtech .org), and **Alliance@IBM** (http://endicottalliance.org/index.php) are chapters of the Communications Workers of America that fight offshoring and H-1B and L-1 abuses.

Follow the reporting of Patrick Thibodeau at *Computerworld*, Julia Hahn at Breitbart.com, Rachel Stolzfoos at the DailyCaller.com, Kenric Ward at Watchdog.org, Norman Oder at Atlantic Yards/Pacific Park Report, and ConservativeReview.com. Use in-depth research resources including the **Center for Immigration Studies** (CIS.org), the **Economic Policy Institute** (EPI.org), U.C. Davis Professor Norman Matloff's H-1B web page (http://heather.cs.ucdavis.edu/h1b.html), the DHS Office of the Inspector General (http://www.oig.dhs.gov/), GOP Sen. Chuck Grassley's immigration issues page (http://www.grassley .senate.gov/issues-legislation/issues/immigration), and GOP Sen. Jeff Sessions's immigration handbook (http://www.sessions.senate .gov/public/_cache/files/67ae7163-6616-4023-a5c4-534c53e6fc26 /immigration-primer-for-the-114th-congress.pdf).

Learn how to file public records requests at http://www.foia.gov /how-to.html and http://www.foiadvocates.com/records.html.

APPENDIX A: LETTER FROM MAJOR CORPORATIONS CALLING FOR MORE CHEAP FOREIGN LABOR

Speaker
United States House of Representatives
Washington, D.C. 20515

The Honorable Nancy Pelosi
Minority Leader
United States House of Representatives
Washington, D.C. 20515

RE: <u>Support for Immigration Reform</u>

Dear Speaker Boehner and Minority Leader Pelosi:

We, the undersigned chief human resource officers of major corporations doing business in the United States, are writing to urge the House to enact legislation to fix the broken immigration system and work with the Senate to ensure that a bill is signed by the President this year. We believe this would be a long overdue step toward aligning our nation's immigration policies with its workforce needs at all skill levels to ensure U.S. global competitiveness, and we are hopeful that the House will address these needs. The Senate bill is not a perfect measure and many of us hope to work with the House to enact more favorable provisions in certain areas.

Two years ago, the HR Policy Association, which represents the most senior human resource executives at the largest companies in the United States—and of which we are all members—issued a *Blueprint for Jobs in the 21st Century*, which provided a number of recommendations for restoring growth and competitiveness in the U.S. Among these was a recommendation that immigration reform "address the reality that there is a global war for talent and that countries are competing to attract and retain the human capital essential to a culture of productivity and innovation." The report contained a number of recommendations aimed at attracting and retaining immigrants with strong science, technology, engineering and math (STEM) skills. The Senate bill includes strong provisions along the lines of our recommendations, and we would encourage the House to adopt a similar approach.

Even with the economy still recovering, many of our companies continue to have difficulty finding sufficient American workers to fill certain lesser-skilled positions. Thus, in addition to addressing the need for more highly skilled immigrants, we strongly support efforts to bolster the availability of a workforce at all skills levels, through a separate visa program as well as by creating a path to legal status for those already here. Finally, we urge you to improve the E-Verify system so employers can rely on its results without fear of legal liability and to preserve federal preemption to ensure uniform application of the enforcement rules across the country.

September 10, 2013
Page 2

The economic benefits of broad immigration reform were recently underscored by the Congressional Budget Office cost estimate regarding the Senate bill. In addition to finding that the bill would reduce the federal deficit by about $197 billion over the next decade, it also estimates the bill would increase real GDP (adjusted for inflation) by 3.3 percent by 2023 and 5.4 percent by 2033. Clearly, the positive human resource impact of the bill plays a key role in these estimates, as CBO projects that the bill would increase the U.S. population by about 10.4 million new residents by 2023 and 16.2 million by 2033, with the U.S. labor force growing by about six million workers (3.5%) by 2023 and about nine million (5%) by 2033.

Our global competitors understand that attracting top talent from around the world is vital to a country's economic success, and many already have rewritten their immigration policies accordingly. We urge Congress not to miss this opportunity to level the playing field for U.S. employers. We can't afford to wait.

Sincerely,

Michele A. Carlin
Senior Vice President, Human Resources and
Communications
Motorola Solutions, Inc.
Chair, Immigration Policy Committee
HR Policy Association

Mirian M. Graddick-Weir
Executive Vice President, Human Resources
Merck & Co., Inc.
Chair
HR Policy Association

David Almeda
Chief People Officer
Kronos Incorporated

Elizabeth B. Amato
Senior Vice President, Human Resources and
Organization
United Technologies Corporation

Marcia J. Avedon
Senior Vice President, Human Resources and
Communications
Ingersoll Rand Company

Dina Barmasse-Gray
Senior Vice President Human Resources
The Cheesecake Factory, Inc.

Mark F. Biegger
Chief Human Resources Officer
The Procter & Gamble Company

Lisa G. Bisaccia
Senior Vice President and Chief Human
Resources Officer
CVS Caremark Corporation

William A. Blase
Senior Executive Vice President, Human
Resources
AT&T Inc.

Robert C. Bloss
Senior Vice President, Human Resources
Hallmark Cards, Inc.

September 10, 2013
Page 3

Cynthia K. Brabander
Executive Vice President, Chief Human
Resources Officer
Eaton

Sharon M. Brady
Senior Vice President, Human Resources
Illinois Tool Works Inc.

Benito Cachinero-Sánchez
Senior Vice President, Human Resources
E.I. du Pont de Nemours & Company

Dean Carter
Chief Human Resources Officer
Sears Holdings Corporation

Rizwan Chand
Vice President, Human Resources and Medical
Chief Human Resources Officer
BNSF Railway Company

Brian J. Cook
Senior Vice President, Human Resources and
Corporate Communications
USG Corporation

Lawrence B. Costello
Executive Vice President, Human Resources
Tyco International

L. Kevin Cox
Chief Human Resources Officer
American Express Company

Bruce Culpepper
Executive Vice President, Human Resources
Americas
Shell Oil Company

Michael D'Ambrose
Senior Vice President, Chief Human Resource
Officer
Archer Daniels Midland Company

Michael L. Davis
Senior Vice President, Global Human
Resources
General Mills, Inc.

Susan F. Davis
Executive Vice President, Human Resources
Johnson Controls, Inc.

Dennis T. Delaney
Executive Vice President, Human Resources
and Administration
Ingram Industries Inc.

James D. DeVries
Executive Vice President and Chief
Administrative Officer
Allstate Insurance Company

John DiBenedetto
Executive Vice President, Chief People Officer
General Parts Inc.

James J. Duffy
Chief Human Resources Officer
Ally Financial Inc.

Robert L. Duffy
Senior Vice President, Human Resources and
Administration
Harris Corporation

Ceree Eberly
Senior Vice President and Chief People Officer
The Coca-Cola Company

Joann M. Eisenhart
Senior Vice President, Human Resources
Northwestern Mutual

David J. Esler
Chief Human Resources Officer
US Foods

September 10, 2013
Page 4

Edward A. Evans
Executive Vice President, Chief Human
Resources Officer
Univar, Inc.

Robyn Ewing
Senior Vice President and Chief
Administrative Officer
The Williams Companies, Inc.

Peter M. Fasolo
Chief Human Resources Officer
Johnson & Johnson

Richard R. Floersch
Executive Vice President, Chief Human
Resources Officer
McDonald's Corporation

Melanie M. Foley
Senior Vice President, Manager, Human
Resources and Administration
Liberty Mutual Group, Inc.

Roger C. Gaston
Senior Vice President, Human Resources
Avaya Inc.

Michael Geary
Corporate Vice President, Human Resources
Kiewit Corporation

Anita Graham
Chief Human Resources and Administrative
Officer
The ADT Corporation

Jennifer L. Grant
Vice President, Human Resources
Air Products and Chemicals, Inc.

Kimberly S. Hauer
Vice President and Chief Human Resources
Officer
Caterpillar Inc.

Joseph C. High
Senior Vice President and Chief People Officer
W.W. Grainger, Inc.

Charles H. Hill
Executive Vice President, Human Resources
Pfizer Inc.

Anne Hill
Senior Vice President, Chief Human Resources
and Communications Officer
Avery Dennison Corporation

Sunita Holzer
Executive Vice President and Chief Human
Resources Officer
Computer Sciences Corporation

Tim Huval
Chief Human Resources Officer
Humana Inc.

Mark R. James
Senior Vice President, Human Resources and
Communications
Honeywell International Inc.

Leslie W. Joyce
Senior Vice President and Chief People Officer
Novelis, Inc.

Paul J. Karre
Senior Vice President, HR and
Communications
International Paper Company

September 10, 2013
Page 5

Tracy Keogh
Executive Vice President, Human Resources
Hewlett-Packard Company

Jay L. Kloosterboer
Senior Vice President, Human Resources
Dover Corporation

Angela S. Lalor
Senior Vice President, Human Resources
Danaher Corporation

Neil E. Marchuk
Executive Vice President, Human Resources
TRW Automotive

William Matson
Chief Human Resource Officer
Analog Devices, Inc.

John McDevitt
Senior Vice President, Human Resources and
Labor Relations
United Parcel Service, Inc.

Michael L. Meyer
Executive Vice President, Human Resources
Ecolab, Inc.

MaryAnn Miller
Senior Vice President, Chief Human Resources
Officer
Avnet, Inc.

Harold Morgan
Senior Vice President, Chief Human Resources
Officer
White Lodging Corporation

Larry L. Myers
Executive Vice President, Human Resources
T-Mobile USA, Inc.

Pamela O. Kimmet
Senior Vice President, Human Resources
Coca-Cola Enterprises, Inc.

Lawrence J. Krema
Senior Vice President of Human Resources
and Corporate Operations
Simon Property Group

Denise Lynn
Senior Vice President – People
American Airlines Inc.

Bill Mateikis
Senior Vice President, HR & Legal
Daikin McQuay Americas

Teresa E. McCaslin
Executive Vice President – Chief Human
Resources & Administrative Officer
Continental Grain Company

Eileen McGuire
Executive Vice President, Human Resources
MSC Industrial Direct Co., Inc.

Kenneth F. Meyers
SVP & Chief Human Resources Officer
Hospira, Inc.

Jeffrey Mook
Executive Vice President & Chief Human
Resources Officer
21st Century Fox

John M. Murabito
Executive Vice President, Human Resources &
Services
Cigna Corporation

Daisy Ng
Senior Vice President, Chief Human Resources
Officer
Darden Restaurants, Inc.

September 10, 2013
Page 6

Jed L. Norden
Senior Vice President Human Resources
The ServiceMaster Company

Susan C. Nutson
Senior Vice President – Human Resources
Saint-Gobain Corporation

Dermot J. O'Brien
Chief Human Resources Officer
Automatic Data Processing, Inc.

Walter M. Oliver
Senior Vice President, Human Resources and
Administration
General Dynamics Corporation

David A. Pace
Executive Vice President and Chief Resource
Officer
Bloomin' Brands Inc.

Jayne Parker
Executive Vice President and Chief Human
Resources Officer
The Walt Disney Company

Kevin Pennington
Executive Vice President of Human Resources
Fiserv, Inc.

Cecile K. Perich
Senior Vice President Human Relations
McCormick & Company, Inc.

Susan P. Peters
Senior Vice President, Human Resources
General Electric Company

Mark A. Petrarca
Senior Vice President, Human Resources and
Public Affairs
A. O. Smith Corporation

Debra Plousha Moore
Chief Human Resources Officer, Executive
Vice President
Carolinas HealthCare System

Marc C. Reed
Chief Administrative Officer
Verizon Communications Inc.

John P. Reing
Senior Vice President, Human Resources
SRA International

David A. Rodriguez
Executive Vice President and Chief Human
Resources Officer
Marriott International, Inc.

Michael G. Rohret
Senior Vice President, Human Resources
Emerson

Sally A. Savoia
Vice President, Human Resources
Praxair, Inc.

Susan J. Schmitt
Senior Vice President, Human Resources
Rockwell Automation, Inc.

Matthew W. Schuyler
Chief Human Resources Officer
Hilton Worldwide

Daniel S. Serbin
Executive Vice President, Human Resources
Parker Hannifin Corporation

Jeffrey S. Shuman
Senior Vice President, Chief Human Resources
Officer
Quest Diagnostics Incorporated

September 10, 2013
Page 7

John M. Steele
Senior Vice President, Human Resources
HCA Inc.

Larry E. Steward
Vice President, Human Resources
DTE Energy Company

Perry Stuckey
Senior Vice President and Chief Human
Resources Officer
Eastman Chemical Company

Susan M. Suver
Vice President, Human Resources
U.S. Steel Corporation

Mara E. Swan
Executive Vice President, Global Strategy and
Talent
ManpowerGroup

Jim M. Sweet
Chief Human Resources Officer
Newell Rubbermaid Inc.

Teresa J. Tanner
Executive Vice President and Chief Human
Resources Officer
Fifth Third Bank

Kurt J. Thomas
Vice President Human Resources
Mortgage Guaranty Insurance Corporation

Johnna G. Torsone
Executive Vice President and Chief Human
Resources Officer
Pitney Bowes Inc.

Peter Vrijsen
Chief Human Resources Officer
Cargill, Incorporated

Sara Wade
Senior Vice President and Chief Human
Resources Officer
Express Scripts, Inc.

Sylvia R. Wagner
Executive Vice President, Human Resources
and Development
Assurant, Inc.

Carole S. Watkins
Chief Human Resources Officer
Cardinal Health, Inc.

Robb Webb
Chief Human Resources Officer
Hyatt Hotels Corporation

Thomas W. Weidenkopf
Executive Vice President, Human Resources
and Communications
Aleris International, Inc.

Scott A. Weisberg
Chief People Officer
The Wendy's Company

Kathleen Weslock
Senior Vice President and Chief Human
Resources Officer
Cisco Systems, Inc.

Eileen G. Whelley
Executive Vice President and Chief Human
Resources Officer
XL Global Services, Inc

September 10, 2013
Page 8

Darla Whitaker
Senior Vice President, Worldwide Human
Resources
Texas Instruments Incorporated

Richard Williams
SVP Human Resources & Interim CHRO
Western Union

Kimberly G. Windrow
Vice President, Human Resources
WESCO International

Christine A. Wolf
Senior Vice President, Human Resources
ATK

APPENDIX B

Email from a Google Recruiter to an Apple employee that violated the tech industry's illegal agreement not to hire each other's employees.

From: Stephanie Buran <sburan@google.com>
Date: March 7, 2007 9:46:13 AM PST
To: mjs@apples.com
Subject: Google.com Engineering Recruitment Team

Hello Maciej,

My name is Stephanie Buran and I am a Recruiter for the "Google.com Engineering" team formally known as the "Site Reliability Engineering" team. I found your contact information on the Internet. I am interested to know more about your past work experience and openness to new opportunities. We currently have positions available at Google that may be a good match for you. If you are open to exploring these opportunities further please send me an updated version of your resume in word, html, or pdf form to me as soon as possible. Let me know when would be a good time to talk, please include your phone number.

Please take a look at these links for more information:

Mountain View:
http://www.google.com/support/jobs/bin/topic.py?dep_id=1058&loc_id=1116

Santa Monica:
http://www.google.com/support/jobs/bin/topic.py?dep_id=1058&loc_id=1118

Kirkland, WA:
http://www.google.com/support/jobs/bin/topic.py?dep_id=1058&loc_id=1123

New York:
http://www.google.com/support/jobs/bin/topic.py?dep_id=1058&loc_id=1122

Ireland:
http://www.google.com/support/jobs/bin/topic.py?dep_id=1058&loc_id=1110

Switzerland:
http://www.google.com/support/jobs/bin/topic.py?dep_id=1058&loc_id=1115

I hope you are not bothered by my networking attempt. If you are not interested or available for this career opportunity, please forward my name and contact information to your friends or colleagues who would be interested.

Thank you and I hope to hear from you soon.

Sincerely,
Stephanie Buran
Site Reliability Engineering (Staffing)
Google Inc.
1600 Amphitheatre Parkway

Mountain View CA 94043
sburan@google.com
650.243.1446

Email from Steve Jobs to Google CEO Eric Schmidt that attached the recruiting email above.

From: Steve Jobs [mailto:sjobs@apple.com]
Sent: Wednesday, March 07, 2007 10:44 PM
To: Eric Schmidt
Subject: Google Recruiting from Apple

Eric,

I would be very pleased if your recruiting department would stop doing this.

Thanks,
Steve

Email from Google CEO Schmidt to Arnnon Geshuri, Google Senior Director, Staffing and HR

Email from Steve Jobs to Eric Schimdt that attached the recruiting email above.

On 3/8/07, Eric Schmidt <eschmidt@google.com> wrote:

I believe we have a policy of no recruiting from Apple and this is a direct inbound request. Can you get this stopped and let me know why this is happening? I will need to send a reponse back to Apple quickly so please let me know.

Thanks Eric.

Arnnon Geshuri's response to Eric Schmidt describing Google participation in the illegal agreement not to hire other companies' employees.

On 3/8/07, Arnnon Geshuri <arnnon@google.com> wrote:

Eric,

On this specific case, the sourcer who contacted this Apple employee should not have and will be terminated within the hour. We are scrubbing the sourcer's records to ensure she did not contact anyone else.

In general, we have a very clear do not call policy (attached) that is given to every staffing professional and I reiterate this message in ongoing communications and staffing meetings. Unfortunately, every six months or so someone makes an error in judgment, and for this type of violation we terminate their relationship with Google.

Please extend my apologies as appropriate to Steve Jobs. This was an isolated incident and we will be careful to make sure this does not happen again.

Thanks,
Arnnon

Email from Shona Brown, Senior VP Google commenting on this exchange.

Arnnon Geshuri's respnse to Eric Schmidt

From: Shona Brown
To: Arnnon Geshuri
Cc: Eric Schmidt; Laszio Bock; Judy Gilbert
Bcc:
Subject: Re: FW: Google Recruiting from Apple

Arnnon-

Appropriate response. Please make a public example of this termination with the group. Please make it a very strong part of the new hire training for the group. I want it clear that we have a zero-tolerance policy for violating our policies. This should (hopefully) prevent future occurrences.

Erik Schmidt's response to Steve Jobs

From: Eric Schmidt <eschmidt@google.com>
Date: March 9, 2007 8:21:25 AM PST
To: sjobs@apple.com
Subject: Google recruiters calling into Apple - isolated incident

Steve, as a followup we investigated the recruiter's actions and she violated our policies. Apologies again on this and I'm including a portion of the email I received from our head of recruiting. Should this ever happen again please let me know immediately and we will handle. Thanks !! Eric

From Google recruiting to me:

On this specific case, the sourcer who contacted this Apple employee should not have and will be terminated within the hour. We are scrubbing the sourcer's records to ensure she did not contact anyone else.

In general, we have a very clear do not call policy (attached) that is given to every staffing professional and I reiterate this message in ongoing communications and staffing meetings. Unfortunately, every six months or so someone makes an error in judgment, and for this type of violation we terminate their relationship with Google.

Please extend my apologies as appropriate to Steve Jobs. This was an isolated incident and we will be careful to make sure this does not happen again.

Steve Jobs message to Danielle Lambert, Apple VP of Human Resources, attaching Eric Schmidt's response

---

From: Steve Jobs <sjobs@apple.com>
Date: March 9, 2007 10:05:26 AM PST
To: Danielle Lambert <lambert@apple.com>
Subject: Fwd: Google recruiters calling into Apple - isolated incident

:)
Steve

APPENDIX C: INFOSYS LETTER TEMPLATE USED
TO IMPORT WORKERS ON B VISITOR VISAS

Case 2:11-cv-00217-MHT-CSC   Document 117-5   Filed 08/13/12   Page 1 of 2

Infosys   B-1 Invitation Letter

Date:

Name of the SBU Head
Senior Vice President
Infosys Technologies Ltd.
Bangalore - 561 229

**PLAINTIFF'S
EXHIBIT**
44

Dear ......,

We are glad to award.................... project to Infosys Technologies Limited, Bangalore.

In this connection, we would like Mr. / Ms. .... to visit our facility at ....(city), ...(state), starting from................ 2002. During this visit, he will be involved in .... We anticipate that this exercise would be completed in about 4-6 weeks.

Will you therefore, arrange through the US consulate for the necessary travel documents for Mr. / Ms .... This project is highly critical and will require him/her to be at our facility starting from ....

We look forward to receiving your confirmation to enable us to make necessary arrangements for the visit of Mr. / Ms. ....

With best regards,

Signature with title

Case 2:11-cv-00217-MHT-CSC   Document 117-5   Filed 08/13/12   Page 2 of 2

▬ ▪ ▪ ▬ ▪ ▪ ▬ ▪ ▪ ▬ ▪ ▬ ▪ ▪ ▬ ▪ ▪ ▬ ▪ ▪ ▬ ▪ ▬ ▪ ▪ ▬ ▪ ▪ ▬ ▪ ▪ ▬ ▪ ▬ ▪ ▪ ▬

Do's

* Consultant - Instead of this, you may use the Project Leader / Module Leader / Project Co-ordinator, etc.,but don't use the terms like Programmer Analyst, Programmer, etc.,

* Purpose - Please mention purpose like: business discussions, meetings, requirement analysis, requirement study, training, etc.

To the extent possible justify the period of stay. It would be more advantageous if details are given.

Don'ts

Kindly make sure that the duration of the trip mentioned in the invite letter **should not exceed BEYOND 4-6** *weeks* at any point of time

Do not mention activities like implementation, design & testing, consulting etc., which sound like work.

Also do not use words like, work, activity, etc., in the invitation letter. DO NOT TELL THEM YOUR WORKING. Speak little English.

Please do not mention anything about the contract rates as your on a B-1 Visa

Basically, the letter should have:

a)   association with Infosys (awarding some project)
b)   purpose of the visit of our employee name(s) should be mentioned
c)   duration
d)   start date
e)   request for visa
f)   arrangements made to receive our employee & confirmation

APPENDIX D

From Microsoft
November 15, 2007
The Honorable Michael Chcrtoff
Secretary
United States Department of Homeland Security
Washington, D.C. 20528

Dear Secretary Chertoff:

I appreciated very much the chance to speak with you recently at the dinner that Ed and Debra Cohen hosted to discuss, immigration reform issues. I am writing to follow up in more detail on the suggestion we briefly discussed for action that the Department of Homeland Security can take easily and immediately, as part of its administrative reforms initiative, to help address the H-1B visa shortage. That is, DHS can extend the period of Optional Practical Training ("OPT') - the period of employment that students are permitted in connection with their degree program - beyond its current maximum of one year. Additional suggestions relating to visa programs for the highly skilled follow as well.

Fulfilling a Key Part of DHS's August 10, 2007 Administrative Reform Initiative

Microsoft believes that it was wise of the Administration, after Congress failed to move forward on comprehensive immigration reform, to commit to exploring changes it could make to strengthen the immigration system without congressional action. As part of the twenty-six point plan that you announced on August 10, 2007, DHS committed, along with the Department of Labor, to explore "potential administrative reforms to visa programs for the highly skilled." DHS has properly recognized that reforms of visa categories for professionals should be given a high priority, because America's talent crisis has reached emergency levels.

The H-1B Shortage and American Competitiveness

Our high-skilled immigration policies are blocking access to crucial foreign talent. With demand in fields like science, technology, math, and engineering far surpassing the supply of American workers, America's employers find themselves unable to get the people they need on the job. The H-1B program, with its severely insufficient base annual cap of 65,000 visas, is at the center of the problem. This year, on April 2 – the very first day that employers could seek an H-1B visa tor the coming fiscal year – DHS received about twice as many requests as there were visas available, *for the entire year*. This means that (1) employers stood only a one-in-two chance of getting a visa at all for critical recruits; (2) employers could not even ask for an H-IB visa tor students about to graduate the next month *from our own universities;* (3) employers arc now in the midst of a staggering *eighteen-month blackout period* before they can put a worker on the job with as visa from the following year's supply; (4) the chances of even getting one of those visas In the first place will be even worse than this year's throw of the dice.

These restrictive policies are a stark contrast to the policies of many other countries, which are now streamlining their immigration programs to attract highly skilled professionals. Notably, the European Union recently proposed a "Blue Card" program, under which skilled workers would be able to obtain a temporary work visa, similar to an H-1B visa, in just one to three months.

Microsoft has long made it a top-level company priority to center its development work in the United States, and we have devoted a great deal of energy into trying to help shape the policy changes that would permit us to continue to do so. To compete globally, however, Microsoft – like other employers of the highly skilled across America – must have access to the talent it needs.

How Extending OPT Will Help

True reform of the H-1B program, of course, will require congressional action. Yet the Administration, consistent with it August 10 commitment, can take a simple, immediate step to help address this crisis: extend from twelve to twenty-nine months the period that students can work in their field of study for OPT. Today OPT exists solely by regulation; no statutory change is necessary to make this needed adjustment. The current regulations provide for OPT to last up to twelve months [see 8 C.F.R. 214.2(f)(10)-(11)]. This period of employment is typically a crucial bridge to a more stable position in the American workforce through an H-1B visa. With this year's historic H-1B cap crisis, however, OPT will expire long before it can bridge the gap to an H-1B. Without corrective action, the same can be expected next year. As a result, U.S. employers will lose recruits to competition overseas. Soon, by necessity, U.S. jobs will follow. Extending OPT to twenty-nine months would permit U.S. employers to hire those students and keep them in service until longer-term visas become available.

OPT can be extended quickly. It would require no more than the issuance of a regulation to replace the word "twelve" with "twenty-nine" in 8 C.F.R. 214.2(f)(11). This simple extension of a critical existing program would provide tremendous relief in this emergency situation. Immediate action is necessary to initiate and announce this change so that U.S. companies and their recruits can make decisions knowing that relief is coming.

Timing of OPT Extension

A commitment to extend OPT should be announced immediately, and a regulation effectuating the extension should be in place no later than next spring. The regulation must be in place by next spring because OPT must be requested before the completion of the student's academic program. We suggest that an interim regulation and comment period would be fully permissible under the Administrative Procedures Act and would facilitate the regulation being in place on time. The announcement must be made now so both employers and students can plan for the recruitment cycle. An announcement now will give employers the assurance that, of they recruit on campus but lose the H-1B lottery, they will not have to lose their recruits and can again seek an H-IB for them when the next year's supply becomes available. It will also give highly prized students considering their employment options the knowledge that they will have reliable work authorization for a period sufficient to move into a longer-term Immigration status.

Other Administrative Reforms

There are other significant steps the Administration can take to alleviate the talent crisis facing the U.S. These steps would help to address the retention and other problems that result from the extreme waits that face most professionals seeking employment-based green cards.

Multi-year work and travel authorization documents

DHS could issue multi-year employment authorization documents ("EADs") and advance parole documents. These documents are typically issued for only one year and, during the several-year green card wait, must be renewed multiple times. Given its massive adjudications caseload, DHS often is unable to process renewal applications promptly, and often cannot meet the 90-day deadline that its regulations provide for EAD adjudications. This literally means professionals must come off the job, as employers cannot lawfully continue to employ any employees who do not have evidence of employment authorization, even where timely filed renewal applications have not been adjudicated within the regulatory deadline.

This problem would be alleviated greatly if DHS were to issue EADs and advance paroles that were valid for two or three years rather than one. DHS has full authority to issue multi-year documents. It already issues multi-year EADs to certain nonimmigrants, including the spouses of E and L visa holders. There is no statutory or regulatory limit on the validity periods for EADs and advance paroles, and the Secretary of Homeland Security has wide discretion under section 103 of the Immigration and Nationality Act to "establish such regulations; ... issue such instructions; and perform such other acts as he deems necessary for carrying out his authority under the provisions of this Act."

Moreover, it is in the strong interest of DHS itself to issue multi-year EADs and advance paroles. By doing so, USCIS would greatly reduce the adjudicative burden it now faces, unnecessarily, as a result of annual renewals. This is especially significant now, when USCIS is struggling with at major front-log and is having difficulty even receipting incoming petitions. In this situation, any elimination of unnecessary adjudication workload should be highly desirable to DHS. In addition to this efficiency incentive, DHS has a financial incentive as well. Under the new USCIS fee regulations that took effect on July 30, 2007, applicants who have paid the fee for Form I-485 to adjust to lawful permanent resident status do not have to pay an additional fee to renew an EAD or advance parole. This means that DHS will collect no additional revenue for all the additional work it performs to renew EADs and advance paroles repeatedly for these applicants.

Pre-certification

DHS also could establish a "pre-certification" process to allow employers who petition USCIS frequently for visas to submit petitions via an expedited system. Under such a system, USCIS would review an employer's organizational documents to establish certain generic information, such as the employer's ability to pay employees, and would pre-certify the employer. When a pre-Certified employer submitted a visa application, it would not mean an automatic approval; USCIS would analyze the particular foreign national's eligibility for the visa. It would simply relieve users of the burden of re-adjudicating, over and over, the criteria that have already been determined through pre-certification. Such a system would reduce the burden on USCIS and allow employers to obtain the visas they need in a more efficient and expeditious manner.

Conclusion

We are very grateful to you for your commitment to administrative reforms of the visa programs for the highly skilled. If there is anything that Microsoft can do to be of assistance to your efforts, please do not hesitate to contact me.

Jack Krumholtz
Managing Director of Federal Government Affairs
Associate General Counsel

APPENDIX E: HOW THE H-1B QUOTA WOULD HAVE READ
UNDER "COMPREHENSIVE IMMIGRATION REFORM"

8 U.S.C. § 1182(g) (proposed)

(1) The total number of aliens who may be issued visas or otherwise provided nonimmigrant status during any fiscal year—

(A) under section 101(a)(15)(H)(i)(b) may not exceed the sum of—

(i) the base allocation calculated under paragraph (9)(A); and

(ii) the allocation adjustment calculated under paragraph (9)(B); and

. . . .

(5) The numerical limitations contained in paragraph (1)(A) shall not apply to any nonimmigrant alien issued a visa or otherwise provided status under section 1101(a)(15)(H)(i)(b) of this title who—

(A) is employed (or has received an offer of employment) at an institution of higher education (as defined in section 1001(a) of title 20), or a related or affiliated nonprofit entity;

(B) is employed (or has received an offer of employment) at a nonprofit research organization or a governmental research organization; or

(C) has earned a master's or higher degree, in a field of science, technology, engineering, or math included in the Department of Education's Classification of Instructional Programs taxonomy within the summary groups of computer and information sciences and support services, engineering, mathematics and statistics, biological and biomedical sciences, and physical sciences, from a United States institution of higher education (as defined in section 101(a) of the Higher Education Act of 1965 (20 U.S.C. 1001(a)) until the number of aliens who are exempted from such numerical limitation during such year exceed 25,000.

. . . .

(9)(A) Except as provided in subparagraph (C), the base allocation of nonimmigrant visas under section 101(a)(15)(H)(i)(b) for each fiscal year shall be equal to—

(i) the sum of—

(I) the base allocation for the most recently completed fiscal year; and

(II) the allocation adjustment under subparagraph (B) for the most recently completed fiscal year;

(ii) if the number calculated under clause (i) is less than 115,000, 115,000; or

(iii) if the number calculated under clause (i) is more than 180,000, 180,000.

(B)(i) If the number of cap-subject non-immigrant visa petitions accepted for filing under section 101(a)(15)(H)(i)(b) during the first 45 days petitions may be filed for a fiscal year is equal to the base allocation for such fiscal year, an additional 20,000 such visas shall be made available beginning on the 46th day on which petitions may be filed for such fiscal year.

(ii) If the base allocation of cap-subject non-immigrant visa petitions accepted for filing under section 101(a)(15)(H)(i)(b) for a fiscal year is reached during the 15-day period ending on the 60th day on which petitions may be filed for such fiscal year, an additional 15,000 such visas shall be made available beginning on the 61st day on which petitions may be filed for such fiscal year.

(iii) If the base allocation of cap-subject non-immigrant visa petitions accepted for filing under section 101(a)(15)(H)(i)(b) for a fiscal year is reached during the 30-day period ending on the 90th day on which petitions may be filed for such fiscal year, an additional 10,000 such visas shall be made available beginning on the 91st day on which petitions may be filed for such fiscal year.

(iv) If the base allocation of cap-subject non-immigrant visa petitions accepted for filing under section 101(a)(15)(H)(i)(b) for a fiscal year is reached during the 85-day period ending on the 275th day on which petitions may be filed for such fiscal year, an additional 5,000 such visas shall be made available beginning on the date on which such allocation is reached.

(v) If the number of cap-subject nonimmigrant visa petitions accepted for filing under section 101(a)(15)(H)(i)(b) for a fiscal year is at least 5,000 fewer than the base allocation, but is not more than 9,999 fewer than the base allocation, the allocation adjustment for the following fiscal year shall be 5,000.

(vi) If the number of cap-subject nonimmigrant visa petitions accepted for filing under section 101(a)(15)(H)(i)(b) for a fiscal year is at least 10,000 fewer than the base allocation, but not more than 14,999 fewer than the base allocation, the allocation adjustment for the following fiscal year shall be –10,000.

(vii) If the number of cap-subject nonimmigrant visa petitions accepted for filing under section 101(a)(15)(H)(i)(b) for a fiscal year is at least 15,000 fewer than the base allocation, but not more than 19,999 fewer than the base allocation, the allocation adjustment for the following fiscal year shall be 15,000.

(viii) If the number of cap-subject nonimmigrant visa petitions accepted for filing under section 101(a)(15)(H)(i)(b) for a fiscal year is at least 20,000 fewer than the base allocation, the allocation adjustment for the following fiscal year shall be –20,000.

(C) An allocation adjustment under clause (i), (ii), or (iv) of subparagraph (B)—

(i) may not increase the numerical limitation contained in paragraph (9)(A) to a number above 180,000; and

(ii) may not take place to make additional nonimmigrant visas available for any fiscal year in which the national occupational unemployment rate for 'Management, Professional, and Related Occupations', as published by the Bureau of Labor Statistics each month, averages 4.5 percent or greater over the 12-month period preceding the date of the Secretary's determination of whether the cap should be increased or decreased.

Notes

INTRODUCTION

1   Greg Fox, "Walt Disney World information technology workers laid off,"
    WESH.com (January 30, 2015); available online at: http://www.wesh.com
    /news/walt-disney-world-information-technology-workers-laid-off
    /31015168 [accessed April 18, 2105].

2   Rachel Stoltzfoos, "Qualcomm lays off 4,500 workers while demanding more
    H-1Bs," *Daily Caller* (July 29, 2015); available online at: http://dailycaller
    .com/2015/07/29/qualcomm-lays-off-4500-workers-while-demanding
    -more-h-1bs/ [accessed August 21, 2015].

3   "Intel to cut over 5,000 jobs," CNNMoney (January 17, 2014); available
    online at: http://money.cnn.com/2014/01/17/technology/intel-jobs/ [ac-
    cessed April 18, 2015].

4   Steve Johnson, "Cisco execs try to put best face on 6,000 layoffs," *San Jose Mer-
    cury News* silicon beat blog (August 20, 2014); available online at: http://www
    .siliconbeat.com/2014/08/20/cisco-execs-try-to-put-best-face-on-6000
    -layoffs/ [accessed April 19, 2015].

5   Mike Hughlett, "Cargill to outsource IT services; 900 jobs affected," *Min-
    neapolis Star-Tribune* (March 27, 2014).

6   Stuart Johnston, "Microsoft Won't Layoff H-1B Before U.S. Workers,"
    Datamation (March 4, 2009); available online at: http://www.datamation
    .com/cnews/article.php/3808516/Microsoft-Wont-Layoff-H-1B-Before-US
    -Workers.htm [accessed April 20, 2105].

7   Reuters, "Bank Of America Planning To Cut 16,000 Jobs By Year End" (September 20, 2012); available online at: http://www.huffingtonpost.com /2012/09/20/bank-of-america-layoffs-16000_n_1899691.html [accessed April 19, 2015].

8   Patrick Thibodeau, "Southern California Edison IT workers 'beyond furious' over H-1B replacements," *Computerworld* (February 4, 2015); available online at: http://www.computerworld.com/article/2879083/southern -california-edison-it-workers-beyond-furious-over-h-1b-replacements .html [accessed April 18, 2015].

9   Susan Hall, "Harley-Davidson Cuts IT Staff; Shifts Some to Infosys," Dice (July 30, 2012); available online at: http://news.dice.com/2012/07/30/harley -davidson-infosys/ [accessed April 19, 2015].

10 Patrick Thibodeau, "Utility cuts IT workforce, hires Indian outsourcers," *Computerworld* (October 1, 2013); available online at: http://www .computerworld.com/article/2485375/it-leadership/utility-cuts-it-work force-hires-indian-outsourcers.html [accessed April 19, 2015].

11 Kevin Fogarty, "Did Pfizer Force Its Staff to Train Their H-1B Replacements?" eWeek (November 7, 2008); available online at: http://www.eweek .com/c/a/IT-Infrastructure/Did-Pfizer-Force-its-Staff-to-Train-Their -H1B-Replacements [accessed April 19, 2015].

12 Carol Sliwa, "Best Buy Hit With Lawsuit Over Layoffs of IT Workers," *Computerworld* (November 22, 2004); available online at: http://www .computerworld.com/article/2568591/it-careers/best-buy-hit-with-law suit-over-layoffs-of-it-workers.html [accessed April 19, 2015].

13 "Foreign workers fill hundreds of Sacramento-area IT jobs," News 10 (February 24, 2015); available online at: http://www.news10.net/story/news /investigations/2015/02/24/foreign-workers-fill-hundreds-of-sacramento -area-it-jobs/22603549/ [accessed April 18, 2105].

14 Ted Hesson, "Outsourced at home: U.S. workers 'pissed' at H-1B visa program," Fusion (March 17, 2015); available online at: http://fusion.net /story/105274/outsourced-at-home-u-s-workers-pissed-at-h-1b-visa -program/ [accessed April 18, 2105].

15 Patrick Thibodeau, "A restructuring and H-1B use affect the Magic Kingdom's IT operations," *Computerworld*, April 29, 2015; available online at: http://www.computerworld.com/article/2915904/it-outsourcing/fury -rises-at-disney-over-use-of-foreign-workers.html [accessed April 29, 2015].

16 Greg Fox, "Walt Disney World information technology workers laid off," WESH, January 30, 2015, http://www.wesh.com/news/walt-disney -world-information-technology-workers-laid-off/31015168#galleria.

17 Sandra Pedicini, "Disney technology workers lose jobs in restructuring," *Orlando Sentinel*, January 30, 2015.

18 E.g., Patrick Thibodeau, "Fury rises at Disney over use of foreign workers," *Computerworld*, April 29, 2015; available online at: http://www.computer world.com/article/2915904/it-outsourcing/fury-rises-at-disney-over-use -of-foreign-workers.html [accessed August 5, 2015].

19 Ibid.

20 Julia Preston, "Pink Slips at Disney. But First, Training Foreign Replace- ments," *New York Times*, June 3, 2014; available online at: http://www .nytimes.com/2015/06/04/us/last-task-after-layoff-at-disney-train -foreign-replacements.html [accessed August 5, 2015].

21 Rachel Stoltzfoos, "Disney blacklisted displaced American workers," *Daily Caller*, June 9, 2015; available onine at: http://dailycaller.com/2015/06/09 /disney-blacklisted-displaced-american-workers/ [accessed August 5, 2015].

22 Patrick Thibodeau, "In a turnabout, Disney ABC TV cancels plans to out- source IT jobs," *Computerworld*, June 12, 2015; available online at: http:// www.computerworld.com/article/2934978/it-outsourcing/in-a-turnabout -disney-abc-tv-cancels-plans-to-outsource-it-jobs.html [accessed August 5, 2015].

23 Ben Fritz, "Disney CEO's Compensation Worth $46.5 Million: Robert Iger's Pay Increased 35% in the Last Fiscal Year," *Wall Street Journal*, January 16, 2015; available online at: http://www.wsj.com/articles/disney -ceo-robert-igers-compensation-worth-46-5-million-1421449515 [accessed August 16, 2015].

24 Lobbyists and politicians who use the buzzword "STEM" are usually re- ferring to technology workers. Practitioners do not generally use the term STEM. No one says, "I am a STEM worker." S&E (Science and Engineer- ing) is a synonymous term that is indistinguishable from STEM. There is an accepted definition of what fields make up STEM. The physical sciences, engineering, computer fields, and mathematics form the core of STEM. Be- cause the government confers certain benefits on STEM fields (e.g., longer authorization to work on student visas), there is constant lobbying among the soft sciences (e.g., economics, sociology) to be considered STEM fields.

25 See, e.g., the "Bring Jobs Home" Act. Available online at: https://www .congress.gov/bill/113th-congress/senate-bill/2569 [accessed May 12, 2015].

26 Eric Berger, "How come the scientific establishment of the United States hasn't collapsed? Because it has a secret weapon," *Houston Chronicle* SciGuy science blog (June 18, 2011); available online at: http://blog.chron .com/sciguy/2011/06/how-come-the-scientific-establishment-of-the

-united-states-hasnt-collapsed-because-it-has-a-secret-weapon/ [accessed April 19, 2015].

27 Larry Kudlow, "GOP will lose without immigration plan," CNBC (May 8, 2015); available online at: http://finance.yahoo.com/news/kudlow -gop-lose-without-immigration-031719335.html [accessed May 11, 2015].

28 Steve Lohr, "Parsing the Truths About Visas for Tech Workers," *New York Times* (April 15, 2007); available online at: http://www.nytimes.com/2007 /04/15/business/yourmoney/15view.html?_r=0 [accessed April 19, 2015].

29 Gary Beach, "The H-1B Visa: 'A Blunt Instrument That Pleases No One,'" *Wall Street Journal* (April 13, 2015); available online at: http://blogs.wsj .com/cio/2015/04/13/the-h-1b-visa-a-blunt-instrument-that-pleases-no -one/ [accessed April 18, 2105].

30 Ibid.

31 Michael Hiltzik, "A loophole in immigration law is costing thousands of American jobs," *Los Angeles Times* (February 20, 2015); available at: http:// www.latimes.com/business/hiltzik/la-fi-hiltzik-20150222-column.html #page=1 [accessed April 18, 2015].

32 Sen. Jeff Sessions press release (April 9, 2015); available online at: http://www .sessions.senate.gov/public/index.cfm/2015/4/sessions-durbin-lead-bipar tisan-group-of-senators-demanding-federal-investigation-of-socal-edison [accessed April 19, 2015].

33 Jim Puzzanghera, "Labor Department won't investigate alleged Edison H-1B visa abuses," *Los Angeles Times* (April 23, 2015); available online at: http://www.latimes.com/business/la-fi-edison-visas-labor-investigation -20150423-story.html [accessed April 29, 2015].

34 John Miano, "Southern California Edison Workers Just More H-1B Roadkill," Center for Immgiration Studies (February 9, 2015); available online at: http://www.cis.org/miano/southern-california-edison-workers -just-more-h-1b-roadkill [accessed April 19, 2015].

35 Patrick Thibodeau, "10 U.S. senators seek investigation into H-1B-driven layoffs," *Computerworld* (April 9, 2015); available online at: http://www .computerworld.com/article/2908124/10-us-senators-seek-investigation -into-h-1b-driven-layoffs.html [accessed April 19, 2015].

36 U.S. Census Bureau, "Census Bureau Reports Majority of STEM College Graduates Do Not Work in STEM Occupations," Release Number: CB14- 130 (July 10, 2014); available online at: http://www.census.gov/newsroom /press-releases/2014/cb14-130.html [accessed April 18, 2015].

37 Robert N. Charette, "The STEM Crisis is a Myth," IEEE Spectrum (August 30, 2013); available online at: http://spectrum.ieee.org/at-work /education/the-stem-crisis-is-a-myth [accessed April 18, 2015].

38 Stuart Anderson biography, Cato.org, available online at: http://www.cato .org/people/stuart-anderson [accessed May 4, 2015].

39 Challenger, Gray & Christmas, Inc., "2014 December Job Cut Report: 32,640 Cuts Top Off Lowest Job Cutting Year Since 1997" (undated); available online at: http://www.challengergray.com/press/press-releases/2014 -december-job-cut-report-32640-cuts-top-lowest-job-cutting-year-1997 [accessed April 18, 2015].

40 Byron York, "Companies lay off thousands, then demand immigration reform for new labor," *Washington Examiner* (September 11, 2013); available online at: http://www.washingtonexaminer.com/companies-lay-off-thou sands-then-demand-immigration-reform-for-new-labor/article/2535595 [accessed April 18, 2015].

41 Hal Salzman, Daniel Kuehn, and B. Lindsay Lowell, "Guestworkers in the high-skill U.S. labor market," Employment Policy Institute (April 24, 2013); available online at: http://www.epi.org/publication/bp359-guestworkers -high-skill-labor-market-analysis/ [accessed April 18, 2015].

42 AFL-CIO Department of Professional Employees, "DPE Fact Sheet: Guest Worker Visas: The H-1B and L-1" (March 2015); available online at: http://dpeaflcio.org/wp-content/uploads/Guest-Worker-Visas-The-H-1B -and-L-1-2015.pdf [accessed April 19, 2015].

43 Ray Hennessey, "Is the U.S. Too Hungry for Foreign Workers?" *Entrepreneur* (July 24, 2013); available online at: http://www.entrepreneur.com /article/227556 [accessed April 19, 2015].

44 Ibid.

45 Norman Matloff, "New CS Grads' Wages Down 9%," Upon Closer Inspection (January 23, 2015); available online at: https://normsaysno.wordpress .com/2015/01/23/new-cs-grads-wages-down-9/ [accessed April 18, 2015].

46 Hal Salzman, "STEM Grads Are at a Loss," *U.S. News & World Report* (September 15, 2014); available online at: http://www.usnews.com/opinion /articles/2014/09/15/stem-graduates-cant-find-jobs [accessed April 18, 2015].

47 Sen. Jeff Sessions, "Immigration Handbook for the New Republican Majority" (January 2015); available online at: http://www.sessions.senate.gov /public/_cache/files/67ae7163-6616-4023-a5c4-534c53e6fc26/immigration -primer-for-the-114th-congress—final.pdf [accessed April 18, 2015].

48 Russell Roberts, "Obama vs. ATMs: Why Technology Doesn't Destroy Jobs," *Wall Street Journal* (June 22, 2011); available online at: http://www .wsj.com/articles/SB10001424052702304070104576399704275939640 [accessed April 18, 2015].

49 Sen. Jeff Sessions, "CHART: U.S. TO LEGALLY ADMIT MORE NEW IMMIGRANTS OVER NEXT DECADE THAN POPULATION

OF HALF-DOZEN MAJOR AMERICAN CITIES COMBINED" (April 13, 2015); available online at: http://www.sessions.senate.gov/public /index.cfm/news-releases?ID=48826A5A-BD7B-49AE-BFF7-78C4E7 E2A473 [accessed April 18, 2015].

50 Neil Munro, "Immigration rivals agree; Senate bill will legalize more than 30 million migrants," *Daily Caller* (May 6, 2013); available online at: http:// dailycaller.com/2013/05/06/immigration-rivals-agree-senate-bill-will -legalize-more-than-30-million-migrants/ [accessed April 18, 2015].

51 Sen. Jeff Sessions, "Immigration Handbook for the New Republican Majority," op. cit., p. 1. See also: Jessica Vaughan, "Nearly 700,000 Guestworker Visas Issued in 2012," Center for Immigration Studies (April 2, 2013); available online at: http://www.cis.org/vaughan/700000-guestworker-visas -issued-2012 [accessed April 18, 2015].

52 Ann Stock, "Launching the New J-1 Visa Exchange Visitor Program Website," DIPNOTE (U.S. Department of State Official Blog (June 1, 2011); available online at: http://blogs.state.gov/stories/2011/06/01/launching-new -j-1-visa-exchange-visitor-program-website [accessed May 4, 2015].

53 "H-2A Temporary Agricultural Labor Certification Program—Selected Statistics, FY 2014," Office of Foreign Labor Certification, available online at: http://www.foreignlaborcert.doleta.gov/pdf/H-2A_Selected_Statistics _FY2014_Q4.pdf [accessed May 4, 2015].

54 Curtis Ellis, "Trade agreement is a Trojan Horse for Obama's immigration agenda," *The Hill* (April 13, 2015); available online at: http://thehill .com/blogs/pundits-blog/international/238574-trade-agreement-is-a -trojan-horse-for-obamas-immigration [accessed May 4, 2015]. On May 12, 2015, the Senate failed to pass a TPP deal promoted aggressively by immigration expansionist Utah GOP Sen. Orrin Hatch.

55 "Executive actions on immigration," U.S. Department of Homeland Security, available online at: http://www.uscis.gov/immigrationaction [accessed July 25, 2015].

56 John O'Sullivan, "A Suit against One of Obama's Immigration Orders Can Go Ahead, and It's a Setback for the GOP Establishment," *National Review* (December 8, 2014); available online at: http://www.nationalreview .com/corner/394176/suit-against-one-obamas-immigration-orders-can-go -ahead-and-its-setback-gop [accessed April 18, 2015].

57 Save Jobs USA v. U.S. Dep't of Homeland Security, 1:15-cv-00615 (D.C.D.) (Complaint April 23, 2015).

CHAPTER 1. WHEN BARRY MET JENNIFER

1 "Momma Wedel & Family" YouTube channel; available online at: https://www.youtube.com/user/Mommawedel [accessed February 18, 2015].

2 Nancy Scola, "What It's Like When Google Comes to Your House for a Presidential Chat," *Atlantic* (January 31, 2012); available online at: http://www.theatlantic.com/politics/archive/2012/01/what-its-like-when-google-comes-to-your-house-for-a-presidential-chat/252281/ [accessed February 16, 2015].

3 Google Official Blog, "Your Interview with President Obama" (January 23, 2012); available online at: http://googleblog.blogspot.com/2012/01/your-interview-with-president-obama.html [accessed February 16, 2015].

4 The Immigration and Nationality Act defines a number of nonimmigrant visas for various purposes; there are currently more than twenty such categories. See http://www.uscis.gov/working-united-states/temporary-workers/temporary-nonimmigrant-workers. The name of the visa is derived from its location within the act. For example, 8 U.S.C. § 1101(a)(15)(A) defines A visas for diplomats. Similarly, 8 U.S.C. § 1101(a)(15)(B) defines B visa for tourists and business visitors and 8 U.S.C. § 1101(a)(15)(F)(i) defines F-1 visas for students.

5 In their mad rush to pass the 1990 act, lawmakers realized they had forgotten to create a special visa category for fashion models under the O or P visa programs for foreign athletes, artists, and entertainers. Sens. Ted Kennedy and Alan Simpson herded the runway beauties into H-1B. Disgraced former New York Democratic Rep. Anthony Weiner attempted unsuccessfully to expand the number of H-1B visas for foreign models while collecting New York City mayoral campaign cash from top modeling agencies. See Ryan Grim, "Weiner bill looks out for models," *Politico* (June 11, 2008); available online at: http://www.politico.com/news/stories/0608/10997.html [accessed March 19, 2015].

6 K. Sunil Thomas, et al., "Byting the Bait," *The Week* (August 29, 1999); available online at: http://www.the-week.com/99aug29/life7.htm [accessed March 18, 2015].

7 Robert X. Cringely, "H-1B visa abuse limits wages and steals US jobs," Beta News (October 25, 2012); available online at: http://betanews.com/2012/10/25/h-1b-visa-abuse-limits-wages-and-steals-us-jobs/ [accessed April 18, 2015].

8 "O-1 Visa: Individuals with Extraordinary Ability or Achievement," U.S. Citizenship and Immigration Services (July 7, 2015); available online at: http://www.uscis.gov/working-unitedstates/temporary-workers/o-1

-individuals-extraordinary-ability-or-achievement/o-1-visa-individuals
-extraordinary-ability-or-achievement [accessed August 6, 2015].

9 Robert X. Cringely, "What Americans don't know about H-1B visas could hurt us all" (October 23, 2012); available online at: http://www.cringely .com/2012/10/23/what-americans-dont-know-about-h-1b-visas-could -hurt-us-all/ [accessed March 18. 2015].

10 Darin Wedel LinkedIn page; available online at: https://www.linkedin.com /pub/darin-wedel/7/a19/977 [accessed February 16, 2015].

11 Ibid.

12 Catherine Rampell, "Layoffs Spread to More Sectors of the Economy," *New York Times* (January 26, 2009); available online at: http://www.nytimes .com/2009/01/27/business/economy/27layoffs.html?_r=0 [accessed February 16, 2015].

13 Larry Dignan, "Tech layoff parade continues: TI cuts 12 percent of workforce," ZDNet (January 26, 2009); available online at: http://www.zdnet .com/article/tech-layoff-parade-continues-ti-cuts-12-percent-of-work force/ [accessed February 16, 2015].

14 U.S. Department of State, Office of the Historian, "The Immigration and Nationality Act of 1952 (The McCarran-Walter Act)," undated; available online at: https://history.state.gov/milestones/1945-1952/immigration-act [accessed March 18, 2015]. See also: "Documents of American History II"; available online at: http://tucnak.fsv.cuni.cz/~calda/Documents/1950s /McCarran_52.html [accessed March 18, 2015].

15 See House Report 1365, February 14, 1952.

16 "Revising the Laws Relating to Immigration, Naturalization, and Nationality," Report No. 1365 from the U.S. House of Representatives (February 14, 1952); available online at: https://bulk.resource.org/gao .gov/82-414/00002059.pdf [accessed April 29, 2015]. See pp. 41–42.

17 E.g., International Union of Bricklayers & Allied Craftsmen v. Meese, 761 F.2d 798 (D.C. Cir. 1985), International Longshoremen's & Warehousemen's Union v. Meese, 891 F.2d 1374 (9th Cir. Wash. 1989).

18 H.Rept. 101-723, p. 44.

19 Ibid.

20 Immigration Act of 1990, Pub. L. 101-649, § 205, 104 Stat. 4,978, 5,019.

21 Steve Barrett, "White-Collar Jobs Follow the Blues," *Chattanooga Times Free Press* (June 9, 2003).

22 U.S. Government Accountability Office, "H-1B VISA PROGRAM: Reforms Are Needed to Minimize the Risks and Costs of Current Program," op. cit.

23 Joe Kennedy, "Increase H-1B visas as part of the DHS appropriations bill," *The Hill* (March 13, 2015); available online at: http://thehill.com/blogs/con gress-blog/economy-budget/235589-increase-h-1b-visas-as-part-of-the -dhs-appropriations-bill [accessed March 19, 2015].

24 Moira Herbst, "Senators Target Visa 'Loopholes,'" Bloomberg Busi- ness (April 1, 2008); available online at: http://www.bloomberg.com/bw /stories/2008-04-01/senators-target-visa-loopholesbusinessweek-business -news-stock-market-and-financial-advice [accessed March 19, 2015].

25 Norman Matloff, "On the Need for Reform of the H-1B Nonimmigrant Work Visa in Computer-Related Occupations," 36 U. Mich. J.L. Reform 815, 874.

26 Vivek Wadhwa, "Silicon Valley's Dark Secret: It's All About Age," TechCrunch (August 28, 2010); available online at: http://techcrunch.com/2010/08/28 /silicon-valley%E2%80%99s-dark-secret-it%E2%80%99s-all-about-age / [accessed March 24, 2015].

27 Sarah McBride, "Special Report: Silicon Valley's dirty secret—age bias," Reuters (November 27, 2013); accessed February 16, 2015: http://www .reuters.com/article/2012/11/27/us-valley-ageism-idUSBRE8AQ0JK20121127.

28 Mark Coker, "Startup advice for entrepreneurs from Y Combinator," Ven- tureBeat (March 26, 2007); accessed February 16 2015: http://venturebeat .com/2007/03/26/start-up-advice-for-entrepreneurs-from-y-combinator -startup-school/.

29 Sarah McBride, "Silicon Valley's dirty secret—age bias," Reuters, op. cit.

30 Noam Scheiber, "Silicon Valley's brutal ageism," *New Republic* (March 23, 2014); accessed February 18, 2015: http://www.newrepublic.com/article /117088/silicons-valleys-brutal-ageism.

31 Ibid.

32 E.g., DICE.COM, DICE ID "GROM," posted April 22, 2015; DICE ID "RTX1700a8."

33 Verne Kopytoff, "Tech industry job ads: Older workers need not apply" (June 19, 2014); accessed February 18, 2015: http://fortune.com/2014/06/19 /tech-job-ads-discrimination/.

34 AFL-CIO Department for Professional Employees, "Guest Worker Visas: The H-1B and L-1" (March 2015); available online at: http://dpeaflcio.org /programs-publications/issue-fact-sheets/guest-worker-visas-the-h-1b -and-l-1/#_ednref30 [accessed April 15, 2015].

35 Immigration Act of 1990, Pub. L. 101-649, § 205, 104 Stat. 4,978, 5,022.

36 U.S. Government Accountability Office, H-1B Foreign Workers: Better Tracking Needed to Help Determine H-1B Program's Effects on U.S.

Workforce, GAO-03-883 (September 2003), p. 27; available online at: http://www.gao.gov/new.items/d03883.pdf [accessed April 15, 2015].

37   David North, "Technical Note: The Estimate of about 650,000 H-1Bs as of 9/30/09," Center for Immigration Studies (January 28, 2011); available online at: http://www.cis.org/north/estimate-H1B-population [accessed April 20, 2015].

38   Michelle Malkin, Invasion: How America Still Welcomes Terrorists Criminals & Other Foreign Menaces to Our Shores (Washington, D.C.: Regnery, 2002). See also: Michelle Malkin, "A National Security History Lesson for Marco Rubio," michellemalkin.com (April 26, 2013); available online at: http://michellemalkin.com/2013/04/26/a-national-security-history-lesson -for-marco-rubio/ [accessed March 18, 2015].

39   U.S. Department of Homeland Security, "US-VISIT Faces Challenges in Identifying and Reporting Multiple Biographic Identities (Redacted)," OIG-12-111 (August 2012); available online at: http://www.oig.dhs.gov/assets /Mgmt/2012/OIG_12-111_Aug12.pdf [accessed April 4, 2015].

40   Government Accountability Office, "OVERSTAY ENFORCEMENT: Additional Actions Needed to Assess DHS's Data and Improve Planning for a Biometric Air Exit Program," GAO-13-683 (July 2013); available online at: http://www.gao.gov/assets/660/656316.pdf [accessed April 4 2015].

41   Jerry Zremski, "House GOP pulls border biometric testing bill," Buffalo News (January 26, 2015); available online at: http://www.buffalonews .com/city-region/house-gop-pulls-border-biometric-testing-bill-20150126 [accessed April 4, 2015]. See also: Michelle Malkin, "A National Security History Lesson for Marco Rubio," michellemalkin.com (April 26, 2013); available online at: http://michellemalkin.com/2013/04/26/a-national-security -history-lesson-for-marco-rubio/ [accessed April 4, 2015].

42   See Government Accountability Office, "OVERSTAY ENFORCEMENT," op. cit. See also: David Seminara, "New Pew Report Confirms Visa Overstays Are Driving Increased Illegal Immigration," Center for Immigration Studies (September 24, 2013); available online at: http://www.cis.org /seminara/new-pew-report-confirms-visa-overstays-are-driving-increased -illegal-immigration [accessed April 4, 2015]; Sara Murray, "Many in U.S. Illegally Overstayed Their Visas," Wall Street Journal (April 7, 2013); available online at: http://www.wsj.com/articles/SB10001424127887323916304578404960101110032 [accessed April 4, 2015].

43   OpenSecrets.org, profile of Texas Instruments for the year 2008; available online at: http://www.opensecrets.org/lobby/firm_reports.php?id =D000000722&year=2008 [accessed February 18, 2015].

44 *New York Times*, "Do we need foreign technology workers?" (April 8, 2009); available online at: http://roomfordebate.blogs.nytimes.com/2009/04/08/do -we-need-foreign-technology-workers/#norman [accessed February 18, 2015].

45 Hearing before the Subcommittee on Immigration Policy and Enforcement of the Committee on the Judiciary, House of Representatives, "'STEM' THE TIDE: SHOULD AMERICA TRY TO PREVENT AN EXODUS OF FOREIGN GRADUATES OF U.S. UNIVERSITIES WITH AD-VANCED SCIENCE DEGREES?" (October 5, 2011); available online at: http://www.gpo.gov/fdsys/pkg/CHRG-112hhrg70576/html/CHRG-112 hhrg70576.htm [accessed February 18, 2015].

46 Sarah A. Webb, "Ph.Dollars: Does Grad School Make Financial Sense?" *Science* (April 11, 2008); available online at: http://sciencecareers.sciencemag .org/career_magazine/previous_issues/articles/2008_04_11/caredit.a080 0055 [accessed February 18, 2015].

47 Norman S. Matloff, "How Foreign Students Hurt U.S. Innovation" (February 11, 2013); available online at: http://www.bloomberg.com/news/articles /2013-02-12/glut-of-foreign-students-hurts-u-s-innovation [accessed February 18, 2015].

48 William J. Holstein, "Are raises bad for America?" *U.S. News & World Report* (August 30, 1999).

49 Sharon Machlis and Patrick Thibodeau, "Offshore firms took 50% of H-1B visas in 2013," *Computerworld* (April 1, 2014); available online at: http:// www.computerworld.com/article/2489146/technology-law-regulation-off shore-firms-took-50-of-h-1b-visas-in-2013.html [accessed March 18, 2015].

50 Ibid.

51 Microsoft, "Microsoft in India" (undated); available online at: http://www .microsoft.com/en-in/about/about-microsoft/our-offices.aspx [accessed April 29, 2015].

52 Brian Valentine, Senior VP Windows Division, Microsoft, "Thinking About India" (July 2, 2002).

53 Characteristics of Specialty Occupation Workers (FY 2013), U.S. Citizen-ship and Immigration Services, March 24, 2014, p. 6.

54 Patrick Thibodeau and Sharon Machlis, "With H-1B visa, diversity doesn't apply," *Computerworld* (August 10, 2015); available online at: http://www .itworld.com/article/2968356/it-management/with-h-1b-visa-diversity -doesnt-apply.html [accessed August 12, 2015].

55 Ibid.

56 "Best Videos Ever" YouTube channel, "Barack Obama Speech Writing of the 2012 State of the Union Address" (April 15, 2013); available online at:

https://www.youtube.com/watch?v=UDLSXwTNReY [accessed February 18, 2015].

57   Ibid.

58   Laurie Segall, "Instagram goes to Washington," CNN Money (January 25, 2012); available online at: http://money.cnn.com/2012/01/25/technology /instagram_white_house/ [accessed February 18, 2015].

59   Somini Sengupta, Nicole Perlroth, and Jenna Wortham, "Instagram founders were helped by Bay Area connections," *New York Times* (April 13, 2012); available online at: http://www.nytimes.com/2012/04/14/technology/insta gram-founders-were-helped-by-bay-area-connections.html?pagewanted =all&_r=0 [accessed February 18, 2015].

60   White House Office of the Press Secretary, "Guest List for the First Lady's Box at the State of the Union Address" (January 24, 2012); available online at: http://www.whitehouse.gov/the-press-office/2012/01/24/guest-list-first -ladys-box-state-union-address [accessed February 18, 2015].

61   Zachary Mider and Sarah Frier, "Getting a visa took longer than building Instagram, says immigrant co-founder," Bloomberg News (April 8, 2015); available online at: http://www.bloomberg.com/news/articles/2015-04-08 /getting-a-visa-took-longer-than-building-instagram-says-immigrant-co -founder [accessed April 14, 2015].

62   Kate Linthicum, "White House touts economic effect of Obama's immigration program," *Los Angeles Times* (January 26, 2015); available online at: http://www.latimes.com/local/california/la-me-obama-immigration -20150127-story.html [accessed February 18, 2015]. See also: Mike Krieger, "Celebrating Startups in the State of the Union," White House blog (January 31, 2012); available online at: http://www.whitehouse.gov /blog/2012/01/31/celebrating-startups-state-union [accessed February 18, 2015].

63   Laurie Segall, "Instagram goes to Washington," CNN Money (January 25, 2012); available online at: http://money.cnn.com/2012/01/25/technology /instagram_white_house/ [accessed February 18, 2015].

64   White House Office of the Press Secretary, "Remarks by the President in State of the Union Address" (January 24, 2012); available online at: http:// www.whitehouse.gov/the-press-office/2012/01/24/remarks-president -state-union-address [accessed February 18, 2015].

65   White House Jobs Council, Taking Action, Building Confidence: Five Common-Sense Initiatives to Boost Jobs and Competitiveness, President's Council on Jobs and Competitiveness (October 2011); available online at: http://files.jobs-council.com/jobscouncil/files/2011/10/JobsCouncil_Interim Report_Oct11.pdf [accessed February 18, 2015].

66 Rebecca Borison, "More Than A Third Of The Top US Tech Companies Were Founded By People Born Outside The Country," *Business Insider* (May 28, 2014); available online at: http://www.businessinsider.com /top-tech-companies-founded-by-foreigners-2014-5 [accessed February 18, 2015].

67 Cale Guthrie Weissman, "Mary Meeker highlights US immigration hypocrisy," pandodaily (May 29, 2013); available online at: http://pando.com /2013/05/29/mary-meeker-highlights-us-immigration-hypocrisy/ [accessed February 18, 2015].

68 John Bauschard, "It's time to stem the loss of STEM graduates," Yahoo! Finance (July 6, 2014); available online at: http://finance.yahoo.com/news /time-stem-loss-stem-graduates-173056641.html [accessed February 18, 2015].

69 John Miano, "92% of Top Tech Companies Created in the U.S. Were Founded by Native-Born Americans," Center for Immigration Studies (June 3, 2014); available online at: http://www.cis.org/miano/92-top-tech-com panies-created-us-were-founded-native-born-americans [accessed April 12, 2015].

70 Matt Faustman, "How can a startup sponsor an H1B visa?" upcounsel blog (November 18, 2013); available online at: https://www.upcounsel.com /blog/how-can-a-startup-sponsor-an-h1b-visa/ [accessed April 15, 2015].

71 Jennifer Epstein, "President Obama Google+ chat gets personal," *Politico* (January 30, 2012); available online at: http://www.politico.com/news /stories/0112/72185.html [accessed February 18, 2015].

72 Alex Nowrasteh, "Immigrants Did Not Take Your Job," Cato Institute (November 2, 2012); available online at: http://www.cato.org/blog/immigrants -did-not-take-job [accessed February 18, 2015].

73 Norman S. Matloff, "Get used to a life of layoffs," CNN (May 25, 2012); available online at: http://www.cnn.com/2012/05/25/opinion/matloff-hp -layoffs/ [accessed February 18, 2015].

74 Richard Templeton, "A CEO's argument for immigration reform," *Dallas Morning News* (July 14, 2014); available online at: http://www.dallasnews .com/opinion/latest-columns/20140714-a-ceos-argument-for-immigration -reform.ece [accessed February 18, 2015].

75 Korri Kezar, "21 Dallas–Fort Worth companies make the Forbes 2000 list," *Dallas Business Journal* (May 14, 2014); available online at: http://www.biz journals.com/dallas/blog/morning_call/2014/05/21dallas-fort-worth -companies-make-the-forbes-2000.html?page=all [accessed March 25, 2015].

76 White House Office of the Press Secretary, "Press Briefing by Press Secretary Jay Carney, 1/31/12" (January 31, 2012); available online at: http://

www.whitehouse.gov/the-press-office/2012/01/31/press-briefing-press|
-secretary-jay-carney-13112 [accessed February 18, 2015].

77   Ibid.

78   Ibid.

79   Ibid.

80   U.S. Department of Homeland Security, "DHS Reforms To Attract And Retain Highly Skilled Immigrants" (January 31, 2012); available online at: http://www.dhs.gov/news/2012/01/31/dhs-reforms-attract-and-retain -highly-skilled-immigrants [accessed February 18, 2015].

81   Press Briefing by Press Secretary Jay Carney, 1/31/12; available online at: http://www.whitehouse.gov/the-press-office/2012/01/31/press-briefing -press-secretary-jay-carney-13112 [accessed February 18, 2015].

82   PRWEB, "Programmers Guild Files 300 Discrimination Complaints Against H-1B Employers" (June 19, 2006); available online at: http://www .prweb.com/releases/2006/06/prweb400619.htm [accessed February 18, 2015].

83   Rick Merritt, "Consulting firm settles H-1B discrimination case," EE Times (May 2, 2008); available online at: http://www.eetimes.com/document .asp?doc_id=1168476 [accessed February 18, 2015].

84   John Zappe, "Report Says: IT Staffing Firms Discriminate Against American Workers," *Fordyce Letter* (July 9, 2012); available online at: http:// www.fordyceletter.com/2012/07/09/report-says-it-staffing-firms-discrimi nate-against-american-workers/ [accessed February 18, 2015].

85   PRWEB, "No Americans Need Apply Job Ads Exposed; Demands Dice .com Remove Ads" (July 5, 2012); available online at: http://www.bright futurejobs.com/no_americans_need_apply_job_ads_exposed [accessed February 18, 2015].

86   White House Office of the Press Secretary, "Press Briefing by Press Secretary Jay Carney, 1/31/12," op. cit.

87   Anna M. Tinsley, "Texas engineer, whose wife sent Obama his résumé, still unemployed," McClatchy DC (April 9, 2012); available online at: http:// www.mcclatchydc.com/2012/04/09/144558/texas-engineer-who-sent -obama.html [accessed February 18, 2015].

88   Ibid.

89   White House Office of the Press Secretary, "Remarks by the President on Immigration" (June 15, 2012); available online at: http://www.whitehouse .gov/the-press-office/2012/06/15/remarks-president-immigration [accessed February 18, 2015].

90   Ibid.

91 Bureau of Labor Statistics, "Unemployment in June 2012" (July 10, 2012); available online at: http://www.bls.gov/opub/ted/2012/ted_20120710.htm [accessed February 18, 2015].

92 Tommy Christopher, "The Fundamental Problem With Daily Caller's Neil Munro Heckling President Obama," Mediaite (June 19, 2012); available online at: http://www.mediaite.com/online/the-fundamental-problem -with-daily-callers-neil-munro-heckling-president-obama/ [accessed February 18, 2015].

93 Tommy Christopher, "MSNBC Guest Asks If Daily Caller Would Have Heckled A White President," Mediaite (June 15, 2012); available online at: http://www.mediaite.com/tv/msnbc-guest-asks-if-daily-caller-would-have -heckled-a-white-president/ [accessed February 18, 2015].

94 Dylan Byers, "WHCA: Daily Caller heckler 'discourteous,'" *Politico* (June 15, 2012); available online at: http://www.politico.com/blogs/media /2012/06/whca-pres-daily-caller-heckler-discourteous-126329.html [accessed February 18, 2015].

95 Anna M. Tinsley, "Texas engineer, whose wife sent Obama his résumé, still unemployed," op. cit.

96 Sen. Charles Grassley, "Grassley: High-Skilled American Workers Struggling to Find Jobs" (February 7, 2012); available online at: http://www .grassley.senate.gov/news/news-releases/grassley-high-skilled-american -workers-struggling-find-jobs [accessed March 18, 2015].

CHAPTER 2. DEBUNKING THE BIG FAT LIE

1 AAUW, "AAUW Issues: Science, Technology, Engineering, and Mathematics (STEM) Education" (undated); available online at: http://www.aauw .org/what-we-do/public-policy/aauw-issues/stem-education/ [accessed March 28, 2015].

2 Jonathan Rothwell, "Short on STEM Talent: Don't buy claims that the U.S. has too many STEM workers," *U.S. News & World Report* (September 14, 2014); available online at: http://www.usnews.com/opinion/articles /2014/09/15/the-stem-worker-shortage-is-real [accessed March 28, 2015]. See also: Andrew J. Rotherham, "The Next Great Resource Shortage: U.S. Scientists," *Time* (May 26, 2011); available online at: http://content.time .com/time/nation/article/0,8599,2074024,00.html [accessed March 28, 2015].

3 Morgan Reed, "Why Pi Day Matters," *Huffington Post* (March 14, 2015); available online at: http://www.huffingtonpost.com/morgan-reed/why-pi -day-matters_b_6866324.html [accessed March 28, 2015].

4 Issie Lapowski, "Obama has a $100M Plan to Fill the Tech Talent Shortage," *Wired* (March 9, 2015); available online at: http://www.wired.com/2015/03 /techhire-initiative/ [accessed March 28, 2015].

5 American Immigration Lawyers Association, et al. Letter to Sens. Grassley and Leahy (March 16, 2015); available online at https://www.uschamber .com/sites/default/files/multi-association_myths_facts_letter_for_sjc _hearing.pdf [accessed March 22, 2015].

6 Thomas J. Espenshade, "High-End Immigrants and the Shortage of Skilled Labor," Office of Population Research Working Paper No. 99-5 (June 1999); available online at: https://opr.princeton.edu/papers/opr9905.pdf [accessed March 28, 2015].

7 Richard Freeman, "Does Globalization of the Scientific/Engineering Workforce Threaten U.S. Economic Leadership?" National Bureau of Economic Research, 2006; available online at: http://www.nber.org/chapters/c0207.pdf [accessed March 28, 2015].

8 B. Lindsay Lowell and Harold Salzman, "Into the Eye of the Storm: Assessing the Evidence on Science and Engineering Education, Quality, and Workforce Demand," Urban Institute (October 29, 2007); available online at: http://www.urban.org/publications/411562.html [accessed March 28, 2015]. See also: Hal Salzman, "What Shortages? The Real Evidence About the STEM Workforce," *Issues in Science and Technology* (November 21, 2013); available online at: http://issues.org/29-4/what-shortages-the-real -evidence-about-the-stem-workforce/ [accessed March 28, 2015].

9 Titus Galama and James Hosek, "U.S. Competitiveness in Science and Technology," RAND Corporation Monograph MG-674-OSD (2008).

10 Claire Brown and Greg Linden, "Is There a Shortage of Engineering Talent in the U.S.?" IRLE Working Paper No. 163-07 (2008); available online at: http://www.irle.berkeley.edu/workingpapers/163-07.pdf [accessed March 28, 2105].

11 Hal Salzman, Daniel Kuehn, and B. Lindsay Lowell, "Guestworkers in the High-Skill U.S. Labor Market," Economic Policy Institute (April 24, 2013); available online at: http://www.epi.org/publication/bp359-guestworkers -high-skill-labor-market-analysis/ [accessed March 28, 2015].

12 Michael Anft, "The STEM Crisis: Reality or Myth?" *Chronicle of Higher Education* (November 11, 2013); available online at: http://www.rit.edu /news/pdfs/CHE_Hira.pdf [accessed March 28, 2015].

13 Patrick Thibodeau, "An H-1B cap hike would mean a grim future for workers," *Computerworld* (May 19, 2014); available online at: http://www .computerworld.com/article/2489494/it-careers/an-h-1b-cap-hike-would -mean-a-grim-future-for-workers.html [accessed March 28, 2015].

14 Ron Hira, Paula Stephan, et al., "Bill Gates' tech worker fantasy: Column" (July 27, 2014); available online at: http://www.usatoday.com/story/opinion /2014/07/27/bill-gates-tech-worker-wages-reforms-employment-column /13243305/ [accessed March 28, 2015].

15 Karen Zeigler and Steven A. Camarota, "Is There a STEM Worker Shortage? A look at employment and wages in science, technology, engineering, and math," Center for Immigration Studies (May 2014); available online at: http://cis.org/no-stem-shortage [accessed March 28, 2015].

16 Roger Fillion, "The catch-22 of coveted H-1B visas," ZDNet (September 25, 2000); available online at: http://www.zdnet.com/article/the-catch-22-of -coveted-h-1b-visas-5000110681/ [accessed March 28, 2015].

17 Francine Knowles and Shu Shin Luh, "So many IT jobs, so few takers," *Chicago Sun-Times* (September 28, 2000).

18 Patrick Thibodeau, "An H-1B cap hike would mean a grim future for workers," op. cit.

19 Daniel S. Greenberg, *Science, Money, and Politics: Political Triumph and Ethical Erosion* (Chicago: University of Chicago Press, 2003), p. 107.

20 Jeffrey Mervis, "Bloch Fleshes Out Long-term NSF Budget," *The Scientist* (April 6, 1987).

21 Eric Weinstein, "How and Why Government, Universities, and Industry Create Domestic Labor Shortages of Scientists and High-Tech Workers" (undated working draft); available online at: http://users.nber.org/~peat /PapersFolder/Papers/SG/NSF.html [accessed March 28, 2015].

22 Daniel S. Greenberg, *Science, Money, and Politics*, op. cit., p. 122–23.

23 Jeffrey Mervis, "Analysts Debunk Idea Of Scientist Shortage, Citing Defects In Current Economic Models," *The Scientist* (April 29, 1991); available online at: http://www.the-scientist.com/?articles.view/articleNo/11796 /title/Analysts-Debunk-Idea-Of-Scientist-Shortage—Citing-Defects -In-Current-Economic-Models/ [accessed March 28, 2015].

24 Michael S. Teitelbaum, *Falling Behind? Boom, Bust, and the Global Race for Scientific Talent* (Princeton, N.J.: Princeton University Press, 2014), p. 54.

25 Homer A. Neal, Tobin L. Smith, and Jennifer B. McCormick, *Beyond Sputnik: U.S. Science Policy in the 21st Century* (Ann Arbor: University of Michigan Press, 2008), p. 280.

26 Eric Weinstein, "How and Why Government, Universities, and Industry Create Domestic Labor Shortages of Scientists and High-Tech Workers," op. cit.

27 Richard B. Freeman and Daniel Goroff, eds., *Science and Engineering Careers in the United States* (Chicago: University of Chicago Press, 2009), p. 11.

28 U.S. Department of Commerce, Office of Technology Policy, *America's New Deficit: The Shortage of Information Technology Workers* (1997);

available online at: http://wdr.doleta.gov/research/pdf/newdeficit.pdf [accessed March 29, 2015].

29 Ibid.

30 Government Accountability Office, *Information Technology: Assessment of the Department of Commerce's Report on Workforce Demand and Supply*, GAO/HEHS-98-106 (March 1998), pp. 6–7; available online at: http://www.gao.gov/assets/230/225415.pdf [accessed March 29, 2015].

31 Ibid.

32 Ibid., p. 7.

33 Microsoft, "A National Talent Strategy: Ideas for Securing U.S. Competitiveness and Economic Growth" (2012); available online at: http://www.microsoft.com/en-us/news/download/presskits/citizenship/MSNTS.pdf [accessed March 29, 2015].

34 Ibid.

35 Ibid.

36 Sheldon Adelson, Warren Buffett, and Bill Gates, "Break the Immigration Impasse," op. cit.

37 Todd Bishop, "Microsoft cuts another 3,000 jobs, finishing last big phase of layoffs," GeekWire (October 29, 2014); available online at: http://www.geekwire.com/2014/microsoft-cuts-another-3000-jobs-finishing-last-big-phase-layoffs/ [accessed March 29, 2015].

38 Michael Teitelbaum, *Falling Behind?*, op. cit., p. 140.

39 Hal Salzman, Daniel Kuehn, and B. Lindsay Lowell, "Guestworkers in the high-skill U.S. labor market," op. cit.

40 Ibid.

41 Ryan Holeywell, "Campus anxiety rises as crude price falls," *Houston Chronicle* (December 12, 2014); available online at: http://www.houstonchronicle.com/business/energy/article/Campus-anxiety-rises-as-crude-price-falls-5954204.php [accessed March 29, 2015].

42 Michael Teitelbaum, "The Myth of the Science and Engineering Shortage," *Atlantic* (March 19, 2014); available online at: http://www.theatlantic.com/education/archive/2014/03/the-myth-of-the-science-and-engineering-shortage/284359/ [accessed March 29, 2015].

43 Norman Matloff, "Michael Teitelbaum Visits Davis—Invited by the Provost," Upon Closer Inspection blog (October 11, 2014); available online at: https://normsaysno.wordpress.com/2014/10/11/michael-teitelbaum-visits-davis-invited-by-the-provost/ [accessed March 29, 2015].

44 Janet H. Cho, "Google's Eric Schmidt and Jonathan Rosenberg share 'How Google Works' with Cleveland Clinic's Dr. Toby Cosgrove (gallery)," Cleveland.com (October 3, 2014); available online at: http://www.cleveland

.com/business/index.ssf/2014/10/googles_eric_schmidt_and_jonathan
_rosenberg_share_how_google_works_with_cleveland_clinics_dr_toby
_cosgrove.html [accessed March 29, 2015].

45 Kevin Freking, "Google's Eric Schmidt says H-1B visa changes would help economy," Associated Press (March 19, 2015); available online at: http://www.mercurynews.com/business/ci_27739294/googles-eric-schmidt-says-h-1b-visa-changes [accessed March 29, 2015].

46 Byron York, "As tech giant calls for more foreign workers, Senate hears of displaced Americans," *Washington Examiner* (March 19, 2015); available online at: http://www.washingtonexaminer.com/as-tech-giant-calls-for-more-foreign-workers-senate-hears-of-displaced-americans/article/2561766 [accessed March 29, 2015].

CHAPTER 3. MARKETING, MEDIA, AND MYTHS

1 Michael Kinsman, "Problems obtaining foreign worker visas leave some employers scrambling," U-T San Diego (August 27, 2006); available online at: http://www.utsandiego.com/uniontrib/20060827/news_lz1b27hiring.html [accessed April 15, 2015].

2 Judi Hasson, "Stimulus plan restricts H-1B hires," *Fierce CIO* (March 11, 2009); available online at: http://www.fiercecio.com/story/stimulus-plan-restricts-h-1b-hires/2009-03-11 [accessed March 22, 2015].

3 Michael Kinsman, "Problems obtaining foreign worker visas leave some employers scrambling," op. cit.

4 Hiawatha Bray, "High-tech visa quota filled in 5 days," *Boston Globe* (April 6, 2013); available online at: http://www.bostonglobe.com/business/2013/04/05/foreign-worker-visas-snapped-quickly/e9NGVB7zF0iZbtVXt6VhXN/story.html [accessed March 22, 2015].

5 Martha Mendoza and Amy Taxin, "US will let spouses of some highly skilled immigrants work under rule change," Associated Press (February 25, 2015); available online at: http://jobs.aol.com/articles/2015/02/25/highly-skilled-immigrant-spouses-can-soon-work-in-us/ [accessed March 23, 2015].

6 According to the Government Accountability Office only 24 of the top 150 H-1B users in Fiscal Year 2009 were H-1B-dependent. See U.S. Government Accountability Office, "H-1B VISA PROGRAM Reforms Are Needed to Minimize the Risks and Costs of Current Program," op. cit.

7 E.g., Michael Kinsman, "Problems obtaining foreign worker visas leave some employers scrambling," *San Diego Union-Tribune*, Aug. 27, 2006.

8 USCIS, Employment Based Second Preference: EB-2 Visa - General Requirements, available at http://www.uscis.gov/eir/visa-guide/eb-2-employment

-based-second-preference/employment-based-second-preference-eb-2-visa
-general-requirements.

9   Martin Kaste, "Older Tech Workers Oppose Overhauling H-1B Visas," NPR, February 19, 2013, available at http://www.npr.org/2013/02/19/172373123 /older-tech-workers-oppose-increasing-h-1b-visas.

10 Ibid.

11 American Recovery and Reinvestment Act of 2009, Pub. L. No. 111-5, § 1611, 123 Stat. 115.

12 Ibid.

13 To avoid H-1B-dependent status, companies take advantage of regulations that allow them to count all of their employees, including janitors and secretaries, when calculating the ratio of H-1B to non-H-1B workers—and not just workers in the employer's specialty occupation workforce. See Christopher Fulmer, "A CRITICAL LOOK AT THE H-1B VISA PROGRAM AND ITS EFFECTS ON U.S. AND FOREIGN WORKERS—A CONTROVERSIAL PROGRAM UNHINGED FROM ITS ORIGINAL INTENT," *Lewis & Clark Law Review* (Vol. 13:3), p. 827; available online at: http://www.lclark.edu/live/files/2196 [accessed April 15, 2015].

14 U.S. Department of Labor, Strategic Plan for Fiscal Years 2006–2011, p. 35.

15 Nolo Law For All, "Do I really have to pay the H-1B worker more than the prevailing wage?" (undated); available online at: http://www.nolo.com /legal-encyclopedia/do-i-really-pay-the-h-1b-worker-more-the-prevailing -wage.html [accessed April 15, 2015].

16 Peter Coy, "America's Gift to Rival Economies? The Absurd H-1B Visa Cap," Bloomberg Business (May 22, 2013); available online at: http://www .bloomberg.com/bw/articles/2013-05-22/america-s-gift-to-rival-econo mies-the-absurd-h-1b-visa-cap [accessed April 15, 2015].

17 Grant Sovern, "Misconceptions dominate the immigration debate," WTN News (May 1, 2007); available online at: http://wtnnews.com/articles/3888/ [accessed April 15, 2015].

18 H1B Wiki, "Top 10 Myths about H-1B Visa" (July 26, 2012); available online at: http://www.h1bwiki.com/top-10-myths-about-h-1b-visa/ [accessed April 15, 2015].

19 Immigration Act of 1990, Pub. L. 101-649, § 205, 104 Stat. 4,978, 5021.

20 John Miano, "The Bottom of the Pay Scale: Wages for H-1B Computer Programmers," Center for Immigration Studies (December 2005); available online at: http://www.cis.org/PayScale-H1BWages [accessed April 15, 2015].

21 Miscellaneous and Technical Immigration and Naturalization Amendments of 1991, PL 102-232, § 303, 105 Stat 1733.

22 U.S. Government Accountability Office, "H-1B Visa Program: Labor Could Improve Its Oversight and Increase Information Sharing with Homeland Security," GAO-06-720 (June 22, 2006); available online at: http://www .gao.gov/products/GAO-06-720 [accessed April 15, 2015].

23 U.S. Department of Labor, "OVERVIEW AND ASSESSMENT OF VULNERABILITIES IN THE DEPARTMENT OF LABOR'S ALIEN LABOR CERTIFICATION PROGRAMS," Report No. 06-03-007-03-321 (September 30, 2003); available online at: http://www.oig.dol.gov/public /reports/oa/2003/06-03-007-03-321.pdf [accessed April 15, 2015].

24 8 USC 1182, Section 212.

25 8 USC 1182(p)(4).

26 FLC Data Center, Employment and Training Administration Prevailing Wage Determination Policy Guidance Nonagricultural Immigration Programs (revised November 2009); available online at: http://www.flcdata center.com/download/NPWHC_Guidance_Revised_11_2009.pdf [accessed April 15, 2015].

27 U.S. Government Accountability Office, "H-1B VISA PROGRAM:Reforms Are Needed to Minimize the Risks and Costs of Current Program," GAO-11-26 (January 14, 2011); available online at: http://www.gao.gov /products/GAO-11-26 [accessed April 15, 2015].

28 John Miano, "Low Salaries for Low Skills: Wages and Skill Levels for H-1B Computer Workers, 2005," Center for Immigration Studies (April 2007); available online at: http://cis.org/LowSalariesforLowSkills-H1B [accessed April 5, 2015].

29 You can find the actual prevailing wage and the H-1B prevailing wages for any job and location combination at the Foreign Labor Certification web site, FLCDATACENTER.COM.

30 Ibid.

31 Patrick Thibodeau, "H-1B pay and its impact on U.S. workers is aired by Congress," *Computerworld* (March 31, 2011); available online at: http://www .computerworld.com/article/2507602/technology-law-regulation/h-1b -pay-and-its-impact-on-u-s--workers-is-aired-by-congress.html [accessed April 15, 2015].

32 Ibid.

33 Ibid.

34 Mac Lifsher, "SoCal Edison to lay off hundreds in effort to streamline management," *Los Angeles Times* (April 15, 2014); available online at: http:// articles.latimes.com/2014/apr/15/business/la-fi-edison-layoffs-20140415 [accessed April 19, 2015].

35 Ron Hira, "New Data Show How Firms Like Infosys and Tata Abuse the H-1B Program," Employment Policy Institute (February 19, 2015); available online at: http://www.epi.org/blog/new-data-infosys-tata-abuse-h-1b-program/ [accessed April 19, 2015].

36 USCIS is required to accept H-1B visa petitions submitted during the first five days of April of one calendar for approval in the next fiscal year beginning in October of that calendar year. H-1B applicants with master's degrees or higher are sorted from non–master's degree holders. The twenty thousand "masters cap" for advanced degree holders gets used up through a random selection process. "Losers" then enter the sixty-five-thousand-cap pool with the non–master's degree holders for a second bite at the random lottery apple.

37 Kirk Doran, et al., "The Effects of High-Skilled Immigration on Firms: Evidence from H-1B Visa Lotteries," presented at Workshop in Economics of Science and Engineering, Harvard University, April 24, 2015, p. 29; available online at: http://isites.harvard.edu/fs/docs/icb.topic1459278.files/ISEN-Adam_4-24-15_Effect%20of%20High%20Skill%20Immigration_w-Doran-and-Gelber_3-15-15.pdf [last accessed May 7, 2015].

38 Ibid.

39 Josh Barro tweet (November 21, 2012); available online at: https://twitter.com/jbarro/status/271373411446562816 [accessed April 15, 2015].

40 Chemjobber tweet (November 21, 2015); available online at: https://twitter.com/Chemjobber/status/271373776334245888 [accessed April 15, 2015].

41 Josh Barro tweet (November 21, 2012); available online at: https://twitter.com/jbarro/status/271374310030065664 [accessed April 15, 2015].

42 Gary Beach, "Remove the H-1B Visa Cap," *Wall Street Journal* (April 1, 2015); available online at: http://blogs.wsj.com/cio/2015/04/01/remove-the-h1b-visa-cap/ [accessed May 12, 2015].

43 Eric Berger, "How come the scientific establishment of the United States hasn't collapsed? Because it has a secret weapon," *Houston Chronicle* SciGuy blog (June 18, 2011); available online at: http://blog.chron.com/sciguy/2011/06/how-come-the-scientific-establishment-of-the-united-states-hasnt-collapsed-because-it-has-a-secret-weapon/ [accessed March 29, 2015].

44 U.S. Government Accountability Office, "H-1B program: Reforms are needed to minimize the costs and risks of current program" GAO-11-26 (January 2011), p. 35.

45 Kirk Doran, et al., "The Effects of High-Skilled Immigration on Firms: Evidence from H-1B Visa Lotteries," presented at Workshop in Economics of Science and Engineering, Harvard University, April 24, 2015; available online at: http://isites.harvard.edu/fs/docs/icb.topic1459278.files/ISEN

-Adam_4-24-15_Effect%20of%20High%20Skill%20Immigration_w-Doran
-and-Gelber_3-15-15.pdf [last accessed May 7, 2015].

46 David North, "More Foreign Workers = More Patents Argument is Disputed
at DC Session," Center for Immigration Studies (December 10, 2012); available online at: http://cis.org/north/more-foreign-workers-more-patents
-argument-disputed-dc-session [accessed April 20, 2015].

47 Office of Senator Orrin Hatch, "Hatch, Flake promote 21st century workforce
through I-Squared Act," *St. George News* (March 19, 2014); available online at:
https://www.stgeorgeutah.com/news/archive/2015/03/19/hatch-flake-promote
-21st-century-workforce-squared/#.VQx3xlxva-I [accessed March 22, 2015].

48 Michael Kinsman, "Problems obtaining foreign worker visas leave some
employers scrambling," U-T San Diego (August 27, 2006); available online
at: http://www.utsandiego.com/uniontrib/20060827/news_lz1b27hiring
.html [accessed March 22, 2015].

49 Bryan Renk, "Immigration reform vital to Wisconsin bioscience," *Milwau-
kee Journal-Sentinel* (September 16, 2013); available online at: http://www
.jsonline.com/news/opinion/immigration-reform-vital-to-wisconsin-bio
science-b9999393z1-223995341.html [accessed March 22, 2015].

50 James Sherk and Guinevere Nell, "More H-1B Visas, More American Jobs, A
Better Economy," Heritage Foundation (April 30, 2008); available online at:
http://www.heritage.org/research/reports/2008/04/more-h-1b-visas-more
-american-jobs-a-better-economy [accessed March 29, 2015].

51 Joe Green, "The Immigration Bill is out of Committee, what does that mean
and why does it matter?" FWD.us (May 23, 2013); available online at: http://
www.FWD.us/tags/movement?page=2 [accessed March 29, 2015].

52 David Brooks, "The easy problem," *New York Times* (February 1, 2013);
available online at: http://www.nytimes.com/2013/02/01/opinion/brooks
-the-easy-problem.html [accessed March 29, 2015].

53 National Foundation for American Policy, "H-1B Visas and Job Creation"
(March 2008); available online at: http://www.nfap.com/pdf/080311h1b.pdf
[accessed March 29, 2015].

54 Microsoft News Center, "Bill Gates: Testimony before the Committee
on Science and Technology, U.S. House of Representatives" (March 12,
2008); available online at: http://news.microsoft.com/2008/03/12/bill-gates
-testimony-before-the-committee-on-science-and-technology-u-s-house
-of-representatives/ [accessed March 29, 2015].

55 Statement of the American Immigration Lawyers Association et al. to Sen.
Charles Grassley (March 16, 2015); available online at: https://www.us
chamber.com/sites/default/files/multi-association_myths_facts_letter_for
_sjc_hearing.pdf [accessed March 29, 2015].

56 Ibid.

57 National Foundation for American Policy, "H-1B Visas and Job Creation," op. cit.

58 Immigration Policy Center, "The U.S. Economy Still Needs Highly Skilled Foreign Workers" (March 30, 2011); available online at: http://www.immigrationpolicy.org/just-facts/us-economy-still-needs-highly-skilled-foreign-workers [accessed March 29, 2015].

59 Madeline Zavodny, "Immigration and American jobs," American Enterprise Institute (December 5, 2011); available online at: https://www.aei.org/wp-content/uploads/2011/12/-immigration-and-american-jobs_144002688962.pdf [accessed March 29, 2015].

60 U.S. Chamber of Commerce, "Immigration Myths and Facts" (October 24, 2013); available online at: https://www.uschamber.com/sites/default/files/legacy/reports/Immigration_MythsFacts.pdf [accessed March 29, 2015].

61 Laura Collins, "Low H-1B Visa Caps Don't Reflect Market Reality," American Action Forum (April 1, 2014); available online at: http://americanactionforum.org/insights/low-h-1b-visa-caps-dont-reflect-market-reality [accessed March 29, 2015].

62 Carl Bialik, "Work-Visa Numbers Get Squishy—and Get Played," *Wall Street Journal* (March 21, 2009).

63 Norman Matloff email (April 1, 2009); available online at: http://heather.cs.ucdavis.edu/Archive/WSJOnNFAPClaim.txt [accessed March 29, 2015].

64 David Brooks, "The easy problem," op. cit.

65 Madeline Zavodny, "Immigration and American jobs," op. cit., p. 16.

66 R. Davis, "Analysis of Key Finding from 'Immigration and American Jobs'" (undated); available online at: http://econdataus.com/amjobs0.htm [accessed April 19, 2015].

67 Ron Hira, "New Data Show How Firms Like Infosys and Tata Abuse the H-1B Program," Employment Policy Institute (February 19, 2015); available online at: http://www.epi.org/blog/new-data-infosys-tata-abuse-h-1b-program/ [accessed March 29, 2015].

68 FWD.us, "Know the Facts: H-1B Visas," YouTube (September 29, 2014); available online at: https://www.youtube.com/watch?v=iXun0-mEOM8 [accessed March 29, 2015].

69 *New York Daily News*, "Immigration boosts jobs for Americans, study finds" (December 19, 2011); available online at: http://www.nydailynews.com/opinion/immigration-boosts-jobs-americans-study-finds-article-1.992877 [accessed March 29, 2015].

70 Kirk Doran, et al., "The Effects of High-Skilled Immigration on Firms: Evidence from H-1B Visa Lotteries," presented at Workshop in Econom-

ics of Science and Engineering, Harvard University, April 24, 2015, p. 3; available online at: http://isites.harvard.edu/fs/docs/icb.topic1459278.files /ISEN-Adam_4-24-15_Effect%20of%20High%20Skill%20Immigration _w-Doran-and-Gelber_3-15-15.pdf [Last accessed May 7, 2015].

71 American Immigration Lawyers Association, et al., Letter to Sens. Grassley and Leahy (March 16, 2015); available online at https://www.uschamber .com/sites/default/files/multi-association_myths_facts_letter_for_sjc _hearing.pdf [accessed March 22, 2015].

72 Aaron N. Taylor, "Why Law School is Still Worth It," *PreLaw National Jurist* (October 11, 2011) [accessed May 5, 2015].

73 See, e.g., "Microsoft's Vancouver expansion a sharp nudge on immigration reform," *Seattle Post-Intelligencer* (May 11, 2014). See also: David Bier, "Removing H-1B visa quotas will create American jobs," FoxNews.com (April 9, 2012).

74 Ina Fried and Anne Broache, "Microsoft sings 'O Canada' amid immigration challenges," CNET (July 5, 2007); available online at: http://news .cnet.com/Microsoft-sings-O-Canada-amid-immigration-challenges /2100-1014_3-6195049.html [accessed March 29, 2015].

75 Nancy Gohring, "Microsoft Vancouver responds to immigration woes," *Infoworld* (July 5, 2007); available online at: http://www.infoworld.com /article/2663608/techology-business/microsoft-vancouver-responds -to-immigration-woes.html [accessed March 29, 2015].

76 Todd Bishop, "Microsoft plans big Vancouver, B.C., software center," *Seattle Post-Intelligencer* (July 5, 2007); available online at: http://blog .seattlepi.com/microsoft/2007/07/05/microsoft-plans-big-vancouver-b-c -software-center/ [accessed March 29, 2015].

77 Microsoft, "Peter Moore Resigns From Microsoft to Return to Northern California" (July 17, 2007).

78 Janet I. Tu, "Microsoft to create B.C. tech hub, hire Canadian R&D talent," *Seattle Times* (May 1, 2014); available online at: http://www.seattletimes .com/business/microsoft-to-create-bc-tech-hub-hire-canadian-rd-talent / [accessed April 29, 2015].

79 U.S. Government Accountability Office, "H-1B Program: Reforms Are Needed to Minimize the Risks and Costs of Current Program," GAO-11-26 (January 14, 2011); available online at: http://www.gao.gov/assets /320/314501.pdf [accessed March 29, 2015].

80 Tazmin Booth, "Here, there and everywhere," *The Economist* (January 19, 2013); available online at: http://www.economist.com/news/special-report /21569572-after-decades-sending-work-across-world-companies-are -rethinking-their-offshoring [accessed March 29, 2015].

81 Charles Fishman, "The Insourcing boom," *Atlantic* (November 28, 2012); available online at: http://theatlantic.com/magazine/archive/2012/12/the -insourcing-boom/309166/ [accessed April 19, 2015].

82 Tazmin Booth, "Here, there and everywhere," op. cit.

CHAPTER 4. DIG YOUR OWN GRAVE

1 Department of Homeland Security, "DHS Extends Eligibility for Employment Authorization to Certain H-4 Dependent Spouses of H-1B Nonimmigrants Seeking Employment-Based Lawful Permanent Residence" (February 24, 2015); available online at: http://www.uscis.gov/news/dhs-extends-eligibil ity-employment-authorization-certain-h-4-dependent-spouses-h-1b-non immigrants-seeking-employment-based-lawful-permanent-residence.

2 8 U.S.C. § 1182(n)(1).

3 8 U.S.C. § 1182(n)(1)(E).

4 Douglass Crouse, "Competition from abroad: Increasing visas for high-tech workers criticized," *Daily Record* (May 2, 2000).

5 Ibid.

6 Ibid.

7 Ellen Lee, "Job Losses Sap Morale of Workers," *Contra Costa Times* (date unknown); reproduced online at: http://www.engology.com/BobFlanagan .htm [accessed April 8, 2015].

8 Stephanie Armor, "Workers asked to train foreign replacements," *USA Today* (April 6, 2004); available online at: http://usatoday30.usatoday.com /money/workplace/2004-04-06-replace_x.htm [accessed April 8, 2015].

9 Ibid.

10 David Lazarus, "BofA: Train your replacement, or no severance pay for you," *San Francisco Chronicle* (June 9, 2006); available online at: http:// www.sfgate.com/business/article/BofA-Train-your-replacement-or-no -severance-pay-2517604.php [accessed April 8, 2015].

11 Ibid.

12 Kevin Fogarty, "Moving IT to Low-Cost Countries," *eWeek* (November 7, 2008); available online at: http://www.eweek.com/c/a/IT-Infrastructure /Did-Pfizer-Force-its-Staff-to-Train-Their-H1B-Replacements/1 [accessed March 22, 2015].

13 Lee Howard, "Pfizer layoffs slightly larger than projected," *The Day* (February 11, 2013); available online at: http://www.theday.com/article/20130211 /BIZ02/302119958 [accessed March 22, 2015].

14 Ibid.

15 Pfizer, Corporate Procedure #117 (November 3, 2007).

16 Lee Howard, "Pfizer layoffs slightly larger than projected," op. cit.

17 Richard Behar, "Exclusive: World Bank's Web of Ties to 'India's Enron,'" FoxNews.com (January 12, 2009); available online at: http://www.foxnews .com/story/2009/01/12/exclusive-world-bank-web-ties-to-india-enron / [accessed March 22, 2015].

18 Heather Timmons and Bettina Wassener, "Satyam Chief Admits Huge Fraud," *New York Times* (January 8, 2009); available online at: http://www .nytimes.com/2009/01/08/business/worldbusiness/08satyam.html?_r=0 [accessed March 22, 2015].

19 Ibid.

20 "Satyam banned from World Bank," dna India (October 12, 2008); available online at: http://www.dnaindia.com/money/report-satyam-banned-from -world-bank-1197363 [accessed March 22, 2015].

21 Memo from Elahe Hessamfar (March 20, 2000); available online at: http:// www.programmersguild.org/archives/lib/Abuse/dnb20000320elahe.htm [accessed March 22, 2015].

22 Ibid.

23 Ibid.

24 Douglas Crouse, "Dun workers fear layoffs," *Daily Record* (June 3, 2000); available online at: https://www.numbersusa.com/text?ID=78 [accessed March 22, 2015].

25 Stephanie Armour, "Workers asked to train foreign replacements," *USA Today* (April 6, 2004); available online at: http://usatoday30.usatoday.com /tech/news/2004-04-06-replace_x.htm [accessed March 22, 2015].

26 Ibid.

27 Patrick Thibodeau and Jaikumar Vijayan, "Utility sets IT department on path to self-destruction," *Computerworld* (September 23, 2013); available online at: http://www.computerworld.com/article/2484942/it-outsourcing/utility-sets -it-department-on-path-to-self-destruction.html [accessed March 22, 2015].

28 Ibid.

29 Ibid.

30 Jon Chesto, "Eversource CEO awarded $1.3 million pay raise," *Boston Globe* (March 13, 2013); available online at: http://www.bostonglobe.com /business/2015/03/12/eversource-ceo-tom-may-enjoyed-percent-bump -pay/jFlFgmu6oOvJrPAgNE1qYL/story.html [accessed March 22, 2105].

31 Patrick Thibodeau, "Infosys ran 'unlawful' visa scheme, U.S. alleges in set-tlement," *Computerworld* (October 30, 2013); available online at: http://www .computerworld.com/article/2485485/it-outsourcing/infosys-ran--unlawful --visa-scheme--u-s--alleges-in-settlement.html [accessed March 22, 2015].

32 Patrick Thibodeau, "H-1B whistleblower files new federal lawsuit," *Com-puterworld* (October 2, 2014); available online at: http://www.computer

world.com/article/2691106/h-1b-whistleblower-files-new-federal-lawsuit
.html [accessed March 22, 2015].

33 Statement of Jack (Jay) B. Palmer Jr., "Immigration Reforms Needed to
Protect Skilled American Workers," U.S. Senate Judiciary Committee
(March 17, 2015); available online at: http://www.judiciary.senate.gov/imo
/media/doc/Palmer%20Testimony.pdf [accessed March 22, 2015].

34 Ron Hira, "Congress and President Obama Cannot Sit Idly By While Companies Use H-1B Guestworkers to Replace American Workers," Employment Policy Institute (February 10, 2015); available online at: http://www
.epi.org/blog/congress-and-president-obama-cannot-sit-idly-by-while
-companies-use-h-1b-guestworkers-to-replace-american-workers/ [accessed
April 8, 2015].

35 Shilpa Phadnis and Mini Joseph Tejaswi, "HCL inks $200 million deal with
Disney," *Times of India* (June 19, 2012); available online at: http://timesof
india.indiatimes.com/tech/tech-news/HCL-inks-200-million-deal-with
-Disney/articleshow/14270161.cms [accessed April 8, 2015].

36 Ibid.

37 Byron York, "Silenced workers who lost jobs to H-1B visa abuse (quietly) speak out," *Washington Examiner* (March 22, 2015); available online
at: http://www.washingtonexaminer.com/victims-of-visa-abuse-quietly
-speak-out/article/2561856 [accessed March 22, 2015].

38 David North, "The H-1B Program Wins the Triple Crown for Discrimination," Center for Immigration Studies (May 29, 2014); available online at:
http://cis.org/north/h-1b-program-wins-triple-crown-discrimination.

39 Patrick Thibodeau and Sharon Machlis, "With H-1B visa, diversity doesn't
apply," *Computerworld* (August 10, 2015); available online at: http://www
.itworld.com/article/2968356/it-management/with-h-1b-visa-diversity
-doesnt-apply.html [accessed August 13, 2015].

40 Brenda Koehler vs. Infosys Technologies Limited Incorporated, D/B/A Infosys Limited, Case 2:13-cv-00885 (filed August 1, 2013); available online at:
http://www.scribd.com/doc/157691931/Complaint-Proposed-Class-Action
-Infosys#scribd

41 Ibid.

42 Patrick Thibodeau, "IT workers win key ruling against visa-using firm,"
Computerworld, May 26, 2015; available online at: http://www.computer
world.com/article/2926837/it-careers/it-workers-win-key-ruling-against
-visa-using-firm.html [accessed August 7, 2015].

43 Patrick Thibodeau, "Court case offers a peek at how H-1B-fueled discrimination works," *Computerworld* (July 10, 2014); available online at: http://
www.computerworld.com/article/2489900/it-outsourcing/court-case

-offers-a-peek-at-how-h-1b-fueled-discrimination-works.html [accessed April 8, 2015].

44 Brenda Koehler, Kelly Parker, Layla Bolten, and Gregory Handloser vs. Infosys Technologies Limited Inc., and Infosys Public Services, Inc., Civil Action No. 2:13-cv-885 (filed September 27, 2013); available online at: http://www.dealernews.com/sites/www.dealernews.com/files/files/ParkervInfo sys%20%28HD%29.pdf [accessed April 8, 2015].

45 Ibid.

46 Brenda Koehler vs. Infosys Technologies Limited Incorporated, D/B/A Infosys Limited, Case 2:13-cv-00885, op. cit.

47 Brenda Koehler, Kelly Parker, Layla Bolten, and Gregory Handloser vs. Infosys Technologies Limited Inc., and Infosys Public Services, Inc., Civil Action No. 2:13-cv-885, op. cit.

48 Koehler v. Infosys, Civil Action 2:13-cv-885 (E.D.Wis.), Declaration of Samual Marerro, ECF #13-1.

49 Heldt v. Tata Consultancy Services, 15-cv-01696, (N.D. Calif, Complaint filed April, 14, 2015).

50 Ibid., p. 9.

51 Ibid., p. 13.

52 Martin J. Lawler and Margaret Stock, "Saying 'No Thanks' to 87,500 High-Skill Workers," *Wall Street Journal* (May 7, 2014); available online at: http://www.wsj.com/articles/SB10001424052702303647204579544362260141496 [accessed March 22, 2015].

53 Brett Joshpe, "SLICKNESS WITH A STRAIGHT FACE," *American Spectator* (March 9, 2009); available online at: http://spectator.org/articles/41995/slickness-straight-face [accessed March 22, 2015].

54 Andrew Ross Sorkin, "Tech Firms May Find No-Poaching Pacts Costly," *New York Times* (April 7, 2014); available online at: http://dealbook.nytimes.com/2014/04/07/tech-firms-may-find-no-poaching-pacts-costly/ [accessed March 22, 2015].

55 John Ribeiro, "Tech bigwigs send $415M deal with workers back to judge for OK," *Computerworld* (March 2, 2015); available online at: http://www.computerworld.com/article/2891933/tech-bigwigs-send-415m-deal-with-workers-back-to-judge-for-ok.html [accessed March 22, 2015].

56 Grover G. Norquist, "SAMUEL GOMPERS VERSUS REAGAN," *American Spectator* (September 2013); available at: http://spectator.org/articles/55096/samuel-gompers-versus-reagan [accessed March 22, 2015].

57 W. James Antle III, "H-1 B-WARE," *American Spectator* (January–February 2014); available online at: http://spectator.org/articles/57162/h-1-b-ware [accessed March 22, 2015].

58   Hal Salzman, Daniel Kuehn, and B. Lindsay Lowell, "Guestworkers in the high-skill U.S. labor market," Economic Policy Institute (April 24, 2013); available online at: http://www.epi.org/publication/bp359-guestworkers-high-skill-labor-market-analysis/ [accessed March 22, 2015].

59   Gordon H. Hanson and Matthew J. Slaughter, "Talent, Immigration, and U.S. Economic Competitiveness, Compete America Coalition" (May 2013); available online at: http://irps.ucsd.edu/assets/001/504703.pdf [accessed March 22, 2015].

60   Paul Donnelly, "H-1B is just another gov't subsidy," *Computerworld* (July 22, 2002); available online at: http://www.computerworld.com/article /2576945/it-careers/h-1b-is-just-another-gov-t—subsidy.html [accessed April 20, 2015].

61   North Carolina Gov. Pat McCrory, "Cognizant to open new IT delivery and operations center in Charlotte" (November 12, 2014); available online at: http://www.governor.state.nc.us/newsroom/press-releases/20141112/cog nizant-open-new-it-delivery-and-operations-center-charlotte [accessed April 20, 2015].

62   Ibid.

63   Charlotte Chamber, "291 Fortune 500 Companies Represented in the Charlotte MSA, 2014" (undated); available online at: https://charlottechamber.com /clientuploads/Economic_pdfs/Fortune500List.pdf [accessed April 20, 2015].

64   Sue Siens, "Charlotte USA Banking Sector Yields Growth in Back Office Operations," BusinessClimate (published August 22, 2013; updated September 19, 2014); available online at: http://businessclimate.com/charlotte-nc -area-economic-development/charlotte-usa-banking-sector-yields-growth -back-office-operat [accessed April 20, 2015].

65   Ben Bradford, "Off-Shoring Company Cognizant Gets Tax Breaks To Expand In NC," WFAE (December 16, 2014); available online at: http:// wfae.org/post/shoring-company-cognizant-gets-tax-breaks-expand-nc [accessed April 20, 2015].

66   Angelo Young, "North Carolina Taxpayers Are Funding Outsourcing, Critics Of Companies Like Cognizant Want To Know Why," *International Business Times* (December 16, 2014); available online at: http://www.ibtimes .com/north-carolina-taxpayers-are-funding-outsourcing-critics-companies -cognizant-want-1760260 [accessed April 20, 2015].

67   8 U.S.C. § 1324b.

68   Ibid.

69   International Business Machines Corp. Schedule 14A, Filed March 9, 2015 with the Securities and Exchange Commission.

70   Press Release, "U.S. Companies Say H-1B Hires are 'Critical' to Success," VISANOW (April 7, 2014).

71   "PERM Fake Job Ads defraud Americans . . ." YouTube.com (uploaded June 16, 2007); available online at: https://youtu.be/TCbFEgFajGU [accessed March 22, 2015].

72   Ibid.

73   Moira Herbst, "Outsourcing: How to Skirt the Law," *BusinessWeek* (June 22, 2007).

74   "PERM Fake Job Ads defraud Americans . . ." YouTube.com, op. cit.

75   H.R. Rept. 101-723, p.41.

76   Ibid., p. 45

77   Ibid.

78   Sheldon G. Adelson, Warren E. Buffett, and Bill Gates, "Break the Immigration Impasse," op. cit.

79   Anne Broache, "Google: Foreign workers are key to our success," CNET News (June 6, 2007); available online at: http://news.cnet.com/Google-Foreign-workers-are-key-to-our-success/2100-1028_3-6189093.html [accessed March 22, 2015].

CHAPTER 5. 50 SHADES OF H-1B ABUSE

1   Ron Hira, "Top 10 users of H-1B guest worker program are all offshore outsourcing firms," Economic Policy Institute (February 14, 2013); available online at: http://www.epi.org/blog/top-10-h1b-guestworker-offshore-outsourcing/ [accessed March 27, 2015].

2   See, e.g., Ron Hira, "H-1B Workers are in a State of Indentured Servitude," *U.S. News & World Report* (August 27, 2011); available online at: http://www.usnews.com/debate-club/should-h-1b-visas-be-easier-to-get/h-1b-workers-are-in-a-state-of-indentured-servitude [accessed March 27, 2015].

3   Pub. L. 105-277, 112 STAT. 2681-646. October 21, 1998.

4   In *Administrator, Wage & Hour Division v. Greater Pro-Care Providers*, 2008-LCA-026 (2014), the employer claimed liquidated damages of $4,000 for a physical therapist; In *Administrator, Wage & Hour Division v. Kutty*, 2001-LCA-00010 (2002), the employer's agreement contained $350,000 liquidated damages clause for doctors; In *Malik v. Knack Systems*, 2013-LCA00017 (2014), the liquidated damages clause was $15,000 for a computer programmer.

5   Gary Cohn and Walter F. Roche, Jr., "Indentured servants for high-tech trade," *Baltimore Sun* (February 21, 2000); available online at: http://www.baltimoresun.com/bal-visavendors022100-htmlstory.html [accessed March 27, 2015].

6   Stephanie Neil, "H1-B [*sic*] safety net fails IT workers," *PC Week* (November 18, 1998).

7   John Ribeiro, "Tata faces employee lawsuit in the U.S.," *InfoWorld* (February 15, 2006).

8   Tata Consultancy Servs. v. Systems Int'l, 31 F.3d 416 (6th Cir. 1994); Vedachalam v. Tata Am. Int'l Corp., 339 Fed. Appx. 761 (9th Cir. Cal. 2009); Matt Smith, Jennifer Gollan and Adithya Sambamurthy, "Job brokers steal wages and entrap Indian tech workers in US," *Guardian* (October 28, 2014); available online at: http://www.theguardian.com/us-news/2014/oct/28/-sp -jobs-brokers-entrap-indian-tech-workers [accessed March 27, 2015].

9   Matt Smith, Jennifer Gollan, and Adithya Sambamurthy, "Job brokers steal wages and entrap Indian tech workers in US," Reveal News (October 27, 2014); available online at: http://www.revealnews.org/article/job-brokers -steal-wages-entrap-indian-tech-workers-in-us/ [accessed March 27, 2015].

10 Ibid.

11 Norman Matloff, "Stop Blaming Indian Companies for Visa Abuse," BloombergView (August 26, 2013); available online at: http://www.bloom bergview.com/articles/2013-08-26/stop-blaming-indian-companies-for-visa -abuse [accessed March 27, 2015].

12 David Swaim, "An Employer's Guide to the Immigration Process," Tidwell, Swaim and Associates (2012); no longer available online.

13 John Miano, "The Bottom of the Pay Scale: Wages for H-1B Computer Programmers," Center for Immigration Studies (December 2005); available online at: http://www.cis.org/PayScale-H1BWages [accessed March 28, 2015].

14 Associated Press, "Ga. Co. Pleads Guilty in INS Case" (November 24, 1999).

15 U.S. Department of Labor Office of Inspector General, Office of Audit, "The Department of Labor's Foreign Labor Certification Programs: The System Is Broken and Needs To Be Fixed," Final Report No. 06-96-002- 03-321 (May 22, 1996); available online at: http://www.oig.dol.gov/public /reports/oa/pre_1998/06-96-002-03-321.pdf [accessed March 28, 2015].

16 Sharon Machlis and Patrick Thibodeau, "Offshore firms took 50% of H-1B visas in 2013," *Computerworld* (April 1, 2014); available online at: http:// www.computerworld.com/article/2489146/technology-law-regulation-off shore-firms-took-50-of-h-1b-visas-in-2013.html [accessed March 28, 2015].

17 U.S. Government Accountability Office, "H-1B Visa Program: Reforms Are Needed to Minimize the Risks and Costs of Current Program," GAO- 11-26 (January 14, 2011), p. 44; available online at: http://www.gao.gov /products/GAO-11-26 [accessed April 29, 2015].

18 Wipro, Form 10-F, March 31, 2014.

19 KForce, Form K-10, December 31, 2013.

20 Cognizant, Form 10-Q, March 31, 2014.

21 H.R. Rept. 101-723, p. 45.

22 "Satyam scam: Raju, 9 others get 7 years' jail for fudging accounts," *Times of India* (April 10, 2015); available online at: http://timesofindia.indiatimes.com/india/Satyam-scam-Raju-9-others-get-7-years-jail-for-fudging-accounts/articleshow/46869500.cms [accessed April 19, 2015].

23 "TCS to pay $30 million to settle employee class action suit in US," *Economic Times* (February 27, 2013); available online at: http://articles.economictimes.indiatimes.com/2013-02-27/news/37330809_1_gopi-vedachalam-tcs-stock-tax-refund [accessed April 29, 2015].

24 U.S. Citizenship and Immigration Services, "H-1B Benefit Fraud and Compliance Assessment" (September 2008); available online at: http://www.bradreese.com/h1b-fraud.pdf [accessed March 28, 2015].

25 U.S. Citizenship and Immigration Services, "NUMBER OF H-1B PETITIONS APPROVED BY USCIS IN FY 2009 FOR INITIAL BENEFICIARIES," (undated); available online at: http://www.uscis.gov/USCIS/Resources/Reports%20and%20Studies/H-1B/h-1b-fy09%20counts-employers.csv [accessed March 28, 2015]. See also: 2008 Disclosure Data from the Department of Labor.

26 Moira Herbst and Steve Hamm, "America's high-tech sweatshops," Bloomberg Business (October 1, 2009); available online at: http://www.bloomberg.com/bw/magazine/content/09_41/b4150034732629.htm [accessed March 28, 2015].

27 Moira Herbst, "Visa Fraud Sparks Arrests Nationwide," Bloomberg Business (February 12, 2009); available online at: http://www.businessweek.com/bwdaily/dnflash/content/feb2009/db20090212_920784.htm?chan=top+news_top+news+index+-+temp_news+%2B+analysis [accessed March 28, 2015].

28 Vision Systems Group Inc., Employment Offer & Agreement (undated); available online at: http://files.rsdn.ru/64606/Employee_Offer_Agg.pdf [accessed March 28, 2015].

29 Patrick Thibodeau, "Troubled H-1B fraud case ends quietly," *Computerworld* (May 16, 2011); available online at: http://www.computerworld.com/article/2508042/vertical-it/troubled-h-1b-fraud-case-ends-quietly.html [accessed March 28, 2015].

30 Indu Nandakumar, "Cognizant spent $1.95 million on lobbying last year, heftiest among IT peers," *Economic Times* (April 23, 2013); available online at: http://articles.economictimes.indiatimes.com/2013-04-23/news

/38763120_1_cognizant-indian-it-immigration-laws [accessed March 28, 2015].

31 Shilpa Phadnis, "Infosys wins $100-million contract from Microsoft," *Times of India* (June 3, 2014).

32 See, e.g., Gary Endelman, "The World According to Senator Schumer: If It's Not a Chop Shop, it's a Body Shop," Foster: Fostering Global Immigration Solutions (August 15, 2010); available online at: http://blog.fosterquan .com/2010/08/15/the-world-according-to-senator-schumer-if-its-not-a -chop-shop-its-a-body-shop/ [accessed March 28, 2015].

33 Stephen Stock, Julie Putnam, Scott Pham, and Jeremy Carroll, "Silicon Valley's 'Body Shop' Secret: Highly Educated Foreign Workers Treated Like Indentured Servants," NBC Bay Area (November 4, 2014); available online at: http://www.nbcbayarea.com/investigations/Silicon-Valleys -Body-Shop-Secret-280567322.html [accessed March 28, 2105].

34 Michael Matza, "Chesco case highlights H-1B immigration scams," *Philadelphia Inquirer* (March 18, 2015); available online at: http://www.philly .com/philly/news/20150318_Chesco_case_highlights_H-1B_immigration _scams.html [accessed March 28, 2015].

35 http://www.justice.gov/usao-edpa/pr/chester-county-business-owner -admits-immigration-fraud-scheme.

36 Ibid.

37 www.dice.com, Dice ID 0111612, posted August 12, 2008; no longer available online.

38 Available online at: http://www.path2usa.com/forum/archive/index.php/t -35123.html [accessed March 28, 2015].

39 Available online at: http://www.path2usa.com/forum/showthread.php?461 76-H1B-transfer-denial-need-advice-on-next-action [accessed March 28, 2015].

40 Available online at: http://www.path2usa.com/forum/showthread.php?406 20-When-will-this-economy-improve [accessed March 28, 2015].

41 Patrick Thibodeau, "H-1B fraud may cost you your car and 'gorgeous contemporary,'" *Computerworld* (October 17, 2014); available online at: http:// www.computerworld.com/article/2835288/h-1b-fraud-may-cost-you-your -car-and-gorgeous-contemporary.html [accessed March 28, 2015].

42 United States of America v. Atul Nanda et al. (February 209, 2013); available online at https://dl.dropboxusercontent.com/u/27924754/Dibon1%202 -20-13.pdf [accessed March 28, 2015].

43 Patrick Thibodeau, "H-1B fraud may cost you your car and 'gorgeous contemporary.'"

44 David North, "Indian Body Shop Indicted for Abuse of H-1B Program," Center for Immigration Studies (March 5, 2013); available online at: http://cis.org/north/indian-body-shop-indicted-abuse-h-1b-program [accessed March 28, 2015].

45 Robert E. Kessler, "Six men held in immigration fraud scheme," *New York Newsday* (June 10, 2008).

46 Lalita Aloor Amuthan, "Edison official charged with work visa fraud," Gannett News Service (June 13, 2008); available online at: http://www.mycentraljersey.com/apps/pbcs.dll/article?AID=/20080612/NEWS/806120388/1005/NEWS0101 [accessed March 28, 2015].

47 Brian Amaral, "Running mate of former Edison mayor pleads guilty in visa fraud scheme," NJ.com (September 8, 2014); available online at: http://www.nj.com/middlesex/index.ssf/2014/09/edison_man_who_ran_for_council_on_former_mayors_ticket_admits_visa_fraud_scheme.html [accessed March 28, 2015].

48 Ibid.

49 Ibid.

50 Steve Lyttle, "Pineville company president gets 4-year prison term," *Charlotte Observer* (March 20, 2014).

51 U.S. Immigration and Customs Enforcement, "Indian national pleads guilty in false work visa scheme" (March 22, 2013); available online at: https://www.ice.gov/news/releases/indian-national-pleads-guilty-false-work-visa-scheme [accessed March 28, 2015].

52 Ibid.

53 Online at: http://www.vanjarivishwa.com/succ1.html [unable to access due to a virus alert].

54 LinkedIn profile of Ken Kendre; available online at: https://www.linkedin.com/pub/ken-kendre/26/344/762 [accessed March 28, 2015].

55 U.S. Attorney's Office, Middle District of Pennsylvania, "Owner Of Harrisburg-Based Health Care Services Company Sentenced For Visa Fraud And Money Laundering Scheme" (September 20, 2011); available online at: http://www.justice.gov/usao/pam/news/2011/Kendre_09_20_2011.htm [accessed March 28, 2015].

56 Ibid.

57 LinkedIn profile of Ken Kendre, op. cit.

58 Rent to Own Properties Inc. website; available online at: http://rtolisting.com/ [accessed March 28, 2015].

59 David Ferris and Demian Bulwa, "Berkeley Landlord Faces Sex Charge," *Contra County Times* (January 20, 2000).

60 Matthew Yi, "Search for Better Life Ends in Family Tragedy," *San Francisco Examiner* (November 27, 1999).

61 Seetha's real name was Chanti Jyotsna Devi Prattipati. Lilitha's real name has not been released, as she was a minor. See Judith Scherr, "Landlord may face civil charges in death," *Berkeley Daily Planet* (November 11, 2000).

62 Anita Chabria, "His Own Private Berkeley," *Los Angeles Times* (November 21, 2001), describes the culture clash, "For 13 Years, Lakireddy Bali Reddy's Demented Version of India's Caste System Thrived In One of California's Most Progressive Communities. But Truth Doesn't Always Survive a Collision of Culture and Law."

63 Megan Greenwell and Iliana Montauk, "Young Indian Immigrant Dies in Berkeley Apartment," Berkeley (California) *High School Jacket* (December 10, 1999).

64 http://programmersguild.org/archives/lib/Reddy/sfe20000121reddy-1.htm.

65 Matthew Yi, "Teen girl in landlord case died pregnant," *San Francisco Examiner* (March 4, 2000).

66 Brandon Bailey and Pete Carey, "Audit details abuse of worker visa program," *San Jose Mercury News*, (January 22, 2000).

67 Paul McDougall, "India Lodges Complaint Over H-1B Visa Rejections," *InformationWeek* (March 28, 2012).

68 For a description of how brokers arrange fraudulent jobs and sham marriages for H-1B visas see Tina Parekh, Kiran Matur and Prashant Rupera, "H1B Visa Without a Job? Money Gives It All," *Econonic Times* (India) (August 17, 2003).

69 Jim Herron Zamora, "INS Turns Blind Eye to Visas for High Tech," *San Francisco Examiner* (February 25, 2000).

70 "Landlord Gets Jail Time for Immigration Fraud," *Los Angeles Times* (June 20, 2001).

71 Federal Bureau of Prisons, Inmate Locator.

72 Tom McGhee, "Jury finds Kalu guilty of human trafficking," *Denver Post* (July 1, 2013); available online at: http://www.denverpost.com/ci_23577659 /highlands-ranch-businessman-convicted-human-trafficking-case?source =infinite [accessed April 8, 2015].

73 United States Attorney's Office, District of Colorado, "Highlands Ranch Man Sentenced For Forced Labor And Trafficking In Forced Labor As Well As Other Offenses" (February 11, 2014); available online at: http://www .justice.gov/usao/co/news/2014/feb/2-11b-14.html [accessed April 8, 2015].

74 Joseph Lariosa, "Ghost Denver university hires, defrauds dozens of PHL nurses," *Filipino Star News* (October 26, 2013); available online at: http://

www.filipinostarnews.net/news/ghost-denver-university-hires-defrauds
-dozens-phl-nurses.html [accessed April 8, 2015].

75 Anne Usher, "You're Fired, Go Home," *Washington Post* (May 10, 2001).

76 David Swaim, "An Employers Guide to the Immigration Process" (un-dated); available online at http://www.utdallas.edu/career/docs/employers
/employersintlguide2010.pdf [accessed March 28, 2015].

77 Fox News Latino, "Foreign Teachers In Texas Face Deportation Due To School District's Visa Handling Blunder" (March 27, 2014); available online at: http://latino.foxnews.com/latino/news/2014/03/27/twenty-three-texas
-teachers-face-deportation-because-school-district-blunder/ [accessed March 28, 2015].

78 Jacquielynn Floyd, "Garland ISD's H-1B teacher scandal highlights latest trend in exploiting foreign workers," *Dallas Morning News* (April 10, 2014); available online at: http://www.dallasnews.com/news/columnists/jacquie
lynn-floyd/20140410-teachers-are-new-victims-of-old-scam-swindling
-foreign-born.ece [accessed March 28, 2015].

79 Ray Leszcynski, "Garland ISD says former HR director profited from H-1B visa scheme," *Dallas Morning News* (April 8, 2014); available online at: http://www.dallasnews.com/news/community-news/garland-mesquite
/headlines/20140408-garland-isd-offers-details-about-visa-program-mis
use.ece [accessed March 28, 2015].

80 Jacquielynn Floyd, "Garland ISD's H-1B teacher scandal highlights latest trend in exploiting foreign workers," op. cit.

81 Josh Ault, "Former Garland School Leader Accused of Illegally Recruiting Foreign Teachers," NBC Dallas–Fort Worth (April 8, 2014); available online at: http://www.nbcdfw.com/news/local/Former-Garland-School-Leader
-Accused-of-Illegally-Recruiting-Foreign-Teachers-254392001.html [ac-cessed March 28, 2015].

82 Fox News Latino, "Foreign Teachers In Texas Face Deportation Due To School District's Visa Handling Blunder," op. cit.

83 Ray Leszcynski, "Garland ISD says former HR director profited from H-1B visa scheme," op. cit.

84 Richard Ray, "Federal investigation into visa program at GISD not the first, document shows," fox4news.com (April 1, 2014); available online at: http://
www.fox4news.com/story/25135635/federal-investigation-into-visa-pro
gram-at-gisd-not-the-first-documents-show [accessed March 28, 2015].

85 Ray Leszcynski, "Garland ISD says former HR director profited from H-1B visa scheme," op. cit.

86 Erica L. Green, "City school system to reimburse teachers for visa fees," *Bal-timore Sun* (June 13, 2011); available online at: http://articles.baltimoresun

.com/2011-06-13/news/bs-md-ci-filipino-visa-payments-20110613_1_filipino -teachers-dollars-in-recruitment-fees-h-1b [accessed March 28, 2015].

87   Farah Stockman, "Teacher trafficking," *Boston Globe* (June 12, 2013); available online at: http://www.bostonglobe.com/editorials/2013/06/11 /your-child-teacher-victim-human-trafficking/dQz2fYPwg6Xkgt 1aV6HaiL/story.html [accessed March 28, 2015].

88   Department for Professional Employees, AFL-CIO, "Gaming the System" (2009); available online at: http://dpeaflcio.org/pdf/DPE_Gaming_the _System_Report.pdf [accessed March 28, 2015].

89   Ibid.

90   David North, "H-1B + K-12 =?," Center for Immigration Studies (April 2011); available online at: http://www.cis.org/h-1b-teacher-recruitment [accessed March 28, 2015].

91   Ibid.

CHAPTER 6. "BILOH": THE B VISA BOONDOGGLE

1   Confidential email from source to Michelle Malkin, February 2008.

2   United States Department of State, "Visitor Visa" (undated); available online at: http://travel.state.gov/content/visas/english/visit/visitor.html [accessed April 4, 2015].

3   Ibid.

4   United States Department of State, "Visa Denials" (undated); available online at: http://travel.state.gov/content/visas/english/general/denials.html [accessed April 4, 2015].

5   See, e.g., VisaPro Immigration Attorneys, "How do I avoid a Visa Denial?" (undated); available online at: http://www.visapro.com/Immigration-Articles /?a=204&z=84 http://www.nationofimmigrators.com/h-1b-visas/tips-from -an-immigration-insider-how-to-excel-at-a-us-visa-interview/ [accessed April 4, 2015]. See also: Murthy Law Firm, "Success Story: Visitor's Visa Approved After Repeated Denials" (undated); available online at: http:// www.murthy.com/2011/12/02/success-story-visitors-visa-approved -after-repeated-denials/ [accessed April 4, 2015].

6   Consulate General of the United States, Chennai, India, "B1 in lieu of H" (undated); available online at: http://chennai.usconsulate.gov/types_of _visas/temporary-employment-holp/b1-in-lieu-of-h2.html [accessed April 4, 2015].

7   Ibid.

8   Wikileaks, "Viewing cable 09CHENNAI77, India Semi-Annual Fraud Update," Reference ID 09CHENNAI77 (created March 13, 2009); available

online at: https://wikileaks.org/cable/2009/03/09CHENNAI77.html [accessed April 4, 2015].

9   International Union of Bricklayers v. Meese, 761 F. 2d 798—Court of Appeals, District of Columbia Circuit (decided May 17, 1985); available online at: https://scholar.google.com/scholar_case?case=16111462862035123569&q =bricklayers+v+meese&hl=en&as_sdt=6,31 [accessed April 4, 2015].

10   Ibid.

11   Sharon Machlis and Patrick Thibodeau, "Offshore firms took 50% of H-1B visas in 2013," Computerworld (April 1, 2014); available online at: http://www.computerworld.com/article/2489146/technology-law-regulation-offshore-firms-took-50-of-h-1b-visas-in-2013.html [accessed April 4, 2015].

12   Unless otherwise noted, direct quotations from Palmer come from his testimony to the U.S. Senate Judiciary Committee on March 15, 2015.

13   Jon Brodkin, "Indian IT firm accused of discrimination against "stupid Americans," Ars Technica (August 5, 2013); available online at: http://arstechnica.com/information-technology/2013/08/indian-it-firm-accused-of -discrimination-against-stupid-americans/ [accessed April 4, 2015].

14   Julia Preston and Vikas Bajaj, "Indian Company Under Scrutiny Over U.S. Visas," New York Times (June 12, 2011); available online at: http://www.nytimes.com/2011/06/22/us/22infosys.html?_r=0 [accessed April 4, 2015].

15   Palmer v. Infosys, 2:11-cv-00217-MHT, (M.D. Ala.,) "B-1 Invitation Letter," Plaintiff's Exhibit 44 (filed August 13, 2012); available online at: http://www.searchindia.net/images/sib/B1-visa-dos-and-donts.pdf [accessed April 4, 2015].

16   Uttara Choudhury, "High stakes for Infosys as visa fraud case trial begins next week," Firstbiz (undated); available online at: http://m.firstbiz.firstpost.com/corporate/2g-auction-foreign-investors-can-claim-damages-for -quashed-licences-30313.html?most-popular [accessed April 4, 2015].

17   Don Tennant, "Infosys Briefed B-1 Visa Holders on How to Deceive U.S. Immigration Officials," IT BusinessEdge (May 2, 2012); available online at: http://www.itbusinessedge.com/cm/blogs/tennant/infosys-briefed-b-1 -visa-holders-on-how-to-deceive-us-immigration-officials/?cs=50342 [accessed April 4, 2015].

18   Don Tennant, "Second Infosys Whistleblower Documented 'Illegal' Activity, Pleaded for Action," IT BusinessEdge (August 3, 2011); available online at: http://www.itbusinessedge.com/cm/blogs/tennant/second-infosys-whistleblower-documented-illegal-activity-pleaded-for-action/?cs=48119 [accessed April 4, 2015].

19   Don Tennant, "Prospective Witness in Infosys Case Alleges Discrimination, Visa Fraud," IT BusinessEdge (July 29, 2012); available online at: http://

www.itbusinessedge.com/cm/blogs/tennant/prospective-witness-in-infosys -case-alleges-discrimination-visa-fraud/?cs=50875.

20 Palmer v. Infosys, 2:11cv217-MHT (M.D. Ala. August 20, 2012); available online at: https://casetext.com/case/palmer-v-infosys-techs-ltd [accessed April 4, 2015].

21 Julia Preston, "Judge Dismisses Whistle-Blower Suit Against Infosys," *New York Times* (August 20, 2012); available online at: http://www.nytimes .com/2012/08/21/us/alabama-judge-dismisses-infosys-whistle-blower-suit .html [accessed April 4, 2015].

22 Infosys, "Judge Throws Out Palmer Case Against Infosys," press release (August 20, 2012); available online at: http://www.infosys.com/newsroom /press-releases/Documents/2012/judge-throws-out-palmer-case-against -infosys.pdf [accessed April 4, 2015].

23 United States Department of Justice, the United States Attorney's Office, Eastern District of Texas, "Indian Corporation Pays Record Amount To Settle Allegations Of Systemic Visa Fraud And Abuse Of Immigration Processes," press release (October 30, 2013); available online at: http://www .justice.gov/usao-edtx/pr/indian-corporation-pays-record-amount -settle-allegations-systemic-visa-fraud-and-abuse [accessed April 4, 2015].

24 Settlement Agreement for Case 4:13-cv-00634 (filed October 30, 2013); available online at: http://www.ice.gov/doclib/news/releases/2013/131030plano .pdf [accessed April 4, 2015].

25 United States Department of Justice, the United States Attorney's Office, Eastern District of Texas, "Indian Corporation Pays Record Amount To Settle Allegations Of Systemic Visa Fraud And Abuse Of Immigration Processes," op. cit.

26 Settlement Agreement for Case 4:13-cv-00634, op. cit.

27 Ibid.

28 Julia Preston, "Deal Reached in Inquiry Into Visa Fraud at Tech Giant," *New York Times* (October 29, 2013); available online at: http://www .nytimes.com/2013/10/30/us/indian-tech-giant-infosys-said-to-reach -settlement-on-us-visa-fraud-claims.html?_r=0 [accessed April 4, 2015].

29 Covington, "FORMER SECRETARY CHERTOFF JOINS COVINGTON," press release (March 26, 2009); available online at: http://www.cov .com/news/detail.aspx?news=1406 [accessed April 4, 2015].

30 Uttara Choudhury, "Palmer's lawsuit against Infosys gets teeth as allegations snowball," *Firstpost* (September 9, 2011); available online at: http://www .firstpost.com/business/palmers-lawsuit-against-infosys-gets-teeth-as -allegations-snowball-79660.html [accessed April 4, 2015].

31 Don Tennant, "Former DHS Secretary Chertoff Lobbied for Infosys in Visa Fraud Settlement Negotiations," Don Tennant tumblr account (November 3, 2013); available online at: http://dontennant.tumblr.com/post/66004936243 /former-dhs-secretary-chertoff-lobbied-for-infosys [accessed April 4, 2015].

32 Don Tennant, "Infosys Gets Employee Pushback as Damage Control Effort Begins," Don Tennant tumblr account (November 4, 2013); available online at: http://dontennant.tumblr.com/post/66014383396/infosys-gets-employee -pushback-as-damage-control [accessed April 4, 2015].

33 Joshua Alston, "Infosys Accused Of Retaliation In Wake Of FCA Suit," Law360.com, October 3, 2014; available online at: http://www.law360.com /articles/583859/infosys-accused-of-retaliation-in-wake-of-fca-suit [accessed August 7, 2015].

34 Patrick Thibodeau, "H-1B whistleblower files new federal lawsuit," *Computerworld* (October 2, 2014); available online at:, http://www.computer world.com/article/2691106/h-1b-whistleblower-files-new-federal-lawsuit .html [accessed August 7, 2015].

35 Letter from Joseph E. Macmanus (acting assistant secretary of legislative affairs at the U.S. Department of State) to Sen. Charles Grassley (May 13, 2011); available online at: http://www.grassley.senate.gov/sites/default/files /judiciary/upload/Immigration-05-24-11-response-from-State-using-B-1 -to-circumvent-H-1B-doc.pdf [accessed April 4, 2015].

36 LexisNexis® Legal Newsroom Immigration Law, "DOS Cable on B-1 in Lieu of H" (October 5, 2012); available online at: http://www.lexisnexis .com/legalnewsroom/immigration/b/insidenews/archive/2012/10/22/dos -cable-on-b-1-in-lieu-of-h-oct-5-2012.aspx [accessed April 4, 2015].

37 Dominic Gates, "Russian engineers, once turned back, now flowing to Boeing again," *Seattle Times* (April 15, 2012); available online at http:// www.seattletimes.com/business/russian-engineers-once-turned-back-now -flowing-to-boeing-again/ [accessed April 23, 2015].

38 Ibid.

39 Ibid.

40 "Grassley Concerned that Fraudulent Practices May be Used to Circumvent Protections of H-1B Visa," press release (May 1, 2012); available online at: http://www.grassley.senate.gov/news/news-releases/grassley-concerned -fraudulent-practices-may-be-used-circumvent-protections-h-1b [accessed April 24, 2015].

41 Dhanya Ann Thoppil, "Infosys Whistleblower files another lawsuit," *Wall Street Journal* (October 3, 2014); available online at: http://www.wsj.com /articles/infosys-whistleblower-files-another-lawsuit-1412324348 [accessed April 4, 2015].

42 Brenda Koehler vs. Infosys Technologies Limited Incorporated D/B/A Infosys Limited, filed in United States District Court Eastern District of Wisconsin (Case 2:13-cv-00885 filed August 1, 2013); available online at: http://www.scribd.com/doc/157691931/Complaint-Proposed-Class-Action-Infosys#scribd [accessed April 4, 2015].

CHAPTER 7. EB-5: AMERICA'S DISASTROUS CASH-FOR-CITIZENSHIP RACKET

1 Cassius Dio, *Roman History*, published in Volume VII of the Loeb Classical Library edition (1924); available online at: http://penelope.uchicago.edu/Thayer/E/Roman/Texts/Cassius_Dio/60*.html [accessed April 6, 2015].

2 Frederic Huidekoper, *Works of Frederic Huidekoper* (Judaism at Rome, New York: David G. Francis, 1887), footnote 172, p. 240.

3 Stephen Dando-Collins, *Blood of the Caesars: How the Murder of Germanicus Led to the Fall of Rome* (Hobken, N.J.: John Wiley & Sons Inc., 2008). See also: Cassius Dio, *Roman History*, op. cit.

4 Immigration Act of 1990, Pub. L. No. 101-649, § 121, 104 Stat. 4978.

5 "Visas for Dollars: Give me your Gucci-clad masses," *Economist* (December 3, 2011); available online at: http://www.economist.com/node/21541054 [accessed April 6, 2015].

6 Ibid.

7 Making appropriations for the Departments of Commerce, Justice, and State, the Judiciary, and related agencies for the fiscal year ending September 30, 1993, and for other purposes, Pub. L. No. 102-395, § 610, 106 Stat. 1828.

8 U.S. Citizenship and Immigration Services, "Immigrant Investor Regional Centers" (last reviewed/updated April 6, 2015); available online at: http://www.uscis.gov/working-united-states/permanent-workers/employment-based-immigration-fifth-preference-eb-5/immigrant-investor-regional-centers [accessed April 6, 2015].

9 U.S. Citizenship and Immigration Services, "EB-5 Immigrant Investor" (last updated March 31, 2015); available online at: http://www.uscis.gov/eb-5 [accessed April 8, 2015].

10 Ibid.

11 Al Kamen, "An Investment in American Citizenship; Immigration Program Invites Millionaires to Buy Their Way In," *Washington Post* (September 29, 1991).

12 President's Council on Jobs and Competitiveness, "Taking Action, Building Confidence" (October 2011), p. 35; available online at: http://iiusa.org/blog/wp-content/uploads/2011/10/JobsCouncil_InterimReport_Oct11.pdf [accessed April 6, 2015].

13 Michelle Malkin, *Invasion*, op. cit.

14 Charles Lane, "EB-5 visa immigration program is flawed," *Washington Post* (April 15, 2013); available online at: http://www.washingtonpost.com /opinions/charles-lane-eb-5-visa-immigration-program-is-flawed/2013 /04/15/d826758c-a606-11e2-a8e2-5b98cb59187f_story.html [accessed April 6, 2015].

15 David North, "Re-Authorizing the EB-5 Regional Center Program, Center for Immigration Studies," Center for Immigration Studies (December 2011); available online at: http://cis.org/node/3374 [accessed April 6, 2015].

16 Angelo Paparelli, "Senator's saucy request roils EB-5 centers" Nation of Immigrators (March 2, 2014); available online at http://www.nationof immigrators.com/gop-on-immigration/senators-saucy-request-roils-eb-5 -regional-centers-1/ [accessed April 7, 2015].

17 Sen. Tom Coburn, "A Review of the Department of Homeland Security's Missions and Performance" (January 2015), 113th Congress, pp. 76–77; available online at http://www.hsgac.senate.gov/media/minority-media /final-coburn-oversight-report-finds-major-problems-in-dhs [accessed April 7, 2015].

18 Laura Foote Reiff, "EB-5 Coalition Sends Final Letter Supporting H.R. 616, American Entrepreneurship and Investment Act," EB5 Insights (March 19, 2015); available online at http://www.eb5insights.com/2015/03/19/eb-5 -coalition-sends-final-letter-supporting-h-r-616-american-entrepreneur ship-and-investment-act/ [accessed April 29, 2015].

19 U.S. Government Accountability Office, "Immigrant Investor Program: Additional actions needed to better assess fraud risks and report economic benefits," GAO-15-696, August 12, 2015; available online at: http://www .gao.gov/products/GAO-15-696 [accessed August 13, 2015].

20 Bill Straub, "Woman in fund scandal aided McConnell campaign," *Cincinnati Post* (March 14, 1998). See also: "Campaign Finance Key Player: Maria Hsia," *Washington Post* (last updated March 4, 1998); available online at: http://www.washingtonpost.com/wp-srv/politics/special/campfin/players /hsia.htm [accessed April 7, 2015].

21 Pete Yost, "Dems Fund-Raiser Hsia Found Guilty," *Washington Post* (March 2, 2000); available online at: http://www.washingtonpost.com/wp -srv/aponline/20000302/aponline121006_000.htm [accessed April 6, 2015].

22 Robert L. Jackson, "Clinton Donor Riady Pleads Guilty to Conspiracy Charge," *Los Angeles Times* (January 12, 2001); available online at: http:// articles.latimes.com/2001/jan/12/news/mn-11506 [accessed April 6, 2015]. See also: Edward Walsh and Roberto Suro, "Clinton Fund-Raiser Huang to Offer Guilty Plea," *Washington Post* (May 26, 1999); available online at:

http://www.washingtonpost.com/wp-srv/politics/special/campfin/stories/huang052699.htm [accessed April 6, 2015].

23 Kenneth R. Timmerman, "INS Abuse" *American Spectator* (July–August 2000).

24 Walter F. Roche and Gary Cohn, "INS insiders profit on immigrant dreams," *Baltimore Sun* (February 20, 2000); available online at: http://www.baltimoresun.com/bal-visavendors022000-htmlstory.html [accessed April 6, 2015].

25 Ibid.

26 Ibid.

27 Michelle Malkin, *Invasion*, op. cit.

28 Walter F. Roche and Gary Cohn, "INS insiders profit on immigrant dreams," op. cit.

29 Ibid.

30 Dan Richman, "Foreign investments in Sodo raise questions," *Seattle Post-Intelligencer* (July 31, 2007); available online at: http://www.seattlepi.com/local/article/Foreign-investments-in-Sodo-raise-questions-1245260.php [accessed April 6, 2015].

31 P. J. Huffstutter, "In U.S. visa program, money talks," *Los Angeles Times* (September 3, 2011); available online at: http://articles.latimes.com/2011/sep/03/business/la-fi-easy-visa-20110904 [accessed April 6, 2015].

32 Department of Homeland Security Office of the Inspector General, "United States Citizenship and Immigration Services' Employment-Based Fifth Preference (EB5) Regional Center Program," OIG-14-19 (December 2013); available online at: http://www.oig.dhs.gov/assets/Mgmt/2014/OIG_14-19_Dec13.pdf [accessed April 6, 2015].

33 Ibid.

34 Ibid., p. 8.

35 Ibid., pp. 8–9.

36 Peter Elkind and Marty Jones, "The dark, disturbing world of the visa-for-sale program," *Fortune* (July 24, 2014); available online at: http://fortune.com/2014/07/24/immigration-eb-5-visa-for-sale/ [accessed April 6, 2015].

37 Audrey Singer and Camille Galdes, "Improving the EB-5 Investor Visa Program: International Financing for U.S. Regional Economic Development," Brookings-Rockefeller Project on State and Metropolitan Innovation (February 2014); available online at: http://www.brookings.edu/~/media/research/files/reports/2014/02/05-eb5/eb5_report.pdf [accessed April 6, 2015].

38 Peter Elkind, "Promoter of failed EB-5 project is indicted," *Fortune* (August 27, 2014); available online at: http://fortune.com/2014/08/27/eb-5 -promoter-indicted/ [accessed April 6, 2015].

39 U.S. Securities and Exchange Commission, "Investor Alert: Investment Scams Exploit Immigrant Investor Program" (undated); available online at: http://www.sec.gov/investor/alerts/ia_immigrant.htm [accessed April 6, 2015].

40 U.S. Securities and Exchange Commission, "SEC Charges L.A.-Based Immigration Attorneys With Defrauding Investors Seeking U.S. Residency" (September 3, 2014); available online at: http://www.sec.gov/News/Press Release/Detail/PressRelease/1370542843452#.VRROozvF_pC [accessed April 6, 2015].

41 "Newcastle woman charged with immigrant-investor fraud," *Newcastle News* (March 18, 2015); available online at: http://www.newcastle-news .com/2015/03/18/newcastle-woman-charged-with-immigrant-investor -fraud [accessed April 6, 2015].

42 "Canada kills investor visa popular with Chinese," CNN Money (February 12, 2014,); available online at: http://money.cnn.com/2014/02/12/news /canada-chinese-immigration/ [accessed April 6, 2015].

43 Andrew Mitrovica, "Immigrant investor plan denounced as 'massive sham,'" *Globe and Mail* (September 15, 1999).

44 Michelle Malkin, "When will America end cash-for-visas racket?" michelle malkin.com (February 18, 2014); available online at: http://michellemalkin .com/2014/02/28/when-will-america-end-cash-for-visas-racket/ [accessed April 6, 2015].

45 Sheldon Adelson, Warren Buffett, and Bill Gates, "Break the Immigration Impasse," op. cit.

46 Bernd Debusmann, "To create U.S. jobs, bring in immigrants," Reuters (September 13, 2011); available online at: http://blogs.reuters.com/bernd debusmann/2011/09/13/to-create-u-s-jobs-bring-in-immigrants/ [accessed April 6, 2015].

47 Matthew Mosk and Brian Ross, "FBI investigating former White House military aide," ABC News (April 13, 2015); available online at: http:// abcnews.go.com/US/fbi-investigating-white-house-military-aide/story ?id=30176394 [accessed April 13, 2015].

48 Walter F. Roche, Jr., and Gary Cohn, "INS insiders profit on immigrant dreams," op. cit.

49 Seung Min Kim, "Alejandro Mayorkas confirmed for DHS," *Politico* (December 20, 2013); available online at: http://www.politico.com/story

/2013/12/alejandro-mayorkas-department-of-homeland-security-101382 .html [accessed April 6, 2015].

50 Opening statement of Sen. Tom Coburn, Ranking Member, U.S. Senate Homeland Security and Governmental Affairs Committee (December 11, 2013); available online at: http://www.hsgac.senate.gov/download /?id=d0171306-4019-42ac-82a2-616acec43d08 [accessed April 6, 2015].

51 Seung Min Kim, "Alejandro Mayorkas confirmed for DHS," op. cit.

52 "On the Cloture Motion PN640: Alejandro Nicholas Mayorkas, of the District of Columbia, to be Deputy Secretary of Homeland Security," Senate Vote #285, 113th Congress (December 19, 2013); available online at: https://www.govtrack.us/congress/votes/113-2013/s285 [accessed April 6, 2015].

53 John Solomon and David Sherfinski, "VEGAS RULES: Harry Reid pushed feds to change ruling for casino's big-money foreigners," *Washington Times* (December 10, 2013); available online at: http://www.washingtontimes.com /news/2013/dec/10/harry-reids-visa-pressure-cooker/?utm_source=RSS _Feed&utm_medium=RSS [accessed April 6, 2015].

54 Jon Ralston, "Strip casino that Harry Reid helped with federal bureaucracy is represented by his son," RALSTON Reports (December 12, 2013); available online at: https://www.ralstonreports.com/blog/strip-casino-harry -reid-helped-federal-bureaucracy-represented-his-son#.UqneMPRDvSh [accessed April 6, 2015].

55 John Solomon and David Sherfinski, "VEGAS RULES: Harry Reid pushed feds to change ruling for casino's big-money foreigners," op. cit.

56 Josh Hicks, "Senators growing impatient with inspector general under investigation," *Washington Post* (November 1, 2013); available online at: http:// www.washingtonpost.com/blogs/federal-eye/wp/2013/11/01/senators -growing-impatient-with-inspector-general-under-investigation/ [accessed April 6, 2015].

57 Deborah Charles, "Obama's pick for No. 2 at Homeland Security says he did nothing wrong," Reuters (July 25, 2013); available online at: http:// articles.chicagotribune.com/2013-07-25/news/sns-rt-usa-securitymayorkas -20130723_1_senate-homeland-security-investigation-hearing [accessed April 6, 2015].

58 Letter from Sen. Charles Grassley to Alejandro Mayorkas (July 31, 2013); availableonlineat:http://www.grassley.senate.gov/sites/default/files/judiciary /upload/EB-5-07-31-13-Grassley-letter-to-Mayorkas-preferential-treatment .pdf [accessed April 6, 2015].

59 Peter Baker and Susan Schmidt, "President Had Big Role in Setting Donor Perks," *Washington Post* (February 27, 1997); available online at: http://

www.washingtonpost.com/wp-srv/politics/special/campfin/stories/lincoln
.htm [accessed April 6, 2015].

60 Tom Hamburger and Peter Wallsten, "GreenTech formula has made big
profits for McAuliffe," *Washington Post* (September 21, 2013); available
online at: http://www.washingtonpost.com/politics/greentech-formula-has
-made-big-profits-for-mcauliffe/2013/09/21/3c6e332c-2136-11e3-b73c
-aab60bf735d0_story.html [accessed April 6, 2015].

61 GreenTech Automotive website (undated); available at: http://gtaev.com/us
/about/our-vehicles#history [accessed April 6, 2015].

62 "About WM Industries Corp." (undated); available online at: http://wm
industriescorp.com/us/about/about-wm-industries-corp [accessed April 6,
2015].

63 Bertel Schmitt, "Clinton's Sleepover Fundraising Maven Breaks Ground
For 300,000 Car Factory In Inner Mongolia While Chinese Head To
The U.S. On $500,000 Green Cards," thetruthaboutcars.com (August 8,
2011); available online at: http://www.thetruthaboutcars.com/2011/08
/clinton%E2%80%99s-sleepover-fundraising-maven-breaks-ground-for
-300000-car-factory-in-inner-mongolia-while-chinese-head-to-the-u-s
-on-500000-green-cards/ [accessed April 6, 2015].

64 Eric Smith, "Investor Announces $1B Auto Plant for Tunica," *Memphis
Daily News* (October 7, 2009); available online at: http://www.memphisdaily
news.com/editorial/Article.aspx?id=45228 [accessed April 6, 2015].

65 Alexander Burns, "Bobby Jindal, Haley Barbour boosted visa firm," *Politico* (October 17, 2012); available online at: http://www.politico.com
/story/2013/10/bobby-jindal-haley-barbour-boosted-visa-firm-98491.html
[accessed April 6, 2015].

66 Frederick Kunkle and Tom Hamburger, "McAuliffe's business partners receive scrutiny through federal inquiry into GreenTech," *Washington Post*
(August 24, 2013); available online at: http://www.washingtonpost.com
/local/virginia-politics/mcauliffes-business-partners-receive-scrutiny
-through-federal-inquiry-into-greentech/2013/08/24/885f3624-fa25-11e2-8
752-b41d7ed1f685_story.html [accessed April 6, 2015].

67 Ibid.

68 Sushannah Walshie and Chris Good, "In McAuliffe's Former Car Company, Echoes of Romney and Bain," ABC News (August 9, 2013); available
online at: http://abcnews.go.com/Politics/mcauliffes-car-company-echoes
-romney-bain/story?id=19905426&singlePage=true [accessed April 6, 2015].

69 Eric Smith, "Tunica's New Cash Crop?" *Memphis Daily News* (December 7,
2009); available online at: http://www.memphisdailynews.com/editorial
/Article.aspx?id=46501 [accessed April 6, 2015].

70   Huw Evans, "GreenTech Automotive: Too Good To Be True?" hybridcars
     .com (July 9, 2012); available online at: http://www.hybridcars.com/green
     tech-automotive-too-good-be-true-48087/ [accessed April 6, 2015].
71   Eric Smith, "Tunica's New Cash Crop?" op. cit.
72   Laura Vozzella and Frederick Kunkle, "Democrat Terry McAuliffe's role
     in GreenTech scrutinized," *Washington Post* (April 10, 2013); available
     online at: http://www.washingtonpost.com/local/va-politics/democrat-terry
     -mcauliffes-role-in-greentech-scrutinized/2013/04/10/a71f056a-a216-11e2
     -be47-b44febad38_print.html [accessed April 6, 2015].
73   Memo from Jeffrey M. Anderson to The Honorable Patrick O. Gottschalk
     (November 19, 2009); available online at: https://www.documentcloud
     .org/documents/561607-gta-nov-2009.html#document/p8/a87238 [accessed
     April 6, 2015].
74   Kenric Ward, "SEC raids Illinois-based cash-for-visa program," Virginia
     Watchdog.org (April 3, 2013); available online at: http://watchdog.org/77761
     /sec-raids-illinois-based-cash-for-visa-program/ [accessed April 6, 2015].
75   "Michael K Evans," EB5 investors website (undated); available online at:
     http://www.eb5investors.com/directories/economists/michael-k-evans [ac-
     cessed April 6, 2015].
76   Tori Richards, Earl Glynn, and Kenric Ward, "GreenTech courted Obama's
     Solyndra aide," Watchdog.org (August 6, 2013); available online at: http://
     watchdog.org/99627/greentech-courted-obamas-solyndra-aide/ [accessed
     April 6, 2015].
77   Frederick Kunkle, "McAuliffe quietly resigned from electric car firm he
     founded," *Washington Post* (April 5, 2013); available online at: http://www
     .washingtonpost.com/local/va-politics/mcauliffe-quietly-resigned-from
     -electric-car-firm-he-founded/2013/04/05/9a5b2b8e-9e32-11e2-a941-a19b
     ce7af755_story.html [accessed April 6, 2015]. See also: Alexander Burns,
     "Terry McAuliffe left car firm in December," *Politico* (April 5, 2013); avail-
     able online at: http://www.politico.com/story/2013/04/terry-mcauliffe
     -left-controversial-car-firm-in-december-89684.html [accessed April 6, 2015].
78   Cause of Action, "REPORT: GreenTech Automotive: A Venture Capital-
     ized by Cronyism" (September 23, 2013); available online at: http://causeof
     action.org/greentech-automotive-a-venture-capitalized-by-cronyism-2/
     [accessed April 6, 2015].
79   Ibid.
80   Ibid., p. 13.
81   Ibid., p. 5.
82   Memo and attached report from Department of Homeland Security In-
     spector General John Roth to Jeh C. Johnson (stamped March 24, 2015);

available online at: http://www.oig.dhs.gov/assets/Mga/OIG_mga-032415 .pdf [accessed April 6, 2015].

83 Ibid.

84 Ibid., p. 43.

85 Ibid., p. 89.

86 Ibid., pp. 42–43.

87 Ibid., p. 49.

88 Letter from Sen. Charles Grassley to Alejandro Mayorkas (August 9, 2013); available online at: http://www.grassley.senate.gov/sites/default/files /judiciary/upload/EB-5-08-09-13-Mayorkas-letter-no-response-to-first -letters-Mayorkas-AAO-rewrite-email.pdf [accessed April 6, 2015].

89 Josh Meyer, "Alejandro Mayorkas tapped to head immigration agency," *Los Angeles Times* (May 1, 2009); available online at: http://articles.latimes .com/2009/may/01/nation/na-mayorkas1 [accessed April 6, 2015].

90 Sonya Ross, "Clinton pardons more than 100," *Washington Post* (January 20, 2001); available online at: http://www.washingtonpost.com/wp-srv /aponline/20010120/aponline104904_000.htm [accessed August 5, 2015].

91 H.R. Rep. 107-454 (May 14, 2002); available online at: http://www.gpo.gov /fdsys/pkg/CRPT-107hrpt454/html/CRPT-107hrpt454-vol2.htm [accessed April 6, 2015].

92 Memo and attached report from Department of Homeland Security Inspector General John Roth to Jeh C. Johnson (stamped March 24, 2015), op. cit., p. 49.

93 U.S. Department of Homeland Security, "Statement by Secretary Jeh C. Johnson about the DHS Inspector General's Report Concerning Deputy Secretary Mayorkas" (March 24, 2015); available online at: http://www.dhs .gov/news/2015/03/24/statement-secretary-jeh-c-johnson-about-dhs -inspector-generals-report-concerning-0 [accessed April 6, 2015].

94 Ibid.

95 Michael Sheffield, "Tunica company plans street-legal electric car for 2016," *Memphis Business Journal* (October 23, 2014); available online at: http://www.bizjournals.com/memphis/news/2014/10/23/tunica-green tech-plans-street-legal-electric-car.html [accessed April 6, 2015].

96 Chambers Associate, "5 minutes with A.B. Culvahouse" (undated); available online at: http://web.archive.org/web/20140822025812/http://www .chambers-associate.com/Articles/MinutesWith/1300 [accessed April 7, 2015].

97 Tom Hamburger and Rachel Weiner, "Report: Va. governor received special treatment from Homeland Security," *Washington Post* (March 24, 2015); available online at: http://www.washingtonpost.com/politics/report-mcauliffe

-asked-for-and-got-favors-at-homeland-security/2015/03/24/00f62514
-d24e-11e4-a62f-ee745911a4ff_story.html [accessed April 6, 2015].

98 Dave Boyer, "White House calls embattled Mayorkas 'effective leader,'"
Washington Times (March 25, 2015); available online at: http://www.wash
ingtontimes.com/news/2015/mar/25/white-house-calls-embattled-mayorkas
-effective-lea/ [accessed April 6, 2015].

99 Jennifer Oldham and Shai Oster, "Solar Jobs Join Harry Reid to Chinese
Billionaire in Price Drop," Bloomberg Business (April 3, 2012); available
online at: http://www.bloomberg.com/news/articles/2012-04-03/solar-jobs
-join-harry-reid-to-chinese-billionaire-in-price-drop [accessed April 6,
2015].

100 Chuck Neubauer and Richard T. Cooper, "In Nevada, the Name to Know is
Reid," *Los Angeles Times* (June 23, 2003); available online at: http://articles
.latimes.com/print/2003/jun/23/nation/na-sons23 [accessed August 7,
2015].

101 Ibid.

102 Memo and attached report from Department of Homeland Security Inspector General John Roth to Jeh C. Johnson (stamped March 24, 2015), op. cit.,
p. 33.

103 John Solomon and David Sherfinski, "VEGAS RULES: Harry Reid pushed
feds to change ruling for casino's big-money foreigners," op. cit.

104 Ibid.

105 Memo and attached report from Department of Homeland Security Inspector General John Roth to Jeh C. Johnson (stamped March 24, 2015), op. cit.,
p. 32.

106 Ibid., p. 33.

107 Executive Order 13577, June 15, 2011.

108 Sen. Charles E. Grassley, Letter to Colleagues (July 24, 2013); available
online at: http://www.grassley.senate.gov/sites/default/files/issues/upload
/Immigration-07-24-13-letter-to-HSGAC-Intelligence-EB-5-for-release
.pdf [accessed April 6, 2015].

109 Memo and attached report from Department of Homeland Security Inspector General John Roth to Jeh C. Johnson (stamped March 24, 2015), op. cit.,
p. 33.

110 Sen. Charles E. Grassley, Letter to Colleagues, op. cit.

111 Ibid.

112 Ibid., p. 37.

113 Letter from Daniel Epstein, Executive Director of Cause of Action to Sens.
Barbara Boxer and Johnny Isakson (October 23, 2014); available online

at: http://causeofaction.org/assets/uploads/2014/10/2014-10-23-Signed
-Senate-Ethics-Letter-2.pdf [accessed April 6, 2015].

114 Ibid.

115 Ibid.

116 "Cause of Action calls for full investigation into questionable EB-5 visa
program," press release (March 26, 2015); available online at: http://causeof
action.org/cause-of-action-calls-for-full-investigation-into-questionable
-eb-5-visa-program/ [accessed April 14, 2014].

117 T. J. Quinn, et al., "THE SCORE HEARS . . . Ratner's latest shell game,"
New York Daily News (October 9, 2005).

118 Deborah Kolben, " Union workers and ACORN rally for 'jobs, housing,
hoops,'" *Brooklyn Paper* (June 19, 2004); available online at: http://www
.brooklynpaper.com/stories/27/24/27_24nets2.html [accessed April 6, 2015].

119 Norman Oder, "The $6 billion lie: Why Ratner's fiscal claim is Swiss cheese,"
Atlantic Yards/Pacfic Park Report (March 28, 2006); available online at:
http://atlanticyardsreport.blogspot.com/2006/03/6-billion-lie-why-ratners
-fiscal-claim.html [accessed April 6, 2015].

120 Nicholas Confessore, "Routine Changes, or 'Bait and Switch'?" *New
York Times* (November 6, 2005); available online at: http://www.nytimes
.com/2005/11/06/nyregion/06yards.html?pagewanted=all [accessed April 6,
2015].

121 Richard Sandomir and Charles V. Bagli, "Brooklyn Developer Reaches Deal
to Buy New Jersey Nets," *New York Times* (January 21, 2004); available
online at: http://www.nytimes.com/2004/01/21/sports/basketball/21CND
-NETS.html [accessed April 6, 2015].

122 George F. Will, "Avaricious developers and governments twist the meaning of 'blight,'" *Washington Post* (January 3, 2010); available online at:
http://www.washingtonpost.com/wp-dyn/content/article/2010/01/01
/AR2010010101367.html [accessed April 6, 2015].

123 Malcom Gladwell, "The Nets and NBA Economics," Grantland (October 10, 2011); available online at: http://grantland.com/features/the-nets-nba
-economics/ [accessed April 6, 2015].

124 Rich Calder, "Group can $core on Atl. Yards," *New York Post* (Septem-
ber 21, 2009); available online at: http://nypost.com/2009/09/21/group-can
-core-on-atl-yards/ [accessed April 7, 2015].

125 Charles V. Bagli, "$500 million in Bonds Sold in 2 Hours for Nets' Arena,"
New York Times (December 15, 2009); available online at: http://www
.nytimes.com/2009/12/16/sports/basketball/16nets.html [accessed April 7,
2015].

126 Malcolm Gladwell, "The Nets and NBA Economics," op. cit.

127 Eliot Brown, "Ratner Mulls Visa Financing," *Wall Street Journal* (September 21, 2010); available online at: http://www.wsj.com/articles/SB100014240 5274870398930457550411398136810 [accessed April 6, 2015].

128 "Anatomy of an EB-5 investment" (undated); available online at: http://www.icic.org/ee_uploads/images/ICIC_EB5_infographic.pdf [accessed April 6, 2015].

129 Daniel M. Kowalski, "EB-5 'investor visa' program a boon for development funding," LexisNexis Legal Newsroom Immigration Law (January 8, 2012); available online at: http://www.lexisnexis.com/legalnewsroom /immigration/b/outsidenews/archive/2012/01/08/eb-5-investor-visa -program-a-boon-for-development-funding.aspx [accessed April 7, 2015].

130 Eliot Brown, "Ratner Mulls Visa Financing," op. cit.

131 Norman Oder, "Green Cards for Sale? Atlantic Yards Backers Seek Chinese Investors," *Huffington Post* (October 11, 2010); available online at: http://www.huffingtonpost.com/norman-oder/does-the-us-allow-the-sal _b_758331.html?utm_source=observer.com&utm_medium=referral&utm _campaign=pubexchange_article [accessed April 7, 2015].

132 Ibid.

133 Norman Oder, "The missing billionaire: Why nobody pitching EB-5 investments to Chinese millionaires wants to talk about Mikhail Prokhorov," Atlantic Yards/Pacific Park Report (December 13, 2010); available online at: http://atlanticyardsreport.blogspot.com/2010/12/missing-billionaire-why -nobody-pitching.html [accessed April 7, 2015].

134 Norman Oder, "Forest City Ratner to sell 70% stake in Atlantic Yards to Chinese government-owned developer; largest such deal with Chinese backing," Atlantic Yards/Pacific Park Report (October 11, 2013); available online at: http://atlanticyardsreport.blogspot.com/2013/10/forest-city -ratner-sells-70-stake-in.html [accessed April 7, 2015].

135 Norman Oder, "Exclusive: Forest City seeking $249M in cheap financing from immigrant investors (again); Chinese government would profit by selling U.S. green cards to Chinese!" Atlantic Yards/Pacific Park Report (January 30, 2014); available online at: http://atlanticyardsreport.blogspot .com/2014/01/exclusive-forest-city-seeking-249m-in.html [accessed April 7, 2015].

136 Norman Oder, "U.S. State Department protests use of official in marketing 'Atlantic Yards III' EB-5 investment to Chinese, gets mention cut from promotion," Atlantic Yards/Pacific Park Report (October 22, 2014); available online at: http://atlanticyardsreport.blogspot.com/2014/10/us-state-depart ment-protests-use-of.html [accessed April 7, 2015].

137 Ibid.

138 David North, "The EB-5 Program—A Nightmare for Publicists," Center for Immigration Studies (October 23, 2014); available online at: cis.org/north /eb-5-program-nightmare-for-publicists [accessed April 7, 2015].

139 Cause of Action, "Political Profiteering: How Forest City Enterprises Makes Private Profits at the Expense of America's Taxpayers" (August 2, 2013), p. 1; available online at: http://causeofaction.org/assets/uploads/2013/12/131204 -FINAL-Forest-City-Report-III.pdf [accessed April 7, 2015].

140 Ibid., pp. 1–2.

141 Ibid., pp. 2–5.

142 "Million-Dollar Visas," *New York Times* (December 26, 2011); available online at: http://www.nytimes.com/2011/12/27/opinion/million-dollar -investor-visas.html?_r=1 [accessed April 7, 2015].

143 Ibid.

144 Statement of Senator Charles E. Schumer for hearing "Reauthorizing the EB-5 Regional Center Program: Promoting Job Creation and Economic Development in American Communities" (December 7, 2011); available online at: http://www.judiciary.senate.gov/imo/media/doc/11-12-7Schumer Statement.pdf [accessed April 7, 2015].

145 Ibid.

146 Matt A. V. Chaban, "In Arena's Shadow, Holdouts at Atlantic Yards Site Must Now Leave," *New York Times* (February 16, 2015); available online at: http://www.nytimes.com/2015/02/17/nyregion/in-arenas-shadow-hold outs-at-atlantic-yards-site-must-now-leave.html?_r=0 [accessed April 7, 2015].

147 "The Man Behind CanAm," EB5 Investors (February 26, 2014); available online at: http://www.eb5investors.com/magazine/article/man-behind -canam [accessed April 7, 2015].

148 Memo and attached report from Department of Homeland Security Inspec- tor General John Roth to Jeh C. Johnson (stamped March 24, 2015), op. cit., p. 19.

149 Ibid., p. 20.

150 Ibid., p. 25.

151 Ibid., pp. 30–31.

152 Bob Mercer, "Rounds answers reporter's questions on EB-5 scandal," *Black Hills Pioneer* (October 2, 2014); available online at: http://www.bhpioneer .com/news/state_news/article_b50db4-4a4e-11e4-a094-ebc3ba95c021.html [accessed April 7, 2015].

153 "The Rise and Fall of South Dakota: A Cautionary Tale for EB-5 Public Pri- vate Partnerships Part I," eb5news.com (November 7, 2013); available online

at: http://eb5news.com/categories/12-projects/posts/247-the-rise-and-fall
-of-south-dakota-a-cautionary-tale-for-eb-5-public-private-partnerships
-part-i [accessed April 7, 2015].

154 Bob Mercer, "Rounds answers reporter's questions on EB-5 scandal,"
op. cit.

155 David Montgomery, "What you need to know about EB-5 in South Dakota,"
Argus Leader (October 8, 2014); available online at: http://www.argusleader
.com/story/davidmontgomery/2014/10/08/eb-5-primer/16890965/ [ac-
cessed April 7, 2015].

156 David Montgomery, "EB-5: South Dakota's visa-investment program not
unusual," *Argus Leader* (September 23, 2014); available online at: http://
www.argusleader.com/story/davidmontgomery/2014/08/05/eb5-industry
-standard/13616619/ [accessed April 7, 2015].

157 David Montgomery, "EB-5: Investment recruiter took cut of EB-5 money,"
Argus Leader (November 6, 2013); available online at: http://www.argus
leader.com/story/davidmontgomery/2014/08/01/sdrc-money/13471697/
[accessed April 7, 2015].

158 David Montgomery, "EB-5: Benda was 'in a hurry ... but he had nowhere
to go,'" *Argus Leader* (September 23, 2014); available online at: http://
www.argusleader.com/story/davidmontgomery/2014/08/10/benda-profile
/13863215/ [accessed April 7, 2015].

159 Ibid.

160 David Montgomery, "Beef plant investigation: EB-5 results mixed in S.D.,"
Argus Leader (November 10, 2013); available online at: http://archive.argus
leader.com/article/20131110/NEWS/311100031/Beef-plant-investigation
-EB-5-results-mixed-S-D- [accessed April 7, 2015].

161 James Nord, "South Dakota officials wrapping up EB-5 loose ends,"
Associated Press (December 6, 2014); available online at: http://www
.washingtontimes.com/news/2014/dec/6/south-dakota-officials-wrapping
-up-eb-5-loose-ends/ [accessed April 7, 2015].

162 Joe O'Sullivan, "Rounds Defends EB-5 Program," *Rapid City Journal*
(January 16, 2014); available online at: http://rapidcityjournal.com/news
/local/rounds-defends-eb—program/article_597f74d4-56a5-5d9a-b597
-819e45fbba25.html [accessed April 7, 2015].

163 Jeffrey Anderson and Shaun Waterman, "Immigration staffers pressured to
rush visas for wealthy investors," *Washington Times* (November 18, 2013);
available online at: http://www.washingtontimes.com/news/2013/nov/18
/immigration-staffers-pressured-to-rush-visas-for-w/?page=all [accessed
April 7, 2015].

164   Sen. Charles Grassley, Letter to Alejandro Mayorkas (September 10, 2010); available online at: http://www.grassley.senate.gov/sites/default/files/about /upload/2010-09-10-Letter-to-Mayorkas-USCIS.pdf [accessed April 7, 2015].

165   Sen. Tom Coburn, "A Review of the Department of Homeland Security's Missions and Performance" (January 2015), 113th Congress, pp. 76–77; available online at http://www.hsgac.senate.gov/media/minority-media /final-coburn-oversight-report-finds-major-problems-in-dhs [accessed: April 7, 2015].

166   Sen. Charles Grassley, Letter to John Sandweg (December 12, 2013); available online at: http://www.grassley.senate.gov/sites/default/files/issues/up load/EB-5-12-12-13-ICE-memo-security-vulnerabilities.pdf [accessed April 7, 2015].

167   Ibid.

168   Ibid.

CHAPTER 8. THE L VISA: A SECRETIVE "BACK DOOR TO CHEAP LABOR"

1   "Obama to ease norms for L-1B work visas," *Hindu BusinessLine* (March 24, 2015); available online at: http://www.thehindubusinessline.com/features /smartbuy/tech-news/obama-to-ease-norms-for-l1b-work-visas/article 7028758.ece [accessed April 1, 2015].

2   "Obama vows L-1B visa reform to attract global business," greatandhra .com (March 24, 2015); available online at: http://www.greatandhra.com /articles/special-articles/obama-vows-l-1b-visa-reform-to-attract-global -business-64907.html [accessed April 1, 2015].

3   Neha Alawadhi and Jochelle Mendonca, "Indian IT cos rejoice as Obama promises to ease L1 visa process," *Economic Times* (March 25, 2015); available online at: http://articles.economictimes.indiatimes.com/2015-03-25 /news/60475412_1_h1-b-visas-l1-ganesh-natarajan [accessed April 1, 2015].

4   "Boost for Indian IT workers as US L-1B visas now easier to get," *Economic Times* (March 24, 2015); available online at: http://articles.economictimes .indiatimes.com/2015-03-24/news/60439191_1_indian-companies-presi dent-barack-obama-non-immigrant-workers [accessed April 1, 2015].

5   Chidanand Rajghatta, "In boost to Indian companies, US to ease L-1B visas," *Times of India* (March 25, 2015); available online at: http://timesofindia .indiatimes.com/world/us/In-boost-to-Indian-companies-US-to-ease-L -1B-visas/articleshow/46681776.cms [accessed April 1, 2015].

6   Raif Karerat, "L-1B visas to become easier to get: Barack Obama," *American Bazaar* (March 24, 2015); available online at: http://www

.americanbazaaronline.com/2015/03/24/l-1b-visas-to-become-easier-to -get-barack-obama/ [accessed April 1, 2015].

7 Raul Perales, "Modernizing the Visa System to Attract and Retain Global Investment and Global Talent," The White House blog (March 26, 2015); available online at: https://www.whitehouse.gov/blog/2015/03/26/modern izing-visa-system-attract-and-retain-global-investment-and-global-talent [accessed April 1, 2015].

8 "L-1 Visa Alarm for Indian IT," *Indian American Times* (March 26, 2015); available online at: http://www.indiaamericatoday.com/article/l-1-visa -alarm-indian-it [accessed April 1, 2015].

9 National Foundation for American Policy, "Analysis: Data reveal high denial rates for L-1 and H-1B petitions at U.S. Citizenship and Immigration Services," NFAP Policy Brief (February 2012); available online at: http:// www.imminfo.com/NFAP_Policy_Brief-USCIS_and_Denial_Rates_of _L1_and_H-1B_Petitions-February2012.pdf [accessed April 1, 2015].

10 Seema Sirohio, "L-1 Visa Alarm for Indian IT," *Indian America Times* (March 26, 2015); available online at: http://www.indiaamericatoday.com /article/l-1-visa-alarm-indian-it [accessed April 1, 2015].

11 "Testimony by ACIP on L-1 Visas," Statement by Austin T. Fragomen, Man- aging Partner, Fragomen, Del Rey, Bernsen & Loewy, P.C., on behalf of the American Council on International Personnel (ACIP), at a hearing on the L-1 Visa and American Interests in the 21st Century Global Economy before the Senate Judiciary Subcommittee on Immigration (undated); available online at: http://www.aila.org/File/Related/03073059d.pdf [accessed April 1, 2015].

12 Executive Order 13,577 (June 15, 2011).

13 Julie Fei, "Steve Olson Returns to O'Melveny," O'Melveny & Myers Press release (August 1, 2013); available online at: http://www.omm.com/news room/news.aspx?news=3253 [accessed April 1, 2015].

14 National Trade Association biography of Vinai Thummalapally (undated); available online at: http://trade.gov/press/bios/thummalapally.asp [accessed April 1, 2015].

15 James Tapper, "Indian hustle: How fraudsters prey on would-be US tech workers," *Global Post* (February 17, 2014); available online at: http://www .globalpost.com/dispatch/news/regions/asia-pacific/india/140121/india -H1B-fraud-con-artist [accessed April 1, 2015].

16 Patrick Thibodeau, "Inside visa fraud in India," *Computerworld* (April 27, 2011); available online at: http://www.computerworld.com/article/2471242 /technology-law-regulation/inside-visa-fraud-in-india.html [accessed April 1, 2015].

17 Ibid.

18 "Ambassador to Belize: Who is Vinai Thummalapally?" AllGov (August 10, 2009); available online at: http://www.allgov.com/news/appointments-and -resignations/ambassador-to-belize-who-is-vinai-thummalapally?news =839351 [accessed April 1, 2015].

19 "SelectUSA to help resolve visa issues of Indian firms," Live Mint (September 18, 2014); available online at: http://www.livemint.com/Politics /HAvSINgyT5n6WD2g3AiE1H/SelectUSA-to-help-resolve-visa-issues -of-Indian-firms.html [accessed April 1, 2015].

20 Ibid.

21 Embassy of the United States in New Delhi, India, "Top U.S. Official to Visit Five Cities in India to Promote Indian Investment into the United States" (September 15, 2014); available online at: http://newdelhi.usembassy .gov/pr091514.html [accessed April 1, 2015].

22 White House Office of the Press Secretary, "Remarks by the President at the SelectUSA Investment Summit" (March 23, 2015); available online at: https://www.whitehouse.gov/the-press-office/2015/03/23/remarks-presi dent-selectusa-investment-summit [accessed April 1, 2015].

23 8 U.S.C. § 1184(c)(2)(E).

24 "A Mainframe-Size Visa Loophole," Bloomberg Business (March 5, 2003); available online at: http://www.bloomberg.com/bw/stories/2003-03-05/a -mainframe-size-visa-loophole [accessed April 22, 2015].

25 H.R. Rep. No. 91-851 (1970), reprinted in 1970 U.S.C.C.A.N. at 2753-54.

26 U.S. Citizenship and Immigration Services, "L-1B Intracompany Transferee Specialized Knowledge," (last reviewed/updated November 5, 2013); available online at: http://www.uscis.gov/working-united-states/temporary -workers/l-1b-intracompany-transferee-specialized-knowledge [accessed April 1, 2015].

27 Joan Fleischer, "Visa Holders Replace Workers," *Sun Sentinel* (August 10, 2003); available online at: http://articles.sun-sentinel.com/2003-08-10 /news/0308100157_1_visa-holders-foreign-workers-job-market/3 [accessed April 1, 2015].

28 "A Mainframe-Size Visa Loophole," Bloomberg Business (March 5, 2003); available online at: http://www.bloomberg.com/bw/stories/2003-03-05/a -mainframe-size-visa-loophole [accessed April 1, 2015].

29 Carrie Kirby, "Visa's use provokes opposition by techies / L-1 regarded as threat to workers," SFGATE (May 25, 2003); available online at: http:// www.sfgate.com/bayarea/article/Visa-s-use-provokes-opposition-by -techies-L-1-2645714.php [accessed April 1, 2015].

30 Associated Press, "Ultimate job-loss insult: training your own replacement," *USA Today* (August 10, 2003); available online at: http://usatoday30

.usatoday.com/tech/news/2003-08-10-offshoring_x.htm [accessed April 1, 2015].

31 Testimony of Ms. Patricia Fluno (July 29, 2003); available online at: http://www.judiciary.senate.gov/imo/media/doc/fluno_testimony_07_29_03.pdf [accessed April 1, 2015].

32 Ibid.

33 Ibid.

34 Ibid.

35 "A Mainframe-Size Visa Loophole," Bloomberg Business, op. cit.

36 Susan Ladika, "The Use—And Abuse—Of L-1 Visas," *HR Magazine* Vol. 51 Number 7 (July 1, 2006); available online at: http://www.shrm.org/publications/hrmagazine/editorialcontent/pages/0706ladika.aspx [accessed April 1, 2015].

37 Ibid.

38 "L Visas: Losing Jobs Through Laissez Faire Policies?" Hearing before the House International Relations Committee (February 4, 2004); available online at: http://commdocs.house.gov/committees/intlrel/hfa91679.000/hfa91679_0.HTM [accessed April 1, 2015].

39 Ibid.

40 Carrie Kirby, "Visa's use provokes opposition by techies . . ." op. cit.

41 Thomas Hoffman, "Job agency hires foreign help," *Computerworld* (November 17, 2003); available online at: http://www.computerworld.com/article/2573708/it-careers/job-agency-hires-foreign-help.html [accessed April 1, 2015].

42 Thomas Hoffman, "Employment Agency Scuttles India Contract," *Computerworld* (December 1, 2003); available online at: http://www.computerworld.com/article/2573421/it-management/employment-agency-scuttles-india-contract.html [accessed April 1, 2015].

43 John Ribeiro, "India hits back on outsourcing job fears," CIO (December 2, 2003); available online at: http://www.cio.com.au/article/117098/india_hits_back_outsourcing_job_fears/ [accessed April 1, 2015].

44 Ibid.

45 "FAQs RELATING TO WORK RELATED VISAS ISSUED BY INDIA" (undated); available online at: http://mha1.nic.in/pdfs/ForeigD-work_visa_faq.pdf [accessed April 1, 2015].

46 "Employment Visa," Ministry of Home Affairs, India (May 29, 2014); available online at: http://mha1.nic.in/pdfs/EmploymentVisa-300514.pdf [accessed August 6, 2015].

47 Arundhati Ramanathan, "Strict immigration laws affecting quality of research in India, says Nobel laureate," Live Mint (January 18, 2014); available

online at: http://www.livemint.com/Politics/RvOldIPowj2i8ujvmhqRDK
/Strict-immigration-laws-affecting-quality-of-research-in-Ind.html [ac-
cessed April 1, 2015].

48 Rafia Zakaria, "Brown workers and white whiners: The InfoSys visa fraud
case," Dawn.com (November 1, 2013); available online at: http://www.dawn
.com/news/1053389/brown-workers-and-white-whiners-the-infosys-visa
-fraud-case [accessed April 1, 2015].

49 "L Visas: Losing Jobs Through Laissez Faire Policies?" Hearing before the
House International Relations Committee, op. cit.

50 The class-action lawsuit was dismissed in 2000. See Shah v. Wilco Systems Inc. 126 F.Supp.2d 641 (2000); available online at: http://www.leagle
.com/decision/2000767126FSupp2d641_1717.xml/SHAH%20v.%20
WILCO%20SYSTEMS,%20INC. [accessed April 1, 2015]. Shah won a
one-hundred-thousand-dollar New York state settlement with Wilco in
2006. See Shah v. Wilco Systems Inc.; available online at: https://casetext
.com/case/shah-v-wilco-sys-inc [accessed April 1, 2015].

51 Shah v. Wilco Sys., 126 F. Supp. 2d 641, 648–649 (S.D.N.Y. 2000).

52 See, e.g., Zhang v. China Gate, Inc., 2007 U.S. Dist. LEXIS 66643, 5-6 (W.D.
Wash. Sept. 7, 2007).

53 Susan Ladika, "The Use—And Abuse—Of L-1 Visas," op. cit.

54 Department of Homeland Security Office of the Inspector General,
"Review of Vulnerabilities and Potential Abuses of the L-1 Visa Program,"
OIG-06-22 (January 2006); available online at: http://www.oig.dhs.gov
/assets/Mgmt/OIG_06-22_Jan06.pdf [accessed April 1, 2015].

55 Ibid.

56 As part of the "Consolidated Appropriations Act, 2005," Pub. L. No. 108-
447. U.S. Citizenship and Immigration Services press release, "USCIS TO
IMPLEMENT L-1 VISA REFORM ACT OF 2004" (December 9, 2004);
available online at: http://www.uscis.gov/sites/default/files/files/pressrelease
/LVisa_12_9_2004.pdf [accessed April 1, 2015].

57 Pragati Verma and Urmi A Goswami, "L-1 Bill doesn't bother tech majors,"
Economic Times (December 6, 2004); available online at: http://articles
.economictimes.indiatimes.com/2004-12-06/news/27413967_1_wipro-tech
nologies-tech-majors-visas [accessed April 1, 2015].

58 Ibid.

59 Ibid.

60 Sunlight Foundation Influence Explorer profile of Siemens Corporation
(undated); available online at: http://influenceexplorer.com/organization
/siemens-corp/86be094bc6394fbcad1efca7be06704b [accessed April 1,
2015].

61   "The L-1 Visa and American Interests in the 21st Century Global Economy," Hearing before the subcommittee on Immigration, Border Security and Citizenship of the U.S. Senate Judiciary Committee (July 29, 2003); available online at: http://www.loc.gov/law/find/hearings/pdf/00122982476.pdf [accessed April 1, 2015].

62   Department of Homeland Security Office of the Inspector General, "Review of Vulnerabilities and Potential Abuses of the L-1 Visa Program," op. cit.

63   Office of U.S. Senator Charles Grassley, "Grassley, Durbin Release New Information on L Visas," (June 26, 2007); available online at: http://www .grassley.senate.gov/news/news-releases/grassley-durbin-release-new -information-l-visas [accessed April 1, 2015].

64   Marianne Kolbasuk McGee, "Senators Release List of Top L-1 Visa Employers," *Information Week* (June 26, 2007); available online at: http://www .informationweek.com/senators-release-list-of-top-l-1-visa-employers/d/d -id/1056531? [accessed April 1, 2015].

65   Office of U.S. Senator Charles Grassley, "Grassley, Durbin Release New Information on L Visas," op. cit.

66   Daniel Costa, "Little-known temporary visas for foreign tech workers depress wages," *The Hill* (November 11, 2014); available online at: http:// thehill.com/blogs/pundits-blog/technology/223607-little-known-tempo rary-visas-for-foreign-tech-workers-depress [accessed April 1, 2015].

67   Ron Hira congressional testimony, "Immigration Reforms Needed to Protect Skilled American Workers," Employment Policy Institute (March 17, 2015); available online at: http://www.epi.org/publication/congressional -immigration-reforms-needed-to-protect-skilled-american-workers/ [accessed April 1, 2015].

68   U.S. Department of State, Nonimmigrant Visas by Individual Class of Admission, various; available online at: http://travel.state.gov/content/visas /english/law-and-policy/statistics/non-immigrant-visas.html [accessed April 22, 2015].

69   U.S. Department of Labor press release, "US Department of Labor investigation finds Silicon Valley technology employer owed more than $40,000 to foreign workers" (October 22, 2014); available online at: http://www.dol .gov/opa/media/press/whd/WHD20141717.htm [accessed April 1, 2015].

70   Ibid.

71   Congressional testimony given by Ron Hira, "Immigration Reforms Needed to Protect Skilled American Workers" (March 17, 2015); available online at: http://www.judiciary.senate.gov/imo/media/doc/Hira%20Testi mony.pdf [accessed April 1, 2105].

72 Ibid.

73 Ibid.

74 Daniel Costa, "Little-known temporary visas for foreign tech workers depress wages," op. cit.

75 Foreign Labor Certification Data Center Online Wage Library (All Industries database for July 2014 to June 2015); available online at: http://flc datacenter.com/OesQuickResults.aspx?code=49-2011&area=36084&year =15&source=1 [accessed April 1, 2015].

76 Foreign Labor Certification Data Center Online Wage Library (All Industries database for July 2014 to June 2015); available online at: http://flc datacenter.com/OesQuickResults.aspx?code=15-1142&area=36084&year =15&source=1 [accessed April 1, 2015].

77 George Avalos, "Workers paid $1.21 an hour to install Fremont tech company's computers," *San Jose Mercury News* (October 22, 2014); available online at: http://www.mercurynews.com/business/ci_26778017/tech-company -paid-employees-from-india-little-1 [accessed April 1, 2015].

78 EFI press release, "EFI Reports Record Revenue for Fourth Quarter and Full Year 2014," Global News Wire (January 29, 2015); available online at: http://globenewswire.com/news-release/2015/01/29/701331/10117760/en /EFI-Reports-Record-Revenue-for-Fourth-Quarter-and-Full-Year-2014 .html [accessed April 1, 2015].

79 American Immigration Lawyers Association, "Sign-On Letter to President Obama Emphasizes the Importance of L-1 Visa Policy" (March 22, 2012); available online at: http://www.aila.org/advo-media/aila-correspon dence/2011-2012/letter-to-obama-emphasizes-importance-of-l-1-visa [accessed April 1, 2015].

80 Ibid.

81 National Foundation for American Policy Policy Brief, op. cit.

82 Ibid.

83 Ibid.

84 Department for Professional Employees, AFL-CIO, letter to President Barack Obama, "Re: Reform of L1-B Visa 'Specialized Knowledge' Definition" (April 3, 2012); available online at: http://dpeaflcio.org/wp-content /uploads/Ltr-to-POTUS-re-L-1B-visas.pdf [accessed April 1, 2015].

85 U.S. Citizenship and Immigration Services, "USCIS Posts Updated L-1B Adjudications Policy for Public Feedback" (March 24, 2015); available online at: http://www.uscis.gov/news/uscis-posts-updated-l-1b-adjudications -policy-public-feedback [accessed April 1, 2015].

86 Byron York, "Did you know Obama just took new executive action on immigration?" *Washington Examiner* (March 25, 2015); available online at: http://

www.washingtonexaminer.com/did-you-know-obama-just-took-new
-executive-action-on-immigration/article/2562053 [accessed April 1, 2015].

87 U.S. Citizenship and Immigration Services, Memo for Feedback on L-1B
Adjudications Policy (March 24, 2015); available online at: http://www.uscis
.gov/sites/default/files/USCIS/Outreach/Draft%20Memorandum%20
for%20Comment/2015-0324-Draft-L-1B-Memo.pdf [accessed April 1,
2015].

88 Dhanya Ann Thoppil, "Read the New Guide to Getting an L-1B Visa to
Work in the U.S.," *Wall Street Journal* (March 27, 2015); available online at:
http://blogs.wsj.com/indiarealtime/2015/03/27/read-the-new-guide-to-get
ting-an-l-1b-visa-to-work-in-the-u-s/ [accessed April 1, 2015].

**CHAPTER 9. F-1: THE FOREIGN "STUDENT" VISA RUSE
(AKA YET ANOTHER CHEAP FOREIGN WORKER PIPELINE)**

1 William M. Fish, "How to Get Your U.S. Student Visa," Study in the USA
(undated); available online at: http://studyusa.com/en/a/33/how-to-get
-your-u-s-student-visa [accessed April 14, 2015].

2 "Easy ways To Get a Student(F-1) Visa for America," Pressbooks (undated);
available online at: http://immigrationquestion.pressbooks.com/chapter
/easy-ways-to-get-a-studentf-1-visa-for-america/ [accessed April 14, 2015].

3 Jessica Stahl, "Student Visa Tips from Visa Officers," Voice of America (June 27, 2011); available online at: http://blogs.voanews.com/student
-union/2011/06/27/visa-tips-from-visa-officers/ [accessed April 14, 2015].

4 "Student and Exchange Visitor Information System: Summary Quarterly
Review" (April 2, 2012); available online at: http://www.ice.gov/doclib
/sevis/pdf/quarterly_rpt.pdf [accessed April 14, 2015].

5 Neil G. Ruiz, "The Geography of Foreign Students in U.S. Higher Education: Origins and Destinations," Brookings (August 29, 2014); available
online at: http://www.brookings.edu/research/interactives/2014/geography
-of-foreign-students#/M10420 [accessed April 14, 2015]. See footnote 26.

6 U.S. Department of State, Nonimmigrant Visas by Individual Class of Admission, various; available online at: http://travel.state.gov/content/visas
/english/law-and-policy/statistics/non-immigrant-visas.html [accessed
April 22, 2015].

7 U.S. Department of State, "Worldwide NIV Workload by Visa Category
FY 2013" (undated); available at: http://travel.state.gov/content/dam/visas
/Statistics/Non-Immigrant-Statistics/NIVWorkload/FY2013NIVWork
loadbyVisaCategory.pdf [accessed April 14, 2015].

8 Ibid.

9   "10 Points to Remember When Applying for a Nonimmigrant Visa," NAFSA (June 11, 2009); available online at: http://www.nafsa.org/Find_Resources /Supporting_International_Students_And_Scholars/Network_Resources /International_Student_and_Scholar_Services/10_Points_to_Remember _When_Applying_for_a_Nonimmigrant_Visa/ [accessed April 14, 2015].

10 Linwood H. Cousins, ed., *Encyclopedia of Human Services and Diversity* (Sage Publications, 2014).

11 "Institute of International Education—Program, Organizational Structure, History and Development," StateUniversity.com (undated); available online at: http://education.stateuniversity.com/pages/2087/Institute-International -Education.html [accessed April 14, 2015].

12 "A Brief History of the IIE," Institute of International Education (undated); available online at: http://www.iie.org/en/Who-We-Are/History [accessed April 14, 2015].

13 U.S. Department of Justice, "Senator Robert Menendez and Salomon Melgen Indicted for Conspiracy, Bribery and Honest Services Fraud" (April 1, 2015); available online at: http://www.justice.gov/opa/pr/senator -robert-menendez-and-salomon-melgen-indicted-conspiracy-bribery -and-honest-services [accessed April 29, 2015] and Michelle Malkin, "SleazeBob Menendez's 36DD visa program," michellemalkin.com (April 21, 2015); available online at: http://michellemalkin.com/2015/04/21/sleaze bob-menendezs-36dd-visa-program/ [accessed April 29, 2015].

14 Claire Groden, "Dear International Students: Thanks for Your Tuition. Now Go Home. Love, Uncle Sam," *New Republic* (December 2, 2014); available online at: http://www.newrepublic.com/article/120463/immigration -law-discourages-international-students-working [accessed April 14, 2015].

15 Allie Bidwell, "Obama's Immigration Actions Bring Relief for College Students," *U.S. News & World Report* (November 21, 2014); available online at: http://www.usnews.com/news/articles/2014/11/21/obamas-immigration -actions-bring-relief-for-college-students [accessed April 14, 2015].

16 U.S Department of Justice, Immigration and Naturalization Service, "Certificate of Eligibility for Nonimmigrant (F-1) Student Status—For Academic and Language Students," OMB No. 1115-0051 (undated); available online at: http://www.uscampus.com/get_ready/visa/i-20.pdf [accessed April 14, 2015].

17 Marc Benioff tweet posted September 21, 2014; available online at https:// twitter.com/Benioff/status/506666506034626560 [accessed May 13, 2015].

18 David Zweig, "Luring back the Chinese who study abroad," *New York Times* (January 21, 2013); available online at: http://www.nytimes.com

/roomfordebate/2013/01/21/the-effects-of-chinas-push-for-education /luring-back-the-chinese-who-study-abroad [accessed April 17, 2015].

19　David Royce, "Romney, in Orlando, Plays Catch-up On Immigration By Promising More Green Cards," News Service of Florida (June 21, 2012).

20　"Building a 21st Century Immigration System," White House (May 2011); available online at: https://www.whitehouse.gov/sites/default/files/rss _viewer/immigration_blueprint.pdf [accessed April 14, 2015].

21　John Pletz, "TechNexus CEO Howerton joins Silicon Valley lobbying powerhouse," *Crain's Chicago Business* (May 12, 2014); available online at: http://www.chicagobusiness.com/article/20140512/BLOGS11/140519999/ technexus-ceo-howerton-joins-silicon-valley-lobbying-powerhouse [accessed April 14, 2015].

22　Carla Rivera, "Cal State thaws admission freeze for nonresidents," *Los Angeles Times* (August 16, 2012); available online at: http://articles.latimes.com/2012 /aug/16/local/la-me-0817-calstate-20120817 [accessed April 14, 2015].

23　Luiza Ch. Savage, "Courting the Latino vote in the U.S. presidential race," *Maclean's* (July 11, 2012); available online at: http://www.macleans.ca /news/world/hispanic-voters/ [accessed April 14, 2015].

24　U.S. Department of Homeland Security, "School Search" (undated); available online at: http://studyinthestates.dhs.gov/school-search/ [accessed April 14, 2015].

25　U.S. Government Accountability Office, "STUDENT AND EXCHANGE VISITOR PROGRAM: DHS Needs to Assess Risks and Strengthen Oversight Functions," GAO-12-572 (published June 18, 2012); available online at: http://www.gao.gov/products/GAO-12-572 [accessed April 14, 2015].

26　Jon Feere, "20 Years Later: The 1993 WTC Attack and Immigration Failures," Center for Immigration Studies (February 26, 2013); available online at: http://www.cis.org/feere/20-years-later-1993-wtc-attack-and-immigration -failures [accessed April 14, 2015].

27　Jessica Vaughan, "Faisal Shahzad: So Easy, Anyone Can Do It," Center for Immigration Studies (May 7, 2010); available online at: http://cis.org /vaughan/faisal-shahzad [accessed April 14, 2015].

28　"Homeland Security orders visa review for international students," CBS News (May 3, 2013); available online at: http://www.cbsnews.com/news /homeland-security-orders-visa-review-for-international-students/ [accessed April 14, 2015].

29　"9/11 and Terrorist Travel," Staff Report of the National Commission on Terrorist Attacks Upon the United States (August 21, 2004); available online at: http://govinfo.library.unt.edu/911/staff_statements/911_TerrTrav_Mono graph.pdf [accessed April 14, 2015]; see page 8.

30 Barnini Chakraborty, "Boston probe sheds light on 'astonishing' problems in student visa system," Foxnews.com (May 7, 2013); available online at: http://www.foxnews.com/politics/2013/05/07/boston-probe-problems -student-visa-overstays/ [accessed April 14, 2015].

31 Neil G. Ruiz, "The Geography of Foreign Students in U.S. Higher Education: Origins and Destinations," op. cit.

32 U.S. Department of Homeland Security, U.S. Citizenship and Immigration Services, "Students and Employment" (last reviewed/updated July 29, 2013); available online at: http://www.uscis.gov/working-united-states /students-and-exchange-visitors/students-and-employment [accessed April 14, 2015].

33 Kate Bachelder, "How to Save American Colleges," *Wall Street Journal* (April 24, 2015); available online at http://www.wsj.com/articles/how-to -save-american-colleges-1429913861 [accessed April 24, 2015]

34 U.S. Department of Homeland Security, U.S. Citizenship and Immigration Services, "Student and Exchange Visitor Information System" (undated); available online at: http://www.ice.gov/sevis/overview [accessed April 14, 2015].

35 Internal Revenue Service, "Social Security/Medicare and Self-Employment Tax Liability of Foreign Students, Scholars, Teachers, Researchers, and Trainees" (page last reviewed or updated on November 2, 2014); available online at: http://www.irs.gov/Individuals/International-Taxpayers/Foreign -Student-Liability-for-Social-Security-and-Medicare-Taxes [accessed April 14, 2015].

36 Ron Hira, "New Data Show How Firms Like Infosys and Tata Abuse the H-1B Program," February 19, 2015, available at http://www.epi.org/blog /new-data-infosys-tata-abuse-h-1b-program/.

37 Neil G. Ruiz, "The Geography of Foreign Students in U.S. Higher Education: Origins and Destinations," op. cit.

38 Neil G. Ruiz, "Why a Temporary Immigration Solution is Still Problematic for STEM Workers," Brookings (November 20, 2014); available online at: http:// www.brookings.edu/blogs/the-avenue/posts/2014/11/20-immigration -executive-action-stem-ruiz [accessed April 14, 2015].

39 Neil G. Ruiz, "The Geography of Foreign Students in U.S. Higher Education: Origins and Destinations," op. cit.

40 Ibid.

41 Ibid.

42 U.S. Department of Homeland Security, "What is a Designated School Official?" (undated); available online at: https://studyinthestates.dhs.gov /what-is-a-designated-school-official [accessed April 14, 2015].

43 U.S. Government Accountability Office, "STUDENT AND EXCHANGE VISITOR PROGRAM: DHS Needs to Assess Risks and Strengthen Oversight Functions," op. cit.

44 Ibid.

45 David North, "Migration Enforcement Agency Discourages Funds for Its Own Work," Center for Immigration Studies (January 2013); available online at: http://cis.org/sevp-migration-enforcement-agency-discourages -funds-for-Its-own-work [accessed April 14, 2015].

46 Ibid.

47 U.S. Department of Homeland Security, U.S. Citizenship and Immigration Services, "Owner/operator and employee of Miami-based school sentenced for immigration-related fraud" (August 29, 2010); available online at: http://www.ice.gov/news/releases/owneroperator-and-employee-miami -based-school-sentenced-immigration-related-fraud [accessed April 14, 2015].

48 U.S. Department of Homeland Security, U.S. Citizenship and Immigration Services, "Pastor sentenced to 1 year for visa fraud, ordered to forfeit building housing former religious school" (June 13, 2011); available online at: https:// www.ice.gov/news/releases/pastor-sentenced-1-year-visa-fraud-ordered -forfeit-building-housing-former-religious [accessed April 14, 2015].

49 Richard Elliot, "Owner accused of using school to traffic prostitutes," WSB-TV Atlanta (April 12, 2013); available online at: http://www.wsbtv.com /news/news/local/owner-accused-using-school-traffic-prostitutes/nXL BX/ [accessed April 14, 2015].

50 U.S. Attorney's Office, Northern District of Georgia, "English Language School Owner Sentenced For Immigration Fraud" (May 7, 2014); available online at: http://www.justice.gov/usao/gan/press/2014/05-07-14.html [accessed May 7, 2014].

51 Tom Bartlett, Karin Fischer, and Josh Keller, "Little-Known Colleges Exploit Visa Loopholes to Make Millions Off Foreign Students," *Chronicle of Higher Education* (March 20, 2011); available online at: http://chronicle .com/article/Little-Known-Colleges-Exploit/126822/ [accessed April 14, 2015].

52 Lisa M. Krieger, "Universities or Visa Mills?" *San Jose Mercury News* (July 16, 2011); available online at: http://www.mercurynews.com/edito rials/ci_18492754?source=pkg [accessed April 14, 2015].

53 United States of America v. Jerry Wang (filed July 24, 2012); available online at: http://www.justice.gov/archive/usao/can/news/2012/docs/Jerry%20 Wang%20Indictment.pdf [accessed April 14, 2015].

54 U.S. Department of Homeland Security, "Information for Herguan University Students" (undated); available online at: http://web.archive.org

/web/20120928133611/http://www.ice.gov/sevis/alerts/herguan.htm [accessed April 14, 2015].

55 Karen de Sá, "Shirakawa accepts money from Silicon Valley college at center of scandal," *San Jose Mercury News* (February 21, 2013); available online at: http://www.mercurynews.com/ci_22642048/shirakawa-accepts-money-from-silicon-valley-college-at [accessed April 14, 2015].

56 Tom Bartlett, Karin Fischer, and Josh Keller, "Little-Known Colleges Exploit Visa Loopholes to Make Millions Off Foreign Students," op. cit.

57 Ibid.

58 Glenn Wohltmann, "Feds charge university founder with money laundering, fraud," *Pleasanton Weekly* (January 27, 2011); available online at: http://www.pleasantonweekly.com/news/2011/01/27/feds-charge-university-founder-with-money-laundering-fraud [accessed April 14, 2015].

59 U.S. Attorney's Office, Northern District of California, "CEO And President Of East Bay University Sentenced To 198 Months For Fraud Scheme" (November 3, 2014); available online at: http://www.justice.gov/usao-ndca/pr/ceo-and-president-east-bay-university-sentenced-198-months-fraud-scheme [accessed April 14, 2015].

60 See for example "Tri-Valley University—CPT, OPT" (April 5, 2010); available online at: http://www.trackitt.com/usa-discussion-forums/h1b/512950847/tri-valley-university-cpt-opt [accessed April 14, 2015]. See also: "Tri-Valley University" (April 8, 2010); available online at: http://forums.immigration.com/threads/tri-valley-university.291115/ [accessed April 14, 2015].

61 U.S. Attorney's Office, Northern District of California, "President Of East Bay University Convicted In Fraud Scheme" (March 24, 2014); available online at: http://www.justice.gov/usao-ndca/pr/president-east-bay-university-convicted-fraud-scheme [accessed April 14, 2015].

62 U.S. Attorney's Office, Northern District of California, "CEO And President Of East Bay University Sentenced To 198 Months For Fraud Scheme" (November 3, 2014); available online at: http://www.justice.gov/usao-ndca/pr/ceo-and-president-east-bay-university-sentenced-198-months-fraud-scheme [accessed April 14, 2015].

63 Ibid.

64 "India condemns US for radio-tagging duped students," BBC News (January 31, 2011); available online at: http://www.bbc.co.uk/news/world-south-asia-12321193 [accessed April 14, 2015].

65 Jessica Stahl, "The Cautionary Tale of Tri-Valley's 'Sham University,'" Voice of America (February 21, 2011); available online at: http://blogs.voanews.com/student-union/2011/02/21/the-cautionary-tale-of-tri-valleys-sham-university/ [accessed April 14, 2015].

66 Ibid.

67 "300 Tri-Valley students may be sent home," *The Hindu* (October 23, 2011).

68 Chidanand Rajghatta, "Duped Indian students ignored red flags," *Times of India* (January 31, 2011); available online at: http://timesofindia.indiatimes .com/nri/us-canada-news/Duped-Indian-students-ignored-red-flags/article show/7395932.cms [accessed April 14, 2015].

69 Lisa M. Krieger, "Universities or Visa Mills?" op. cit.

70 Chidanand Rajghatta, "Duped Indian students ignored red flags," op. cit.

71 Ibid.

72 "Tri-Valley gave its students a 20% cut to lure buddies: Report," *Economic Times* (February 3, 2011); available online at: http://articles.economictimes .indiatimes.com/2011-02-03/news-by-industry/28432854_1_tri-valley-uni versity-curricular-practical-training-sham-varsity [accessed April 14, 2015].

73 Runa, "The Great TriValley University Scam: How not to come to Am-reeka (Update 3)," Über Desi (January 27, 2011); available online at: http:// uberdesi.com/blog/2011/01/27/the-great-trivalley-university-scam-how -not-to-come-to-amreeka/ [accessed April 14, 2015].

74 Neil G. Ruiz, "The Geography of Foreign Students in U.S. Higher Educa-tion: Origins and Destinations," op. cit.

75 Lisa M. Krieger, "Universities or Visa Mills?" op. cit.

76 Tom Bartlett, Karin Fischer, and Josh Keller, "Little-Known Colleges Ex-ploit Visa Loopholes to Make Millions Off Foreign Students," op. cit.

77 Ibid.

78 "Anyone got CPT from ITU, san jose?" (April 16, 2012); available online at: http://www.trackitt.com/usa-discussion-forums/h1b/993152219/anyone -got-cpt-from-itu-san-jose [accessed April 14 2015].

79 Lisa M. Krieger, "Universities or Visa Mills?" op. cit.

80 Katy Murphy, "San Jose's International Technological University receives stamp of approval," *San Jose Mercury News* (March 29, 2013); available online at: http://www.mercurynews.com/ci_22893549/san-joses-international-tech nological-university-receives-stamp-approval [accessed April 14, 2015].

81 ITU, "FAQs About WASC Accreditation" (last modified July 23, 2014); available online at: http://itu.edu/accreditation/accreditation-home/wasc -faqs/ [accessed April 14, 2015].

82 Letter from Richard Winn to Yau Gene Chan, president of International Technological University (July 17, 2014); available online at: http://itu.edu /wp-content/uploads/2014/07/Letter-to-ITU-071714.pdf [accessed April 14, 2015].

83 ITU, "Summary of ITU Student Visa Process" (undated); available online at: http://itu.edu/ssc/summary-of-itu-student-visa-process/.

84 ITU Google Plus page; available online at: https://plus.google.com/u/0 /108206179954952032402/reviews?hl=en&gl=us [accessed April 14, 2015].

85 Bre Payton, "Soon-to-be shuttered VA university had history of accreditation problems," VirginiaWatchdog.org (July 19, 2013); available online at: http://watchdog.org/96528/soon-to-be-shuttered-va-university-had-history-of-accreditation-problems/ [accessed April 14, 2015].

86 Sandra Davie, "Stop these degree courses, school told," asiaone education (September 15, 2008); available online at: http://news.asiaone.com/News /Education/Story/A1Story20080911-87201.html [accessed April 14, 2015].

87 U.S. Department of Homeland Security, U.S. Immigration and Customs Enforcement, "Update for University of Northern Virginia Students" (undated); available online at: http://www.ice.gov/sevis/students/unva [accessed April 14, 2015].

88 Tom Bartlett, Karin Fischer, and Josh Keller, "Federal Agents Raid Virginia Institution That Draws Many Students From India," *Chronicle of Higher Education* (July 29, 2011); available online at: http://chronicle.com/article /Agents-Raid-Virginia/128433/ [accessed April 14, 2015].

89 Daniel de Vise, "Va. university chancellor resigns over 'sex dungeon' flap," *Washington Post* (August 22, 2011); available online at: http://www.washingtonpost .com/blogs/college-inc/post/va-university-chancellor-resigns-over-sex -dungeon-flap/2011/08/22/gIQAKEYDWJ_blog.html [accessed April 14, 2015].

90 Ibid.

91 David North, "Adventures of a Visa Mill—Moving From Virginia to South Dakota," Center for Immigration Studies (February 18, 2014); available online at: http://cis.org/north/adventures-visa-mill-moving-virginia -south-dakota [accessed April 14, 2015].

92 Lacey Louwagie, "State tells 'university' to get out of town," Courthouse News Service (August 8, 2014); available online at: http://www.courthouse news.com/2014/08/08/70218.htm [accessed April 14, 2015].

93 David North, "Forget the Harvards and Yales, Let's Look at the Other End of the Spectrum," Center for Immigration Studies (May 14, 2014); available online at: http://www.cis.org/north/forget-harvards-and-yales-lets-look -other-end-spectrum [accessed April 14, 2015].

CHAPTER 10. OPT: OPEN-BORDERS BUREAUCRATS RUN AMOK

1 Ron Hira, "Immigration Reforms Needed to Protect Skilled American Workers," Employment Policy Institute (March 17, 2015); available online at: http://www.epi.org/publication/congressional-immigration-reforms -needed-to-protect-skilled-american-workers/ [accessed April 14, 2015].

2 Ibid.

3   U.S. Government Accountability Office, "STUDENT AND EXCHANGE VISITOR PROGRAM: DHS Needs to Assess Risks and Strengthen Oversight of Foreign Students with Employment Authorization," GAO-14-356 (February 27, 2014); available online at: http://gao.gov/products/GAO-14 -356 [accessed April 14, 2015].

4   Ibid.

5   U.S. Government Accountability Office, "STUDENT AND EXCHANGE VISITOR PROGRAM," op. cit.

6   Professor Ron Hira testified before the Senate Judiciary Committee in March 2015 that he personally knew of "OPT workers with STEM degrees who are working without being paid a salary at all."

7   B. Lindsay Lowell and Johanna Avato, "The Wages of Skilled Temporary Migrants: Effects of Visa Pathways and Job Portability," Working Paper of the Institute for the Study of International Migration (March 2007).

8   Ron Hira, "Immigration Reforms Needed to Protect Skilled American Workers," op. cit.

9   Ibid.

10 Part 125—Students, 12 Fed. Reg. 5,355–57 (August 7, 1947) (Codified at 8 C.F.R. part 125)

11 8 C.F.R. § 214.2(f)(10) (1981).

12 Nonimmigrant Classes; Students, F and M Classifications, 56 Fed. Reg. 55,608 (Oct. 29, 1991) (codified at 8 C.F.R. §§ 214, 274a).

13 Ibid.

14 Retention and Reporting of Information for F, J, and M Nonimmigrants; Student and Exchange Visitor Information System (SEVIS), 67 Fed. Reg. 76,256 (December 11, 2002) (codified at 8 C.F.R. §§ 103, 214, 248, 274a).

15 8 U.S.C. § 1101(a)(15)(F)(i).

16 8 C.F.R. 214.2(f)(5).

17 "Bill Gates: U.S. Senate Committee Hearing on Strengthening American Competitiveness," Microsoft News Center (March 7, 2007); available online at: http://news.microsoft.com/2007/03/07/bill-gates-u-s-senate-committee-hear ing-on-strengthening-american-competitiveness/ [accessed April 14, 2015].

18 Letter from Jack Krumholz, managing director of Federal Goverment Affairs, Microsoft, to Michael Chertoff, secretary of Homeland Security (November 15, 2007).

19 Letter from David Castagnetti, executive director, CompeteAmerica, to Michael Chertoff, secretary of Homeland Security (October 29, 2007).

20 Letter from R. Bruce Josten, executive vice president for government affairs, Chamber of Commerce of the United States, to Michael Chertoff, secretary of Homeland Security (November 16, 2007).

21   Letter from Craig R. Barrett, chairman of the board, Intel Corporation, et al., to Michael Chertoff, secretary of Homeland Security (March 11, 2008).

22   Extending Period of Optional Practical Training by 17-Months for F-1 non-immigrant Students with STEM (Science, Technology, Mathematics, and Engineering) Degrees and Expanding Cap-Gap Relief for All F-1 Students with Pending H-1B Petitions, 73 Fed. Reg. 18,944–56 (April 8, 2008) (codified at 8 C.F.R. §§ 214, 274a).

23   18944 Federal Register Vol. 73, No. 68 (April 8, 2008).

24   73 Fed. Reg. 18,953.

25   73 Fed. Reg. 18,947.

26   Committee on Prospering in the Global Economy of the 21st Century: An Agenda for American Science and Technology, *Rising Above the Gathering Storm* (Washington, D.C.: The National Academies Press, 2007).

27   White House press release, "Fact Sheet: Immigration Accountability Executive Action" (November 20, 2014); available online at: https://www.whitehouse.gov/the-press-office/2014/11/20/fact-sheet-immigration-accountability-executive-action [accessed April 14, 2015]. See also: Memorandum from Jeh Johnson to Leon Rodriguez and Thomas Winkowski (November 20, 2014); available online at: http://www.dhs.gov/sites/default/files/publications/14_1120_memo_business_actions.pdf [accessed April 14, 2015].

28   Sen. Charles Grassley, Press Release, "Grassley Concerned with Proposal to Expand Employment Benefits to Foreign Students Enrolled in Program Known for Fraud and Abuse" (June 8, 2015).

29   Programmers Guild, Inc. v. Chertoff, 338 Fed. Appx. 239 (3d Cir. 2009).

30   Match-E-Be-Nash-She-Wish Band of Pottawatomi Indians v. Patchak, 132 S. Ct. 2199, 2210 (2012).

31   Richard J. Pierce, Jr., Is Standing Law or Politics, 77 N.C.L. Rev. 1741.

32   Kent Jackson, "Lawyers argue Hazleton's immigration law in 3rd Circuit Court of Appeals," *Times-Tribune* (August 16, 2012); available online at: http://thetimes-tribune.com/news/lawyers-argue-hazleton-s-immigration-law-in-3rd-circuit-court-of-appeals-1.1359444 [accessed April 14, 2015].

33   Wash. Alliance of Tech. Workers v. United States Dep't of Homeland Sec.; available online at: http://cases.justia.com/federal/district-courts/district-of-columbia/dcdce/1:2014cv00529/165532/17/0.pdf?ts=1416656883 [accessed April 14, 2015].

34   Wash. Alliance of Tech. Workers v. United States Dep't of Homeland Sec., 2014 U.S. Dist. LEXIS 163285 (D.D.C. Nov. 21, 2014).

35   Tony Lee, "Judge greenlights lawsuit against guest-worker program expanded by executive amnesty," Breitbart.com (November 25, 2014); available

online at: http://www.breitbart.com/big-government/2014/11/25/judge
-greenlights-lawsuit-against-guest-worker-program-obama-expanded-via
-exec-action/ [accessed April 14, 2015].

36 Daniel Greenfield, "Facebook's Favorite Part of Amnesty is Already in Trouble," Frontpage Mag (November 28, 2014); available online at: http:// www.frontpagemag.com/2014/dgreenfield/facebooks-favorite-part-of -amnesty-is-already-in-trouble/ [accessed April 14, 2015].

37 Wash. Alliance of Tech. Workers v. United States Dep't of Homeland Sec., Civil Action No. 14-529, 2015 U.S. Dist. Court, August 11, 2015, p. 31.

CHAPTER 11. LEGION OF DOOM

1 Memo to D&B GTO U.S. from Elahe Hessamfar, *Offshore Development* (March 20, 2000). Reproduced online at: http://www.programmersguild .org/archives/lib/Abuse/dnb20000320elahe.htm [accessed March 20, 2015].

2 Lars-Erik Nelson, "Pols Are Going Overboard On Visa Program" *New York Daily News* (May 3, 2000); available online at: http://www.nydailynews .com/archives/opinions/pols-overboard-visa-program-article-1.870203 [accessed March 20, 2015].

3 Juliana Gruenwald, "Committee To Address Bill Eliminating H-1B Cap," *National Journal Technology Daily* (May 5, 2000).

4 "Visa Expansion Surprisingly Unpopular," *Washington Post* (May 22, 2000).

5 Carolyn Lockhead, "Bill to Boost Tech Visas Sails Through Congress," *San Francisco Chronicle* (October 4, 2000).

6 Giovanni Facchini, Anna Maria Mayda, and Prachi Mishra, "Do Interest Groups Affect U.S. Immigration Policy?" IMF Working Paper WP/08/244 October 2008, p. 6.

7 These data are from OpenSecrets.org.

8 "Indian govt, firms spend $10-mn for lobbying in US," Zeenews.com (July 26, 2009).

9 Sara Miles, *How to Hack a Party Line: The Democrats and Silicon Valley* (Berkeley: University of California Press, 2000).

10 Ibid., p. 67.

11 Ibid.

12 Most individuals' net worth fluctuates from day to day. All net worth figures in this chapter were based on data available in March 2015.

13 John K. Waters, *John Chambers and the Cisco Way: Navigating Through Volatility* (Hoboken: John K. Wiley & Sons, 2002), p. 141.

14 Karen Breslau, "Where's Tech Support When You Need It?" *Wired* (December 1999); available online at: http://archive.wired.com/wired/archive/7.12 /gore_pr.html [accessed March 20, 2015].

15 Jim VandeHei, "Bush Endorses High-Tech CEOs' Agenda, Tells Inves-
    tors to Be Patient With Holdings," *Wall Street Journal* (January 5, 2001).
    Reproduced online at: http://www.ibmemployee.com/PDFs/WSJ_Bush
    _Endorses_CEOs_Agenda.pdf [accessed March 20, 2015].

16 Carolyn Said, "VC to Lead Efforts to Shape Tech Policy," *San Francisco
    Chronicle* (March 29, 2001); available online at: http://www.sfgate.com
    /business/article/VC-to-Lead-Efforts-to-Shape-Tech-Policy-2937477.php
    [accessed March 20, 2015].

17 Chris Gaither, "PrivateSector; Valley Elder Goes to Washington," *New
    York Times* (April 8, 2001); available online at: http://www.nytimes.com
    /2001/04/08/business/privatesector-valley-elder-goes-to-washington.html
    [accessed March 20, 2015].

18 Mark Simon and Carla Marinucci, *Silicon Valley Subdued at Clinton Visit,*
    San Francisco Chronicle (September 25, 1998), at A-1.

19 Ibid.

20 John McCormick, "Obama Fires Up His Campaign Cash Machine,"
    Bloomberg Business (April 21, 2011); available online at: http://www
    .bloomberg.com/bw/magazine/content/11_18/b4226031196942.htm [ac-
    cessed March 20, 2015].

21 "Obama's Top Fund-Raisers," *New York Times* (September 13, 2012); avail-
    able online at: http://www.nytimes.com/interactive/2012/09/13/us/politics
    /obamas-top-fund-raisers.html?_r=0 [accessed March 20, 2015].

22 White House Office of the Press Secretary, "President Obama Announces
    his Intent to Appoint Fourteen Individuals to the President's Advisory Com-
    mission on Asian Americans and Pacific Islanders" (April 24, 2014); available
    online at: http://www.whitehouse.gov/the-press-office/2014/04/24/president
    -obama-announces-his-intent-appoint-fourteen-individuals-presid [ac-
    cessed March 20, 2015].

23 Rivali Reddy, "Silicon Valley bets right on Obama," *Peninsula Press* (No-
    vember 6, 2011); available online at: http://archive.peninsulapress.com
    /2012/11/06/silicon-valley-bets-right-on-obama/ [accessed March 20, 2015].

24 Evelyn M. Rusli, "In a Seating Chart, Silicon Valley's Pecking Order,"
    New York Times (February 18, 2011); available online at: http://dealbook
    .nytimes.com/2011/02/18/in-a-seating-chart-silicon-valleys-pecking
    -order/ [accessed March 20, 2015].

25 White House Flickr account, "President Barack Obama joins a toast with
    Technology Business Leaders at a dinner in Woodside, California," Official
    White House Photo by Pete Souza (February 17, 2011); available online at:
    https://www.flickr.com/photos/whitehouse/5455525432/in/photostream/
    [accessed March 20, 2015].

26 See, for example, Mike Rogoway, "Intel: Let spouses of H-1B immigrant employees work, too," *Oregonian* (July 16, 2014); available online at: http://www.oregonlive.com/silicon-forest/index.ssf/2014/07/intel_let_spouses _for_h-1b_emp.html [accessed March 20, 2015].

27 Josh Richman, Nicholas St. Fleur, and Bruce Newman, "Obama completes first day of Silicon Valley visit with fundraising blitz," *San Jose Mercury News* (May 8, 2014); available online at: http://www.mercurynews .com/peninsula/ci_25728199/obama-completes-first-day-silicon-valley -visit-fundraising [accessed March 20, 2015].

28 Ibid.

29 Employment Authorization for Certain H–4 Dependent Spouses, 80 Fed. Reg. 10,284 (February 25, 2015)—codified at 8 C.F.R. parts 214 and 274a.

30 Immigration Reform and Control Act of 1986, Pub. L. No. 99–603, §§ 201, 301, 100 Stat. 3359, 3397, 3399, 3418, 3421, 3428.

31 80 Fed. Reg. 10,294–95.

32 U.S. Citizenship and Immigration Services, "DHS Extends Eligibility for Employment Authorization to Certain H-4 Dependent Spouses of H-1B Nonimmigrants Seeking Employment-Based Lawful Permanent Residence" (February 24, 2015); available online at: http://www.uscis.gov /news/dhs-extends-eligibility-employment-authorization-certain-h-4 -dependent-spouses-h-1b-nonimmigrants-seeking-employment-based -lawful-permanent-residence [accessed March 20, 2105].

33 Save Jobs USA v. U.S. Department of Homeland Security (Civil Action No. Case 1:15-cv-615); Filed April 23, 2015, p. 12; available online at: https:// www.balglobal.com/Portals/0/news/SAVE_JOBS_USA_v_US_DEPART MENT_OF_HOMELAND_SECURITY_Docket_No_115c.pdf [accessed May 3, 2015].

34 Immigration Reform Law Institute, "Displaced American Workers Sue Government for Alleged Illegal Issuance of Work Authorization to Foreign Labor" (April 23, 2015); available online at: irli.org/displaced-american -workers-sue-government-for-alleged-illegal-issuance-of-work-authoriza tion-to-foreign-labor/ [accessed May 3, 2015].

35 "TechNet Statement on H-4 Visa Rule Change," TechNet (February 24, 2015); available online at: http://www.technet.org/technet-statement-on-h -4-visa-rule-change/ [accessed March 20, 2015].

36 Ibid.

37 Mark Zuckerberg, "Immigrants are the key to a knowledge economy," *Washington Post* (April 10, 2013); available online at: http://www.washingtonpost .com/opinions/mark-zuckerberg-immigrants-are-the-key-to-a-knowledge

-economy/2013/04/10/aba05554-a20b-11e2-82bc-511538ae90a4_story.html [accessed March 20, 2015].

38 Michael Beckel tweet (April 22, 2015); available online at: https://twitter .com/mjbeckel/status/590988852044689408 [accessed April 29, 2015].

39 Ibid.

40 Elizabeth Llorente, "With a little help from Mark Zuckerberg, Joe Green applies high tech strategies to immigration advocacy," Fox News Latino (December 19, 2013); available online at: http://latino.foxnews.com/latino/ politics/2013/12/19/with-little-help-from-mark-zuckerberg-joe-green -applies-high-tech-strategies-to/ [accessed March 20, 2015].

41 Reid J. Epstein, "Mark Zuckerberg immigration group's status: Looking for footing," *Politico* (April 4, 2013); available online at: http://www.politico .com/story/2013/04/mark-zuckerberg-immigration-groups-status -stumbling-89652.html [accessed March 20, 2015].

42 Ibid.

43 FWD.us, "Jared Lero's Post Card" (undated); available online at: https:// app.fwd.us/selfies/207 [accessed March 20, 2015].

44 Sarah Flocken and Rory Slatko, "Facebook Turns 10, 'Leaning In' to Washington," OpenSecrets.org (February 5, 2014); available online at: http:// www.opensecrets.org/news/2014/02/facebook-turns-10-leaning-in-to -washington/ [accessed March 20, 2015].

45 Deepak Chitnis, "Mark Zuckerberg's huge campaign for immigration reform, increase in H-1B visas, comes to a grinding halt," *American Bazaar* (July 9, 2014); available online at: http://www.americanbazaaronline .com/2014/07/09/mark-zuckerbergs-huge-campaign-immigration-reform -increase-h-1b-visas-comes-grinding-halt/ [accessed March 20, 2015].

46 Benjamin Bell, "Mark Zuckerberg: Immigration Reform One of the 'Biggest Civil Rights Issues of Our Time,'" ABC News (November 24, 2013); available online at: http://abcnews.go.com/blogs/politics/2013/11/mark -zuckerberg-immigration-reform-one-of-the-biggest-civil-rights-issues -of-our-time/ [accessed March 20, 2015].

47 Innovation Policy Connection, "Rep. Issa unveils SKILLS Visa Act to boost high-tech, STEM visa reform" (June 14, 2013); available online at: http:// connectpolicyblog.com/2013/06/14/rep-issa-unveils-skills-visa-act-to -boost-high-tech-stem-visa-reform/ [accessed March 20, 2015].

48 Jennifer Martinez, "Issa's tech-backed Skills Visa Act passes House Judiciary panel," *The Hill* (June 28, 2013); available online at: http://thehill.com /policy/technology/308439-issas-tech-backed-skills-visa-act-passes-house -judiciary-panel [accessed March 20, 2015].

49 Peter Wallsten, Jia Lynn Yang, and Craig Timberg, "Facebook flexes political muscle with carve-out in immigration bill," *Washington Post* (April 16, 2015); available online at: http://www.washingtonpost.com/business/econ omy/facebook-flexes-political-muscle-with-carve-out-in-immigration -bill/2013/04/16/138f718e-a5e7-11e2-8302-3c7e0ea97057_story.html [accessed March 20, 2015].

50 Ibid.

51 "For Mark Zuckerberg, Discriminating against American Workers is Good for Business," Federation for American Immigration Reform (March 2014); available online at: http://www.fairus.org/issue/for-mark-zuckerberg-br -discriminating-against-american-workers-is-good-for-business [accessed March 20, 2015].

52 Patrick Thibodeau, "H-1B politics shifts to backroom as vote nears," *Computerworld* (May 16, 2013); available online at: http://www.computerworld .com/article/2497624/technology-law-regulation/h-1b-politics-shifts-to -backroom-as-vote-nears.html [accessed March 20, 2015].

53 Dave Jamieson, "Senate Immigration Bill's Visa Rules A 'Landslide' For Tech Lobby," *Huffington Post* (July 1, 2013); available online at: http://www .huffingtonpost.com/2013/07/01/senate-immigration-bill-visa-tech -companies_n_3529241.html [accessed March 20, 2015].

54 Ibid.

55 Council for American Job Growth, "Who We Are" (undated); available online at: http://www.councilforamericanjobgrowth.com/who_we_are [accessed March 20, 2015].

56 Influence Explorer, "Real-Time Federal Campaign Finance"; available online at: http://realtime.influenceexplorer.com/committee/council-for -american-job-growth/C90015090/ [accessed March 20, 2015].

57 FactCheck.org, "Council for American Job Growth" (April 25, 2014); available online at: http://www.factcheck.org/2014/04/council-for-american-job -growth/ [accessed March 20, 2015].

58 Alex Wilhelm, "Zuckerberg-Linked Group Releases Ad Blasting House GOP For Immigration Reform Intransigence," TechCrunch (March 3, 3014); available online at: http://techcrunch.com/2014/03/03/zuckerberg -linked-group-releases-ad-blasting-house-gop-for-immigration-reform -intransigence/ [accessed March 20, 2015].

59 Alexander Burns, "Mark Zuckerberg group launches TV blitz," *Politico* (April 23, 2013); available online at: http://www.politico.com/story/2013/04 /mark-zuckerberg-immigration-group-launches-tv-blitz-90511.html [accessed March 20, 2015].

60 Michael Scherer, "What Haley Barbour Didn't Tell Fox News: He Lobbied For Mexico On 'Amnesty,'" *Time* (February 13, 2011); available online at: http://swampland.time.com/2011/02/13/what-haley-barbour-didnt
-tell-fox-news-he-lobbied-for-mexico-on-amnesty/ [accessed March 20,
2015].

61 Ibid.

62 Matthew Boyle, "ZUCKERBERG RUSHES TO RENEE ELLMERS'
RESCUE WITH 'NO AMNESTY' ADS," Breitbart.com (March 18, 2014);
available online at: http://www.breitbart.com/big-government/2014/03/18/
zuckerberg-rushes-to-ellmers-rescue-on-amnesty-with-eye-popping-ad
-buy/ [accessed March 20, 2015].

63 Mike Isaac, "Elon Musk and David Sacks Depart Fwd.us, Mark Zuckerberg's Political Action Group," All Things D (May 10, 2013); available online at: http://allthingsd.com/20130510/elon-musk-and-david-sacks-depart
-fwd-us-mark-zuckerbergs-political-action-group/ [accessed March 20, 2015].

64 Seung Min Kim, "Facebook-linked group drops $1M on Shaheen," *Po-
litico* (October 10, 2014); available online at: http://www.politico.com
/story/2014/10/mark-zuckerberg-jeanne-shaheen-new-hampshire-111786
.html [accessed March 20, 2015].

65 Dolia Estevez, "Is Mexican Billionaire Carlos Slim The New Role Model
For Facebook's Mark Zuckerberg?" *Forbes* (September 8, 2014); available
online at: http://www.forbes.com/sites/doliaestevez/2014/09/08/is-mexican
-billionaire-carlos-slim-the-new-role-model-for-facebooks-mark-zucker
berg/ [accessed March 20, 2015].

66 Norman Matloff, "Another PR Gaffe by FWD.us," Norm Says No, May 11,
2015; available online at: https://normsaysno.wordpress.com/2015/05/11
/another-pr-gaffe-by-fwd-us/ [accessed May 11, 2015].

67 Anne Broache, "Gates calls for 'infinite' H-1Bs, better schools," CNET
News (March 7, 2007); available online at: http://news.cnet.com/Gates
-calls-for-infinite-H-1Bs,-better-schools/2100-1014_3-6165166.html [ac-
cessed March 20, 2015].

68 Ibid.

69 Ibid.

70 Rajiv Chandrasekaran, "Competitors, Senators Assail Gates at Hearing,"
Washington Post (March 4, 1998); available online at: http://www.wash
ingtonpost.com/wp-srv/washtech/longterm/discussionlinks/dell0304.htm
[accessed March 20, 2015].

71 Timothy P. Carney, "How Hatch forced Microsoft to play K Street's game,"
Washington Examiner (June 24, 2012); available online at: http://www

.washingtonexaminer.com/carney-how-hatch-forced-microsoft-to-play-k
-streets-game/article/2500453 [accessed March 20, 2015].

72 Matthew Continetti, *The K Street Gang: The Rise and Fall of the Republican Machine* (New York: Doubleday, 2006).

73 Michael Teitelbaum, *Falling Behind?*, op. cit., p. 103.

74 Jeffrey H. Birnbaum and Dan Balz, "Case Bringing New Scrutiny to a System and a Profession," *Washington Post* (January 4, 2006); available online at: http://www.washingtonpost.com/wp-dyn/content/article/2006/01/03/AR2006010301536.html [accessed March 20, 2015].

75 Philip Shenon, "Former DeLay aide pleads guilty to conspiracy," *New York Times* (November 22, 2005); available online at: http://www.nytimes.com/2005/11/22/politics/22scanlon.html?hp&ex=1132635600&en=7c3a51fbdc7194&ei=5094&partner=homepage&_r=0 [accessed March 20, 2015].

76 Teitelbaum, *Falling Behind?*, op. cit., pp. 102–5.

77 Charles Pope, "Microsoft defends ties to Ralph Reed," *Seattle Post-Intelligencer* (April 26, 2005); available online at: http://www.seattlepi.com/business/article/Microsoft-defends-ties-to-Ralph-Reed-1171885.php [accessed March 20, 2015]. See also: Rick Anderson, "A Bug in Windows GOP," *Seattle Weekly* (October 9, 2006); available online at: http://www.seattleweekly.com/2005-06-01/news/a-bug-in-windows-gop/ [accessed March 20, 2015].

78 Philip Shenon, "Senate Report Lists Lobbyist's Payments to Ex-Leader of Christian Coalition," *New York Times* (June 23, 2006); available online at: http://www.nytimes.com/2006/06/23/washington/23abramoff.html?_r=3& [accessed March 20, 2015].

79 Jamie Glazov, "The Muslim Brotherhood Infiltrates the GOP," *Front Page Magazine* (November 8, 2011); available online at: http://www.frontpagemag.com/2011/jamie-glazov/the-muslim-brotherhood-penetrates-the-republican-party/. See also Sperry, *Infiltration* [accessed March 20, 2015].

80 U.S. Department of Justice press release, "Former GSA Chief of Staff David Safavian Sentenced for Obstruction of Justice and Making False Statements" (October 16, 2009); available online at: http://www.justice.gov/opa/pr/former-gsa-chief-staff-david-safavian-sentenced-obstruction-justice-and-making-false [accessed March 20, 2015].

81 John Heilemann, "Do You Know the Way to Ban Jose?" *Wired* (undated); available online at: http://archive.wired.com/wired/archive/4.08/netizen_pr.html [accessed March 20, 2015].

82 Gene A. Nelson, "The Greedy Gates Immigration Gambit," *The Social Contract* Volume 18, Number 1 (Fall 2007); available online at: http://

www.thesocialcontract.com/artman2/publish/tsc_18_1/tsc_18_1_nelson _printer.shtml [accessed March 20, 2015].

83 Anu Narayanswamy, "Immigration: Give me your poor, your tired . . . your lobbyists?" Sunlight Foundation (March 21, 2013); available online at: http://sunlightfoundation.com/blog/2013/03/21/immigration-2/ [accessed March 20, 2015].

84 Ibid. Technically, Microsoft filed the most LCAs. The Indian offshore outsourcing companies file fewer LCAs, but hire more H-1B workers.

85 Brad Smith, "Strengthening American Competitiveness and Creating Opportunity for the Next Generation," Microsoft on the Issues (September 27, 2012); available online at: http://blogs.microsoft.com/on-the-issues/2012 /09/27/strengthening-american-competitiveness-and-creating-opportunity -for-the-next-generation/ [accessed April 7, 2015].

86 Josh Harkinson, "Microsoft 'Bait and Switch' Could Mean a Huge Increase in Foreign Tech Workers," *Mother Jones* (March 12, 2013); available online at: http://www.motherjones.com/politics/2013/03/microsoft-stem-education -coalition-h1b-visa-outsourcing [accessed March 20, 2015].

87 Ibid.

88 Microsoft, "A National Talent Strategy" (undated); available online at: http://news.microsoft.com/download/presskits/citizenship/MSNTS.pdf [accesed May 3, 2015].

89 Lyndsey Layton, "How Bill Gates pulled off the swift Common Core revolution," *Washington Post* (June 7, 2014); available online at: http://www .washingtonpost.com/politics/how-bill-gates-pulled-off-the-swift -common-core-revolution/2014/06/07/a830e32e-ec34-11e3-9f5c-9075d 5508f0a_story.html [accessed May 3, 2015]; Michelle Malkin, "Get to Know the Common Core Marketing Overlords," Creators Syndicate (March 21, 2014); available online at: http://www.creators.com/opinion /michelle-malkin/get-to-know-the-common-core-marketing-overlords .html [accessed May 3, 2015].

90 Michelle Malkin, "Jeb Bush, Common Core cronie$, Pearson, PARCC, and your kids' privacy," michellemalkin.com (March 18, 2015); available online at: http://michellemalkin.com/2015/03/18/jeb-bush-common-core-cronie -pearson-parcc-and-your-kids-privacy/ [accessed May 3, 2015].

91 Michelle Malkin, "Get to Know the Common Core Marketing Overlords," op. cit.

92 Eric Owens, "Follow the Money: Microsoft's plan to cash in on Common Core," *Daily Caller* (April 7, 2012); available online at: http://dailycaller .com/2014/07/12/follow-the-money-microsofts-plan-to-cash-in-on -common-core/ [accessed May 4, 2015].

93 Lyndsey Layton, "Full Interview: Bill Gates on the Common Core," *Washington Post TV* (June 5, 2014); available online at: http://www.washing tonpost.com/posttv/national/full-interview-bill-gates-on-the-common -core/2014/06/07/e4c14cae-ecdc-11e3-b10e-5090cf3b5958_video.html [accessed May 4, 2015].

94 Microsoft, "A National Talent Strategy," p. 26.

95 Josh Harkinson, "Microsoft 'Bait and Switch' Could Mean a Huge Increase in Foreign Tech Workers," op. cit.

96 OpenSecrets.org profile of Spencer Abraham (undated); available online at: https://www.opensecrets.org/revolving/rev_summary.php?id=35953 [accessed March 20, 2015].

97 Gebe Martinez, "High-tech firms help Abraham," *Detroit News* (September 5, 2000).

98 Mark Tapscott, "Are Most Techies Libertarians?" The Next Right (December 30, 2008); available online at: http://www.thenextright.com/blogs /marktapscott [accessed March 20, 2015].

99 Ruth Ellen Wasem, "Immigration: Nonimmigrant H-1B Specialty Worker Issues and Legislation," Congressional Research Service (August 4, 1998), p. 7.

100 Transcript of FAIR ads, available online at: http://www.programmersguild .org/archives/lib/ads/fair2000.htm [accessed March 20, 2015].

101 Michael Isikoff, "The Secret Money Chase," *Newsweek* (June 5, 2000); available online at: http://www.newsweek.com/secret-money-chase-160567 [accessed March 20, 2015].

102 Gebe Martinez, "GOP Tapped Tech Execs to Aid Abraham," *Detroit News* (May 17, 2000).

103 Michael Isikoff, *The Secret Money Chase*, op. cit.

104 Mike Allen, "GOP Pressures Tech Firms To Help Michigan Senator," *Washington Post* (May 16, 2000).

105 Ibid.

106 John R. Wilke, "Microsoft Is Source of 'Soft Money' Funds Behind Ads in Michigan's Senate Race," *Wall Street Journal* (October 16, 2000).

107 American Competitiveness in the Twenty-first Century Act of 2000, Pub. L. 106-313, 114 Stat 1251 (2000).

108 Ibid.

109 Joseph Trento, "Spencer Abraham Cashes In," The Bulldog Blog (February 2, 2012); available online at: http://www.dcbureau.org/201202026986 /natural-resources-news-service/spencer-abraham-cashes-in.html [accessed March 20, 2015].

110 David A. Fahrenthold and Paul Kane, "Paul Ryan: Midwesterner, Catholic, intellectual," *Washington Post* (August 11, 2012); available online at: http://www.washingtonpost.com/politics/paul-ryan-midwesterner-catholic-intellectual/2012/08/11/0a7bdc1e-e3bd-11e1-ae7f-d2a13e249eb2_story.html [accessed March 20, 2015].

111 Michelle Malkin, *Invasion*, op. cit., and Mark Krikorian, "Visa Overstays: Can We Bar the Terrorist Door?" Center for Immigration Studies (May 11, 2006); available online at: http://cis.org/node/558 [accessed March 20, 2015].

112 Nicholas Confessore, "Borderline Insanity," *Washington Monthly* (May 2002); available online at: http://www.washingtonmonthly.com/features/2001/0205.confessore.html [accessed March 20, 2015].

113 Business Wire, "NFAP Study to Report on 'Extraordinary Proportion' of Top U.S. Math and Science High School Students with Immigrant Roots: To Be Released in Washington DC on Monday, July 19" (July 16, 2004); available online at: http://www.businesswire.com/news/home/20040716005306/en/NFAP-Study-Report-Extraordinary-Proportion-Top-U.S.#.VQaDJmR4rLc [accessed March 20, 2015].

114 Fawn Johnson, "Norquist Says Ending Birthright Citizenship Is a Tax," *National Journal* (March 5, 2012); available online at: http://www.nationaljournal.com/congress/norquist-says-ending-birthright-citizenship-is-a-tax-20120305 [accessed March 20, 2015].

115 National Foundation for American Policy (NFAP) research papers are available online at: http://www.issuelab.org/organizations/profile/national_foundation_for_american_policy_nfap [accessed March 20, 2015].

116 Chris Chmielenski, "Exposing Tea Party Express Co-Founder's Amnesty Ties," Richard Viguerie's ConservativeHQ (May 15, 2014); available online at: http://www.conservativehq.com/article/17257-exposing-tea-party-express-co-founders-amnesty-ties [accessed April 12, 2015].

117 Emma Dumain, "Immigration Overhaul Backed by Growing Number of Tea Partyers (Video)," *Roll Call* (May 14, 2014); available online at: http://blogs.rollcall.com/218/immigration-reform-backed-by-tea-party-coalition/?dcz= [accessed April 12, 2015].

118 Russ Choma, "Tea Party Express Loses Steam for Candidates," OpenSecrets.org (June 10, 2014); available online at: http://www.opensecrets.org/news/2014/06/tea-party-express-loses-steam-for-candidates/ [accessed April 12, 2015].

119 See Michael Teitelbaum, *Falling Behind*, op. cit., pp. 92–94, for a detailed explanation of the study's flaws and policy impact.

120 Austen R. Fragomen bio at http://www.fragomen.com/austin-t-fragomen / [accessed March 20, 2015].

121 Senate Democratic Policy Committee Hearing, "Shipping American Jobs Overseas: A Hearing on the Bush Administration's Claim That Outsourcing is Good for the U.S. Economy" (March 5, 2004); available online at: http://www.dpc.senate.gov/hearings/hearing13/bios.pdf [accessed March 20, 2015].

122 David North, "Warning: Harris Miller, Immigration Uber-Lobbyist, Has a New Job," Center for Immigration Studies (March 19, 2010); available online at: http://www.cis.org/north/harris-miller-career-colleges [accessed March 20, 2015].

123 Dale Eisman, " 'Wonky' executive Miller thinks it's his time for Senate seat," *Virginian Pilot* (June 1, 2006); available online at http://hamptonroads.com /node/108901 [accessed April 6, 2015].

124 Lisa Rein, "Democrat's bid begins with a salvo," *Washington Post* (April 19, 2006); available online at: http://www.washingtonpost.com/wp-dyn/content /article/2006/04/18/AR2006041801631.html [accessed April 6, 2015].

125 Todd R. Weiss, "Former ITAA head Harris Miller: 'No regrets' in failed Senate bid," *Computerworld* (June 15, 2006); available online at: http://www .computerworld.com/article/2546365/it-outsourcing/former-itaa-head -harris-miller-no-regrets-in-failed-senate-bid.html [accessed April 6, 2015].

126 Info Tech Guy, "Harris Miller and the American job loss nightmare," Daily Kos (May 2, 2006); available online at: http://www.dailykos.com/story /2006/05/02/206820/-Harris-Miller-and-the-American-job-loss-night mare# [accessed March 20, 2015].

127 Influence Explorer profile of the Council for Global Immigration (undated); available online at: http://influenceexplorer.com/organization/council-for -global-immigration/2913f5bbfcce4b83a327c462a8396ba0 [accessed April 7, 2015].

128 Council for Global Immigration website (undated); available online at: http://www.councilforglobalimmigration.org/membership.

129 Irish America Gall of Fame—2013, profile of Bruce Morrison (undated); available online at: http://irishamerica.com/2013/03/bruce-morrison/ [accessed April 7, 2015].

130 c.cur, "IEEE-USA releases 'Misfortune 500' list of displaced high-tech workers," programd.com (October 14, 1998); available online at: http:// www.programd.com/7_dbc170113da1fd4f_1.htm [accessed April 7, 2015].

131 Ibid.

132 Teitelbaum, *Falling Behind?*, op. cit., p. 115.

133   John B. Judis, "Temporary Help," *New Republic* (June 19, 2000); available online at: http://www.newrepublic.com/article/politics/temporary-help [accessed April 7, 2015].

134   Fawn Johnson, "Green cards offered as solution for high-tech firms," *National Journal* (March 31, 2011); available online at: http://www.national journal.com/tech/green-cards-offered-as-solution-for-high-tech-firms -20110331 [accessed April 7, 2015].

135   Influence Explorer profile of Morrison Public Affairs Group (undated); available online at: http://influenceexplorer.com/organization/morrison -public-affairs-group/253fc60a24474345852721b50ed9b17e [accessed April 7, 2015].

136   Mike Ciandella, "Soros Boasts of Spending $100 Million on U.S. Immigration Reform Push," CNS News (October 24, 2013); available online at: http:// www.cnsnews.com/mrctv-blog/mike-ciandella/soros-boasts-spending -100-million-us-immigration-reform-push [accessed March 20, 2015].

137   Discover the Networks profile of the National Immigration Forum available online at: http://www.discoverthenetworks.org/groupProfile.asp?gr pid=6506 [accessed March 20, 2015].

138   John Heilemann, "Do You know the Way to Ban Jose?" op. cit.

139   Maggie Haberman, "GOP mega-donor backs immigration reform," *Politico* (April 29, 2013); available online at: http://www.politico.com/story/2013/04 /gop-donor-paul-singer-immigration-reform-90726.html [accessed March 20, 2015].

140   Mark Krikorian, "Strange Bedfellows: Left and Right on Immigration," Center for Immigration Studies / National Review Online (March 31, 2004); available online at: http://cis.org/node/372 [accessed May 20, 2015].

141   Nicholas Laham, *Ronald Reagan and the Politics of Immigration Reform* (Westport, Conn.: Praeger Publishers, 2000).

142   Matthew Boyle, "NATIONAL IMMIGRATION FORUM FUNDED BY SOROS AND THE LEFT," Breitbart.com (June 2, 2013); available online at: http://www.breitbart.com/big-government/2013/06/02/national -immigration-forum-lead-evangelical-jim-wallis-funded-by-george-soros -other-bastions-of-institutional-left/ [accessed March 20, 2015].

143   Katherine Burton, "Druckenmiller Backs Zuckerberg's Immigration Reform Group," Bloomberg Business (July 12, 2013); available online at: http://www.bloomberg.com/news/articles/2013-07-12/druckenmiller -backs-zuckerberg-s-immigration-reform-group [accessed March 20, 2015].

144   Lucy Fyler, "IMMIGRATION-FOCUSED AD TO AIR AT DAYTONA 500," National Immigration reform press release (February 20, 2015); available

online at: http://immigrationforum.org/blog/immigration-focused-ad
-to-air-at-daytona-500/ [accessed March 20, 2015].

145 Patrick Thibodeau, "Mayor Bloomberg calls H-1B visa caps 'national suicide,'" *Computerworld* (September 29, 2011); available online at: http://
www.computerworld.com/article/2511562/it-outsourcing/mayor-bloom
berg-calls-h-1b-visa-caps—national-suicide-.html [accessed March 20,
2015].

146 Patrick Thibodeau, "H-1B Visa Cap Must Go, Says NYC Mayor," *Computerworld* (October 10, 2011); available online at: http://www.computerworld
.com/article/2550224/data-center/h-1b-visa-cap-must-go--says-nyc-mayor
.html [accessed March 20, 2015].

147 Elizabeth Flock, "Bloomberg Deploys Hundreds of CEOs to Move Lawmakers on Immigration," *U.S. News & World Report* (January 18, 2013); available online at: http://www.usnews.com/news/blogs/washington-whispers
/2013/01/18/bloomberg-deploys-hundreds-of-ceos-to-move-lawmakers
-on-immigration [accessed March 20, 2015].

148 Press release from the office of the New York mayor, "MAYOR BLOOMBERG
JOINS MAYORS AND BUSINESS LEADERS TO FORM *PARTNER-
SHIP FOR A NEW AMERICAN ECONOMY*," News from the Blue
Room, June 24, 2010; available online at: http://www.nyc.gov/portal/site
/nycgov/menuitem.c0935b9a57bb4ef3daf2f1c701c789a0/index.jsp?page
ID=mayor_press_release&catID=1194&doc_name=http%3A%2F%2F
www.nyc.gov%2Fhtml%2Fom%2Fhtml%2F2010a%2Fpr287-10.html&cc
=unused1978&rc=1194&ndi=1 [accessed March 20, 2015].

149 http://www.renewoureconomy.org/news/updates/press-release-top
-national-republican-donors-call-immigration-reform/.

150 Susan Crabtree, "White House's Valerie Jarrett dines with Rupert Murdoch to plot immigration strategy," *Washington Examiner* (June 20, 2014);
available online at: http://www.washingtonexaminer.com/white-houses
-valerie-jarrett-dines-with-rupert-murdoch-to-plot-immigration-strategy
/article/2549994 [accessed March 20, 2015].

151 Rupert Murdoch, "Immigration Reform Can't Wait," *Wall Street Journal*
(June 18, 2014); available online at: http://www.wsj.com/articles/rupert
-murdoch-immigration-reform-cant-wait-1403134311 [accessed March 20,
2015].

152 "In Praise of Huddled Masses," *Wall Street Journal* (July 3, 1984); available online at: http://www.bizzyblog.com/ThereShallBeOpenBorders_WSJ
070384.html [accessed March 20, 2015].

153 Peter Weber, "Rupert Murdoch is immigration reform's biggest booster,
and obstacle," *The Week* (June 20, 2014); available online at: http://theweek

.com/articles/445969/rupert-murdoch-immigration-reforms-biggest
-booster-obstacle [accessed March 20, 2015].

154 Devin Dwyer, "Immigration Reform: Rupert Murdoch and the Fox
News Factor," ABC News (February 2, 2013); available online at: http://
abcnews.go.com/Politics/OTUS/immigration-reform-rupert-murdoch
-fox-news-factor/story?id=18378960 [accessed March 20, 2015].

155 Amy Chozick and Michael Barbaro, "Again for Murdoch, Romney Can Do
No Right," *New York Times* (January 27, 2015); available online at: http://
www.nytimes.com/2015/01/28/us/politics/as-in-2012-romney-can-do-no
-right-in-murdochs-eyes.html?_r=0 [accessed March 20, 2015].

156 John Bussey tweet (December 1, 2014); available online at: https://twitter
.com/johncbussey/status/539566657841020929 [accessed March 20, 2015].

157 James Rainey, "Adelson talks his liberal agenda . . . and intent to give big to
GOP," *Los Angeles Times* (December 6, 2012); available online at: http://
articles.latimes.com/2012/dec/06/news/la-pn-sheldon-adelson-liberal
-stances-abortion-immigration-20121205 [accessed March 20, 2015].

158 Peter Gemma, "Sheldon Adelson's Spider Web—Where special interests in-
tersect with immigration," *Social Contract*, Volume 24, Number 4 (Summer
2014); available online at: http://www.thesocialcontract.com/artman2
/publish/tsc_24_4/tsc_24_4_gemma.shtml [accessed March 20, 2015].

159 Sheldon G. Adelson, Warren E. Buffett, and Bill Gates, "Break the Immigration Impasse," *New York Times* (July 10, 2014); available online at: http://
www.nytimes.com/2014/07/11/opinion/sheldon-adelson-warren-buffett
-and-bill-gates-on-immigration-reform.html#permid=12254564 [accessed
March 20, 2015].

160 Ibid.

161 Ibid.

162 Philip Rucker and Tom Hamburger, "Billionaires Adelson and Saban,
at odds in campaigns, unite on Israel and hit Obama," *Washington Post*
(November 9, 2014); available online at: http://www.washingtonpost.com
/politics/billionaires-adelson-and-saban-at-odds-in-campaigns-unite-on
-israel-and-hit-obama/2014/11/09/92a40f68-6835-11e4-b053-65cea7903f2e
_story.html?hpid=z5 [accessed March 20, 2015].

163 Andrew Wroe, *The Republican Party and Immigration Politics: From Proposition 187 to George W. Bush* (New York: Palgrave MacMillan, 2008).

164 Cox News Service, "Employers Win Fight On Immigration Simpson To
Strip Limits On Foreign Job-Seekers From His Bill," *Spokesman-Review*
(March 8, 1996); available online at: http://www.spokesman.com/stories
/1996/mar/08/employers-win-fight-on-immigration-simpson-to/ [accessed
March 20, 2015].

165 For more, see Teitelbaum, *Falling Behind?*, op. cit.

166 Fawn Johnson, "Will to compete," *National Journal* (April 16, 2008); available online at: http://www.nationaljournal.com/congressdaily/oia_200804 16_8896.php [accessed March 20, 2015].

167 CompeteAmerica, "Immigration Reform: Fact or Fiction"; available online at: http://www.competeamerica.org/category/immigration-reform -fact-or-fiction/ [accessed March 20, 2015].

168 Shilpa Phadnis and Mini Joseph Tejaswi, "Nasscom engages lobbying firm in the U.S.," *Times of India* (May 7, 2013); available online at http://timesof india.indiatimes.com/business/india-business/Nasscom-engages-lobbying -firm-in-US/articleshow/19924148.cms [accessed April 6, 2015].

169 "Nasscom hires lobbyist, PR and law firms on US immigration Bill," Live Mint.com (July 29, 2013); available online at: http://www.livemint.com /Industry/xQ4lOv80FAH2I6R5GJGY9O/Nasscom-hires-lobbyist-PR -and-law-firms-on-US-immigration-B.html [accessed April 6, 2015].

170 Influence Explorer profile of the Lande Group (undated); available online at: http://influenceexplorer.com/organization/lande-group/01f223009b854340 af145dd6e9ffcfcd [accessed April 7, 2015].

171 Influence Explorer profile of the National Association of Software & Services Companies (undated); available online at: http://influenceexplorer.com /organization/natl-assn-of-software-services-cos/c22261be55bb46498530 edd80af4e7.

172 http://articles.economictimes.indiatimes.com/2003-07-05/news/275 25763_1_indian-middle-indian-companies-outsourcing.

173 Phil Muncaster, "India's outsourcers fume over new US immigration bill," *The Register* (June 21, 2013); available online at: http://www.theregister .co.uk/2013/06/21/india_outsourcing_us_immigration_bill/ [accessed April 7, 2015]. See also: "Infosys visa row: Nasscom slams US," *Indian Express* (May 21, 2012); available online at: http://archive.indianexpress.com/ news/infosys-visa-row-nasscom-slams-us/951946/0 [accessed April 7, 2015].

174 "Nasscom terms U.S. move discriminatory." *The Hindu* (September 9, 2010); available online at: http://www.thehindu.com/todays-paper/tp -business/nasscom-terms-us-move-discriminatory/article622034.ece [accessed April 7, 2015].

175 http://www.computerworld.com/article/2531957/it-personnel/india-inc --gets-white-house-meeting-on-h-1b-visas.html.

176 Michelle Malkin, "The U.S. Chamber of Commerce vs. America," michelle malkin.com (January 24, 2014); available online at: http://michellemalkin .com/2014/01/24/the-u-s-chamber-of-commerce-vs-america/ [accessed March 20, 2015].

177 Fredreka Schouten, "Chamber of Commerce plans big push on immigration," *USA Today* (January 8, 2014); available online at: http://www.usatoday.com/story/news/politics/2014/01/08/us-chamber-of-commerce-immigration-election-tea-party/4372125/ [accessed March 20, 2015].

178 Jeffrey Lord, "KARL ROVE AND THE GOP SOCIALISTS," *American Spectator* (January 2, 2014); available online at: http://spectator.org/articles/57314/karl-rove-and-gop-socialists [accessed March 20, 2015].

179 T. W. Farnam, "Head of Crossroads GPS once a McConnell aide, now his political ally," *Washington Post* (October 30, 2012); available online at: http://www.washingtonpost.com/politics/decision2012/head-of-crossroads-gps-once-a-mcconnell-aide-now-his-political-ally/2012/10/30/9f17e2-1329-11e2-ba83-7396e6b2a7_story.html [accessed March 20, 2015].

180 Patrick O'Connor, "U.S. Chamber of Commerce Pushes Priorities in Congress," *Wall Street Journal* (December 26, 2014); available online at: http://www.wsj.com/articles/u-s-chamber-of-commerce-pushes-priorities-in-congress-1419631349 [accessed March 20, 2015].

181 OpenSecrets.org, "American Action Network"; available online at: http://www.opensecrets.org/outsidespending/detail.php?cmte=American%20Action%20Network [accessed March 20, 2015].

182 Michael Crowley, "The New GOP Money Stampede," *Time* (September 16, 2010); available online at: http://content.time.com/time/magazine/article/0,9171,2019611,00.html [accessed April 7, 2015].

183 Dan Eggen, "Interest groups prepared to spend record amounts in 2010 elections," *Washington Post* (June 3, 2010); available online at: http://www.washingtonpost.com/wp-dyn/content/article/2010/06/02/AR2010060204451.html [accessed April 7, 2015].

184 Ian Tuttle, "Jeb Bush's Ties to Big-Money Immigration 'Reform' Backers," *National Review* (March 30, 2105); available online at: http://www.nationalreview.com/article/416158/jeb-bushs-ties-big-money-immigration-reform-backers-ian-tuttle [accessed April 7, 2015].

185 Sung Min Kim, "New ad for immigration reform," *Politico* (July 8, 2013); available online at: http://www.politico.com/story/2013/07/new-ad-for-immigration-reform-93802.html [accessed April 7, 2015].

186 Cameron Joseph, "Hispanic group to GOP congressmen: Watch your language," *The Hill* (January 28, 2013); available online at: http://thehill.com/blogs/ballot-box/senate-races/279753-hispanic-republican-group-to-gop-congressmen-watch-your-language-on-immigration [accessed April 7, 2015].

187 Tony Lee, "ERIC CANTOR SENDS ANOTHER DECEPTIVE ANTI-AMNESTY MAILER," Breitbart.com (June 2, 2014); available

online at: http://www.breitbart.com/big-government/2014/06/02/eric
-cantor-sends-another-deceptive-anti-amnesty-mailer/ [accessed March 20,
2015].

188 Ibid.

189 Reid Epstein, "Who Is David Brat? Meet the Economics Professor Who
Defeated Eric Cantor," *Wall Street Journal* (June 10, 2014); available online
at: http://blogs.wsj.com/washwire/2014/06/10/who-is-david-brat-meet-the
-economics-professor-who-defeated-eric-cantor/ [accessed March 20, 2015].

190 Byron Tau and Tarini Parti, "How Big Money failed to rescue Eric Cantor,"
Politico (June 11, 2014); available online at: http://www.politico.com
/story/2014/06/2014-virginia-primary-big-money-eric-cantor-107699.html
[accessed March 20, 2015].

191 Reid Epstein, "Who Is David Brat? Meet the Economics Professor Who Defeated Eric Cantor," op. cit.

192 Lawrence Delevingne, "Wall Street loses a good friend in Eric Cantor,"
CNBC (June 12, 2014); available online at: http://www.cnbc.com/id/101
751982 [accessed March 20, 2015].

193 Kent Cooper, "Meet David Brat's Core Contributors," *Roll Call* (June 11,
2014); available online at: http://blogs.rollcall.com/moneyline/meet-david
-brats-core-contributors/ [accessed March 20, 2015].

194 Jake Sherman, "Chemistry Council to run Eric Cantor ads," *Politico* (May 16,
2014); available online at: http://www.politico.com/story/2014/05/eric
-cantor-dave-brat-chemistry-council-primary-virginia-106758.html [ac-
cessed March 20, 2015].

195 Reid Epstein, "David Brat Pulls Off Cantor Upset Despite Raising Just
$231,000," *Wall Street Journal* (June 10, 2014); available online at: http://
www.wsj.com/articles/david-brat-beats-eric-cantor-despite-raising-just
-231-000-1402455265 [accessed March 20, 2015].

196 Richard Cameron, "Eric Cantor's immigration capitulation," CDN (June 9,
2014); available online at: http://www.commdiginews.com/politics-2/eric
-cantors-primary-election-highwire-act-19176/ [accessed March 20, 2015].

CHAPTER 12. EXPOSED: HOW BELTWAY CRAPWEASELS COOKED UP THE GANG
OF EIGHT'S "COMPREHENSIVE IMMIGRATION REFORM"

1 Scott Adams, "Things I Don't Understand" (October 14, 2008); available
online at: http://blog.dilbert.com/post/102544367946/things-i-dont-under
stand [accessed April 15, 2015].

2 Dave Boyer, "Obama welcomes new U.S. citizens, vows to fix 'broken'
immigration system," *Washington Times* (July 4, 2014); available online at:

http://www.washingtontimes.com/news/2014/jul/4/obama-welcomes-new
-us-citizens-vows-to-fix-broken-/?page=all [accessed April 15, 2015].

3   Fawn Johnson, "Draft Principles Show GOP Is Evolving on Immigration,"
    National Journal (January 30, 2014); available online at: http://www.national
    journal.com/congress/draft-principles-show-gop-is-evolving-on-immigra
    tion-20140130 [accessed April 15, 2015].

4   House Democrats, "Reforming Our Broken Immigration System" (un-
    dated); available online at: http://www.dems.gov/immigrationreform/ [ac-
    cessed April 15, 2015].

5   C-SPAN, "Senators on Bipartisan Immigration Legislation" (April 18, 2013);
    available online at: http://www.c-span.org/video/?312156-1/gang-eight
    -senators-unveils-bipartisan-immigration-bill [accessed April 15, 2015].

6   See, e.g., Immigration Policy Center, "How the United States Immigration
    System Works: A Fact Sheet" (March 1, 2014); available online at: http://
    www.immigrationpolicy.org/just-facts/how-united-states-immigration
    -system-works-fact-sheet [accessed April 15, 2015].

7   Ibid.

8   Ibid.

9   Federation for American Immigration Reform (FAIR), "Does Your House
    Member Support Boehner's Amnesty Proposal?" ImmigrationReform
    .com (February 27, 2014); available online at: http://immigrationreform
    .com/2014/02/27/does-your-house-member-support-boehners-amnesty
    -proposal/ [accessed April 15, 2015].

10 Border Security, Economic Opportunity, and Immigration Modernization
    Act, S.744, 113th Congress.

11 Erica Werner, "Senators Close in on Immigration Deal," Associated Press
    (March 22, 2013); available online at: http://news.yahoo.com/senators
    -close-immigration-deal-223210868—politics.html [accessed April 15,
    2015].

12 Ryan Lizza, "Getting to Maybe," *New Yorker* (June 24, 2013); available
    online at: http://www.newyorker.com/magazine/2013/06/24/getting-to
    -maybe [accessed April 15, 2015].

13 Ibid.

14 Ibid.

15 He announced his candidacy on April 13, 2015.

16 Neil Munro, "Rubio hires immigration lawyer who imports workers for
    companies," *Daily Caller* (March 21, 2013); available online at: http://daily
    caller.com/2013/03/21/rubio-hires-democratic-lawyer-to-help-write
    -immigration-bill/ [accessed April 15, 2015].

17 Fragomen website, Enrique Gonzalez III profile (undated); available online at: http://www.fragomen.com/enrique-gonzalez-iii/ [accessed April 15, 2015].

18 Neil Munro, "Rubio hires immigration lawyer who imports workers for companies," op. cit.

19 Matt O'Brien, "Immigration reform a boon for lawyers," *San Jose Mercury News* (June 27, 2013); available online at: http://www.mercurynews.com /ci_23547008/immigration-reform-boon-lawyers [accessed April 15, 2015].

20 Ibid.

21 Ibid.

22 Federation for American Immigration Reform (FAIR), "The Gang of Eight's Backroom Deals" (June 30, 2013); available online at: http://www .fairus.org/DocServer/amnesty_2013_debate/The_Gang-of-Eight_Back room_Deals_6-30-13.pdf [accessed April 15, 2015].

23 Sec. 4211(d), p. 918.

24 Sec. 4211(f), p. 919.

25 Sec. 4416, p. 995.

26 Sec. 1107, p. 83.

27 Sec. 4101, p. 862.

28 Sec. 4211, p. 914.

29 Ibid., p. 917.

30 S.744—Border Security, Economic Opportunity, and Immigration Modernization Act, 113th Congress (2013-14); available online at: https://www .congress.gov/bill/113th-congress/senate-bill/744 [accessed April 15, 2015].

31 Ross Eisenbrey, "Gang of 8 bill could give nearly half of new IT jobs requiring a college degree to guestworkers," Employment Policy Institute (April 25, 2013); available online at: http://www.epi.org/publication/gang-of-8-bill -new-it-jobs-college-degree-guestworker-h1-b/ [accessed April 15, 2015].

32 Ibid.

33 Immigration Act of 1990, Pub. L. 101-649, §205, 104 Stat. 4,978, 5,019 8 U.S.C. § 1184(g)(1991).

34 8 U.S.C. § 1184(g)(2014).

35 "Experts analyze summary of Senate immigration bill," *Los Angeles Times* (April 16, 2013); available online at: http://documents.latimes.com/anno tated-immigration-plan/ [accessed April 15, 2015].

36 Federation for American Immigration Reform (FAIR), "Summary of S. 744— The Border Security, Economic Opportunity, and Immigration Modernization Act" (June 6, 2013); available online at: http://www.fairus.org/DocServer /amnesty_2013_debate/FAIR_Summary_of_Gang-of-8_Nonimmigrant -Visa_Provisions._TitleIV_H-1B_6-6-13.pdf [accessed April 15, 2015].

37 Norman Matloff, "Ten-Minute Summary of the H-1B Work Visa" (undated); available online at: http://heather.cs.ucdavis.edu/h1b10min.html [accessed April 15, 2015].

38 S.744, § 4211, p. 923–24.

39 Anna R. Khanna, "Navigating the Headwinds: Mitigating Contention in India-US Business Engagement," Indian Council for Research on International Economic Relations (March 2014); available online at: http://icrier .org/ICRIER_Wadhwani/Index_files/US_%20Immigration_Reform.pdf [accessed April 15, 2015].

40 Fragomen website, "Senate Passes Immigration Bill with Major Provisions Affecting Employers" (June 27, 2013); available online at: http://www.frag omen.com/united-states-06-27-2013/ [accessed April 15, 2015].

41 Federation for American Immigration Reform (FAIR), "Summary of S. 744" op. cit.

42 Ibid.

CHAPTER 13. WHERE DO THE 2016 CANDIDATES STAND?

1 Jamie Weinstein, "Did Trump just come out for amnesty," *Daily Caller* (July 24, 2015); available online at: http://dailycaller.com/2015/07/24/donald -trump-on-amnesty-if-somebodys-been-outstanding-we-try-and-work -something-out-video/ [accessed August 21, 2015].

2 "Immigration reform that will make America great again," DonaldJTrump .com; available online at: https://www.donaldjtrump.com/positions/im migration-reform [accessed August 16, 2015].

3 Jeremy Diamond, "Donald Trump undermines his own immigration policy," CNN.com; available online at http://www.cnn.com/2015/08/18/politics /donald-trump-immigration-policy-tweets/index.html [accessed August 18, 2015].

4 Norman Matloff, "¡Ay, Caramba! It Took Only a Few Days for Trump to Reverse His Stance," Norm Says No blog; available online at: https://norm saysno.wordpress.com/2015/08/18/ay-caramba-it-took-only-a-few-days -for-trump-to-reverse-his-stance/ [accessed August 18, 2015].

5 Ibid.

6 http://www.bloomberg.com/politics/articles/2015-07-12/a-tonal-shift-in -the-long-hot-summer-of-trump.

7 See note 61 in chapter 1. In their mad rush to pass the 1990 act, lawmakers realized they had forgotten to create a special visa category for fashion models under the O or P visa programs for foreign athletes, artists, and entertainers. Senators Ted Kennedy and Alan Simpson herded the runway beauties into H-1B. Disgraced former New York Democratic representative

Anthony Weiner attempted unsuccessfully to expand the number of H-1B visas for foreign models while collecting New York City mayoral campaign cash from top modeling agencies. See Ryan Grim, "Weiner bill looks out for models," *Politico* (June 11, 2008); available online at: http://www.politico.com/news/stories/0608/10997.html [accessed March 19, 2015].

8 "Hillary Clinton Pushes For More H1B Visas and OutSourcing," video posted on YouTube on June 4, 2007; available online at: https://www.youtube.com/watch?v=UhLBSLLIhUs [accessed April 19, 2015].

9 Peter Wallsten, "Clinton's free-trade advocacy is hitting labor where it lives," *Los Angeles Times* (July 30, 2007); available online at: http://articles.latimes.com/2007/jul/30/nation/na-buffalo30 [accessed April 19, 2015].

10 Tata Consultancy Services, "Asia's largest technology firm opens office in Buffalo" (March 10, 2003); available online at: http://www.tata.com/article/inside/1frsPFlB2b8=/TLYVr3YPkMU= [accessed April 19, 2015].

11 "Sen. Hillary Clinton in India," *India Review* (April 1, 2005); available online at: http://www.indianconsulateatlanta.org/pdf/india_review/2005/April2005.pdf [accessed April 19, 2015].

12 Patrick Thibodeau, "'Elena's Inbox' details H-1B battle in Clinton White House," *Computerworld* (July 2, 2010); available online at: http://www.computerworld.com/article/2518662/technology-law-regulation/-elena-s-inbox—details-h-1b-battle-in-clinton-white-house.html?page=2 [accessed April 19, 2015].

13 "Obama apologizes over 'Hillary Clinton (D-Punjab)' memo" (June 19, 2007); available online at: http://www.nytimes.com/2007/06/19/world/americas/19iht-obama.1.6203898.html [accessed April 19, 2015].

14 My Visa Jobs, profile of Cisco Systems Inc. (undated); available at: http://www.myvisajobs.com/Visa-Sponsor/Cisco-Systems/113035.htm [accessed April 19, 2015].

15 Brad Reese, "Cisco caught in maelstrom over fake job ads to hire H-1B visa holders," *Networkworld* (June 29, 2007); available online at: http://www.networkworld.com/article/2347853/cisco-subnet/cisco-caught-in-maelstrom-over-fake-job-ads-to-hire-h-1b-visa-holders.html [accessed April 19, 2015].

16 "Hillary Clinton (D-Punjab)'s personal financial and political ties to India" (undated); available online at: http://graphics8.nytimes.com/packages/pdf/politics/memo1.pdf [accessed April 19, 2015].

17 Eric Zorn, "Obama too fast to retreat from 'Punjab' jab," *Chicago Tribune* (June 19, 2007); available online at: http://blogs.chicagotribune.com/news_columnists_ezorn/2007/06/punjab.html [accessed April 19, 2015].

18 "Bernie Sanders on immigration," FeelTheBern.com; available online at: http://feelthebern.org/bernie-sanders-on-immigration/ [accessed August 15, 2015].

19 Dylan Matthews, " 'This is a massive effort to attract cheap labor.' Why Sen. Bernie Sanders is skeptical of guest workers," *Washington Post* (May 25, 2013); available online at: http://www.washingtonpost.com/blogs/wonkblog /wp/2013/05/25/this-is-a-massive-effort-to-attract-cheap-labor-why-sen -bernie-sanders-is-skeptical-of-guest-workers/ [accessed April 29, 2015].

20 Lisa Mascaro and Brian Bennett, "Support for immigration overhaul rises among GOP senators," *Los Angeles Times* (June 22, 2013); available online at: http://articles.latimes.com/2013/jun/22/news/la-pn-immigration-over haul-gop-senators-20130622 [accessed April 29, 2015].

21 Catalina Camia, "Jim Webb announces 2016 exploratory bid for president," *USA Today* (November 20, 2014); available online at: http://onpolitics.usa today.com/2014/11/20/jim-webb-president-2016-exploratory-committee/ [accessed April 29, 2015].

22 Patrick Thibodeau, "A new H-1B fight looms with the Democratic Congress," *Networkworld* (January 4, 2007); available online at: http://www .networkworld.com/article/2302550/infrastructure-management/a-new-h -1b-fight-looms-with-the-democratic-congress.html [accessed April 29, 2015].

23 https://martinomalley.com/the-latest/immigration/.

24 Matt Cover, "Jeb Bush Changes Position—Again—on 'Pathway to Citizenship' for Illegals," CNS News (March 11, 2013); available online at: http:// cnsnews.com/news/article/jeb-bush-changes-position-again-pathway-citi zenship-illegals [accessed April 19, 2015].

25 Jeb Bush and Clink Bolick, *Immigration Wars: Forging an American Solution* (New York: Simon & Schuster Inc., 2013).

26 Suzy Khimm, "We read Jeb Bush's immigration book so you don't have to," *Washington Post* (March 5, 2013); available online at: http://www.washing tonpost.com/blogs/wonkblog/wp/2013/03/05/we-read-jeb-bushs-immi gration-book-so-you-dont-have-to/ [accessed April 19, 2015].

27 Khalil AlHajal, "Jeb Bush's Detroit visit offers glimpse of what's to come in presidential race," mlive.com (February 5, 2015); available online at: http:// www.mlive.com/news/detroit/index.ssf/2015/02/jeb_bushs_detroit_visit _offers.html [accessed April 19, 2015].

28 Sen. Rand Paul, immigration reform speech (March 18, 2013); transcript available online at: http://www.paul.senate.gov/files/documents/USHCC .pdf [accessed April 19, 2015].

29 Patrick Thibodeau, "Rand Paul's tangled approach to H-1B visas," *Computerworld* (April 7, 2015); available online at: http://www.computerworld .com/article/2907072/rand-pauls-tangled-approach-to-h-1b-visas.html [accessed April 19, 2015].

30 Darren Samuelsohn, "Rand Paul eyes tech-oriented donors, geeks in Bay Area," *Politico* (July 17, 2014); available online at: http://www.politico .com/story/2014/07/rand-paul-tech-donors-bay-area-108998.html [accessed April 19, 2015].

31 Mike Allen, "WHERE RAND PAUL SPENT HIS WEEKEND— JOE LOCKHART is 55: Check out pic of youthful Joe on Santa's lap— MAUREEN DOWD unloads on the Clintons—HOW THIS WORLD CUP changed the game," *Politico* (July 13, 2014); available online at: http:// www.politico.com/playbook/0714/playbook14612.html [accessed April 20, 2015].

32 Sen. Ted Cruz press release, "Sen. Cruz Presents Measure to Strengthen, Improve Legal Immigration" (May 14, 2014); available online at: http:// www.cruz.senate.gov/?p=press_release&id=137 [accessed April 20, 2015].

33 Ibid.

34 Tony Lee, "Hatch, Rubio, Flake co-sponsor bill to increase H-1B guest-worker visas," Breitbart.com (January 13, 2015); available online at: http:// www.breitbart.com/big-government/2015/01/13/hatch-rubio-flake-co -sponsor-bill-to-increase-h-1b-guest-worker-visas/ [accessed April 18, 2015].

35 Laura Meckler, "Bipartisan Senate Bills Would Increase Visas and Green Cards for High-Tech Workers," *Wall Street Journal* (January 13, 2015); available online at: http://www.wsj.com/articles/bipartisan-senate-bills -would-increase-visas-and-green-cards-for-high-tech-workers-1421191748 [accessed April 18, 2015].

36 Anne Broache, "Governors throw support behind H-1B increase," CNET (September 11, 2007); available online at: http://www.cnet.com/news/gover nors-throw-support-behind-h-1b-increase/ [accessed April 20, 2015].

37 Alex Swoyer, "Huckabee promotes American workers, slams H-1B visa fraud and abuse by tech companies," *Daily Caller*; available online at: http:// www.breitbart.com/big-government/2015/06/01/huckabee-promotes -american-workers-slams-h1b-visa-fraud-and-abuse-by-tech-companies / [accessed August 8, 2015].

38 Jenna Portnoy, "Chris Christie trumpets signing of Dream Act in Union City," NJ Advance Media (January 7, 2014); available online at: http://www .nj.com/politics/index.ssf/2014/01/chris_christie_trumpets_signing_of _dream_act_in_union_city.html [accessed April 20, 2015].

39 Matt Arco, "Christie supporting lawsuit challenging Obama immigration reform," NJ Advance Media (March 25, 2015); available online at: http://www.nj.com/politics/index.ssf/2015/03/christie_immigration_lawsuit .html [accessed April 20, 2015].

40 http://www.computerworld.com/article/2943695/it-outsourcing/a-look-at -californias-effort-to-build-an-h-1b-firewall.html.

41 Scott Woolley, "Carly Fiorina's troubling telecom past," *Fortune* (October 5, 2010); available online at: http://fortune.com/2010/10/15/carly-fiorinas -troubling-telecom-past/ [accessed April 29, 2015].

42 Jolie Lee, "Short stint, big payout: View CEO severance packages," *USA Today* (April 17, 2014); available online at: http://www.usatoday.com/story /news/nation-now/2014/04/17/ceos-severance-packages-yahoo/7826743 / [accessed April 29, 2015].

43 Jeff Stone, "Who Is Carly Fiorina? Former HP CEO Jumps Into Presidential Race As GOP Candidate," *International Business Times* (April 23, 2015); available online at: http://www.ibtimes.com/who-carly-fiorina-former-hp-ceo -jumps-presidential-race-gop-candidate-1894274 [accessed April 23, 2014].

44 Rachel Stoltzfoos, "Fiorina Slams Disney, Then Admits She Used H-1B Program At HP," *Daily Caller*, June 10, 2015; available online at: http://daily caller.com/2015/06/10/fiorina-slams-disney-admits-she-used-h-1b-pro gram-at-hp/#ixzz3iTaObU57 [accessed August 7, 2015].

45 Matthew Boyle, "Exclusive: Rick Santorum lays out plan to reduce immigration by 25 percent," Breitbart.com, May 7, 2015; available online at: http://www .breitbart.com/big-government/2015/05/07/exclusive-rick-santorum-lays-out -plan-to-reduce-immigration-by-25-percent/ [accessed August 8, 2015].

46 Rachel Stoltzfoos, "This is the only 2016 candidate committed to reducing legal immigration," *Daily Caller*, June 4, 2015; available online at: http:// dailycaller.com/2015/06/04/this-is-the-only-2016-candidate-committed -to-reducing-legal-immigration/ [accessed August 8, 2015].

47 Gabriel Debendetti, "Scott Walker's immigration problem," *Politico* (February 18, 2015); available online at: http://www.politico.com/story/2015/02 /scott-walkers-immigration-problem-115303.html [accessed August 8, 2015].

48 Eliana Johnson, "Walker's flip-flop-flip on amnesty?" *National Review* (March 26, 2015); available online at: http://www.nationalreview.com /corner/416052/walkers-flip-flop-flip-amnesty-eliana-johnson [accessed April 20, 2015].

49 Matthew Boyle, "Scott Walker lays out pro-American worker stance on immigration," Breitbart.com (April 20, 2015); available online at: http:// www.breitbart.com/big-government/2015/04/20/scott-walker-lays-out -pro-american-worker-stance-on-immigration/.

50 Mackenzie Ryan, "Rubio calls for reformed economic policies at Soapbox," *Des Moines Register*, August 19, 2015; available online at: http://www.des moinesregister.com/story/news/elections/presidential/caucus/2015/08/18 /marco-rubio-register-soapbox-iowa-caucuses/31916575/?hoot PostID=0cd7de07ec5b150a28d285a6938f8e11 [accessed August 19, 2015].

51 Tony Romm, "Hillary Clinton courts Silicon Valley," *Politico* (May 3, 2015); available online at: http://www.politico.com/story/2015/05/hillary -clinton-courts-silicon-valley-117563.html [accessed August 15, 2015].

52 HillaryClinton.com [accessed August 20, 2015].

CONCLUSION. PRO-AMERICAN IMMIGRATION REFORM

1 Ireland has this policy. It tells prospective guest workers: "The employer must employ you directly—this means that applications from recruitment agencies, agents, intermediaries or companies who intend to outsource or subcontract you to work in another company are not accepted." See Citizens Information Board, "Coming to work in Ireland" (undated); available online at: http://www.citizensinformation.ie/en/moving_country/moving_to _ireland/working_in_ireland/coming_to_work_in_ireland.html [accessed April 22, 2015].

Acknowledgments

Michelle wishes to thank Jesse Malkin, Glenn Beck, Kevin Balfe, Mitchell Ivers and Natasha Simons, Jennifer Wedel, Norman Oder, and many sources and friends who must remain nameless as they continue to fight the good fight for our country.

John wishes to thank Ralph Miano, Margaret Miano, David Huber, Norman Matloff, Hal Salzman, Michael Zimmer, Ahmed Bubulia, Jeremy Beck, Peter Brimelow, David North, and Mark Krikorian.

Index